Bloody+Mary

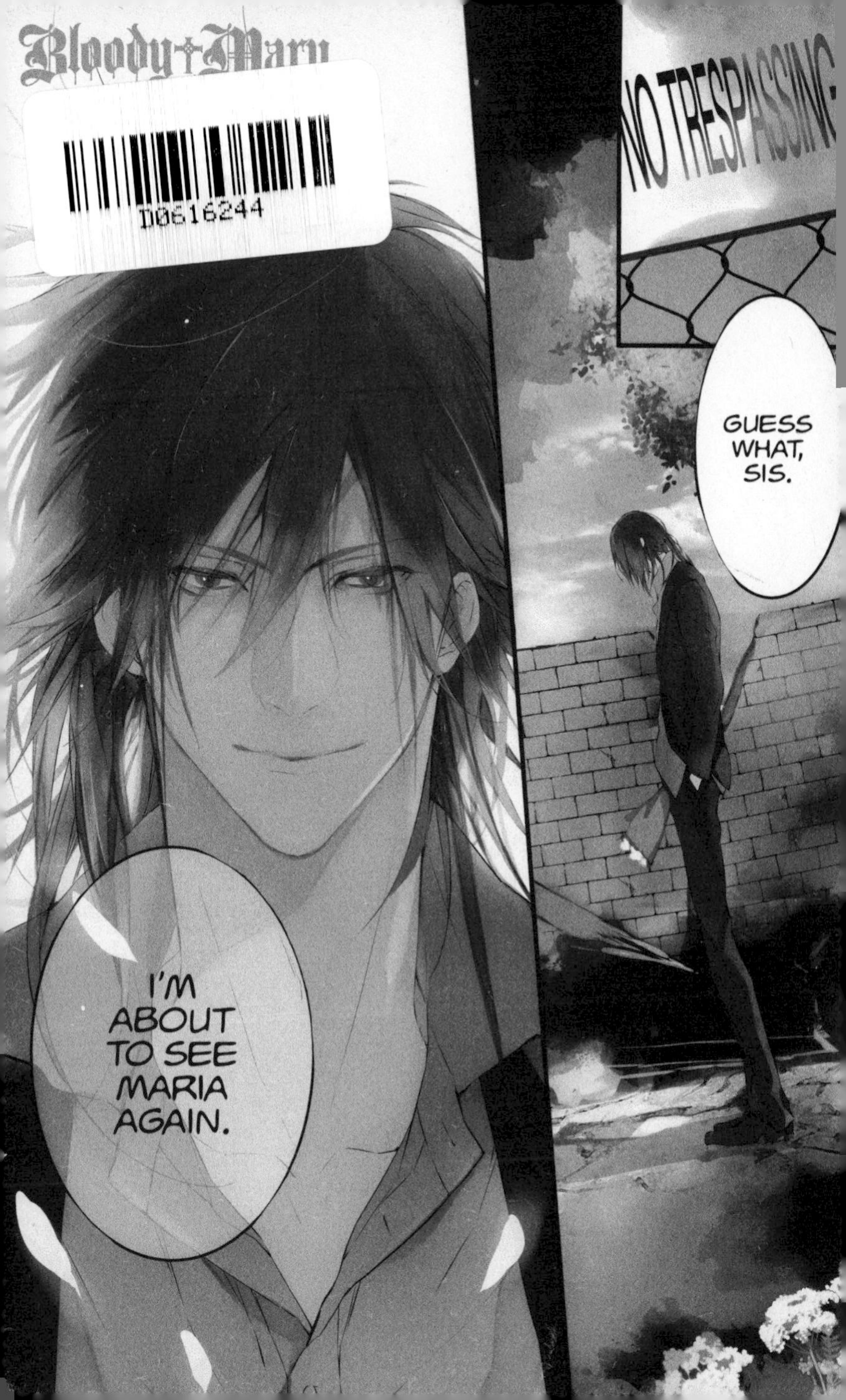
NO TRESPASSING
GUESS WHAT, SIS.
I'M ABOUT TO SEE MARIA AGAIN.

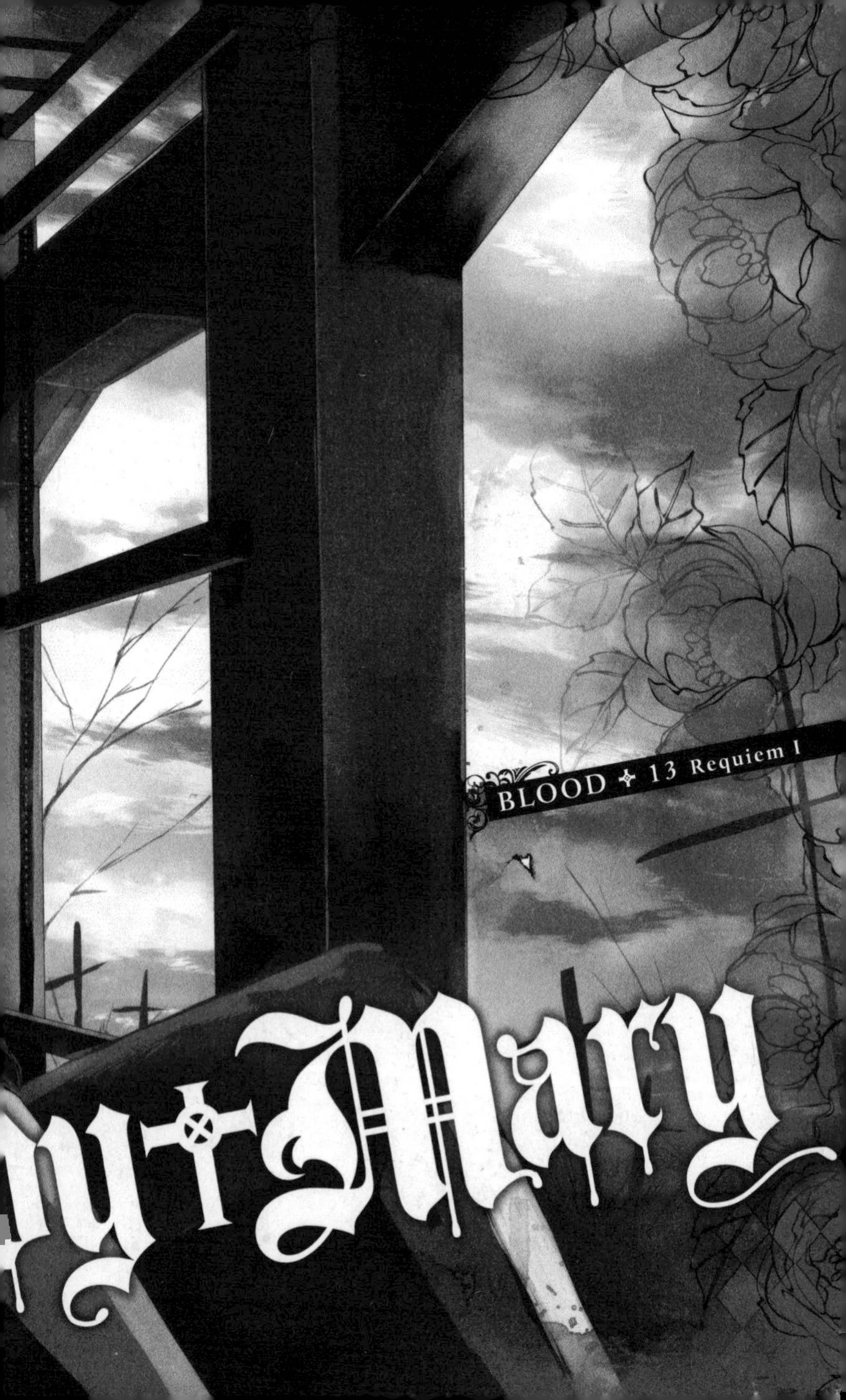
BLOOD ✝ 13 Requiem I
Mary

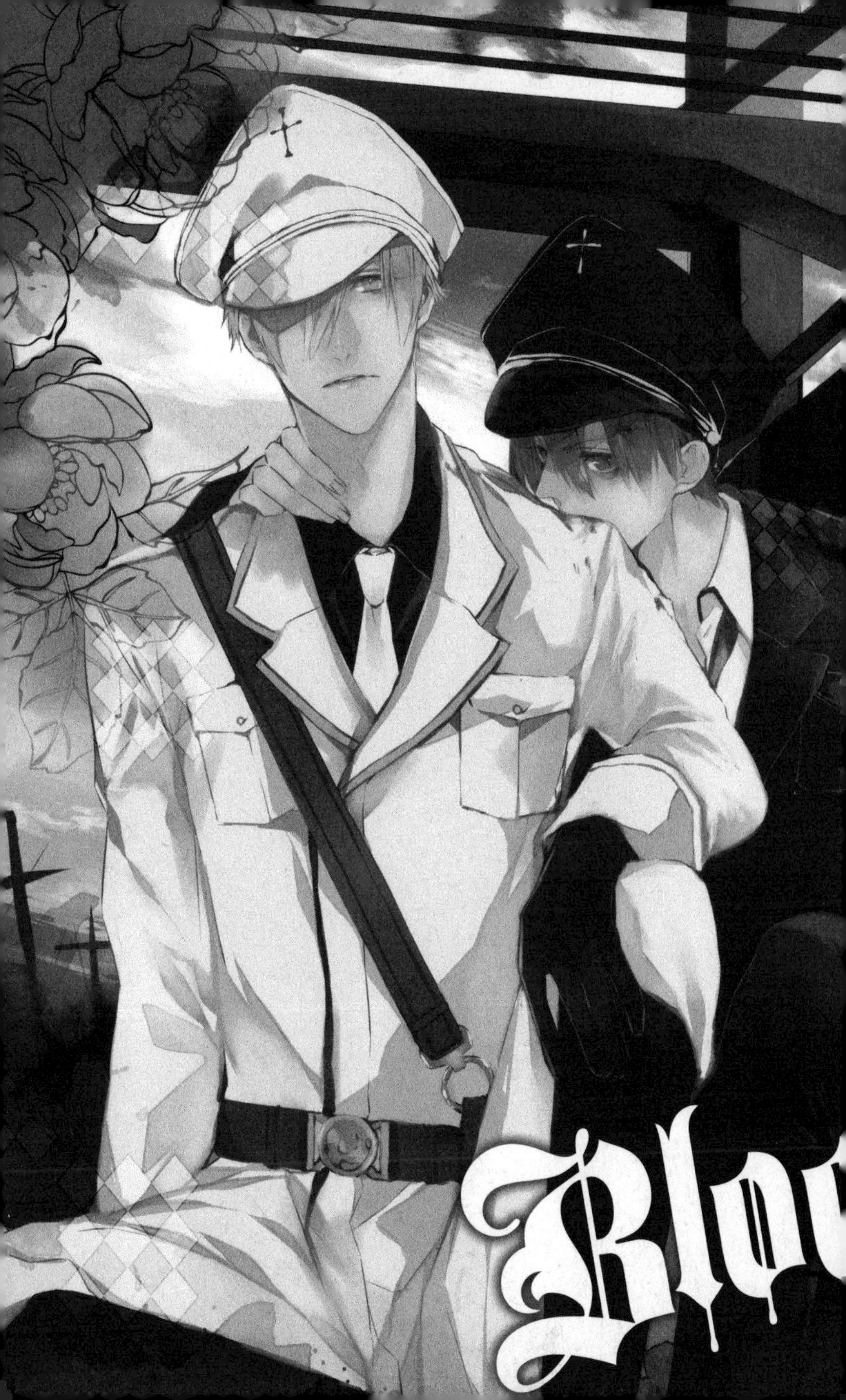
Blo

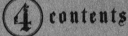

Bloody✝Mary

④ contents

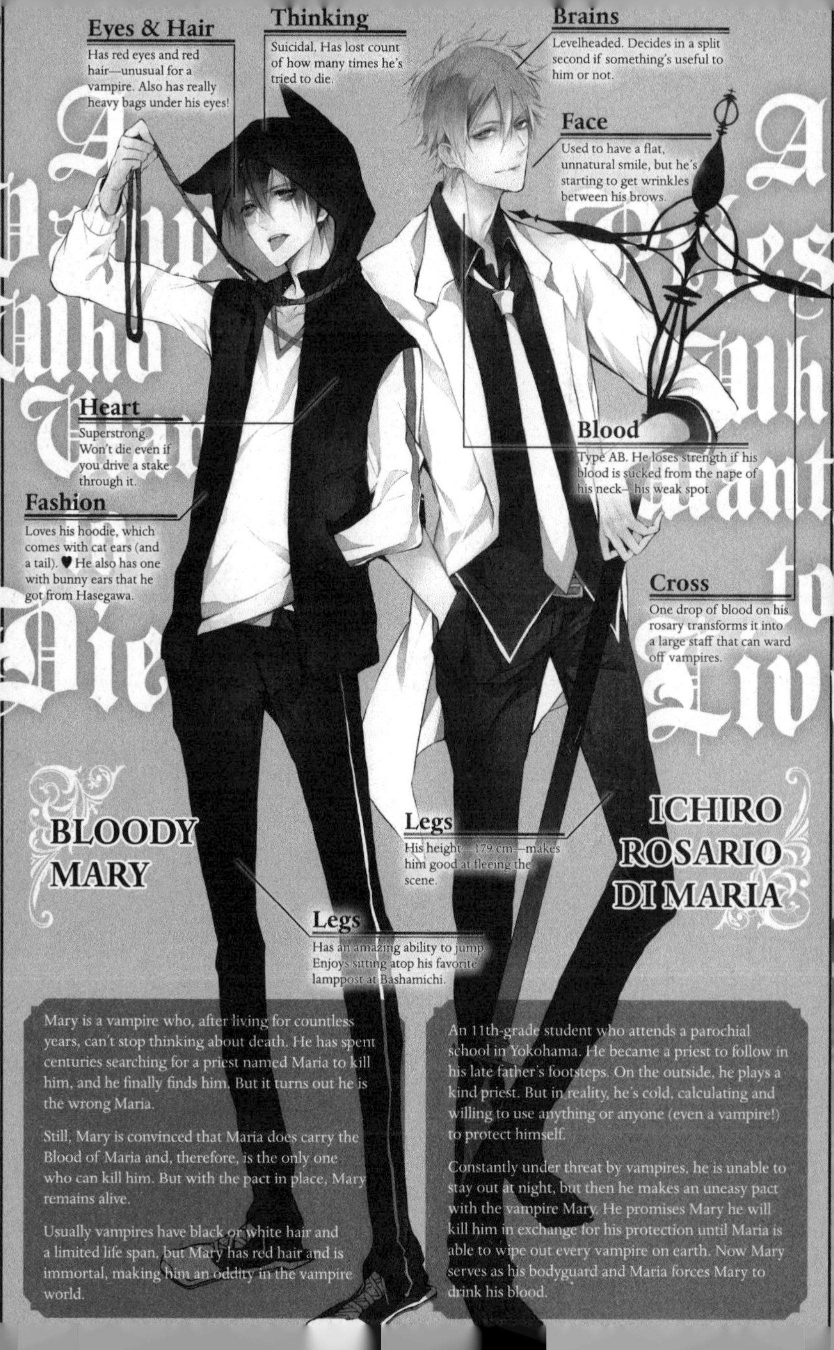
A Vampire Who Wants to Die
A Priest Who Wants to Live
Eyes & Hair
Has red eyes and red hair—unusual for a vampire. Also has really heavy bags under his eyes!
Thinking
Suicidal. Has lost count of how many times he's tried to die.
Heart
Superstrong. Won't die even if you drive a stake through it.
Fashion
Loves his hoodie, which comes with cat ears (and a tail). ♥ He also has one with bunny ears that he got from Hasegawa.
BLOODY MARY
Legs
Has an amazing ability to jump. Enjoys sitting atop his favorite lamppost at Bashamichi.
Brains
Levelheaded. Decides in a split second if something's useful to him or not.
Face
Used to have a flat, unnatural smile, but he's starting to get wrinkles between his brows.
Blood
Type AB. He loses strength if his blood is sucked from the nape of his neck—his weak spot.
Cross
One drop of blood on his rosary transforms it into a large staff that can ward off vampires.
ICHIRO ROSARIO DI MARIA
Legs
His height—179 cm—makes him good at fleeing the scene.

Mary is a vampire who, after living for countless years, can't stop thinking about death. He has spent centuries searching for a priest named Maria to kill him, and he finally finds him. But it turns out he is the wrong Maria.

Still, Mary is convinced that Maria does carry the Blood of Maria and, therefore, is the only one who can kill him. But with the pact in place, Mary remains alive.

Usually vampires have black or white hair and a limited life span, but Mary has red hair and is immortal, making him an oddity in the vampire world.

An 11th-grade student who attends a parochial school in Yokohama. He became a priest to follow in his late father's footsteps. On the outside, he plays a kind priest. But in reality, he's cold, calculating and willing to use anything or anyone (even a vampire!) to protect himself.

Constantly under threat by vampires, he is unable to stay out at night, but then he makes an uneasy pact with the vampire Mary. He promises Mary he will kill him in exchange for his protection until Maria is able to wipe out every vampire on earth. Now Mary serves as his bodyguard and Maria forces Mary to drink his blood.

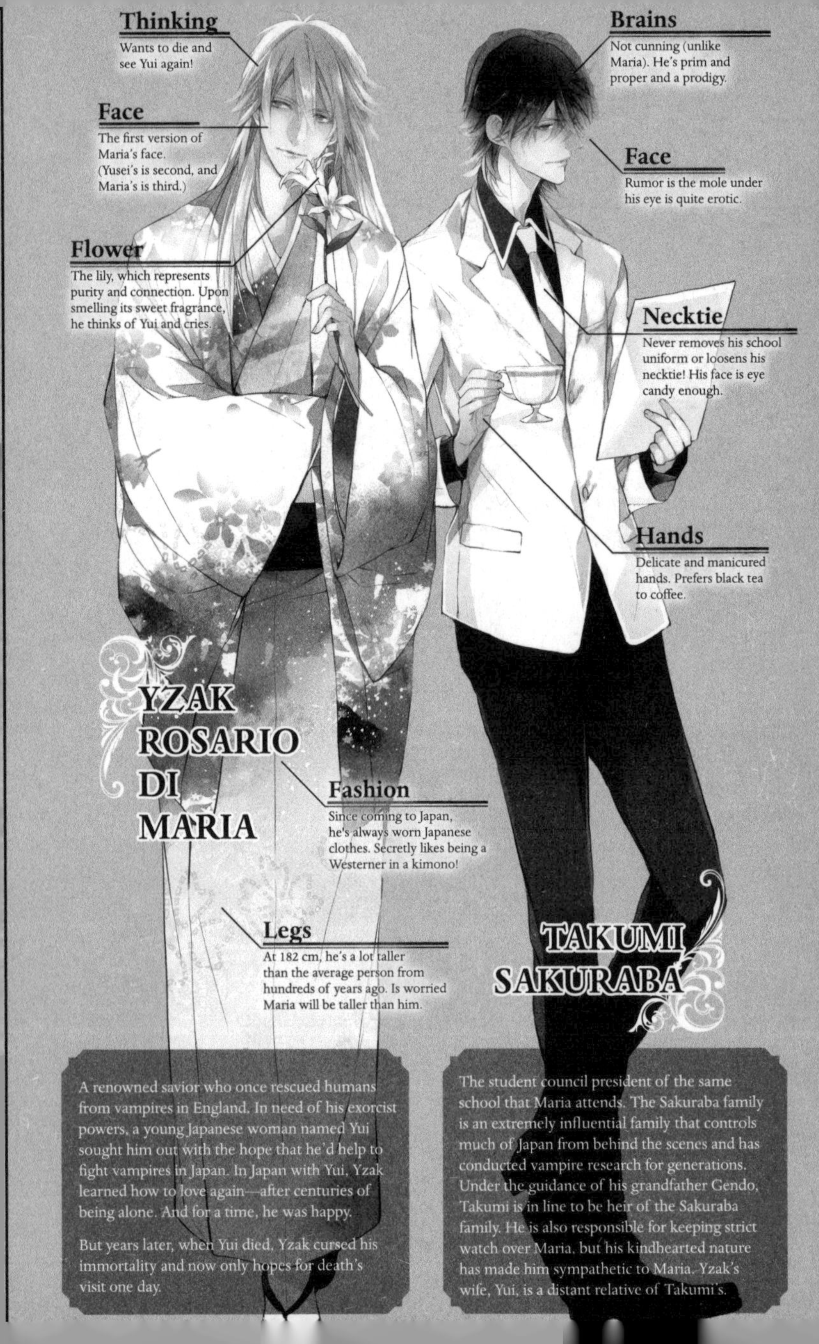
Thinking
Wants to die and see Yui again!
Face
The first version of Maria's face. (Yusei's is second, and Maria's is third.)
Flower
The lily, which represents purity and connection. Upon smelling its sweet fragrance, he thinks of Yui and cries.
YZAK ROSARIO DI MARIA
Fashion
Since coming to Japan, he's always worn Japanese clothes. Secretly likes being a Westerner in a kimono!
Legs
At 182 cm, he's a lot taller than the average person from hundreds of years ago. Is worried Maria will be taller than him.
Brains
Not cunning (unlike Maria). He's prim and proper and a prodigy.
Face
Rumor is the mole under his eye is quite erotic.
Necktie
Never removes his school uniform or loosens his necktie! His face is eye candy enough.
Hands
Delicate and manicured hands. Prefers black tea to coffee.
TAKUMI SAKURABA

A renowned savior who once rescued humans from vampires in England. In need of his exorcist powers, a young Japanese woman named Yui sought him out with the hope that he'd help to fight vampires in Japan. In Japan with Yui, Yzak learned how to love again—after centuries of being alone. And for a time, he was happy.

But years later, when Yui died, Yzak cursed his immortality and now only hopes for death's visit one day.

The student council president of the same school that Maria attends. The Sakuraba family is an extremely influential family that controls much of Japan from behind the scenes and has conducted vampire research for generations. Under the guidance of his grandfather Gendo, Takumi is in line to be heir of the Sakuraba family. He is also responsible for keeping strict watch over Maria, but his kindhearted nature has made him sympathetic to Maria. Yzak's wife, Yui, is a distant relative of Takumi's.

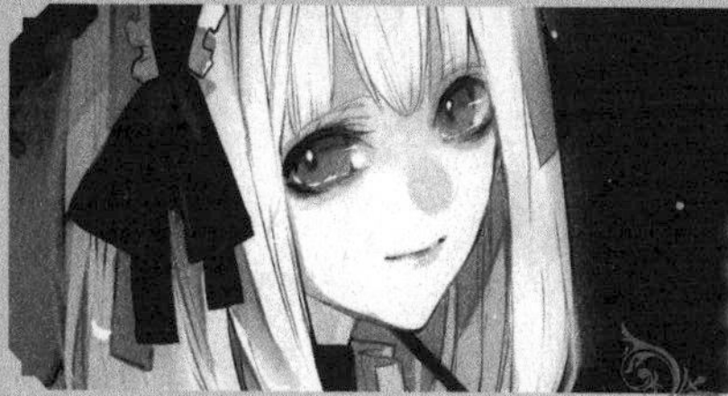

HYDRA

A young-looking female vampire (who's actually older than Mary). She seems to know Mary (the suicidal masochist), though Mary has no memory of her. And she has strong disdainful feelings for the other "Mary" inside of him, so she has more contempt for Masochist Mary than necessary.

Main point

MARY (BLOODY)

Why does he want to die? Why can't he remember his past? Why does he hate being called Mary? Even he himself doesn't know. And he doesn't know anything about the other "Mary" (the non-masochist within him). He's full of mysteries.

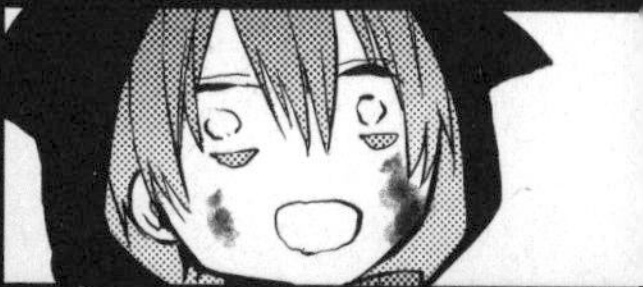

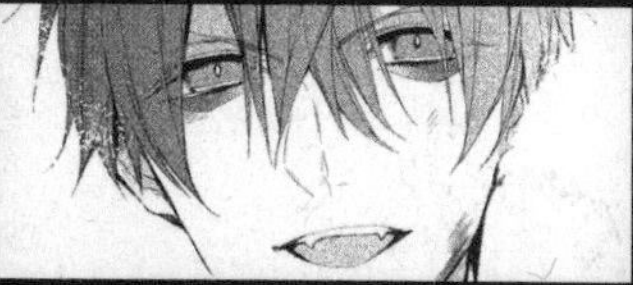

"MARY"

An alter ego hiding within Mary? Did he kill Yusei? He's also full of mysteries (but all we know is that he's not the same as Masochist Mary).

MARIA

After he took away his father Yusei's ever-present rosary, Yusei was left defenseless against vampires and was ultimately killed. Maria blames himself for his father's death and has vowed to annihilate every last vampire. He's full of regrets.

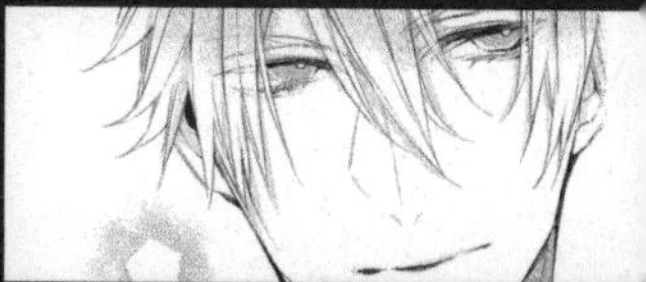

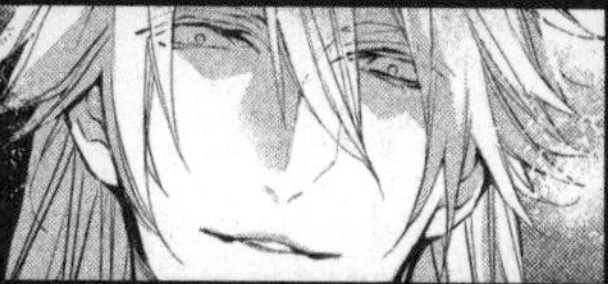

YZAK

He wants "Mary" to kill him, so he sealed away Maria's Power of Exorcism so Maria couldn't exorcise "Mary." He's currently in a deep sleep after getting battered by "Mary." He's full of sorrow.

Story line

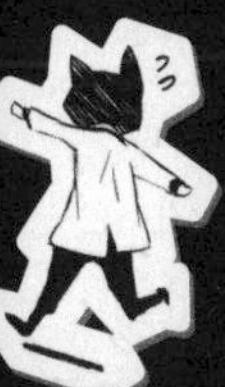

Mary comes down with a cold (even though he won't admit it), and Maria nurses him back to health. In the throes of a feverish dream, Mary mutters, "Don't leave me, Mary." He has no memory of what he said, but Maria, who overhears, is left wondering exactly who this "Mary" is. Later that same night, a mysterious man appears at Yokohama Station, and he's looking for Maria...

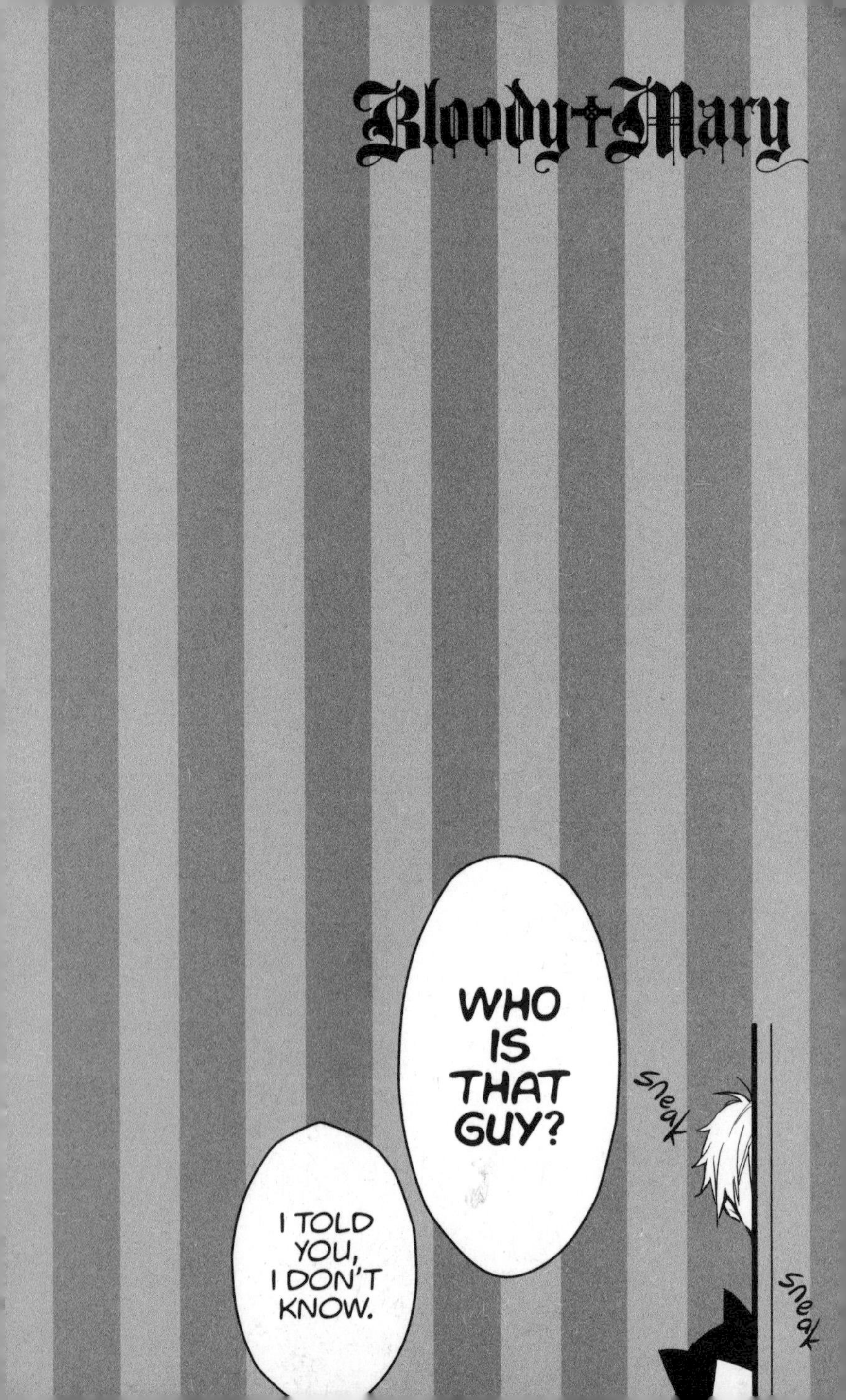
Bloody+Mary
sneak
WHO IS THAT GUY?
sneak
I TOLD YOU, I DON'T KNOW.

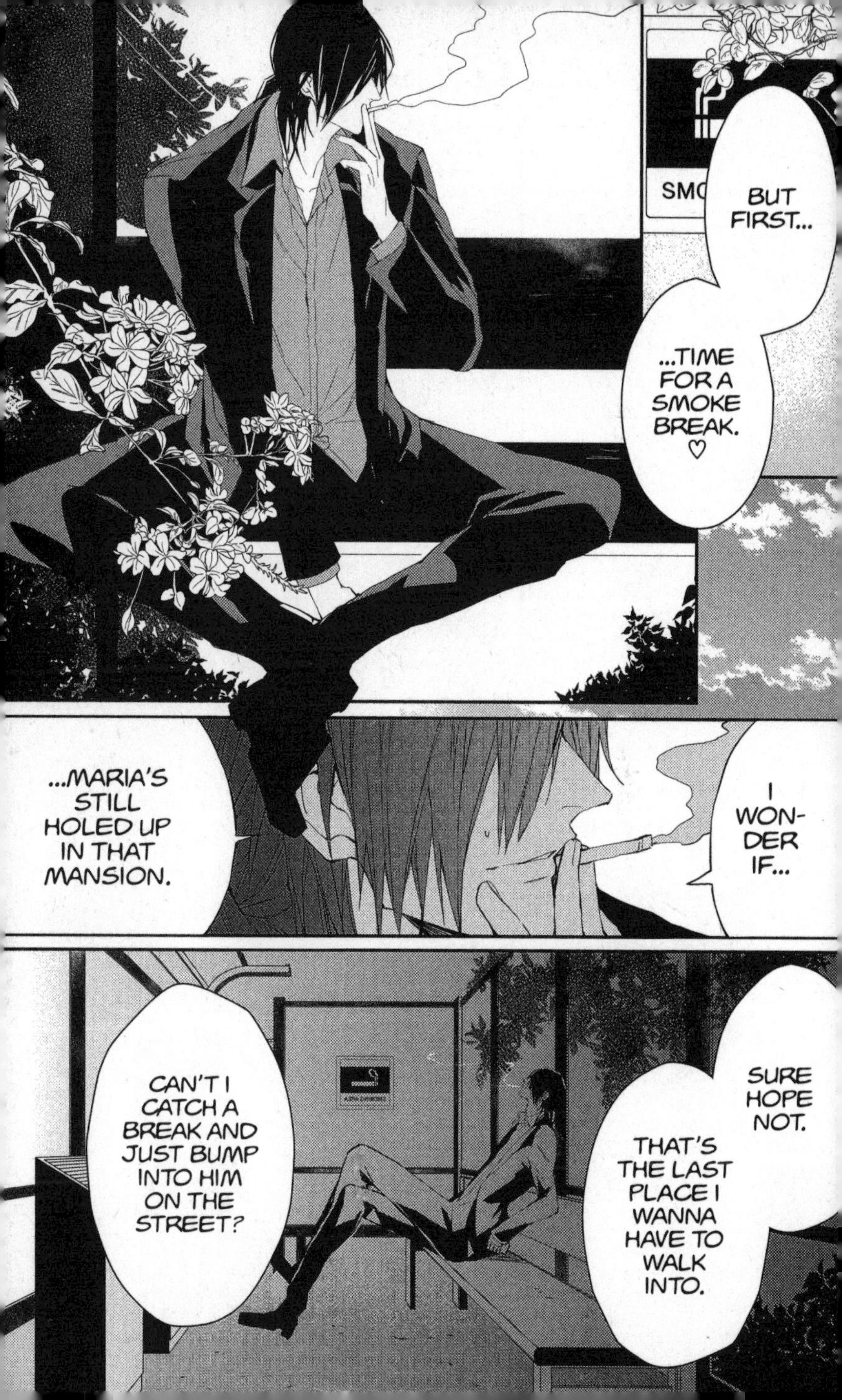
BUT FIRST...
...TIME FOR A SMOKE BREAK. ♡
I WONDER IF...
...MARIA'S STILL HOLED UP IN THAT MANSION.
SURE HOPE NOT.
THAT'S THE LAST PLACE I WANNA HAVE TO WALK INTO.
CAN'T I CATCH A BREAK AND JUST BUMP INTO HIM ON THE STREET?

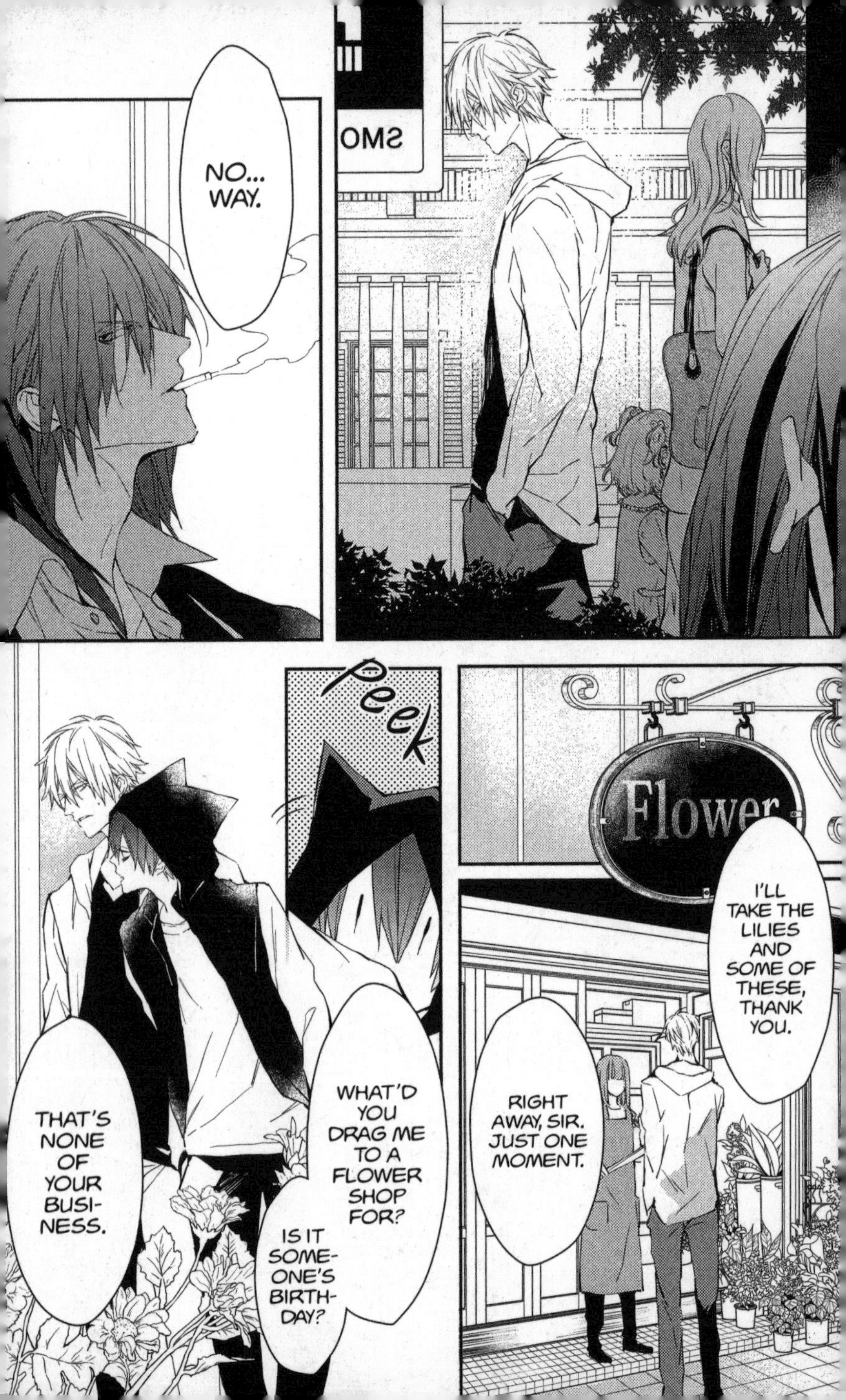
NO... WAY.
Flower
I'LL TAKE THE LILIES AND SOME OF THESE, THANK YOU.
RIGHT AWAY, SIR. JUST ONE MOMENT.
peek
WHAT'D YOU DRAG ME TO A FLOWER SHOP FOR?
IS IT SOMEONE'S BIRTHDAY?
THAT'S NONE OF YOUR BUSINESS.

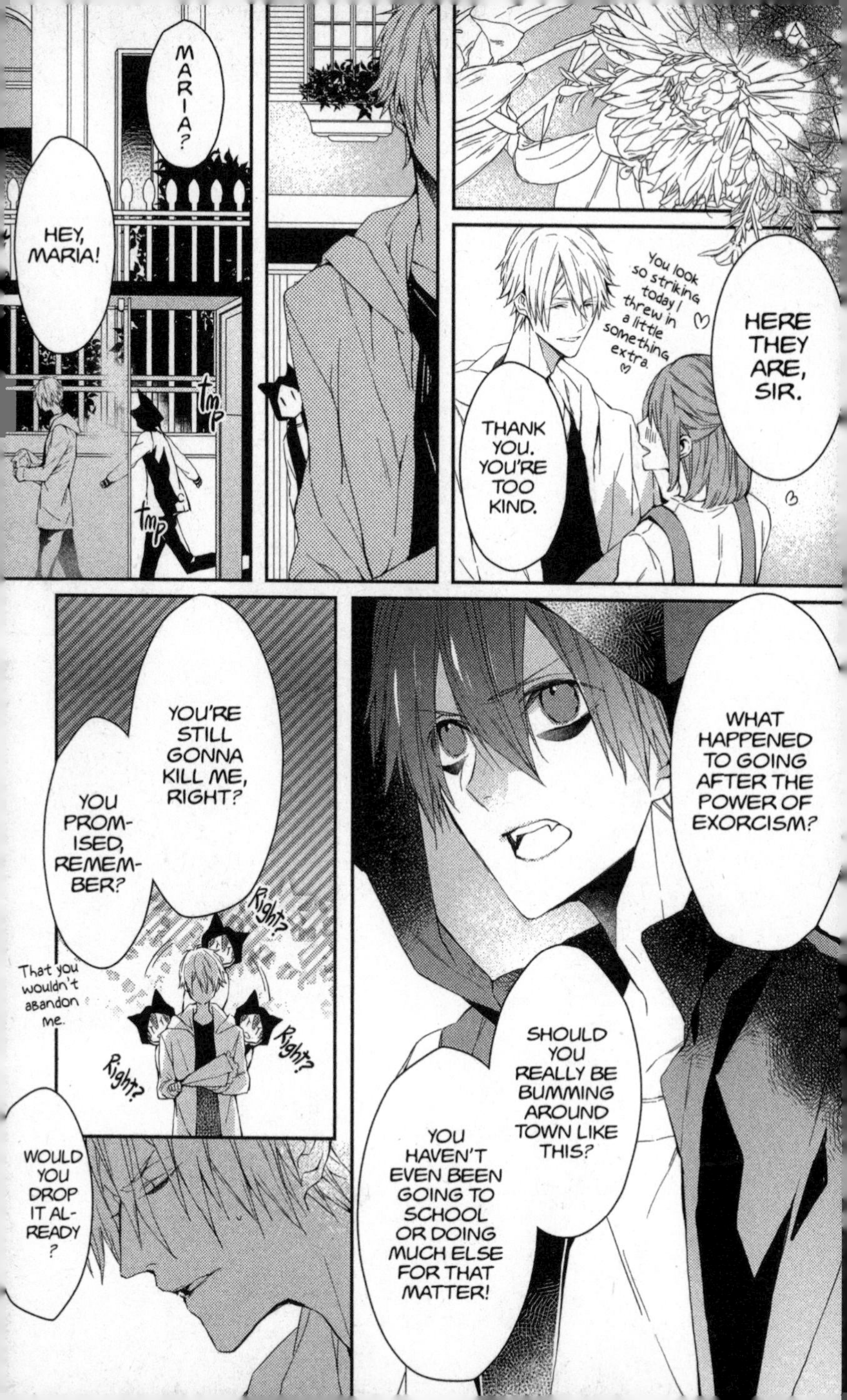
HERE THEY ARE, SIR.
You look so striking today I threw in a little something extra.
THANK YOU. YOU'RE TOO KIND.
MARIA?
HEY, MARIA!
tmp
tmp
WHAT HAPPENED TO GOING AFTER THE POWER OF EXORCISM?
SHOULD YOU REALLY BE BUMMING AROUND TOWN LIKE THIS?
YOU HAVEN'T EVEN BEEN GOING TO SCHOOL OR DOING MUCH ELSE FOR THAT MATTER!
YOU'RE STILL GONNA KILL ME, RIGHT?
YOU PROMISED, REMEMBER?
That you wouldn't abandon me.
Right?
Right?
Right?
WOULD YOU DROP IT ALREADY?

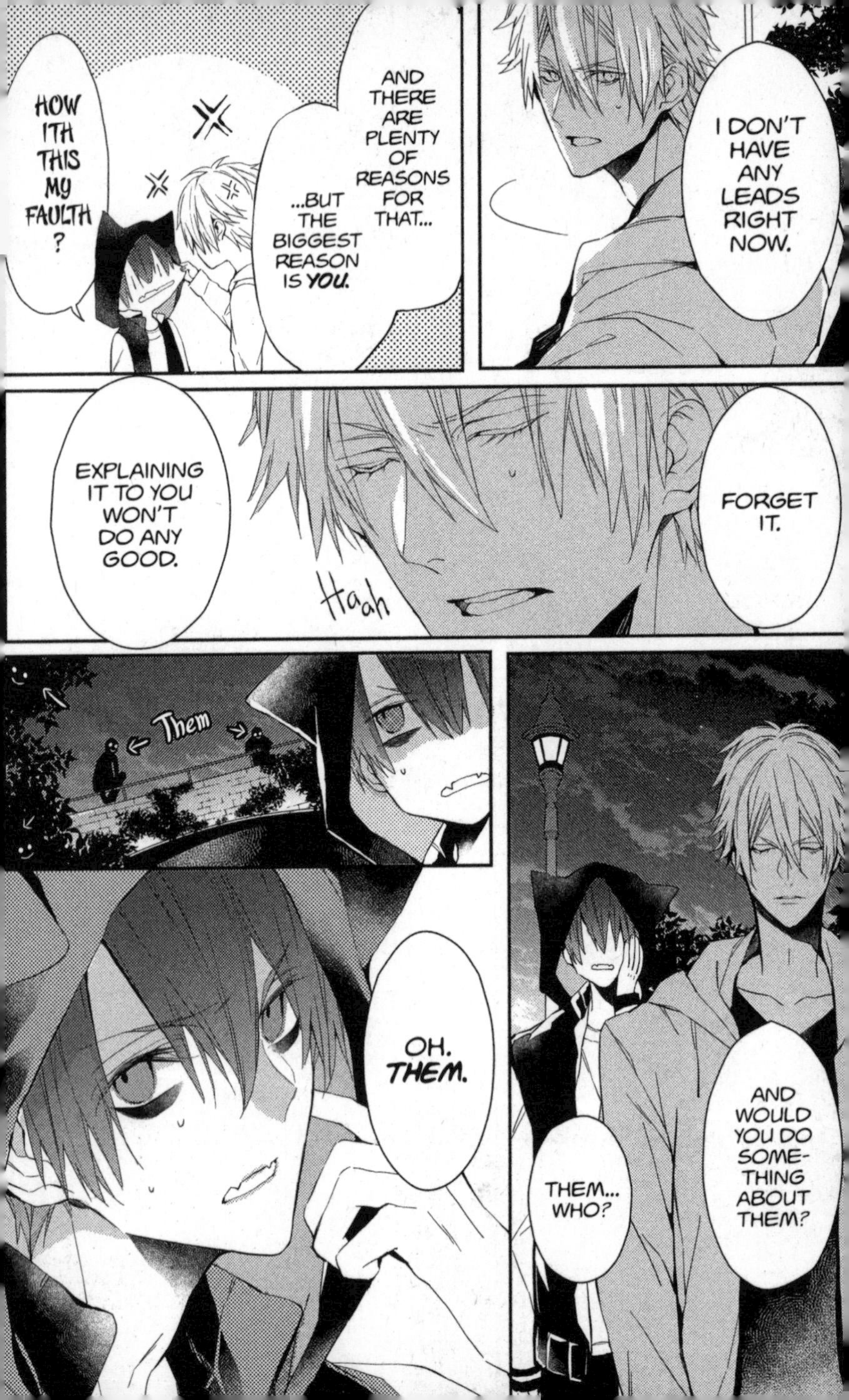
I DON'T HAVE ANY LEADS RIGHT NOW.
AND THERE ARE PLENTY OF REASONS FOR THAT...
...BUT THE BIGGEST REASON IS *YOU.*
HOW ITH THIS MY FAULTH?
FORGET IT.
EXPLAINING IT TO YOU WON'T DO ANY GOOD.
Haah
AND WOULD YOU DO SOME-THING ABOUT THEM?
THEM... WHO?
Them
OH. *THEM.*

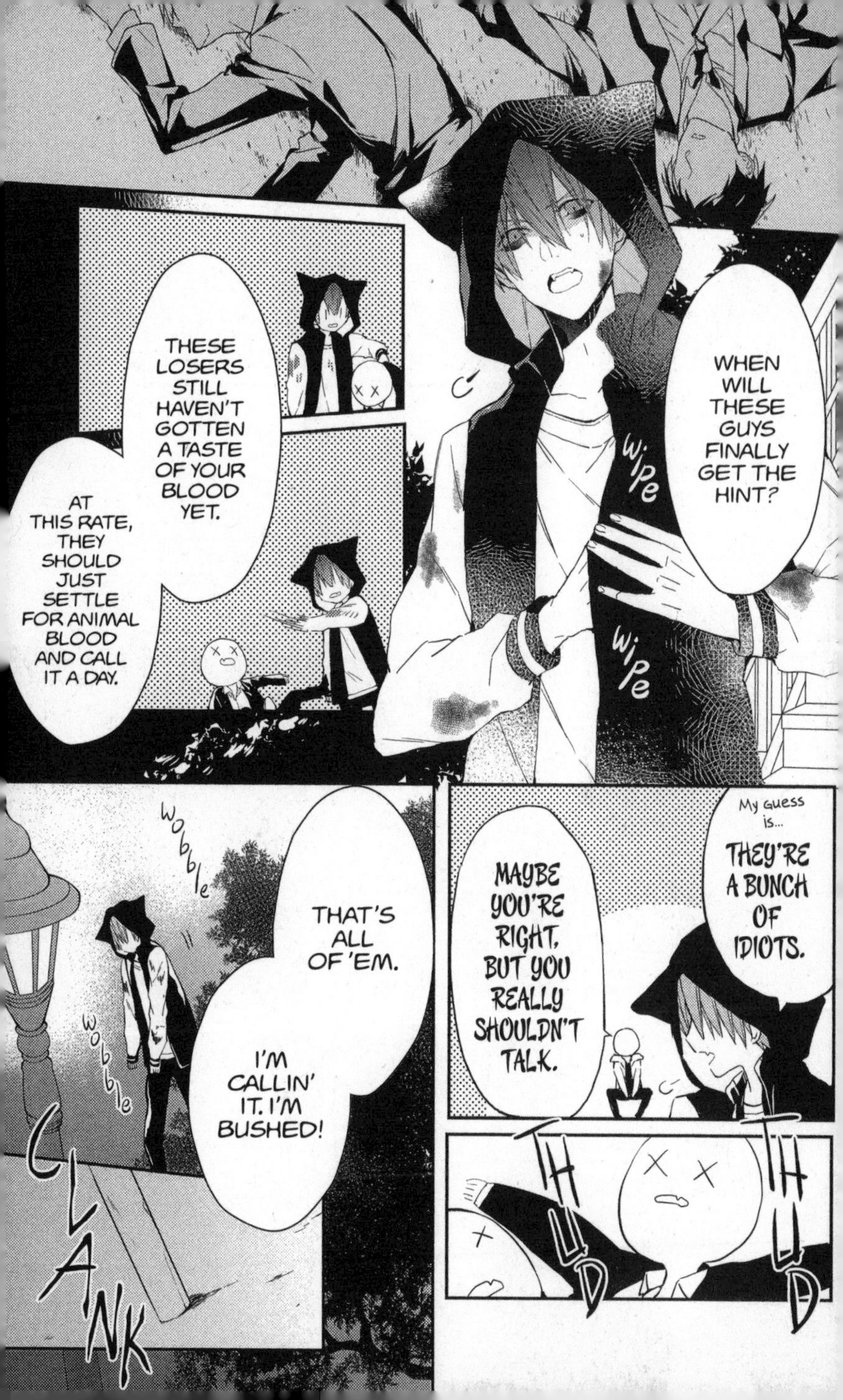
WHEN WILL THESE GUYS FINALLY GET THE HINT?
wipe
wipe
THESE LOSERS STILL HAVEN'T GOTTEN A TASTE OF YOUR BLOOD YET.
AT THIS RATE, THEY SHOULD JUST SETTLE FOR ANIMAL BLOOD AND CALL IT A DAY.
My guess is...
THEY'RE A BUNCH OF IDIOTS.
MAYBE YOU'RE RIGHT, BUT YOU REALLY SHOULDN'T TALK.
THUD
THUD
wobble
wobble
THAT'S ALL OF 'EM.
I'M CALLIN' IT. I'M BUSHED!
CLANK

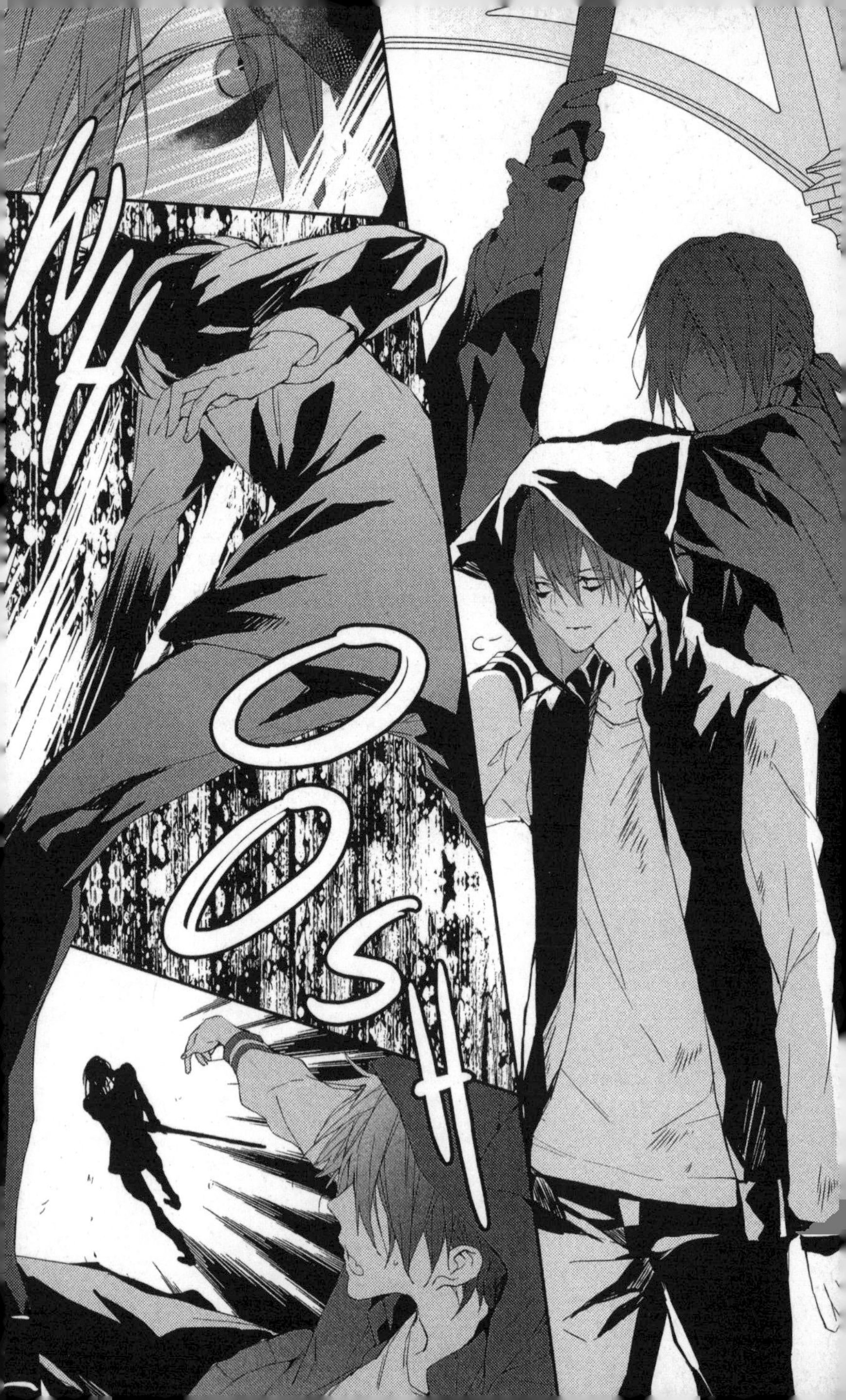
WHOOOSH

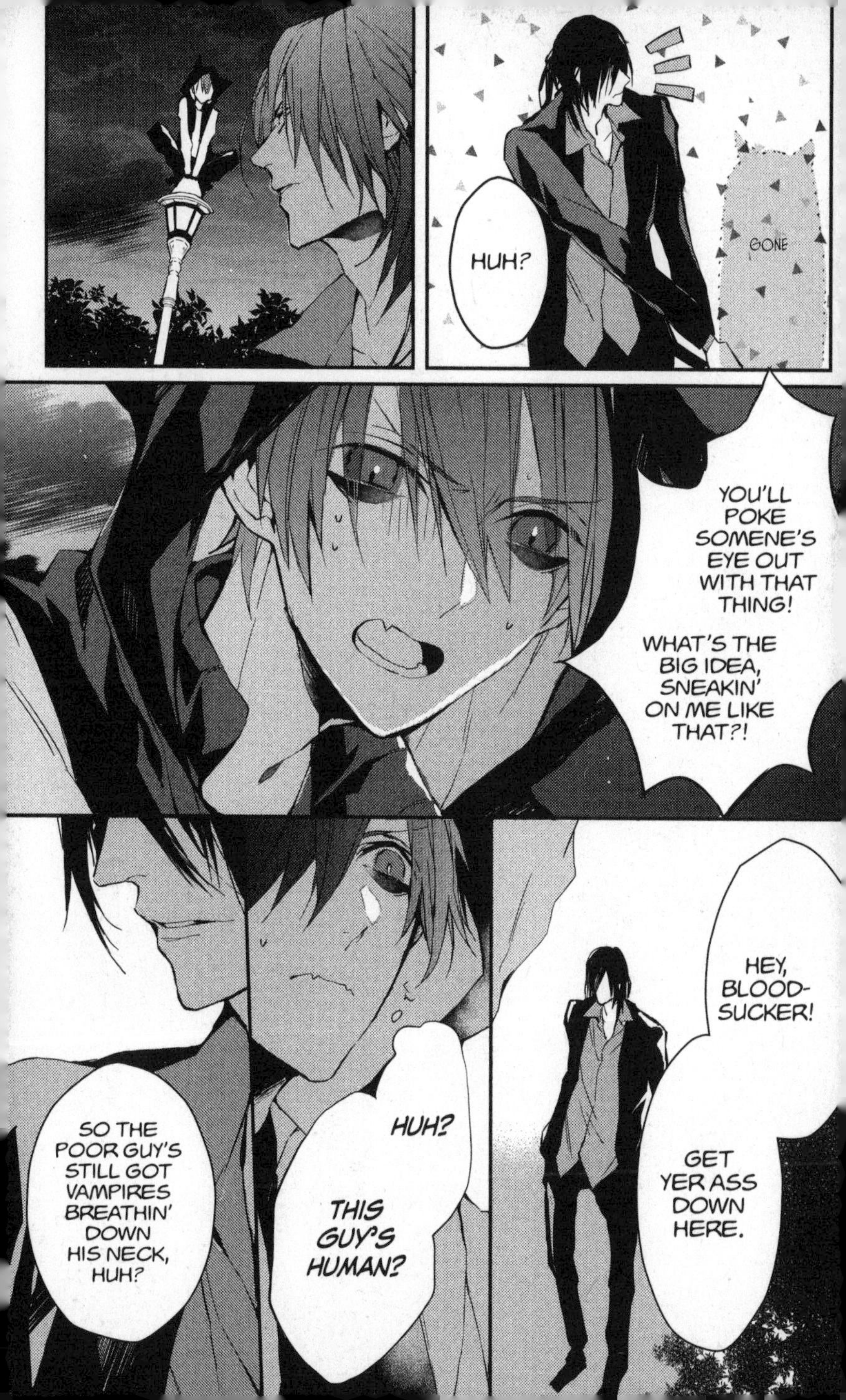
HUH?
GONE
YOU'LL POKE SOMENE'S EYE OUT WITH THAT THING!
WHAT'S THE BIG IDEA, SNEAKIN' ON ME LIKE THAT?!
HEY, BLOOD-SUCKER!
GET YER ASS DOWN HERE.
HUH?
THIS GUY'S HUMAN?
SO THE POOR GUY'S STILL GOT VAMPIRES BREATHIN' DOWN HIS NECK, HUH?

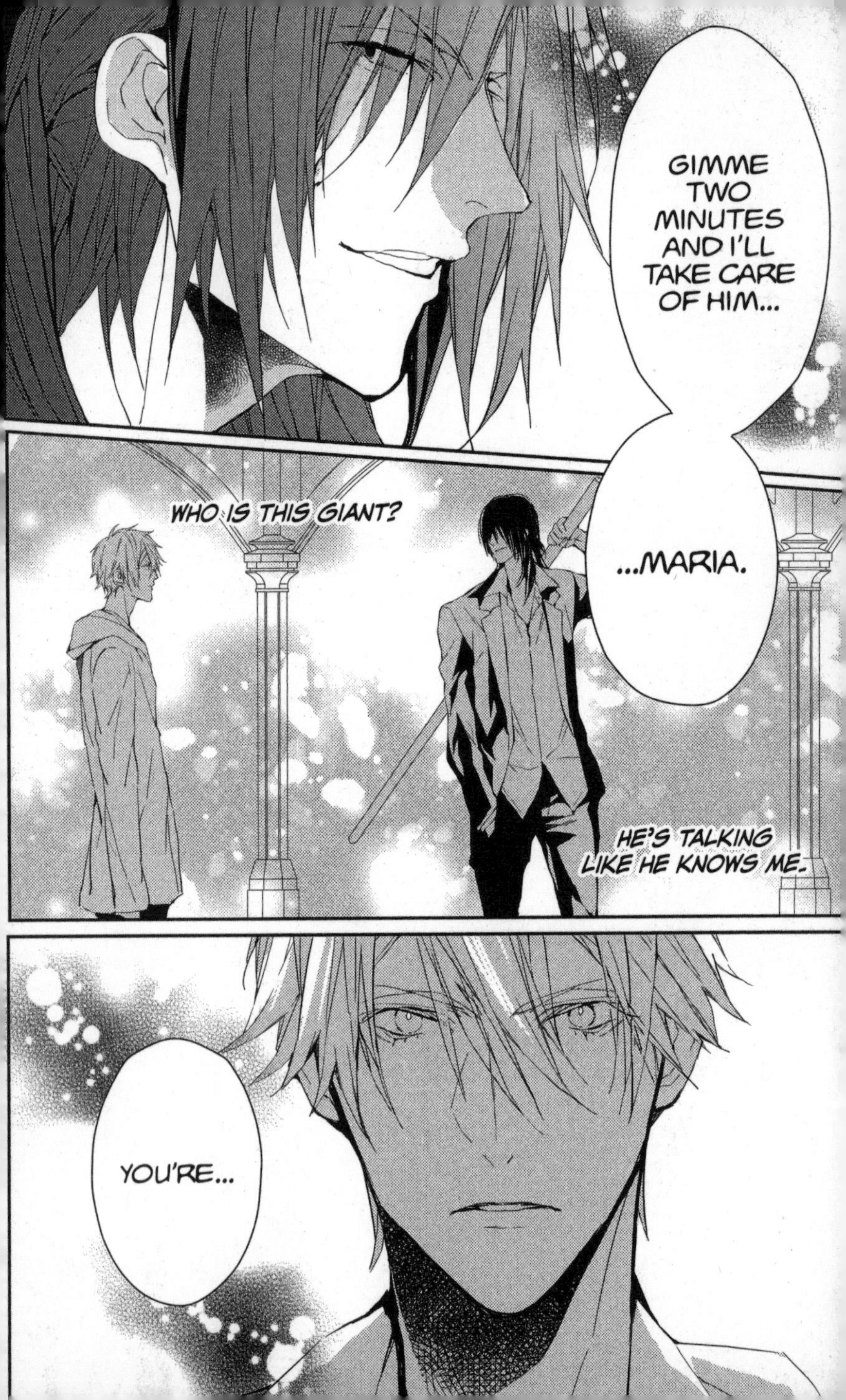
GIMME TWO MINUTES AND I'LL TAKE CARE OF HIM...
...MARIA.
WHO IS THIS GIANT?
HE'S TALKING LIKE HE KNOWS ME.
YOU'RE...

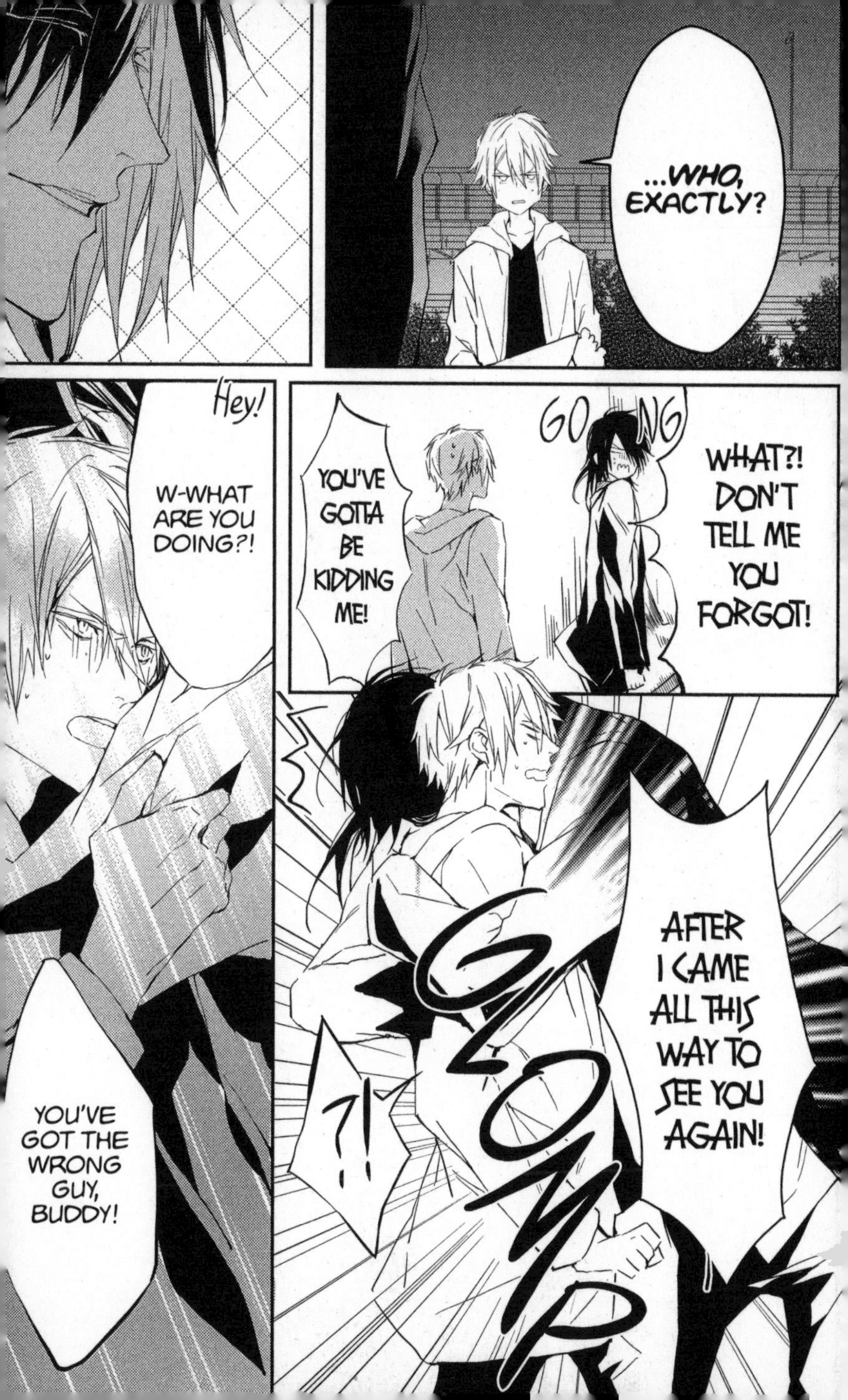
...WHO, EXACTLY?
GONG
WHAT?! DON'T TELL ME YOU FORGOT!
YOU'VE GOTTA BE KIDDING ME!
AFTER I CAME ALL THIS WAY TO SEE YOU AGAIN!
CHOMP
?!
Hey!
W-WHAT ARE YOU DOING?!
YOU'VE GOT THE WRONG GUY, BUDDY!

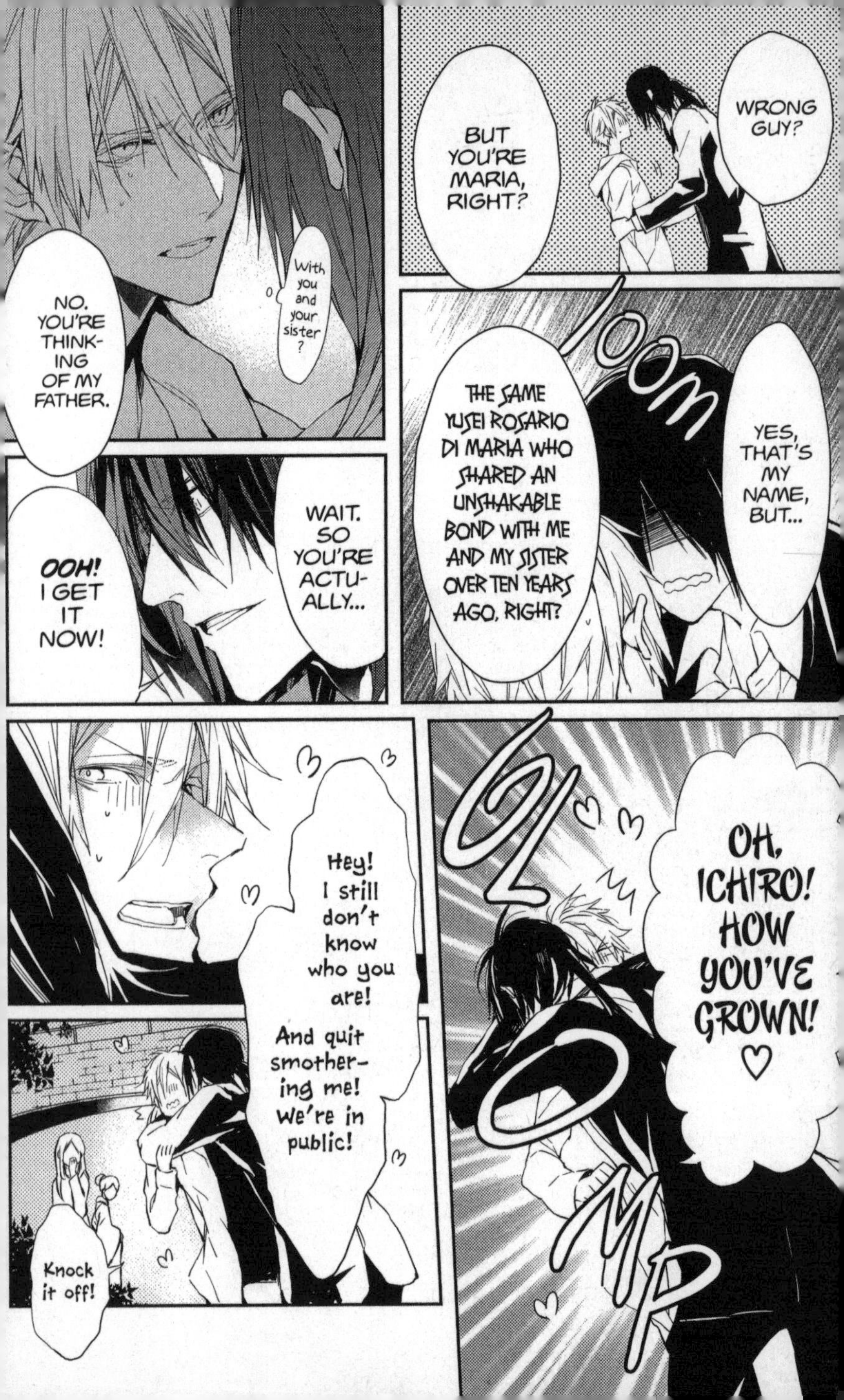
WRONG GUY?
BUT YOU'RE MARIA, RIGHT?
YES, THAT'S MY NAME, BUT...
LOOM
THE SAME YUSEI ROSARIO DI MARIA WHO SHARED AN UNSHAKABLE BOND WITH ME AND MY SISTER OVER TEN YEARS AGO, RIGHT?
With you and your sister?
NO. YOU'RE THINKING OF MY FATHER.
WAIT. SO YOU'RE ACTU-ALLY...
OOH! I GET IT NOW!
OH, ICHIRO! HOW YOU'VE GROWN! ♡
GLOMP
Hey! I still don't know who you are!
And quit smother-ing me! We're in public!
Knock it off!

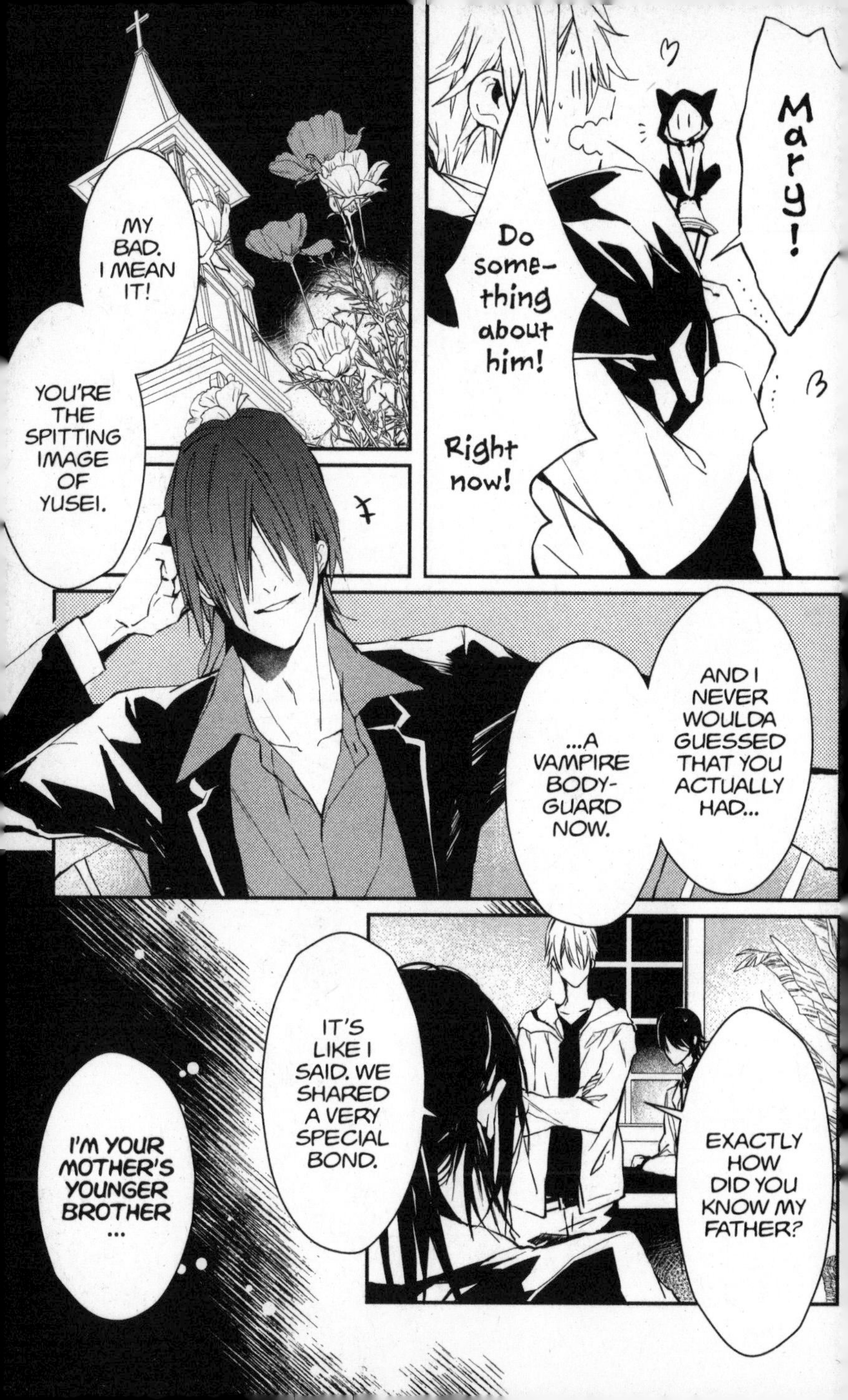
Mary!
Do some-thing about him!
Right now!
MY BAD. I MEAN IT!
YOU'RE THE SPITTING IMAGE OF YUSEI.
AND I NEVER WOULDA GUESSED THAT YOU ACTUALLY HAD...
...A VAMPIRE BODY-GUARD NOW.
EXACTLY HOW DID YOU KNOW MY FATHER?
IT'S LIKE I SAID. WE SHARED A VERY SPECIAL BOND.
I'M YOUR MOTHER'S YOUNGER BROTHER...

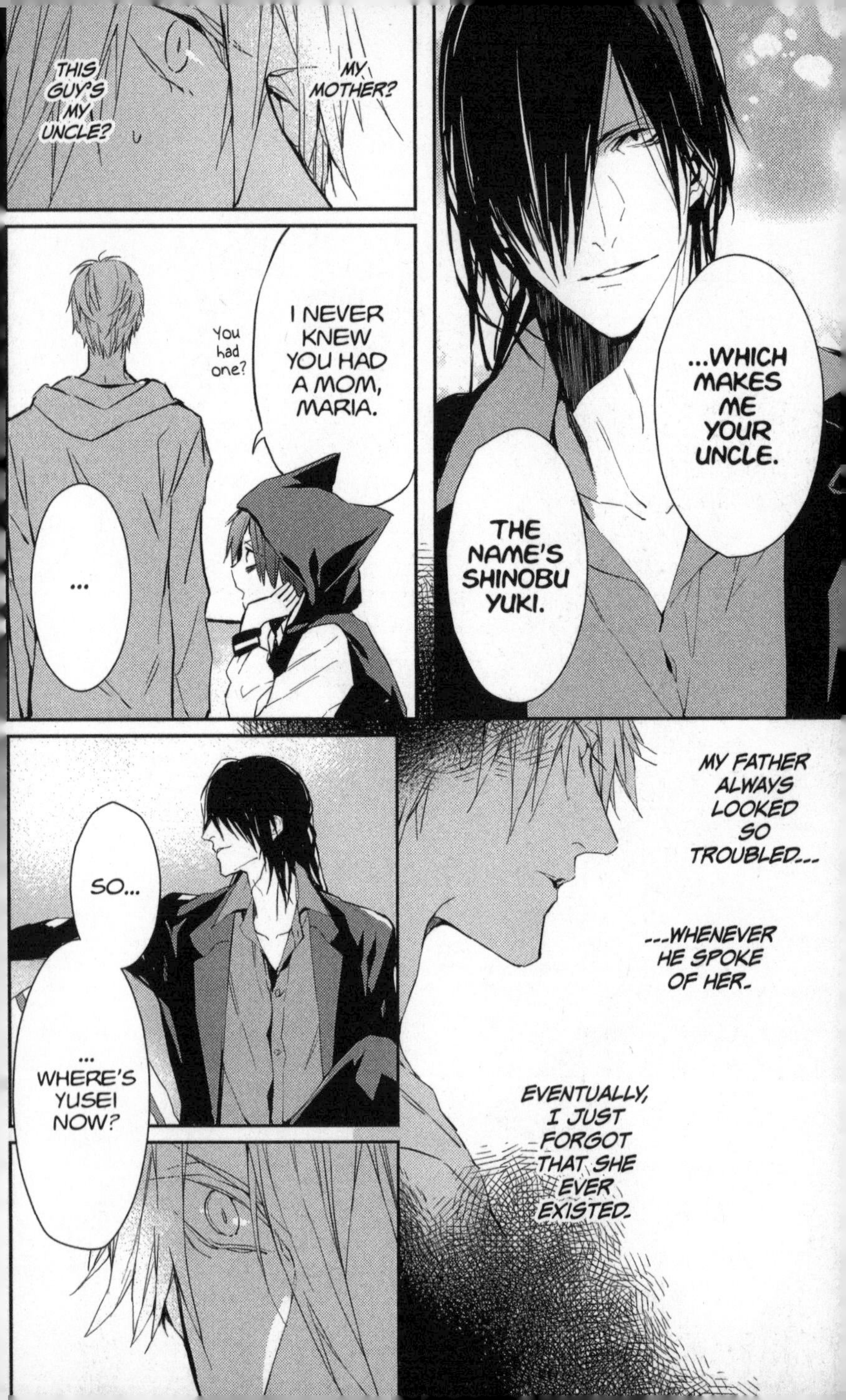
...WHICH MAKES ME YOUR UNCLE.
THE NAME'S SHINOBU YUKI.
MY MOTHER?
THIS GUY'S MY UNCLE?
I NEVER KNEW YOU HAD A MOM, MARIA.
You had one?
...
MY FATHER ALWAYS LOOKED SO TROUBLED...
...WHENEVER HE SPOKE OF HER.
EVENTUALLY, I JUST FORGOT THAT SHE EVER EXISTED.
SO...
...WHERE'S YUSEI NOW?

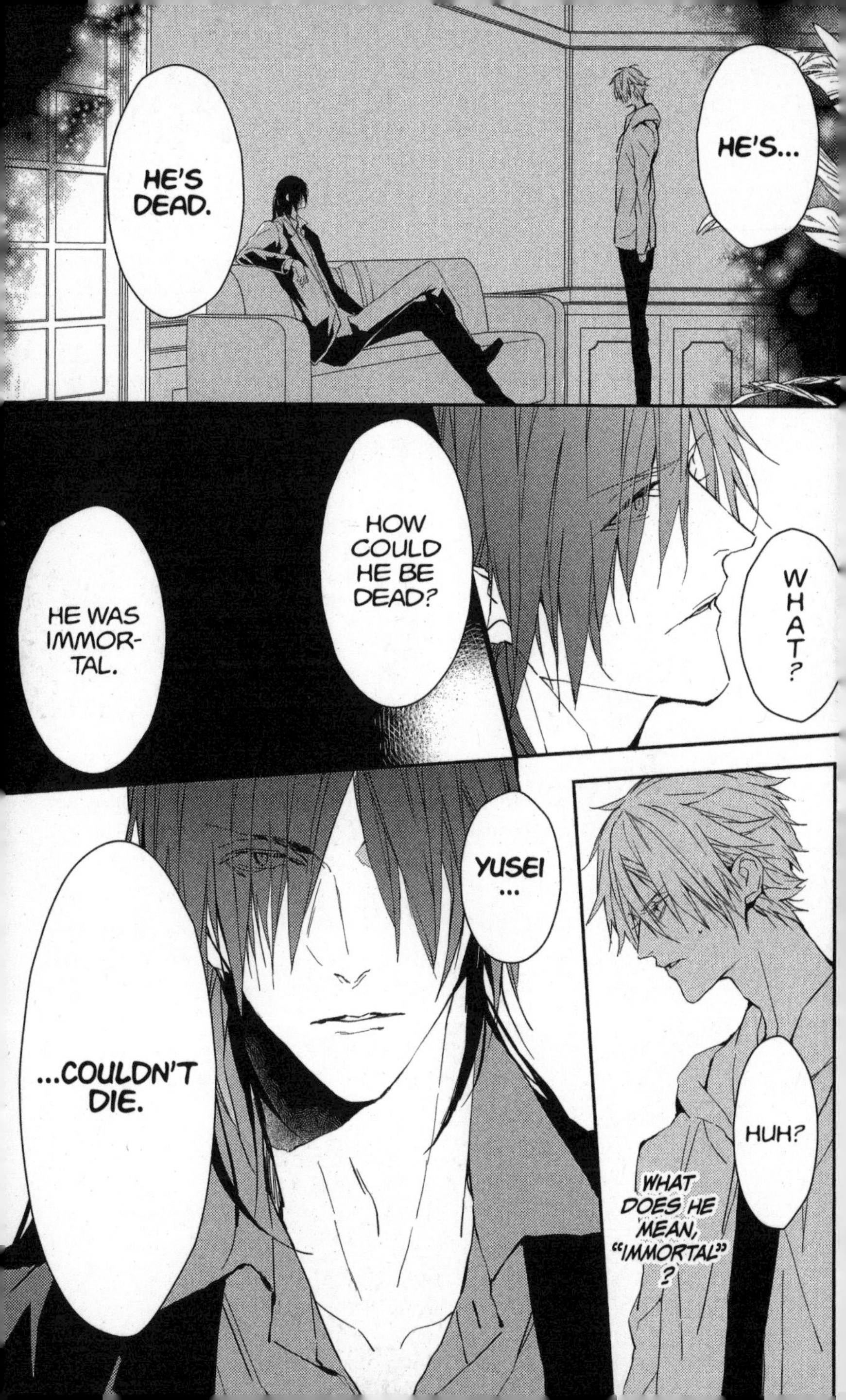
HE'S...
HE'S DEAD.
WHAT?
HOW COULD HE BE DEAD?
HE WAS IMMOR-TAL.
HUH?
WHAT DOES HE MEAN, "IMMORTAL"?
YUSEI...
...COULDN'T DIE.

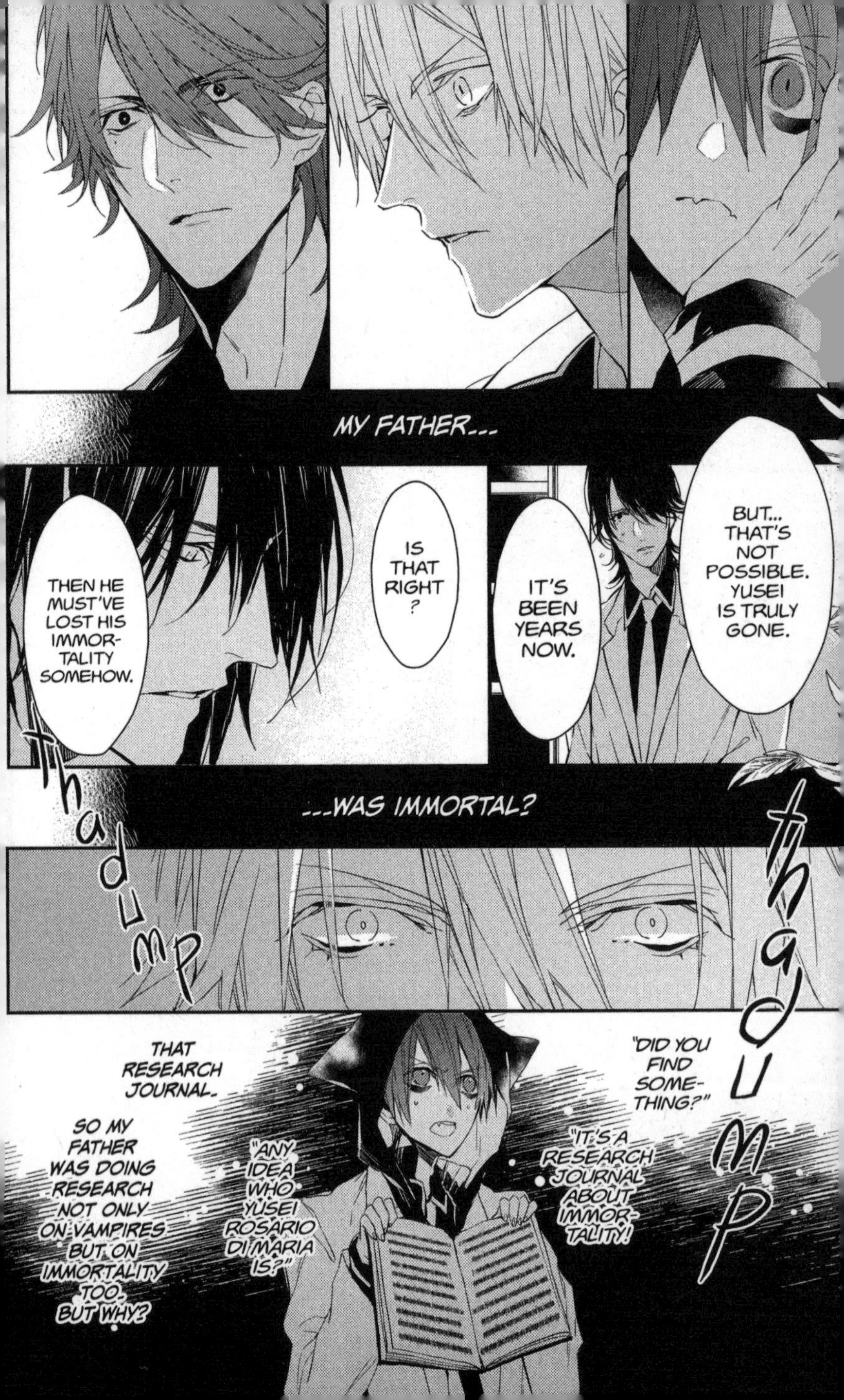
MY FATHER...
BUT... THAT'S NOT POSSIBLE. YUSEI IS TRULY GONE.
IT'S BEEN YEARS NOW.
IS THAT RIGHT?
THEN HE MUST'VE LOST HIS IMMORTALITY SOMEHOW.
thadump
...WAS IMMORTAL?
thadump
"DID YOU FIND SOMETHING?"
"IT'S A RESEARCH JOURNAL ABOUT IMMORTALITY!"
"ANY IDEA WHO YUSEI ROSARIO DI MARIA IS?"
THAT RESEARCH JOURNAL...
SO MY FATHER WAS DOING RESEARCH NOT ONLY ON VAMPIRES BUT ON IMMORTALITY TOO. BUT WHY?

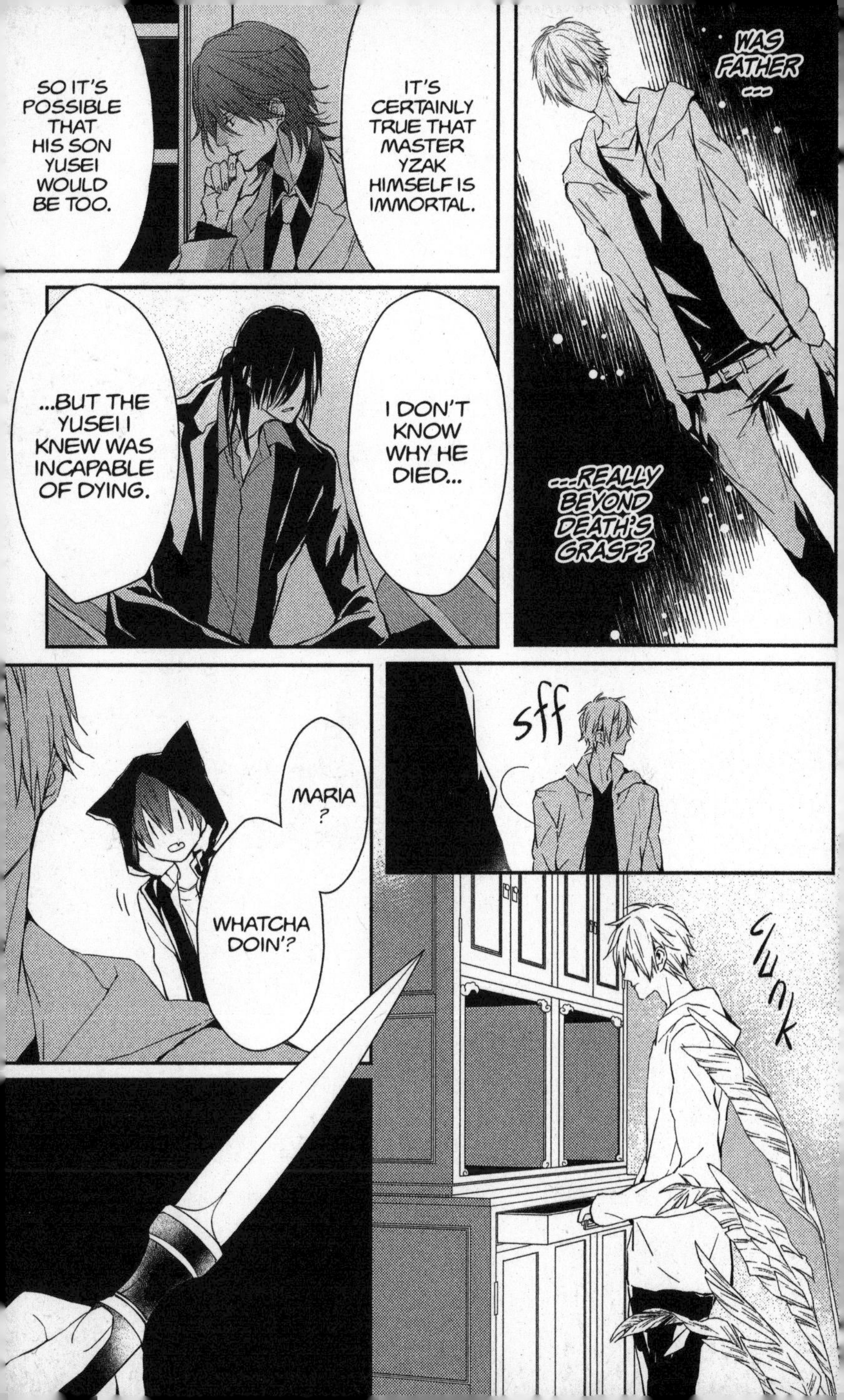
WAS FATHER ---
---REALLY BEYOND DEATH'S GRASP?
IT'S CERTAINLY TRUE THAT MASTER YZAK HIMSELF IS IMMORTAL.
SO IT'S POSSIBLE THAT HIS SON YUSEI WOULD BE TOO.
I DON'T KNOW WHY HE DIED...
...BUT THE YUSEI I KNEW WAS INCAPABLE OF DYING.
sff
MARIA?
WHATCHA DOIN'?
clunk

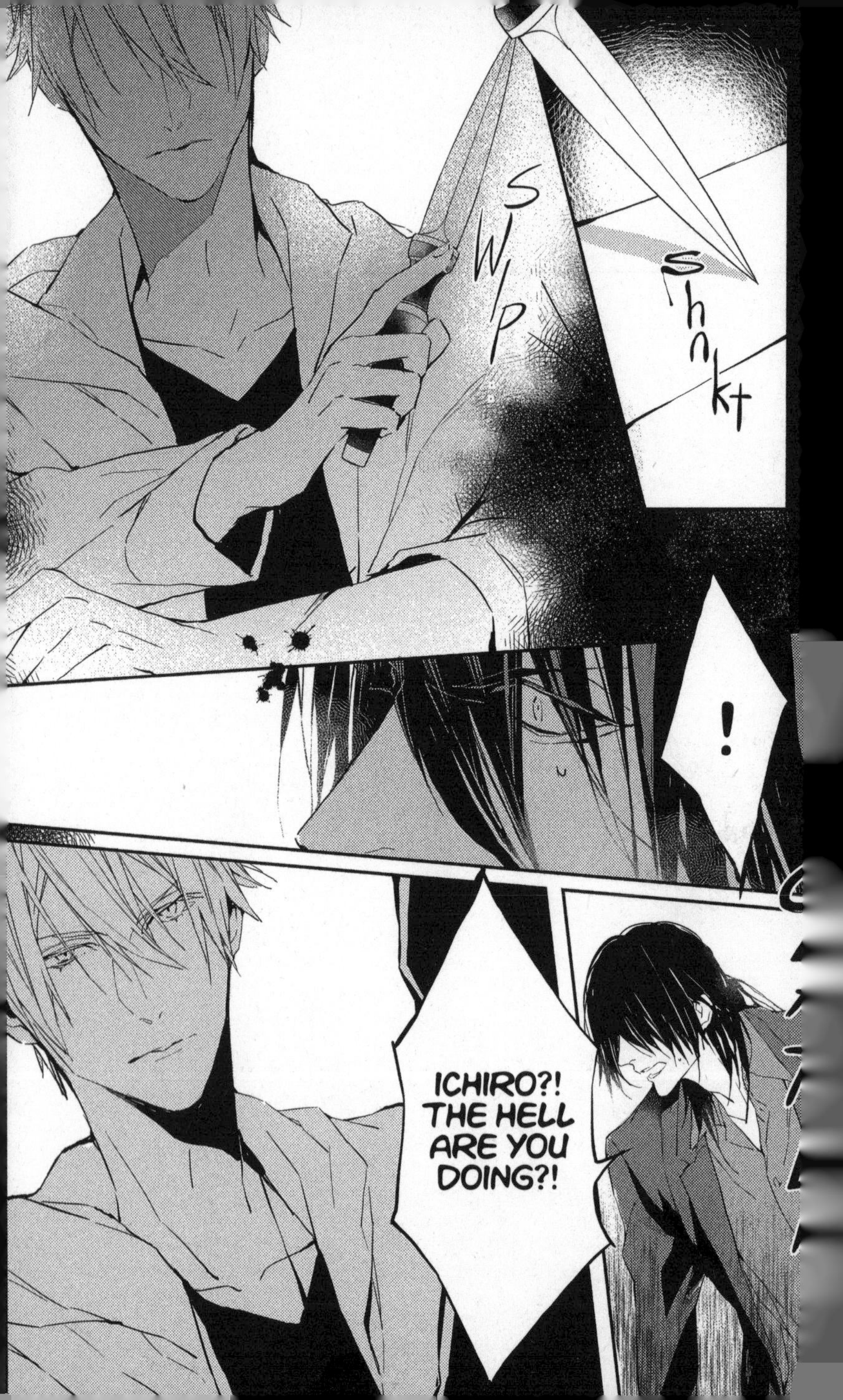
SWP
shnkt
!
ICHIRO?! THE HELL ARE YOU DOING?!

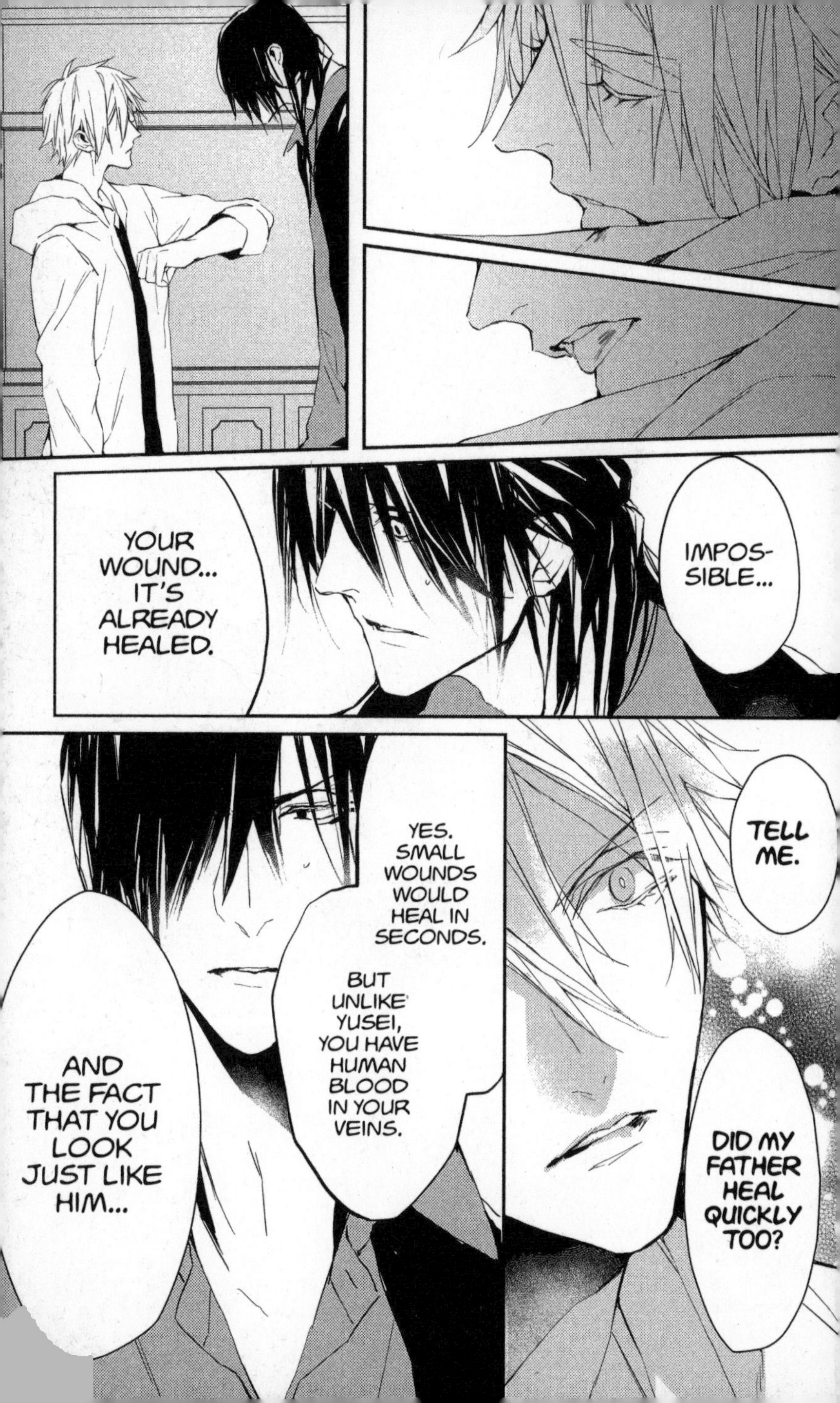
IMPOSSIBLE...
YOUR WOUND... IT'S ALREADY HEALED.
TELL ME.
DID MY FATHER HEAL QUICKLY TOO?
YES. SMALL WOUNDS WOULD HEAL IN SECONDS.
BUT UNLIKE YUSEI, YOU HAVE HUMAN BLOOD IN YOUR VEINS.
AND THE FACT THAT YOU LOOK JUST LIKE HIM...

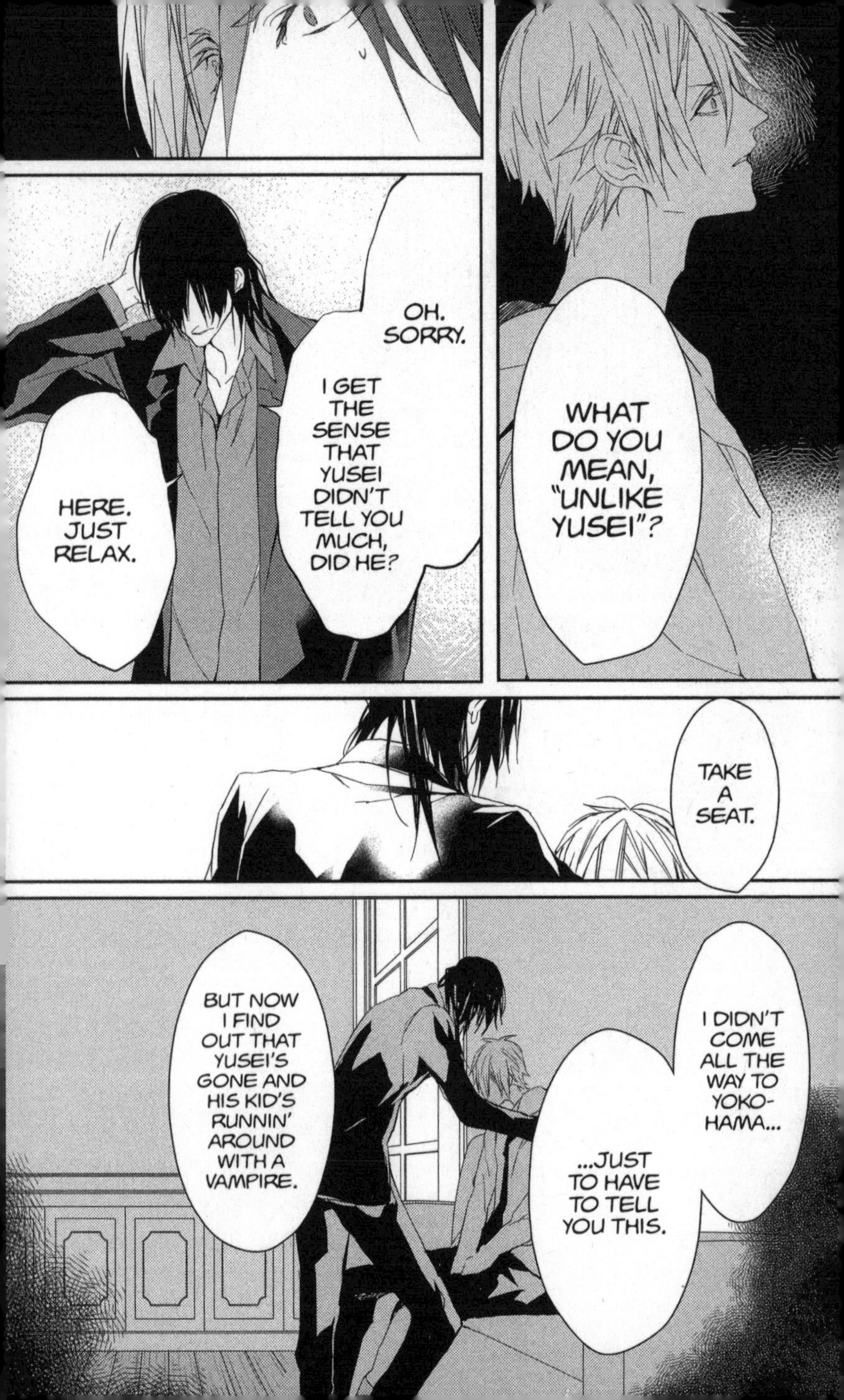
WHAT DO YOU MEAN, "UNLIKE YUSEI"?
OH. SORRY.
I GET THE SENSE THAT YUSEI DIDN'T TELL YOU MUCH, DID HE?
HERE. JUST RELAX.
TAKE A SEAT.
I DIDN'T COME ALL THE WAY TO YOKO-HAMA...
...JUST TO HAVE TO TELL YOU THIS.
BUT NOW I FIND OUT THAT YUSEI'S GONE AND HIS KID'S RUNNIN' AROUND WITH A VAMPIRE.

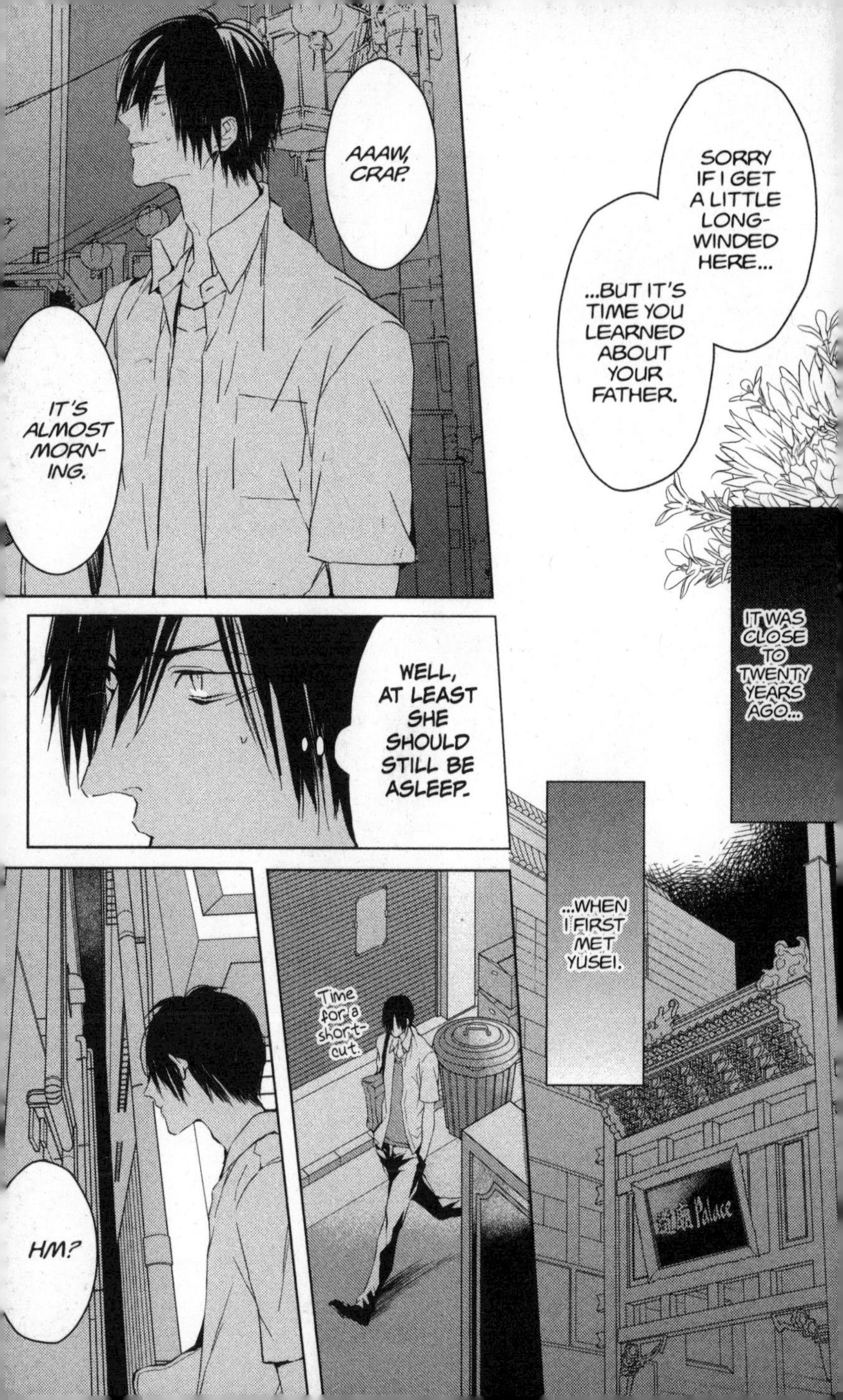
SORRY IF I GET A LITTLE LONG-WINDED HERE...
...BUT IT'S TIME YOU LEARNED ABOUT YOUR FATHER.
IT WAS CLOSE TO TWENTY YEARS AGO...
...WHEN I FIRST MET YUSEI.
AAAW, CRAP.
IT'S ALMOST MORNING.
WELL, AT LEAST SHE SHOULD STILL BE ASLEEP.
Time for a short-cut.
HM?

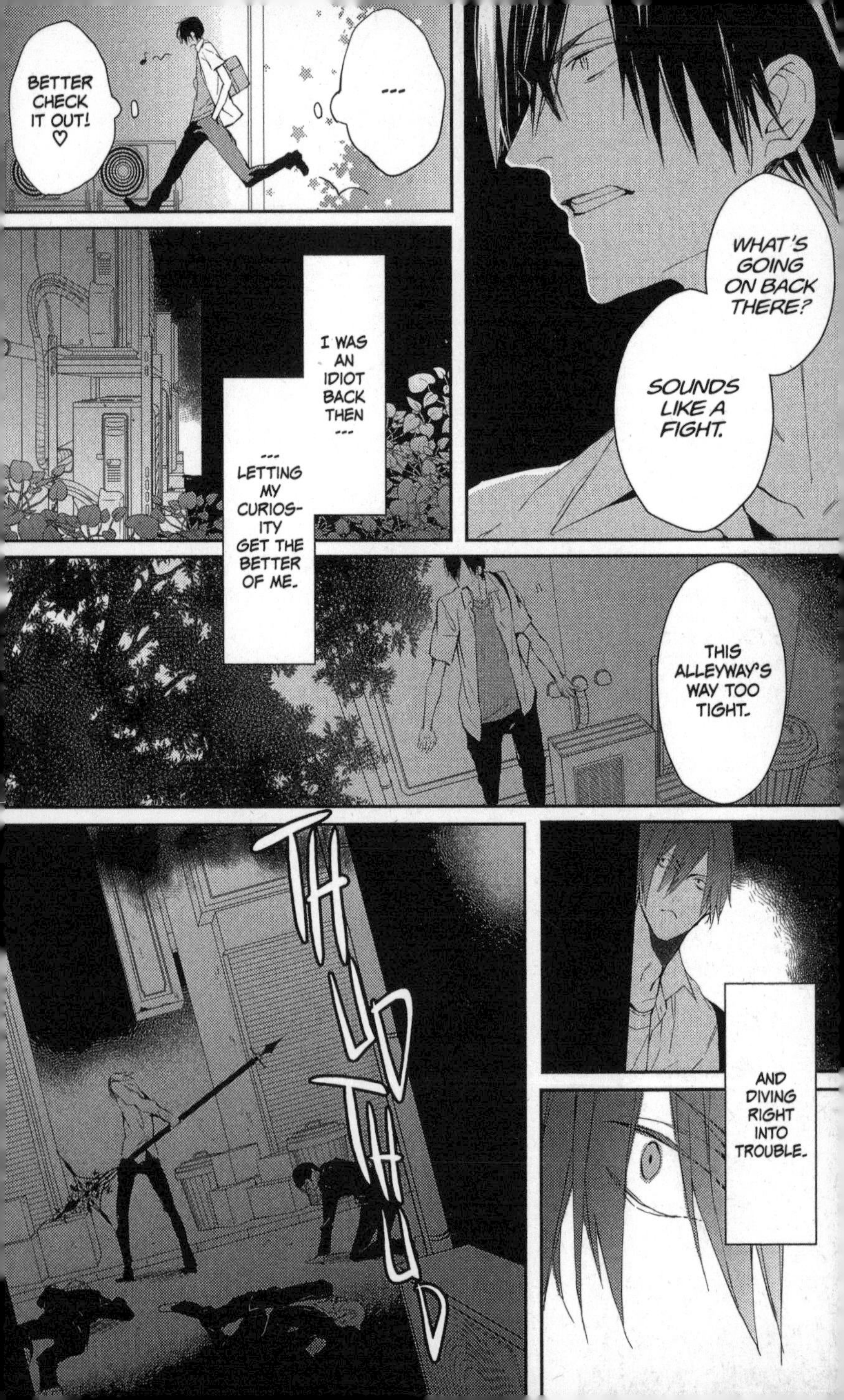
WHAT'S GOING ON BACK THERE?
SOUNDS LIKE A FIGHT.
...
BETTER CHECK IT OUT! ♡
I WAS AN IDIOT BACK THEN...
...LETTING MY CURIOSITY GET THE BETTER OF ME.
THIS ALLEYWAY'S WAY TOO TIGHT.
AND DIVING RIGHT INTO TROUBLE.
THUD THUD

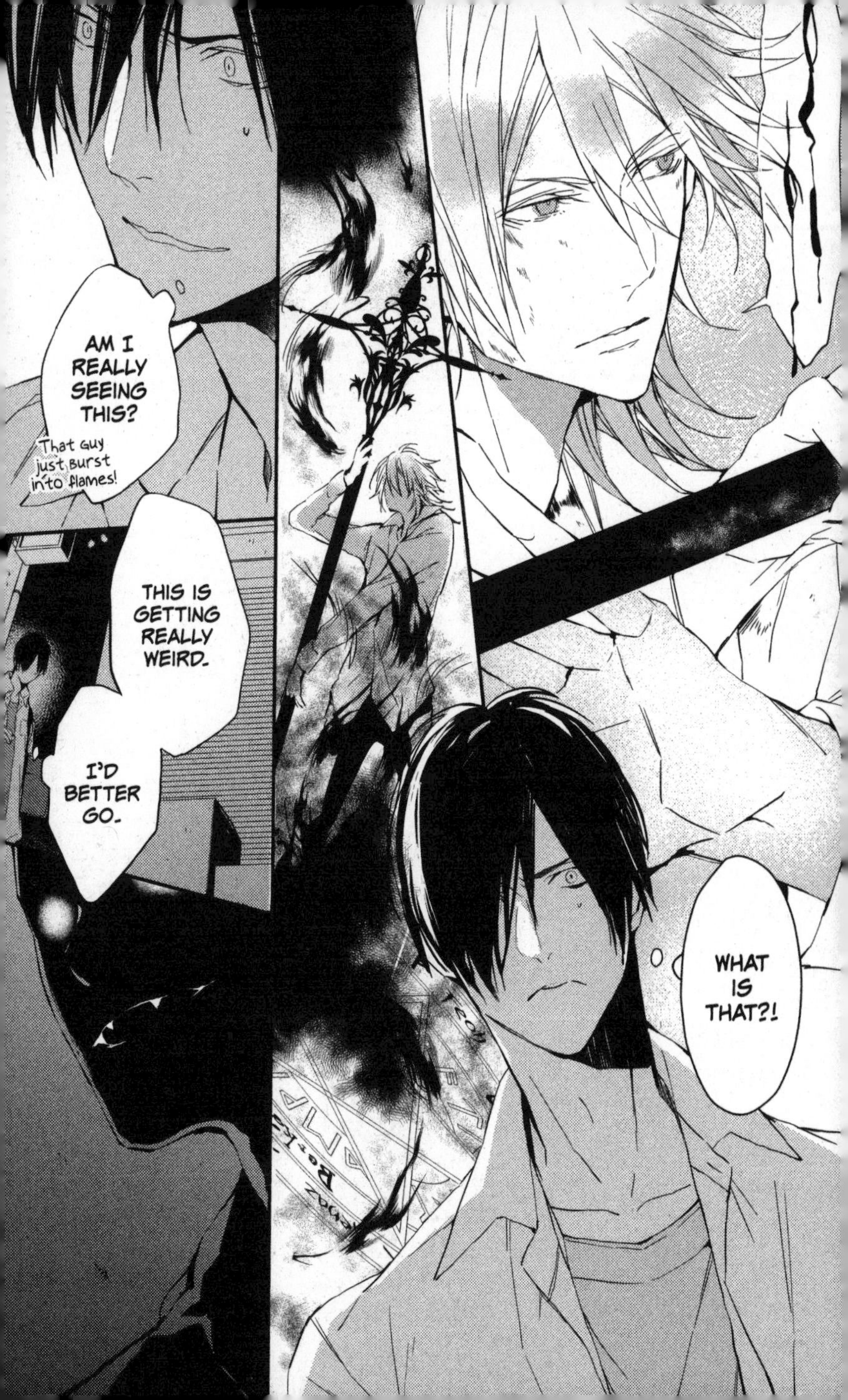
WHAT IS THAT?!
AM I REALLY SEEING THIS?
That guy just burst into flames!
THIS IS GETTING REALLY WEIRD.
I'D BETTER GO.

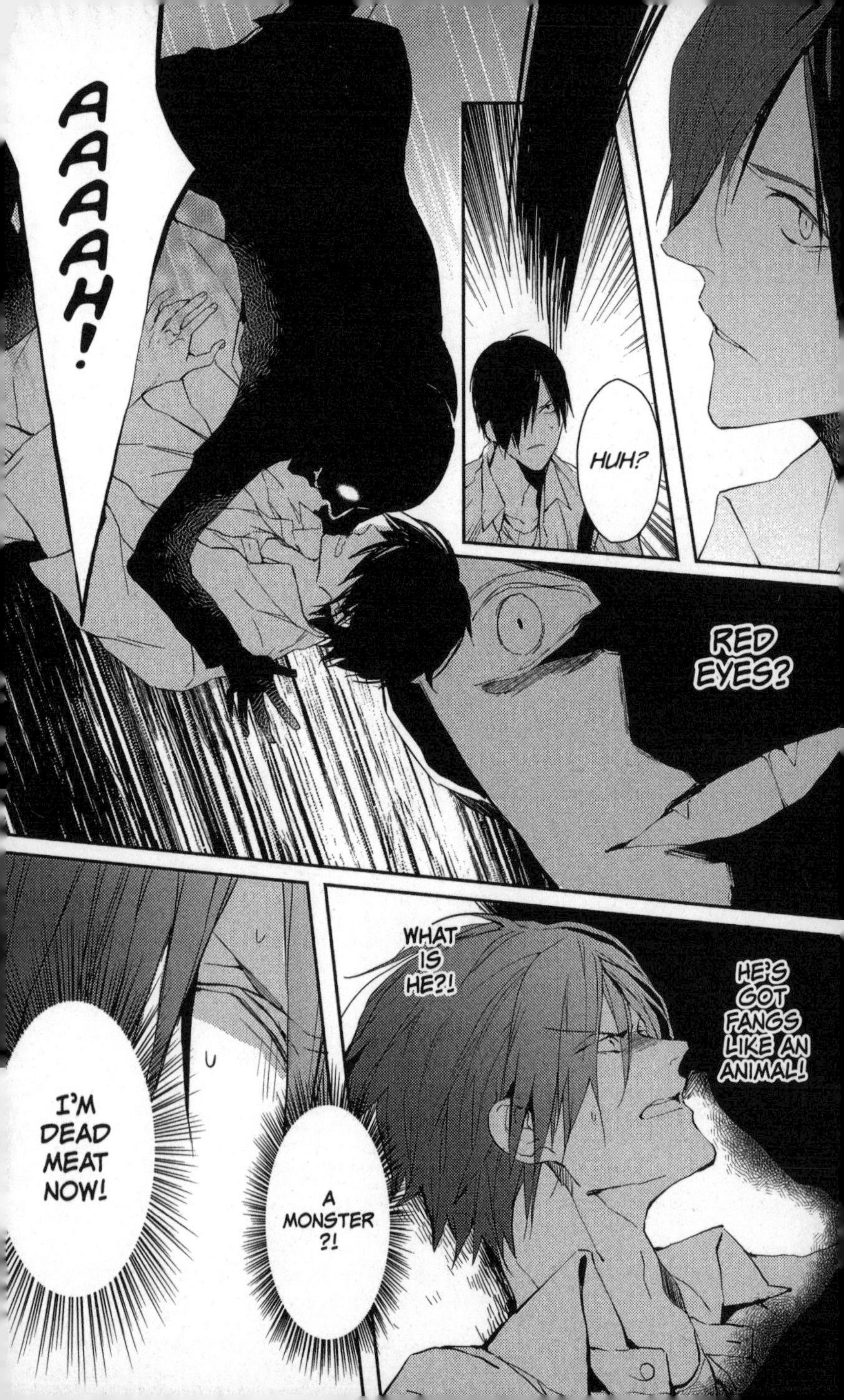
HUH?
AAAAAH!
RED EYES?
HE'S GOT FANGS LIKE AN ANIMAL!
WHAT IS HE?!
A MONSTER?!
I'M DEAD MEAT NOW!

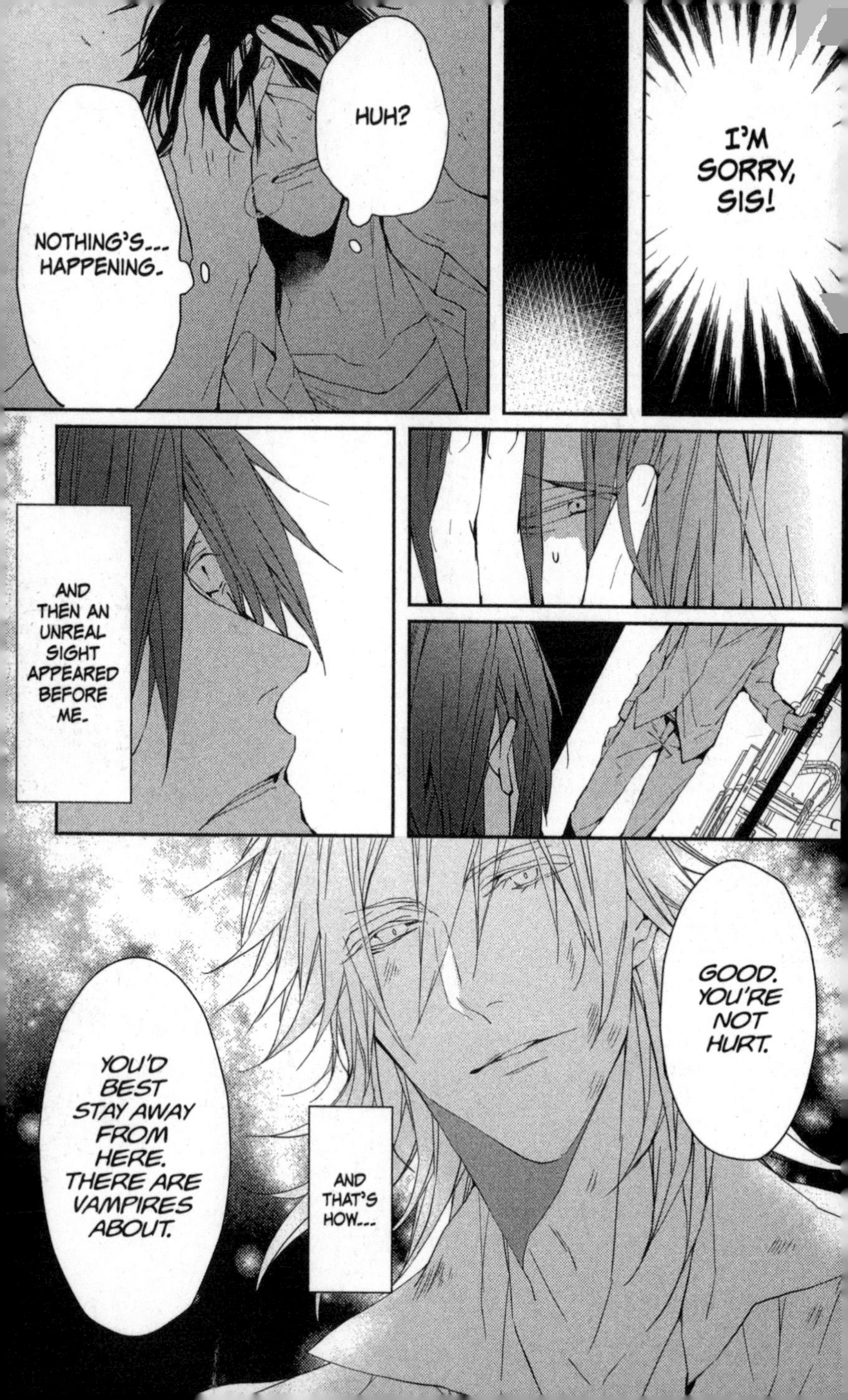
I'M SORRY, SIS!
HUH?
NOTHING'S... HAPPENING.
AND THEN AN UNREAL SIGHT APPEARED BEFORE ME.
GOOD. YOU'RE NOT HURT.
AND THAT'S HOW...
YOU'D BEST STAY AWAY FROM HERE. THERE ARE VAMPIRES ABOUT.

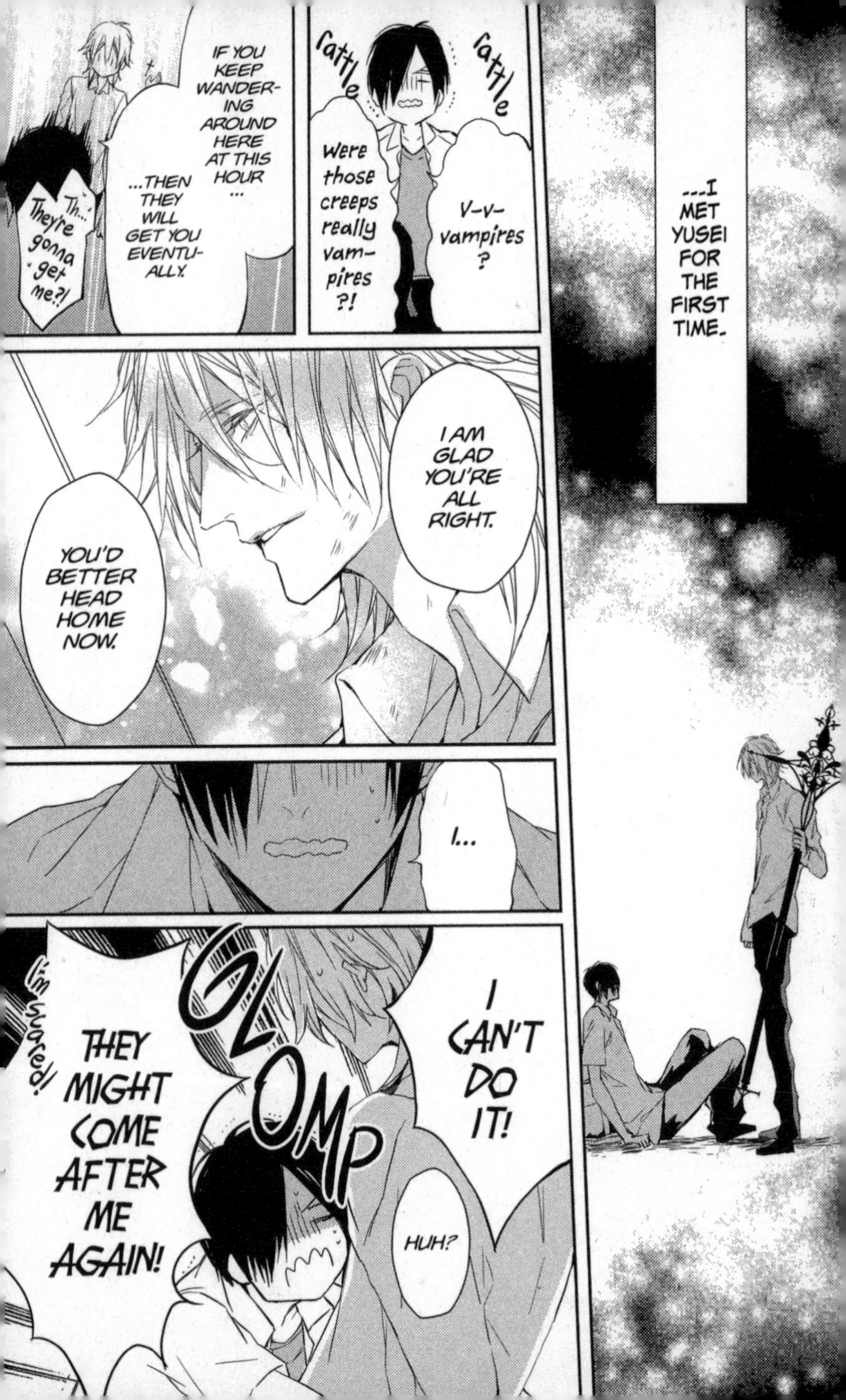
---I MET YUSEI FOR THE FIRST TIME.
rattle
rattle
V-v-vampires?
Were those creeps really vampires?!
IF YOU KEEP WANDERING AROUND HERE AT THIS HOUR...
...THEN THEY WILL GET YOU EVENTUALLY.
Th... They're gonna get me?!
I AM GLAD YOU'RE ALL RIGHT.
YOU'D BETTER HEAD HOME NOW.
I...
I CAN'T DO IT!
GLOMP
HUH?
THEY MIGHT COME AFTER ME AGAIN!
I'm scared!

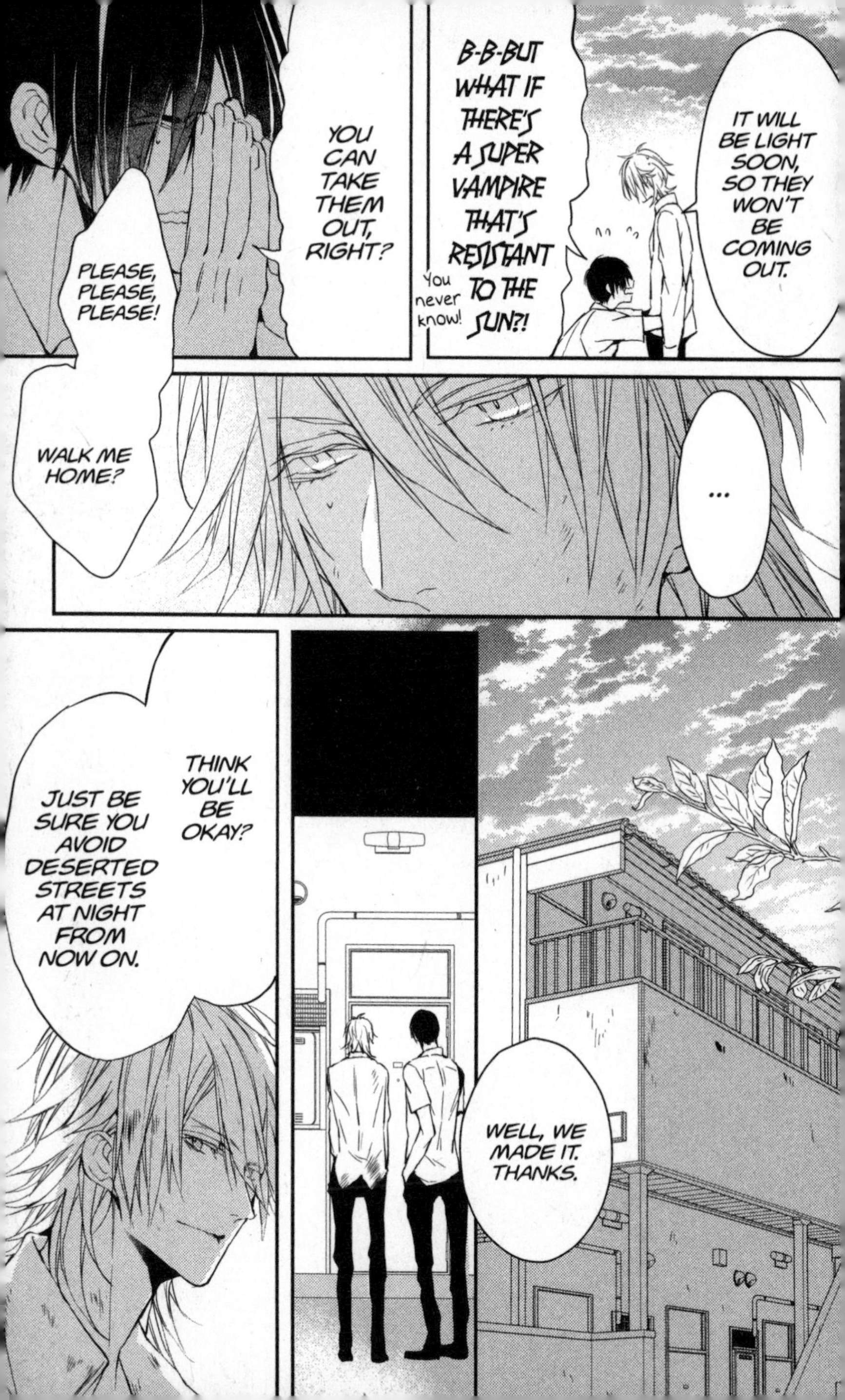
IT WILL BE LIGHT SOON, SO THEY WON'T BE COMING OUT.
B-B-BUT WHAT IF THERE'S A SUPER VAMPIRE THAT'S RESISTANT TO THE SUN?!
You never know!
YOU CAN TAKE THEM OUT, RIGHT?
PLEASE, PLEASE, PLEASE!
WALK ME HOME?
...
WELL, WE MADE IT. THANKS.
THINK YOU'LL BE OKAY?
JUST BE SURE YOU AVOID DESERTED STREETS AT NIGHT FROM NOW ON.

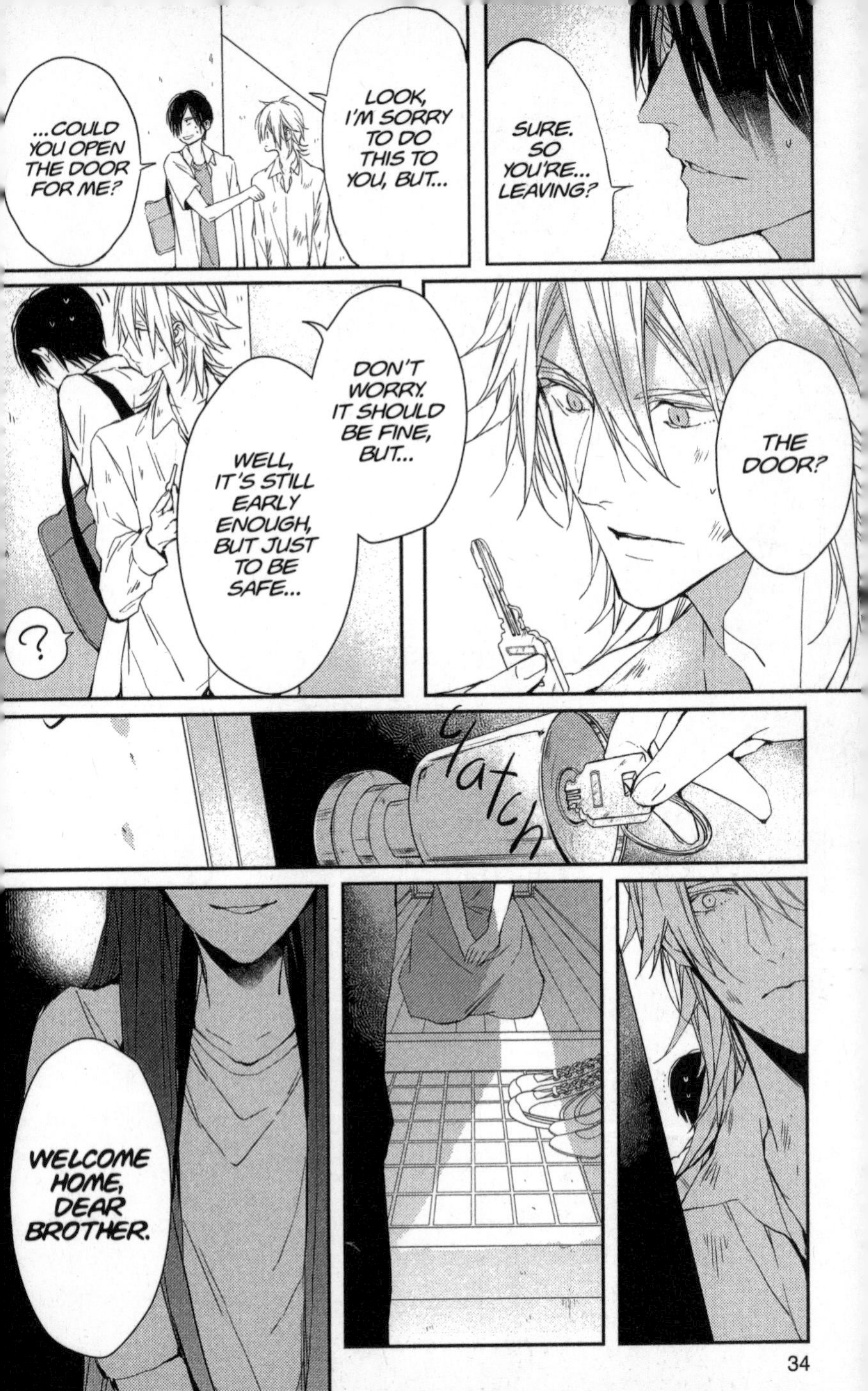
SURE. SO YOU'RE... LEAVING?
LOOK, I'M SORRY TO DO THIS TO YOU, BUT...
...COULD YOU OPEN THE DOOR FOR ME?
THE DOOR?
DON'T WORRY. IT SHOULD BE FINE, BUT...
WELL, IT'S STILL EARLY ENOUGH, BUT JUST TO BE SAFE...
?
gatch
WELCOME HOME, DEAR BROTHER.

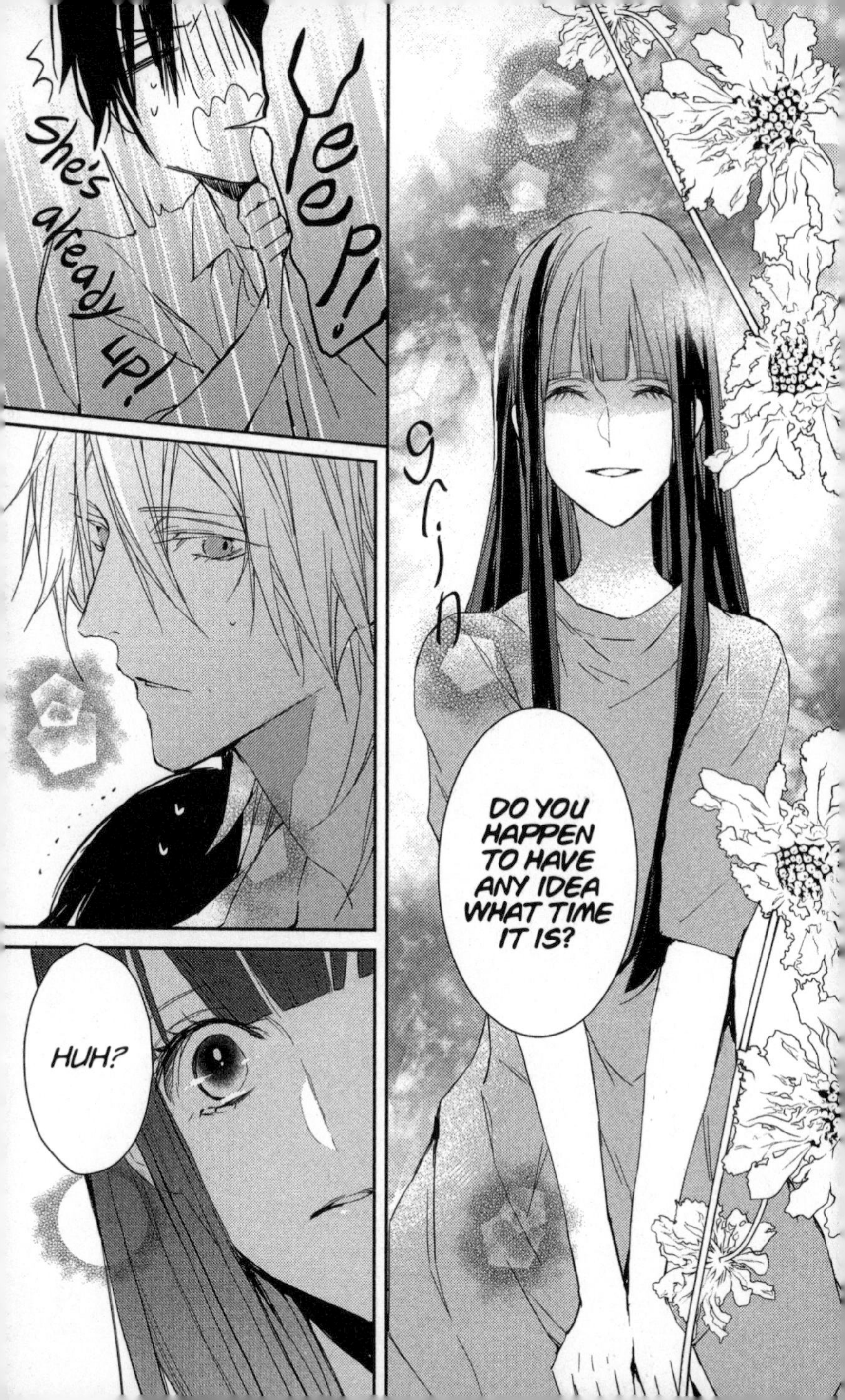
grin
DO YOU HAPPEN TO HAVE ANY IDEA WHAT TIME IT IS?
YEP!
She's already up!
HUH?

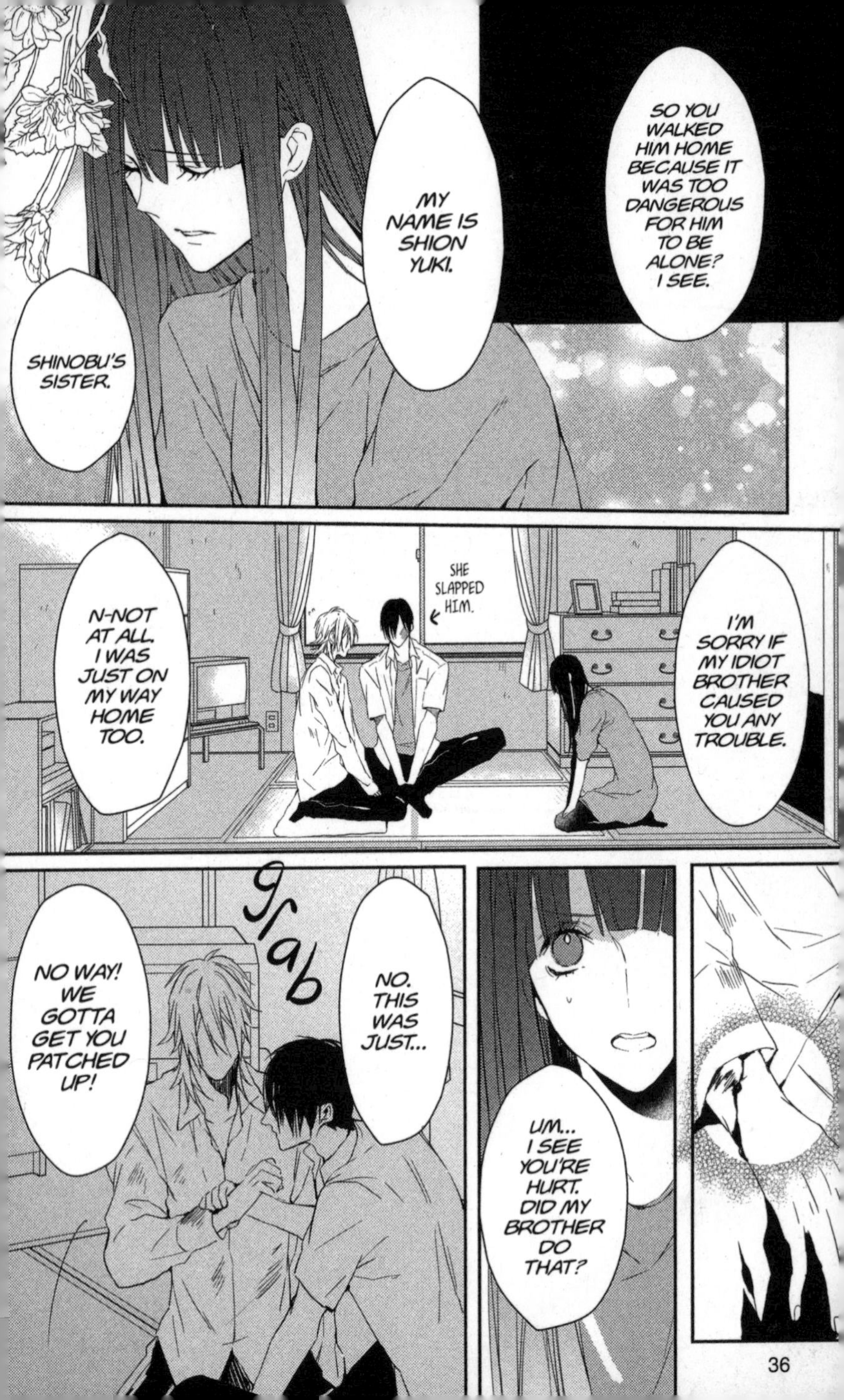
SO YOU WALKED HIM HOME BECAUSE IT WAS TOO DANGEROUS FOR HIM TO BE ALONE? I SEE.
MY NAME IS SHION YUKI.
SHINOBU'S SISTER.
I'M SORRY IF MY IDIOT BROTHER CAUSED YOU ANY TROUBLE.
SHE SLAPPED HIM.
N-NOT AT ALL. I WAS JUST ON MY WAY HOME TOO.
UM... I SEE YOU'RE HURT. DID MY BROTHER DO THAT?
grab
NO. THIS WAS JUST...
NO WAY! WE GOTTA GET YOU PATCHED UP!

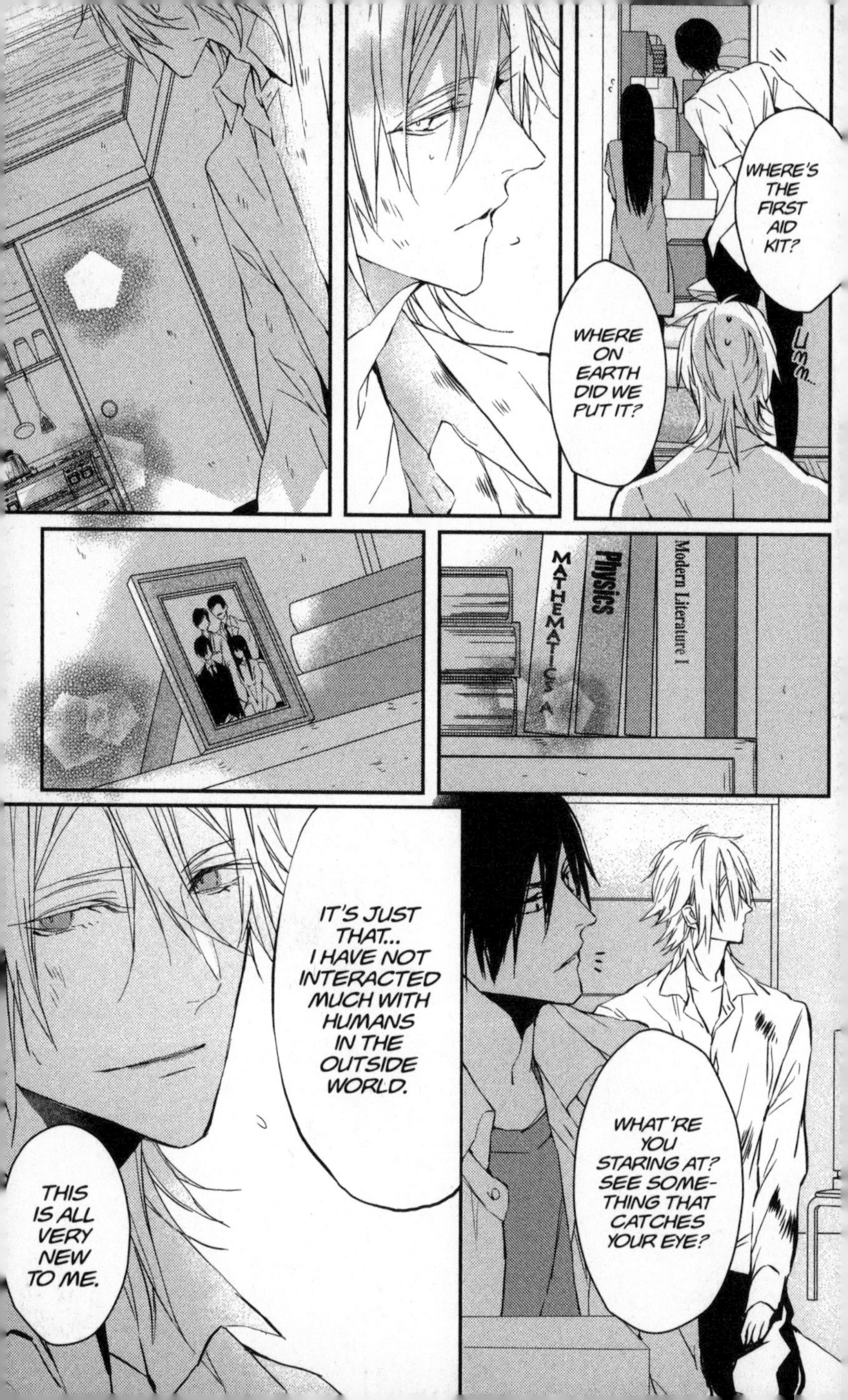
WHERE'S THE FIRST AID KIT?
WHERE ON EARTH DID WE PUT IT?
UMM...
Physics
MATHEMATICS A
Modern Literature I
WHAT'RE YOU STARING AT? SEE SOME-THING THAT CATCHES YOUR EYE?
IT'S JUST THAT... I HAVE NOT INTERACTED MUCH WITH HUMANS IN THE OUTSIDE WORLD.
THIS IS ALL VERY NEW TO ME.

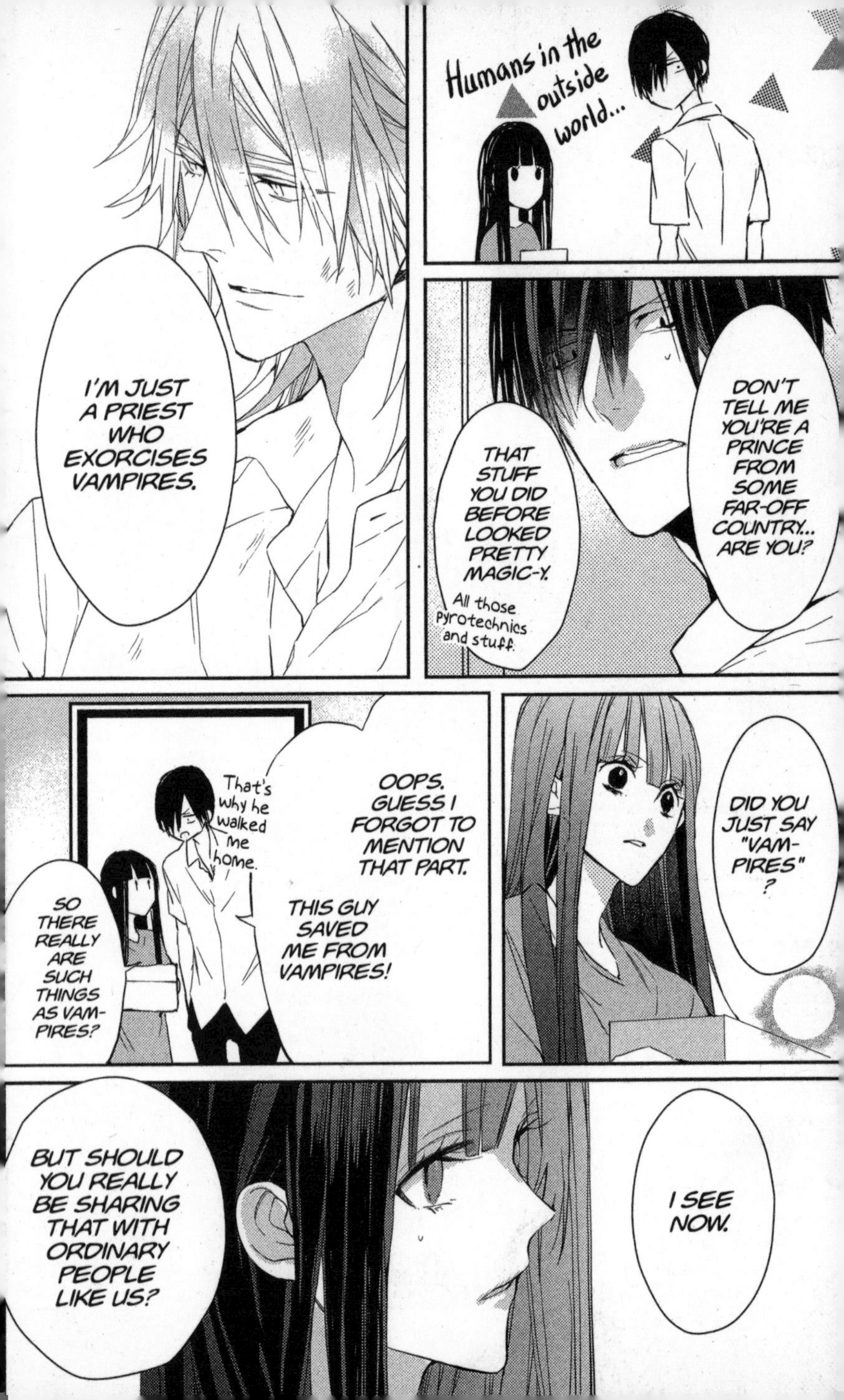
Humans in the outside world...
DON'T TELL ME YOU'RE A PRINCE FROM SOME FAR-OFF COUNTRY... ARE YOU?
THAT STUFF YOU DID BEFORE LOOKED PRETTY MAGIC-Y.
All those pyrotechnics and stuff.
I'M JUST A PRIEST WHO EXORCISES VAMPIRES.
DID YOU JUST SAY "VAM-PIRES"?
OOPS. GUESS I FORGOT TO MENTION THAT PART.
THIS GUY SAVED ME FROM VAMPIRES!
That's why he walked me home.
SO THERE REALLY ARE SUCH THINGS AS VAM-PIRES?
I SEE NOW.
BUT SHOULD YOU REALLY BE SHARING THAT WITH ORDINARY PEOPLE LIKE US?

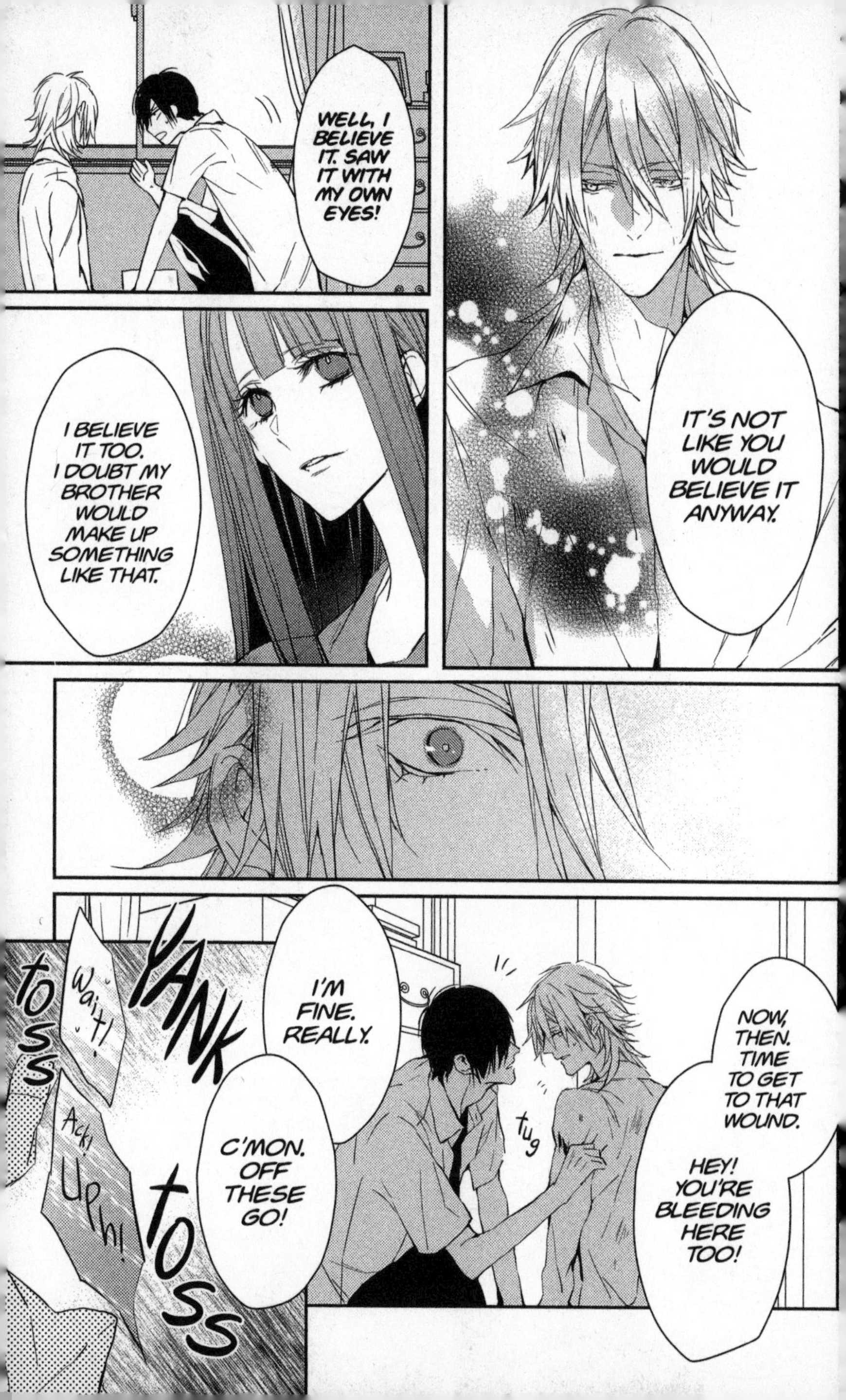
IT'S NOT LIKE YOU WOULD BELIEVE IT ANYWAY.
WELL, I BELIEVE IT. SAW IT WITH MY OWN EYES!
I BELIEVE IT TOO. I DOUBT MY BROTHER WOULD MAKE UP SOMETHING LIKE THAT.
NOW, THEN. TIME TO GET TO THAT WOUND.
HEY! YOU'RE BLEEDING HERE TOO!
I'M FINE. REALLY.
tug
C'MON. OFF THESE GO!
YANK
Wait!
TOSS
Ack!
Uph!
TOSS
TOSS

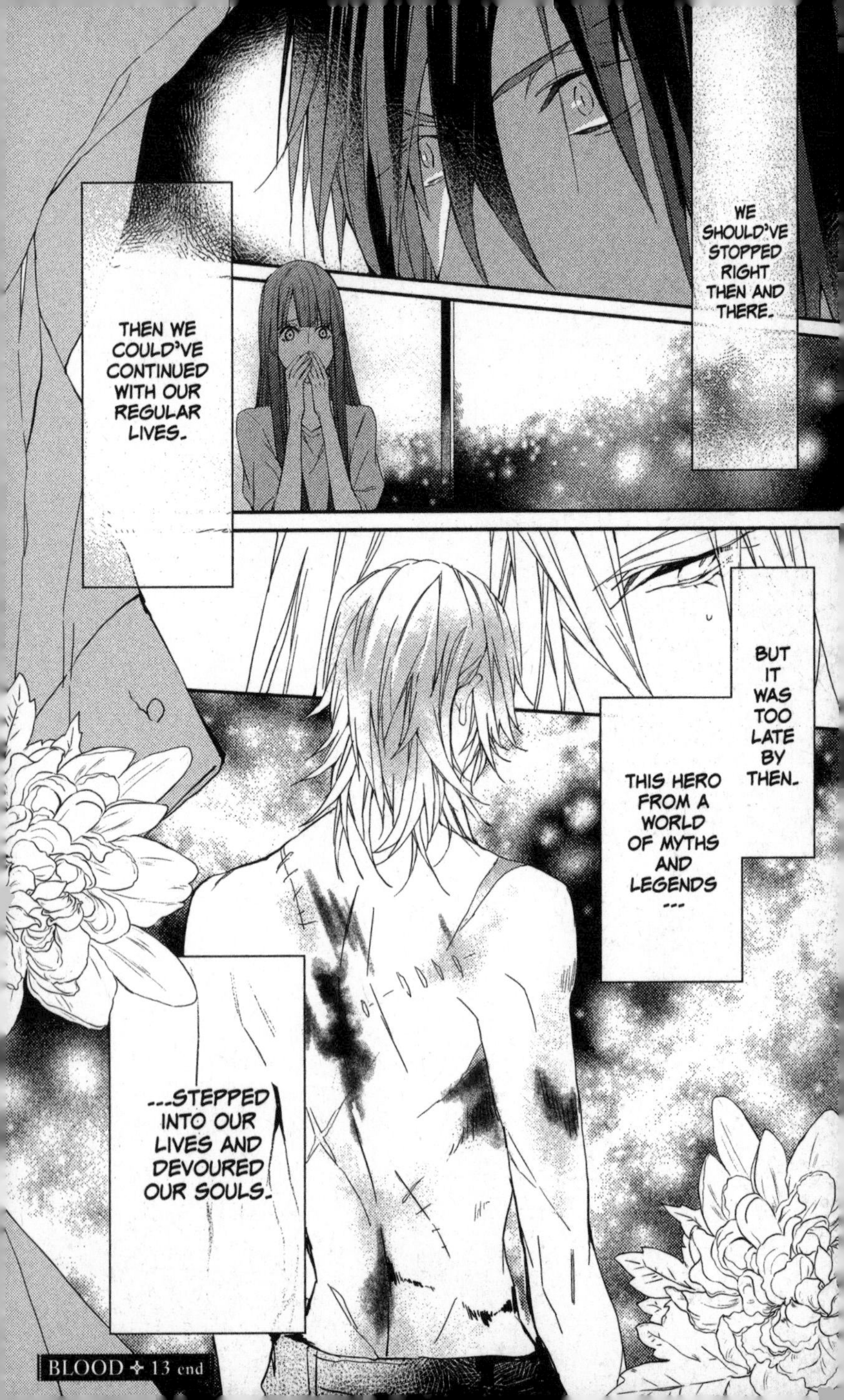
WE SHOULD'VE STOPPED RIGHT THEN AND THERE.
THEN WE COULD'VE CONTINUED WITH OUR REGULAR LIVES.
BUT IT WAS TOO LATE BY THEN.
THIS HERO FROM A WORLD OF MYTHS AND LEGENDS---
---STEPPED INTO OUR LIVES AND DEVOURED OUR SOULS.
BLOOD ✧ 13 end

Bloody+Mary

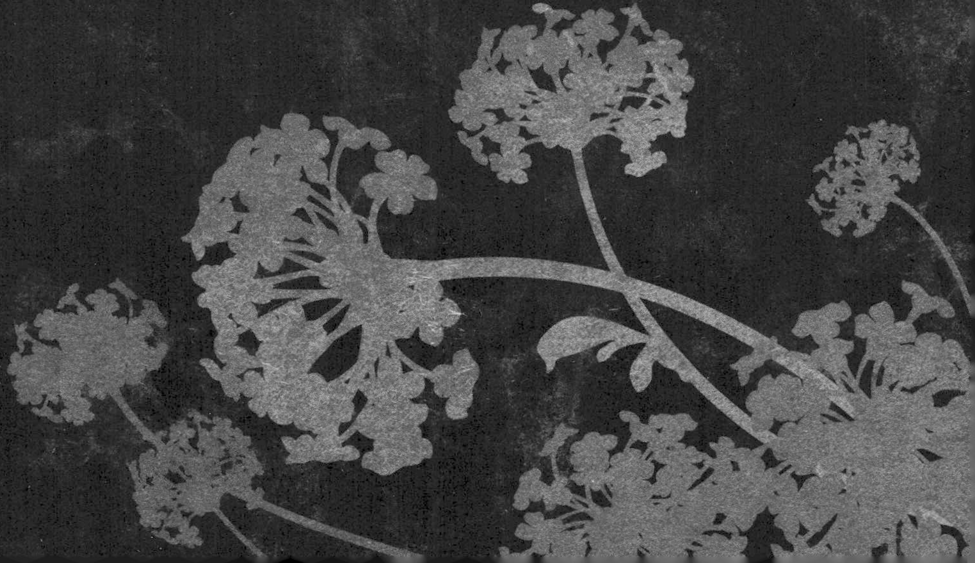

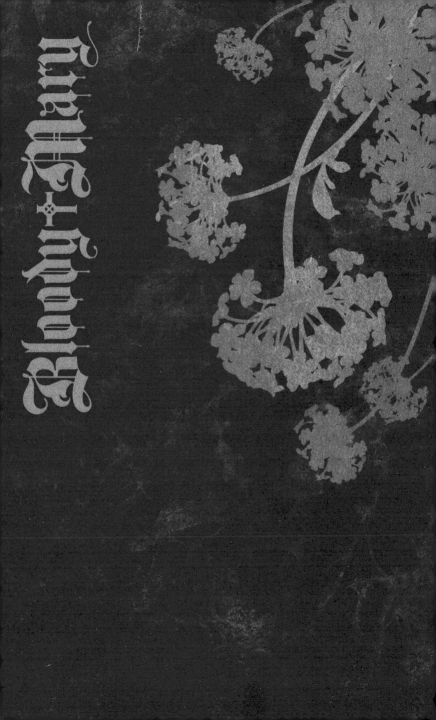

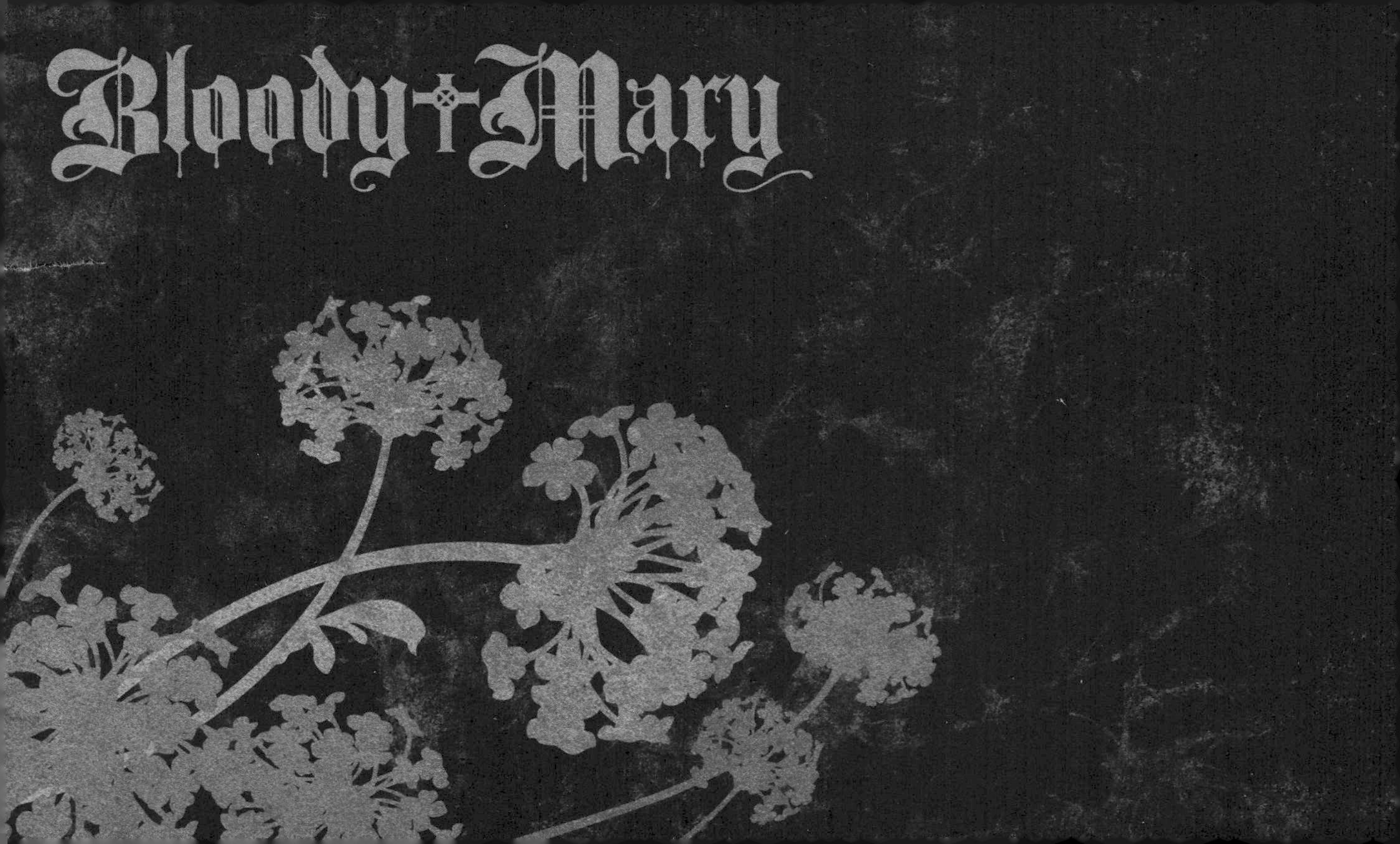
Bloody+Mary

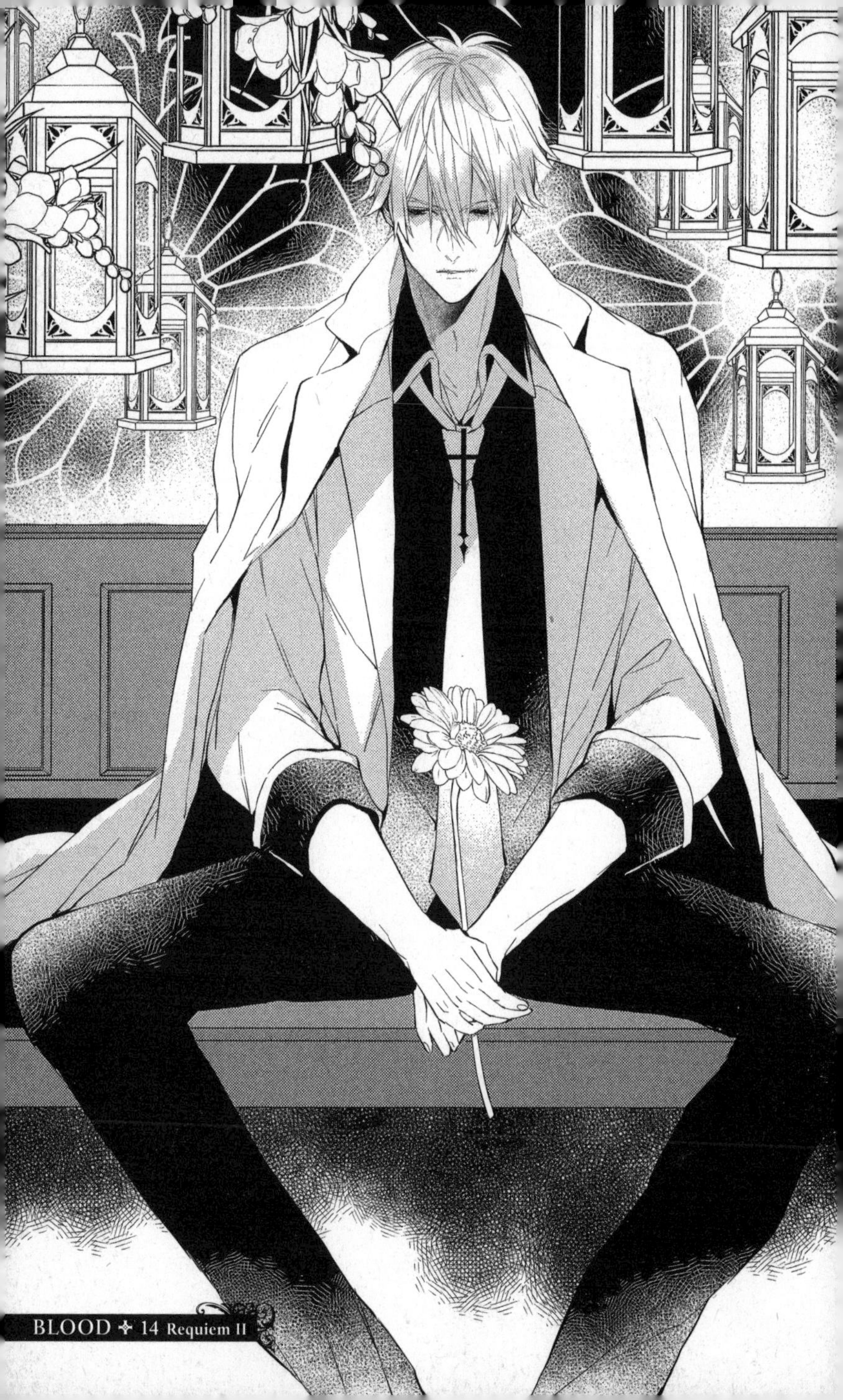

BLOOD ✣ 14 Requiem II

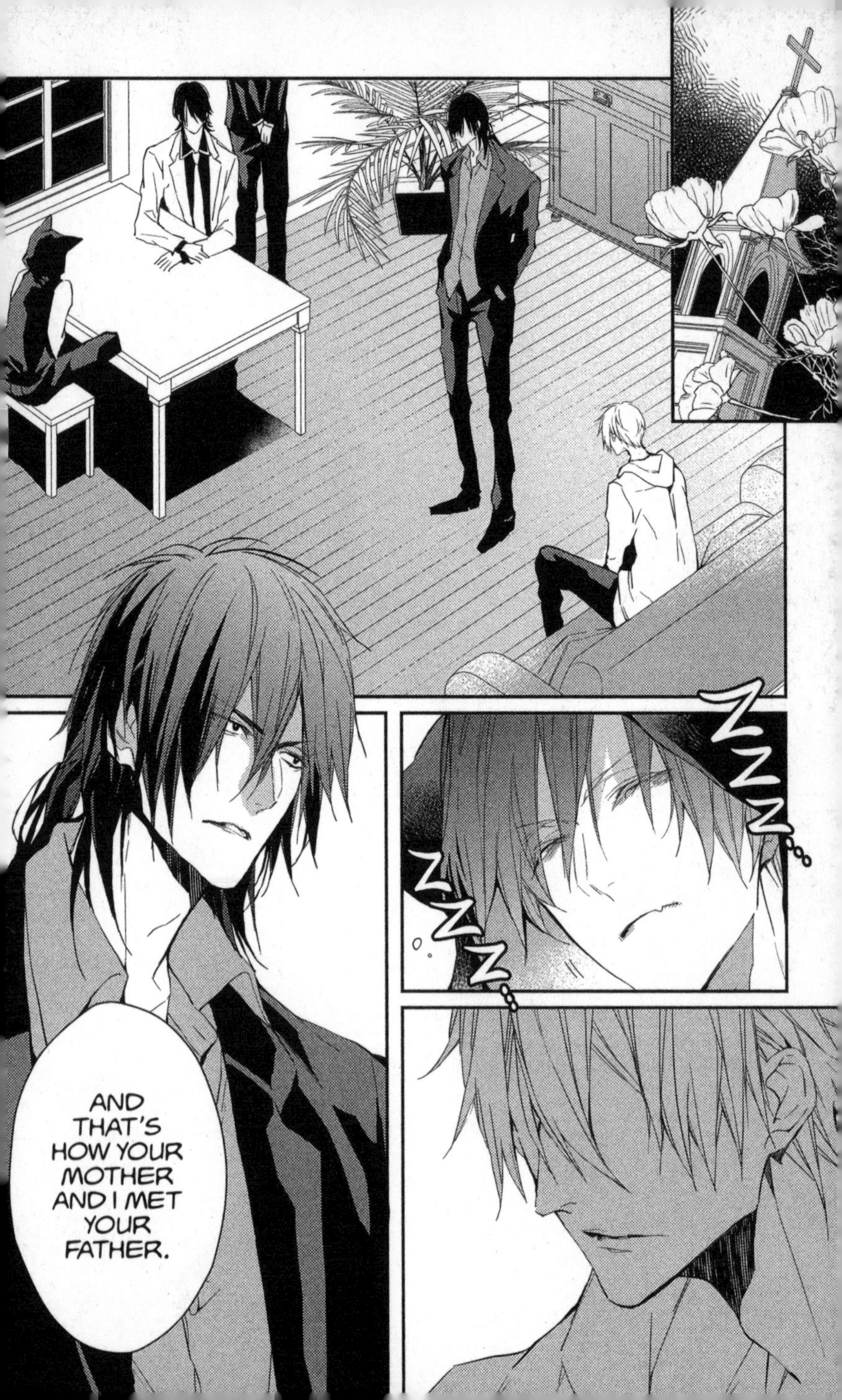

ZZZ...
ZZZ...
AND THAT'S HOW YOUR MOTHER AND I MET YOUR FATHER.

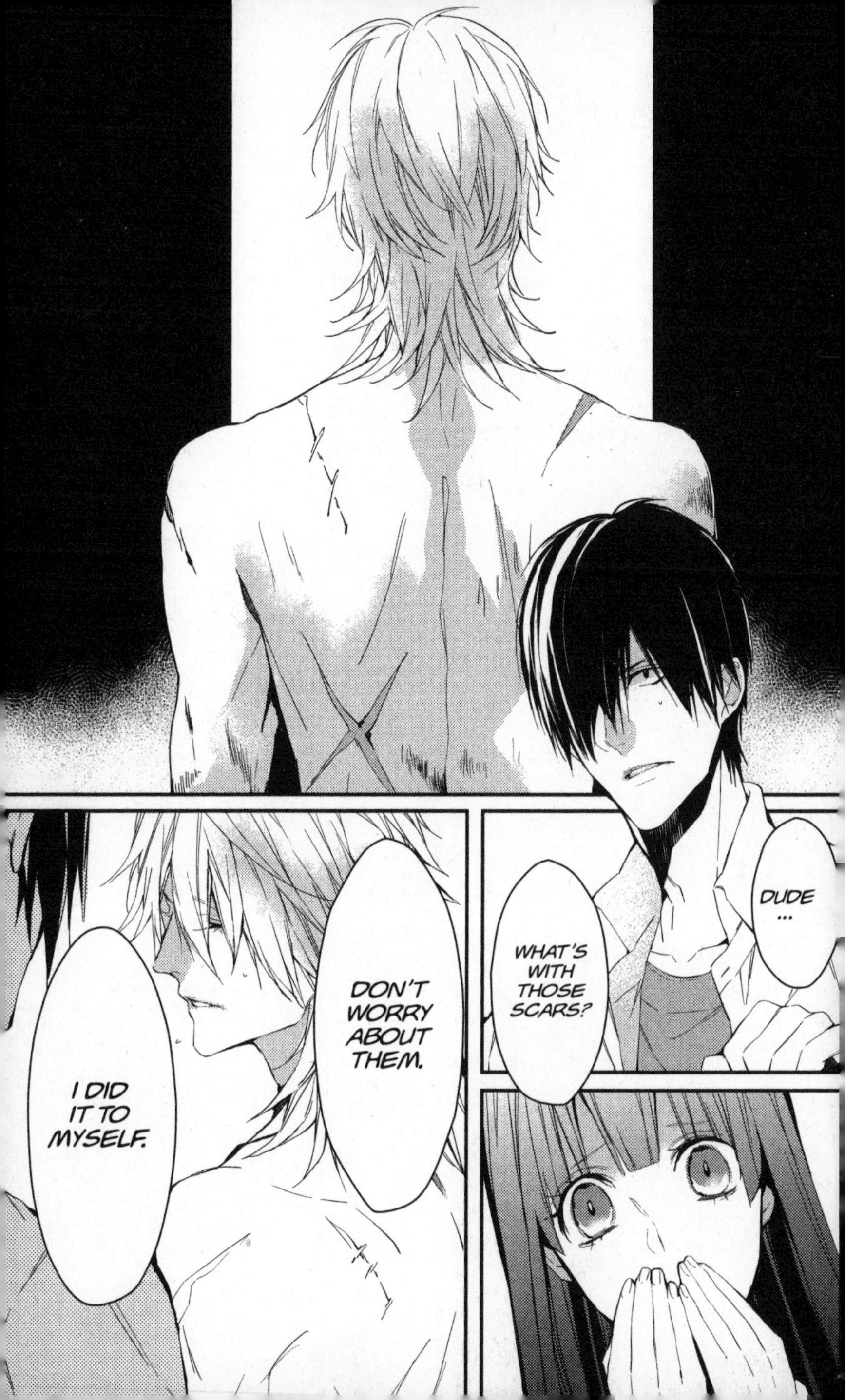
DUDE ...
WHAT'S WITH THOSE SCARS?
DON'T WORRY ABOUT THEM.
I DID IT TO MYSELF.

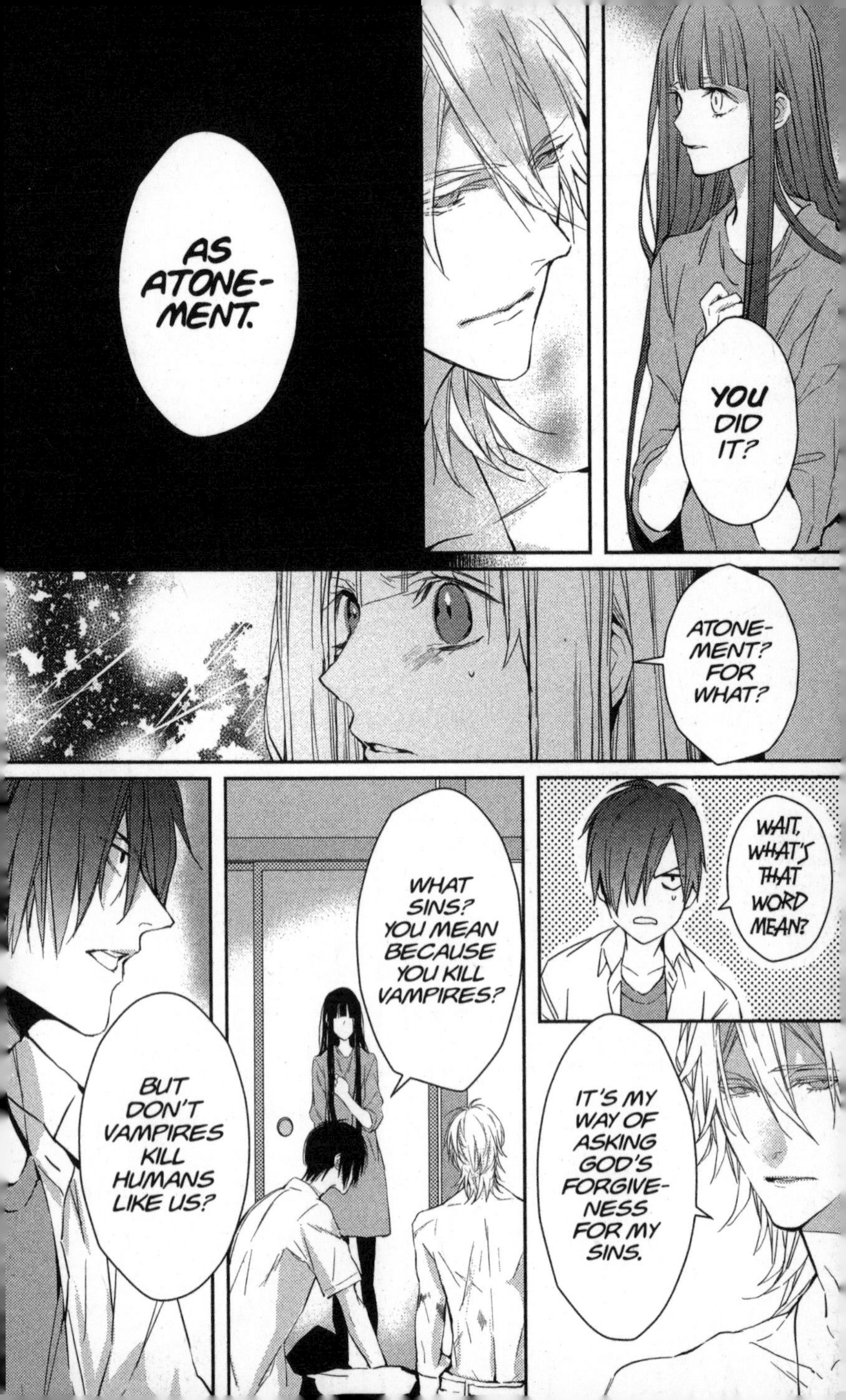
YOU DID IT?
AS ATONE-MENT.
ATONE-MENT? FOR WHAT?
WAIT, WHAT'S THAT WORD MEAN?
IT'S MY WAY OF ASKING GOD'S FORGIVE-NESS FOR MY SINS.
WHAT SINS? YOU MEAN BECAUSE YOU KILL VAMPIRES?
BUT DON'T VAMPIRES KILL HUMANS LIKE US?

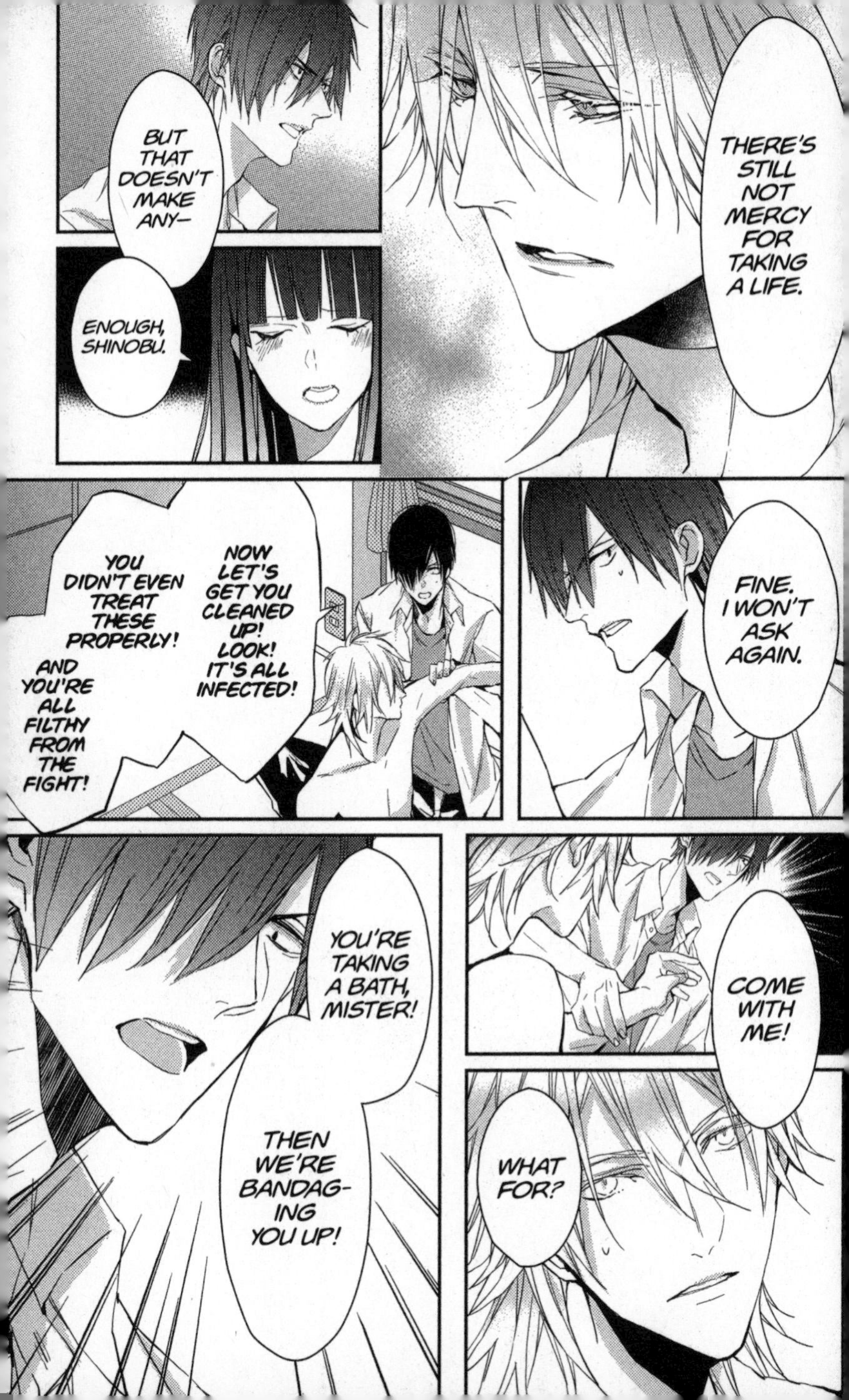
THERE'S STILL NOT MERCY FOR TAKING A LIFE.
BUT THAT DOESN'T MAKE ANY—
ENOUGH, SHINOBU.
FINE. I WON'T ASK AGAIN.
NOW LET'S GET YOU CLEANED UP! LOOK! IT'S ALL INFECTED!
YOU DIDN'T EVEN TREAT THESE PROPERLY!
AND YOU'RE ALL FILTHY FROM THE FIGHT!
COME WITH ME!
WHAT FOR?
YOU'RE TAKING A BATH, MISTER!
THEN WE'RE BANDAGING YOU UP!

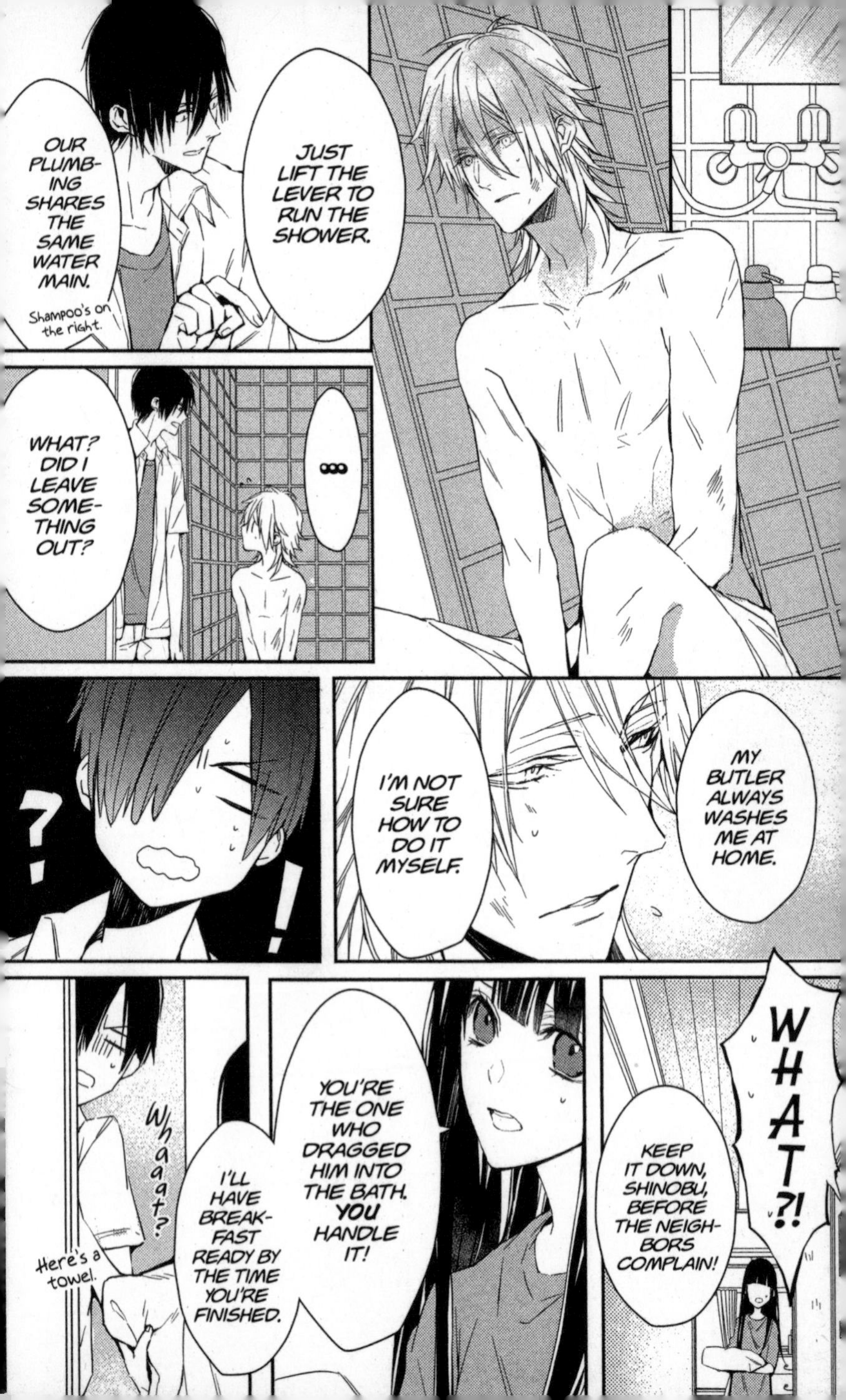
JUST LIFT THE LEVER TO RUN THE SHOWER.
OUR PLUMBING SHARES THE SAME WATER MAIN.
Shampoo's on the right.
...
WHAT? DID I LEAVE SOMETHING OUT?
MY BUTLER ALWAYS WASHES ME AT HOME.
I'M NOT SURE HOW TO DO IT MYSELF.
?!
WHAT?!
KEEP IT DOWN, SHINOBU, BEFORE THE NEIGHBORS COMPLAIN!
YOU'RE THE ONE WHO DRAGGED HIM INTO THE BATH. **YOU** HANDLE IT!
I'LL HAVE BREAKFAST READY BY THE TIME YOU'RE FINISHED.
Whaaaat?
Here's a towel.

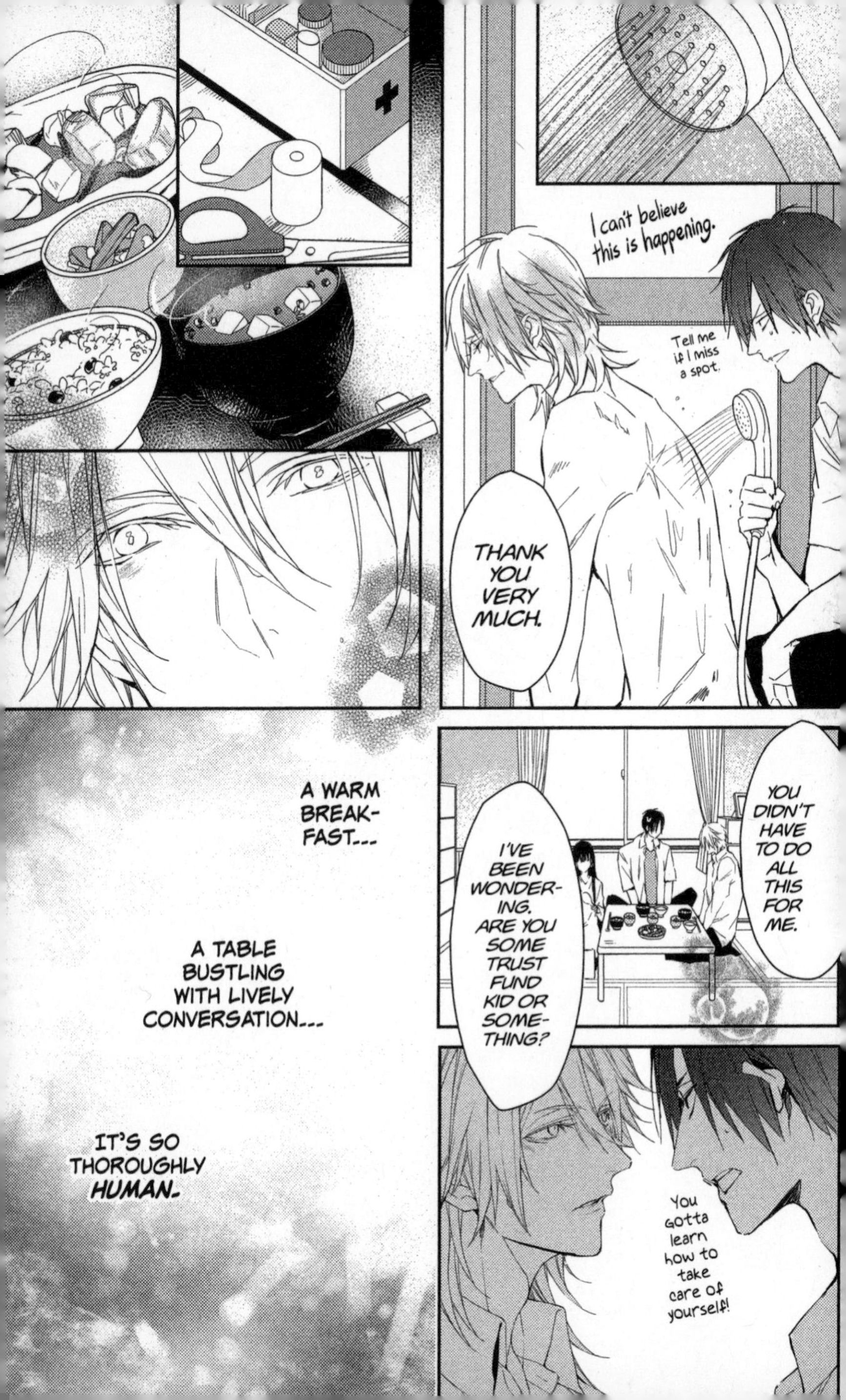
I can't believe this is happening.
Tell me if I miss a spot.
THANK YOU VERY MUCH.
YOU DIDN'T HAVE TO DO ALL THIS FOR ME.
I'VE BEEN WONDERING. ARE YOU SOME TRUST FUND KID OR SOMETHING?
You gotta learn how to take care of yourself!
A WARM BREAKFAST...
A TABLE BUSTLING WITH LIVELY CONVERSATION...
IT'S SO THOROUGHLY HUMAN.

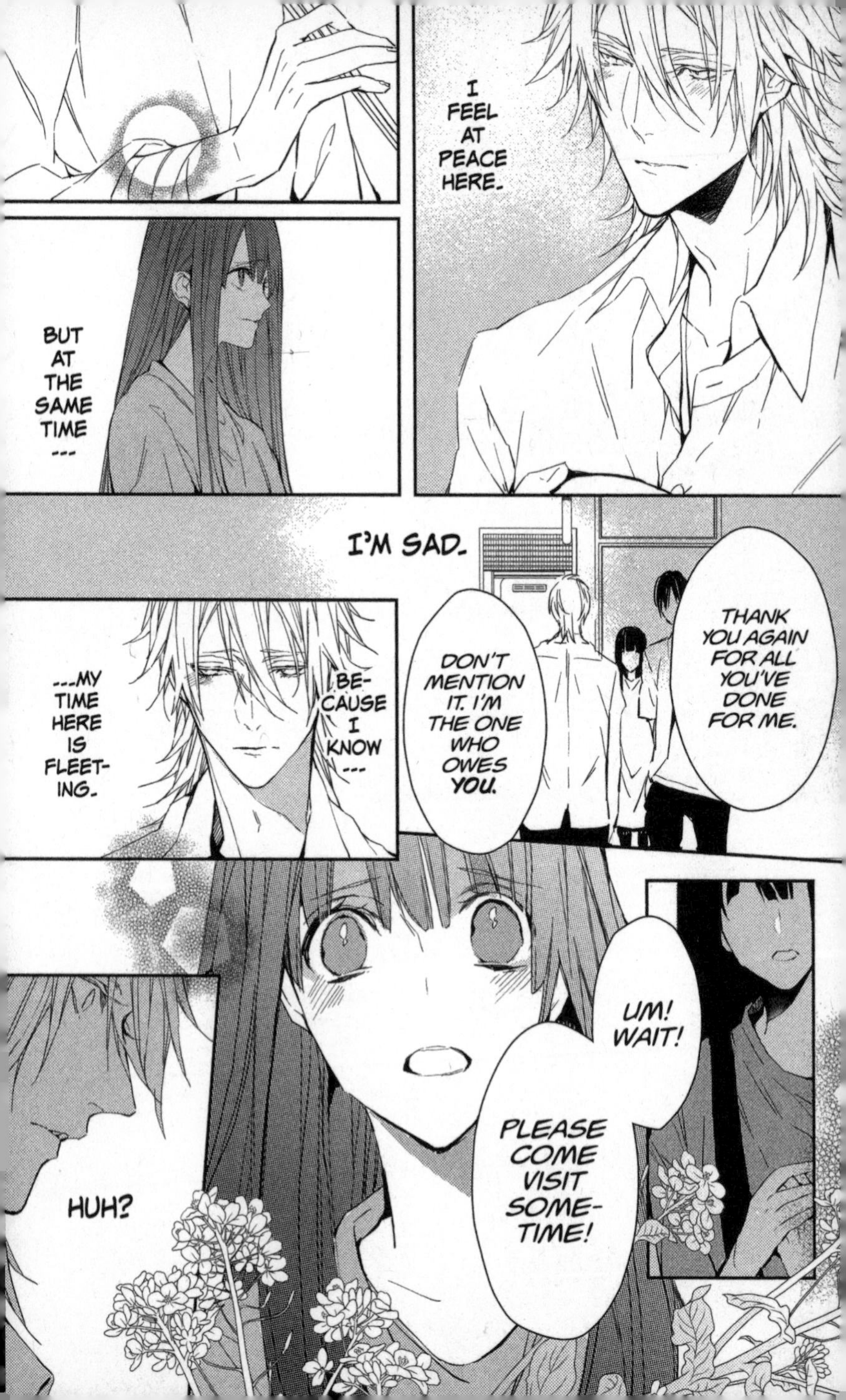
I FEEL AT PEACE HERE.
BUT AT THE SAME TIME---
I'M SAD.
THANK YOU AGAIN FOR ALL YOU'VE DONE FOR ME.
DON'T MENTION IT. I'M THE ONE WHO OWES YOU.
BE-CAUSE I KNOW---
---MY TIME HERE IS FLEET-ING.
UM! WAIT!
PLEASE COME VISIT SOME-TIME!
HUH?

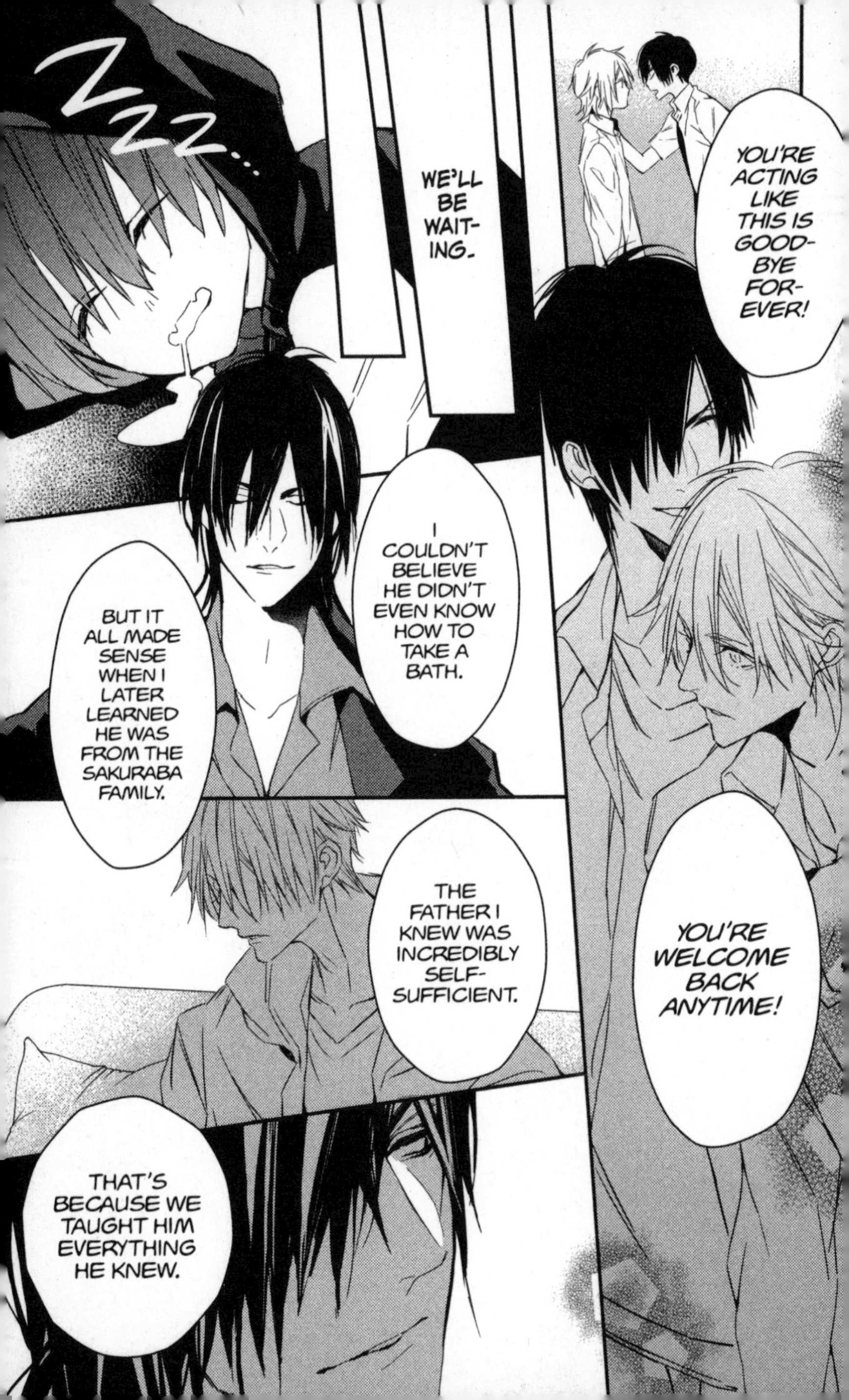
YOU'RE ACTING LIKE THIS IS GOOD-BYE FOR-EVER!
YOU'RE WELCOME BACK ANYTIME!
WE'LL BE WAIT-ING.
ZZZ...
I COULDN'T BELIEVE HE DIDN'T EVEN KNOW HOW TO TAKE A BATH.
BUT IT ALL MADE SENSE WHEN I LATER LEARNED HE WAS FROM THE SAKURABA FAMILY.
THE FATHER I KNEW WAS INCREDIBLY SELF-SUFFICIENT.
THAT'S BECAUSE WE TAUGHT HIM EVERYTHING HE KNEW.

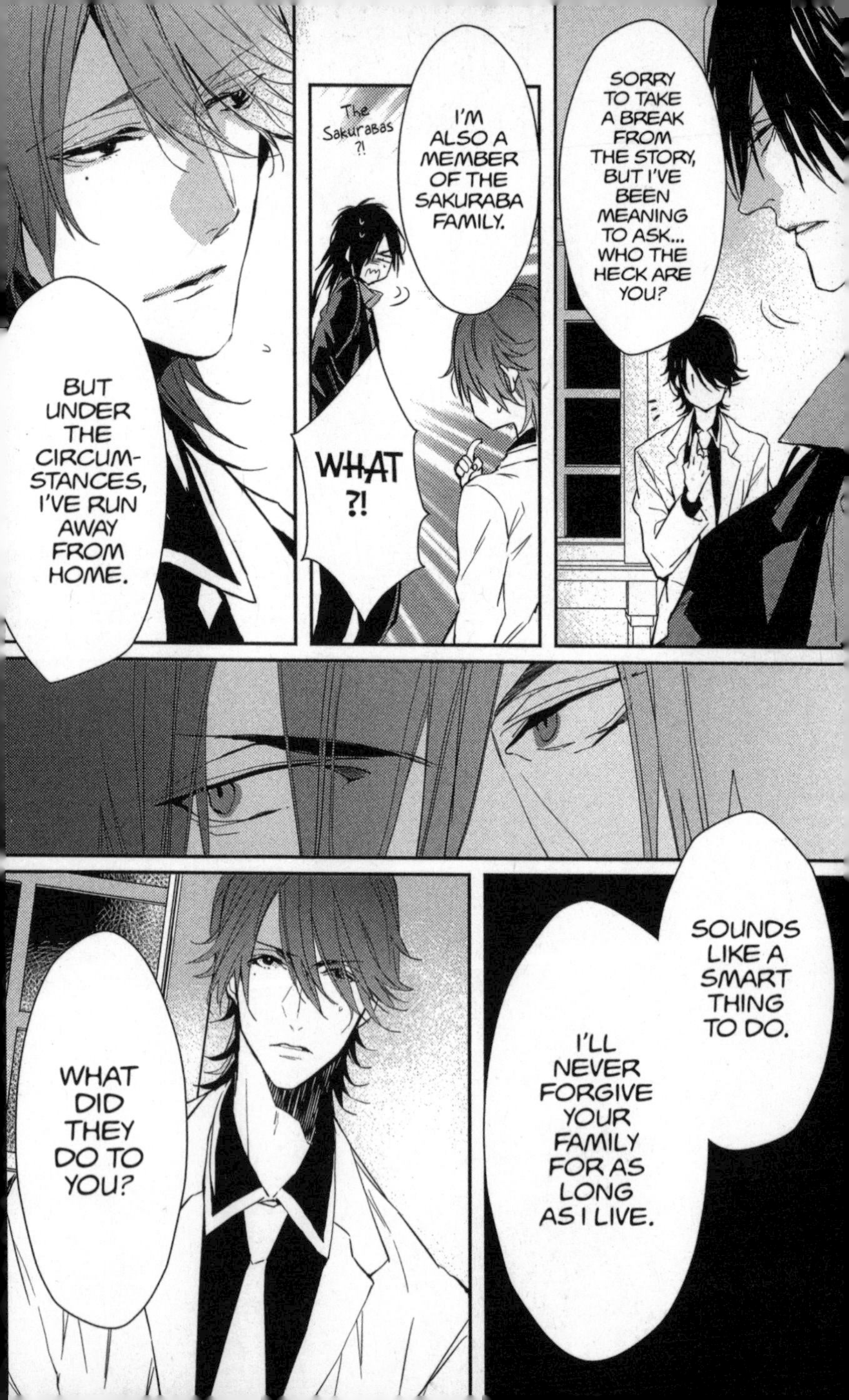
SORRY TO TAKE A BREAK FROM THE STORY, BUT I'VE BEEN MEANING TO ASK... WHO THE HECK ARE YOU?
I'M ALSO A MEMBER OF THE SAKURABA FAMILY.
The Sakurabas ?!
WHAT ?!
BUT UNDER THE CIRCUM-STANCES, I'VE RUN AWAY FROM HOME.
SOUNDS LIKE A SMART THING TO DO.
I'LL NEVER FORGIVE YOUR FAMILY FOR AS LONG AS I LIVE.
WHAT DID THEY DO TO YOU?

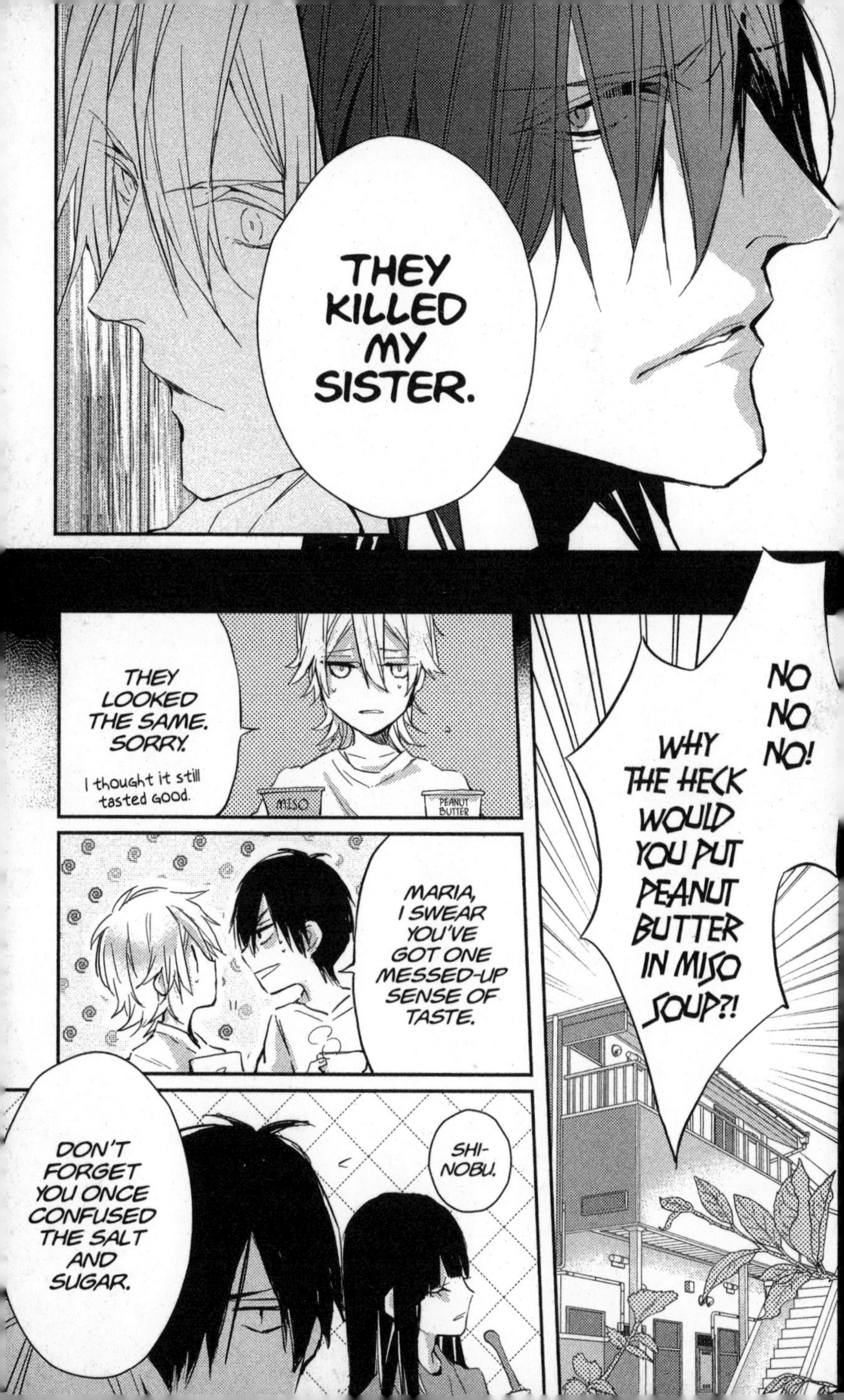
THEY KILLED MY SISTER.
NO NO NO!
WHY THE HECK WOULD YOU PUT PEANUT BUTTER IN MISO SOUP?!
THEY LOOKED THE SAME. SORRY.
I thought it still tasted good.
MISO
PEANUT BUTTER
MARIA, I SWEAR YOU'VE GOT ONE MESSED-UP SENSE OF TASTE.
SHI-NOBU.
DON'T FORGET YOU ONCE CONFUSED THE SALT AND SUGAR.

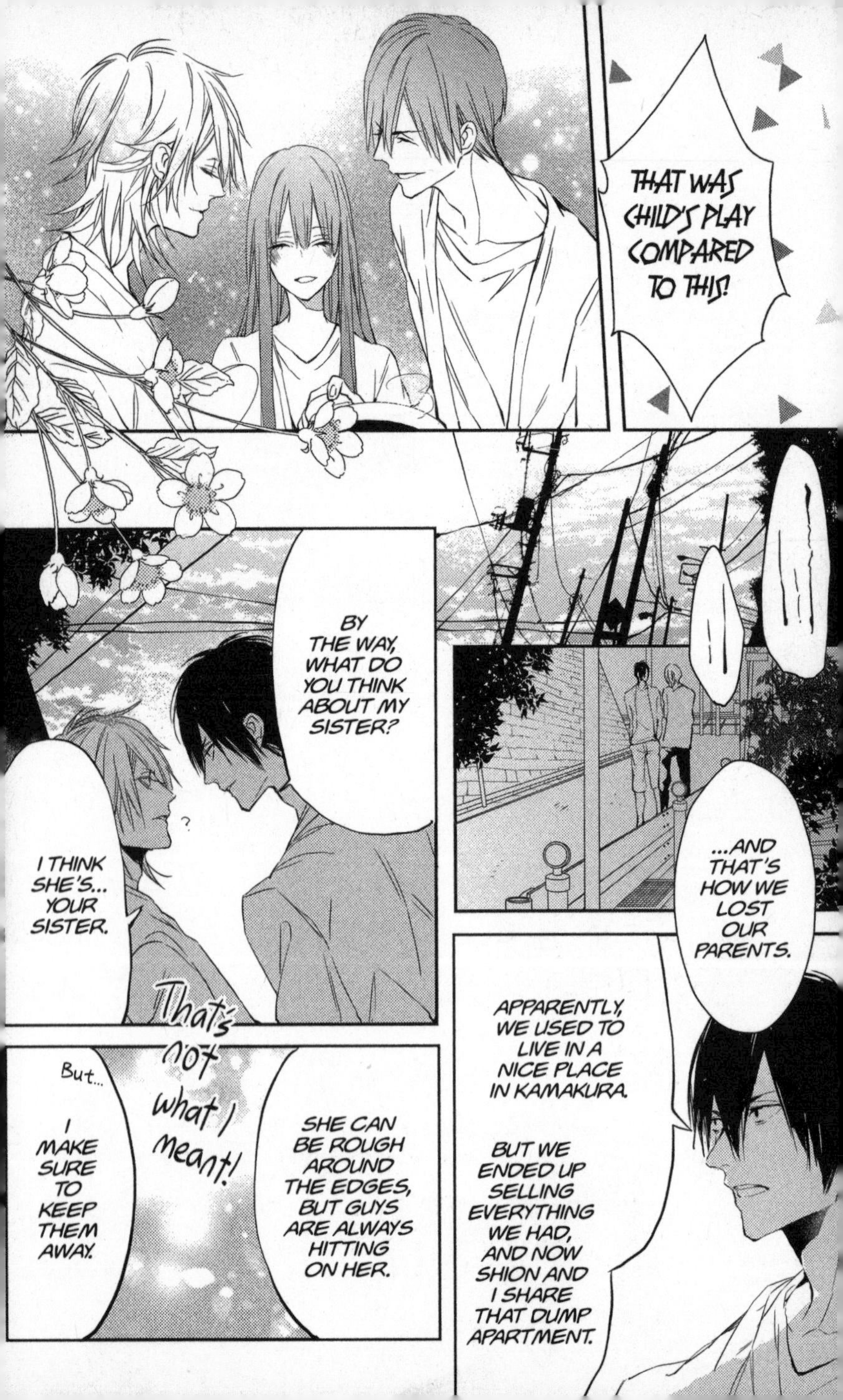
THAT WAS CHILD'S PLAY COMPARED TO THIS!
!
...AND THAT'S HOW WE LOST OUR PARENTS.
APPARENTLY, WE USED TO LIVE IN A NICE PLACE IN KAMAKURA.
BUT WE ENDED UP SELLING EVERYTHING WE HAD, AND NOW SHION AND I SHARE THAT DUMP APARTMENT.
BY THE WAY, WHAT DO YOU THINK ABOUT MY SISTER?
?
I THINK SHE'S... YOUR SISTER.
That's not what I meant!
SHE CAN BE ROUGH AROUND THE EDGES, BUT GUYS ARE ALWAYS HITTING ON HER.
But...
I MAKE SURE TO KEEP THEM AWAY.

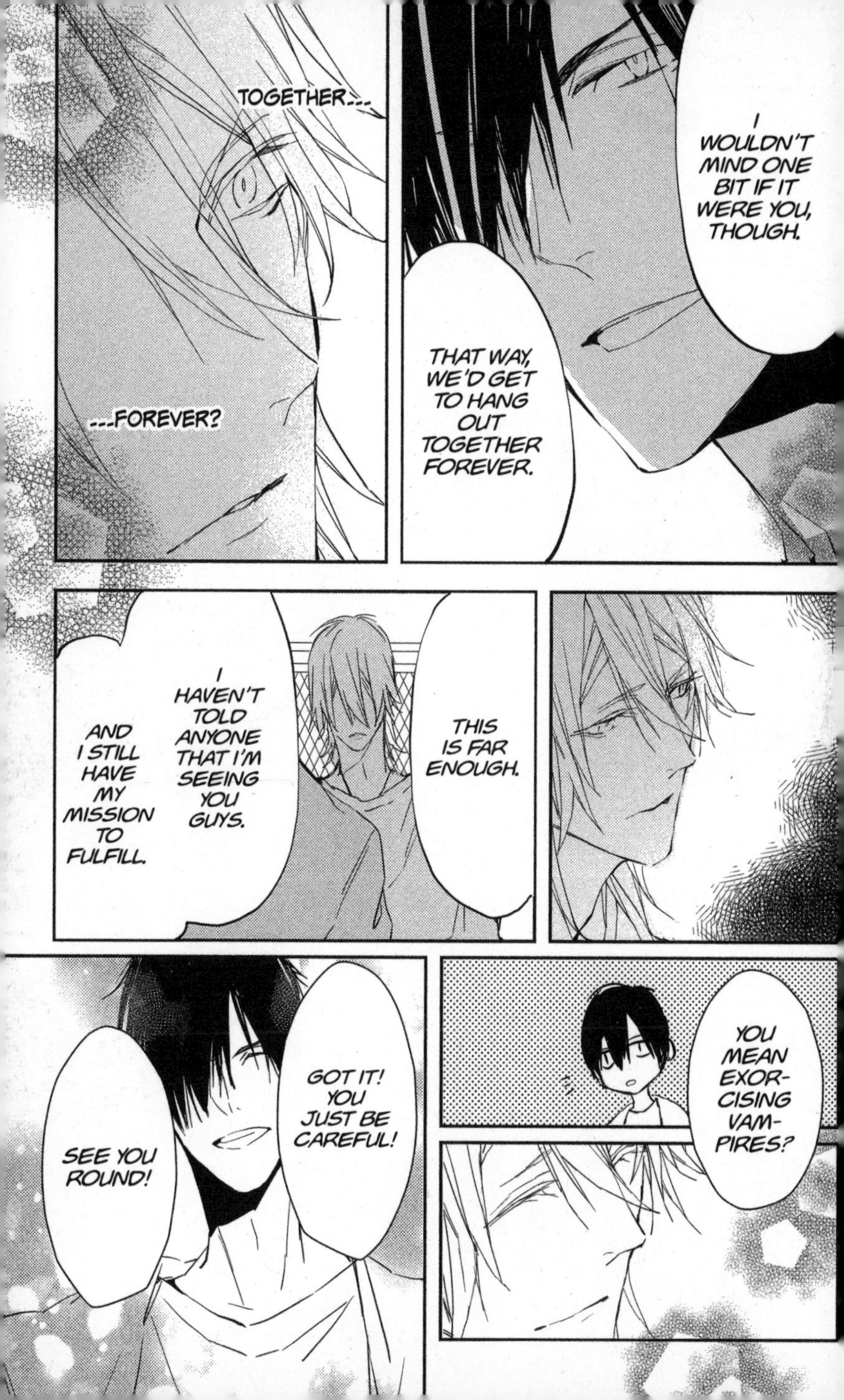
I WOULDN'T MIND ONE BIT IF IT WERE YOU, THOUGH.
THAT WAY, WE'D GET TO HANG OUT TOGETHER FOREVER.
TOGETHER...
...FOREVER?
THIS IS FAR ENOUGH.
I HAVEN'T TOLD ANYONE THAT I'M SEEING YOU GUYS.
AND I STILL HAVE MY MISSION TO FULFILL.
YOU MEAN EXOR-CISING VAM-PIRES?
GOT IT! YOU JUST BE CAREFUL!
SEE YOU ROUND!

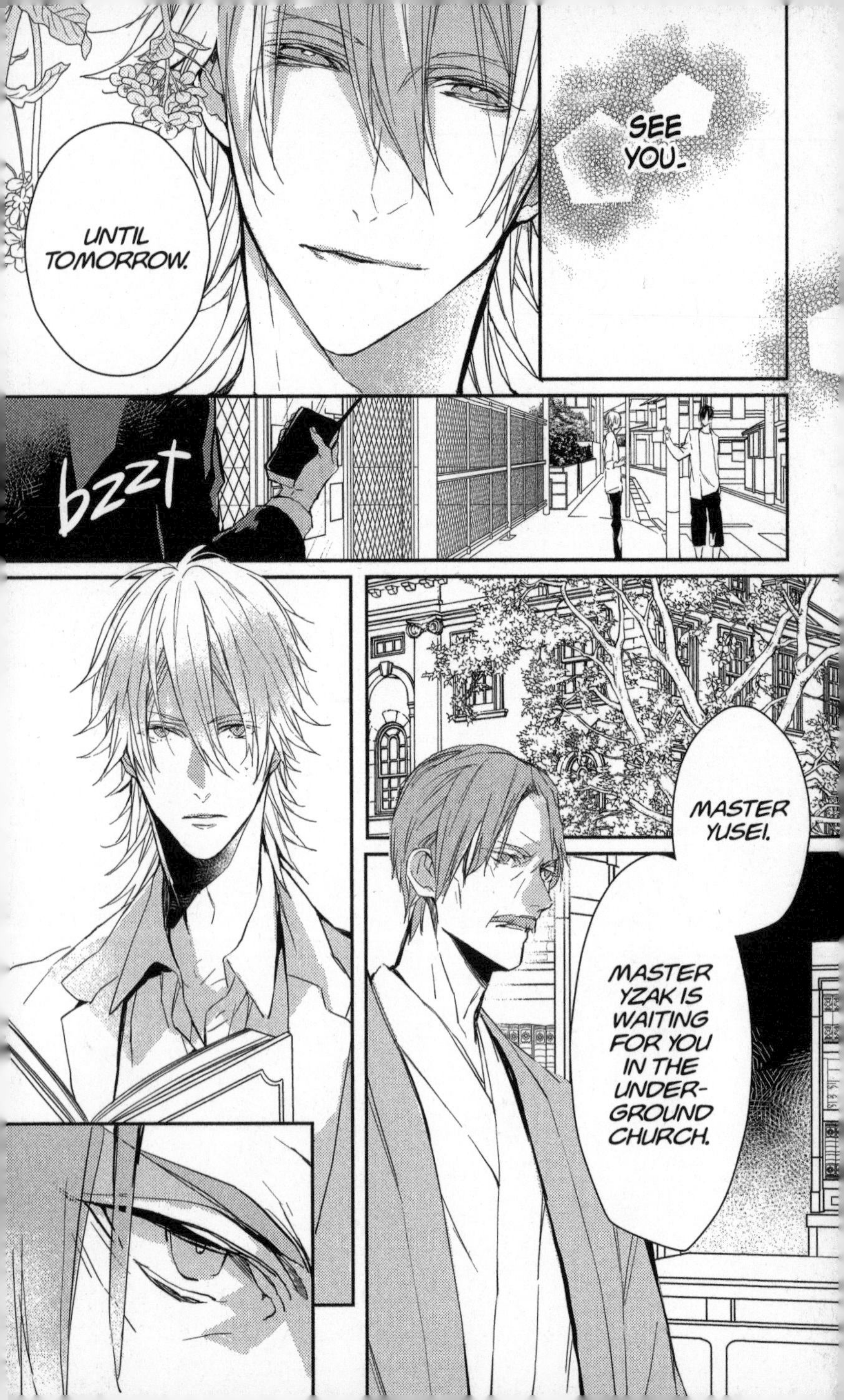
SEE YOU...
UNTIL TOMORROW.
bzzt
MASTER YUSEI.
MASTER YZAK IS WAITING FOR YOU IN THE UNDER-GROUND CHURCH.

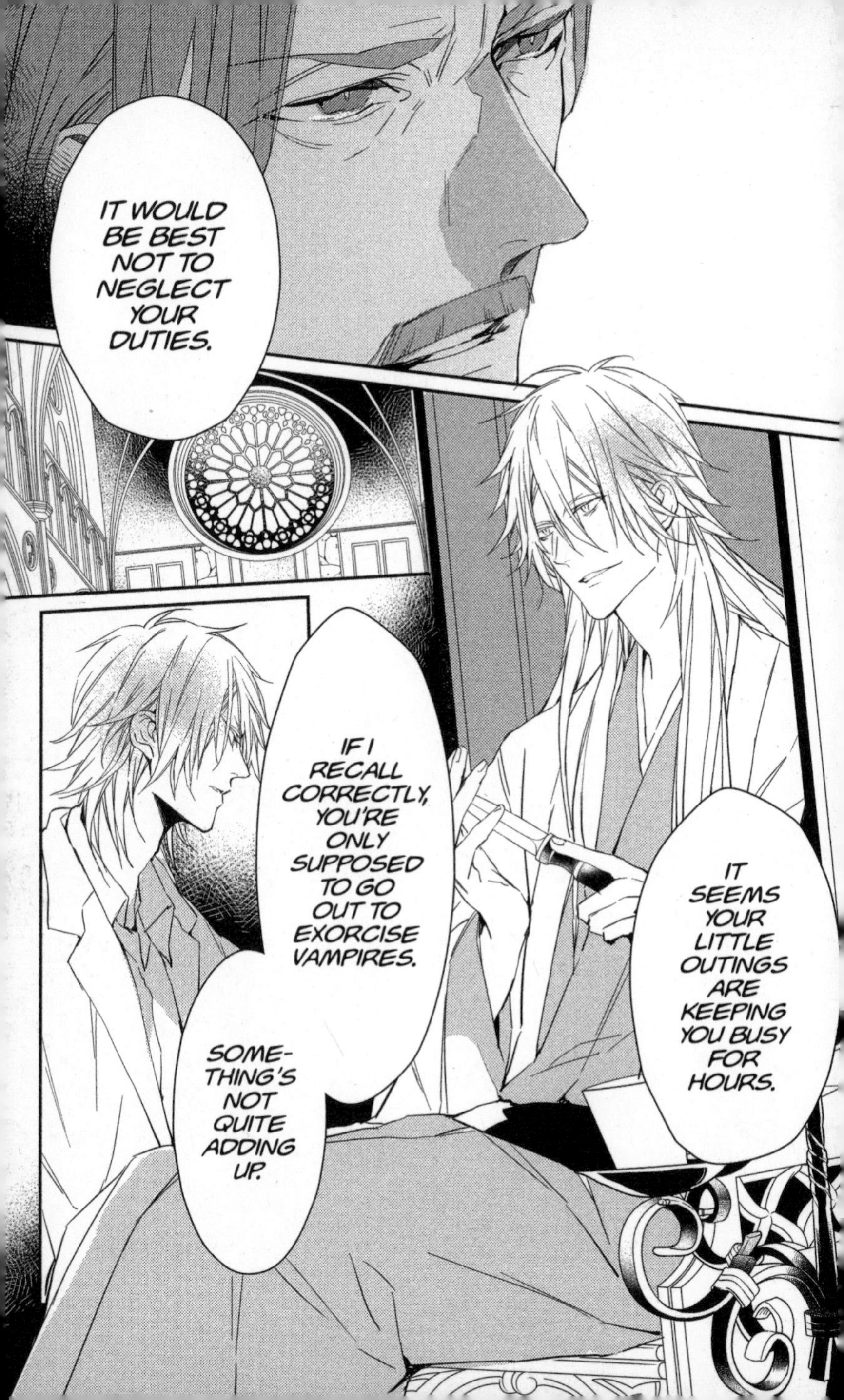
IT WOULD BE BEST NOT TO NEGLECT YOUR DUTIES.
IT SEEMS YOUR LITTLE OUTINGS ARE KEEPING YOU BUSY FOR HOURS.
IF I RECALL CORRECTLY, YOU'RE ONLY SUPPOSED TO GO OUT TO EXORCISE VAMPIRES.
SOME-THING'S NOT QUITE ADDING UP.

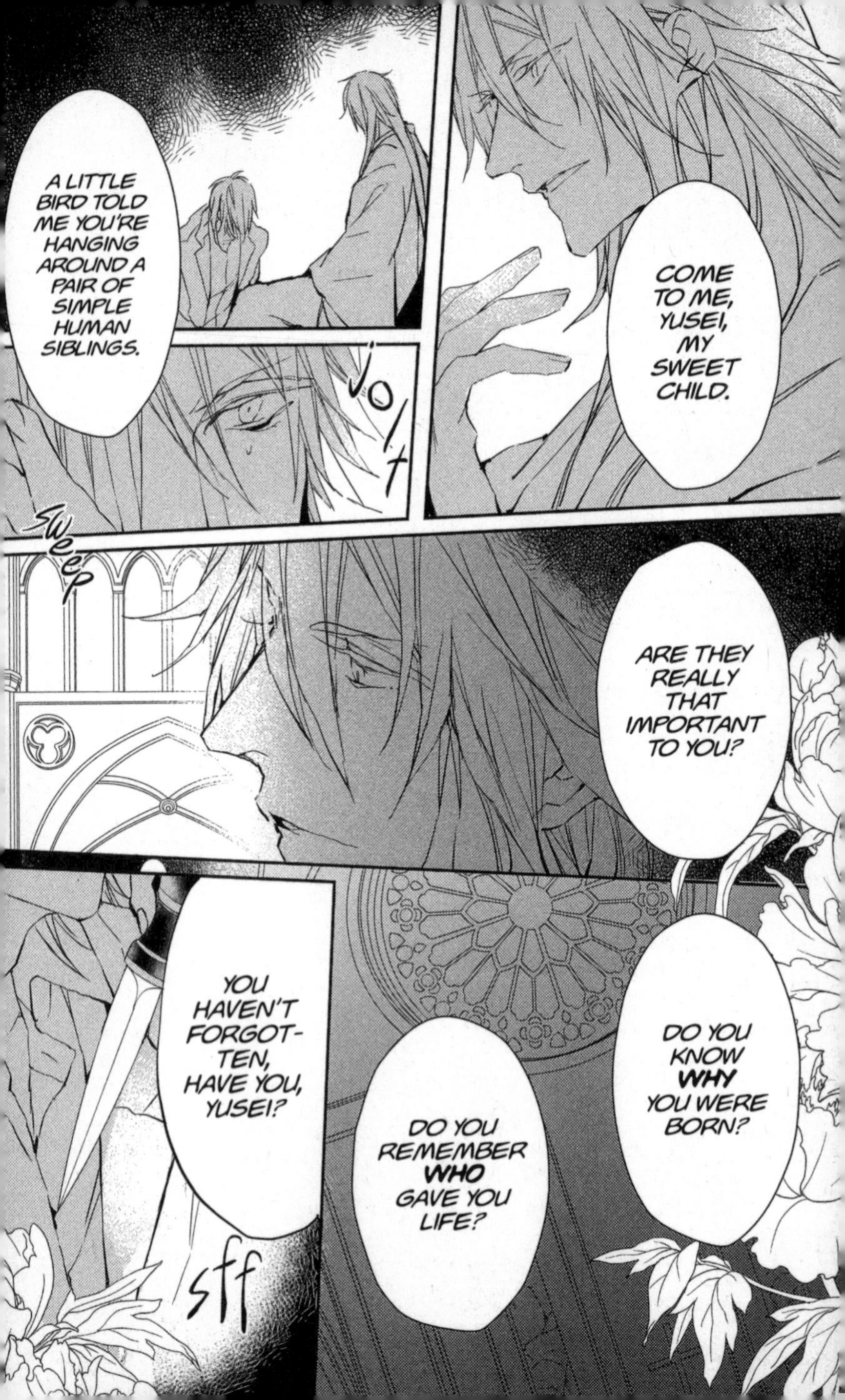
COME TO ME, YUSEI, MY SWEET CHILD.
A LITTLE BIRD TOLD ME YOU'RE HANGING AROUND A PAIR OF SIMPLE HUMAN SIBLINGS.
jolt
sweep
ARE THEY REALLY THAT IMPORTANT TO YOU?
DO YOU KNOW **WHY** YOU WERE BORN?
DO YOU REMEMBER **WHO** GAVE YOU LIFE?
YOU HAVEN'T FORGOT-TEN, HAVE YOU, YUSEI?
sff

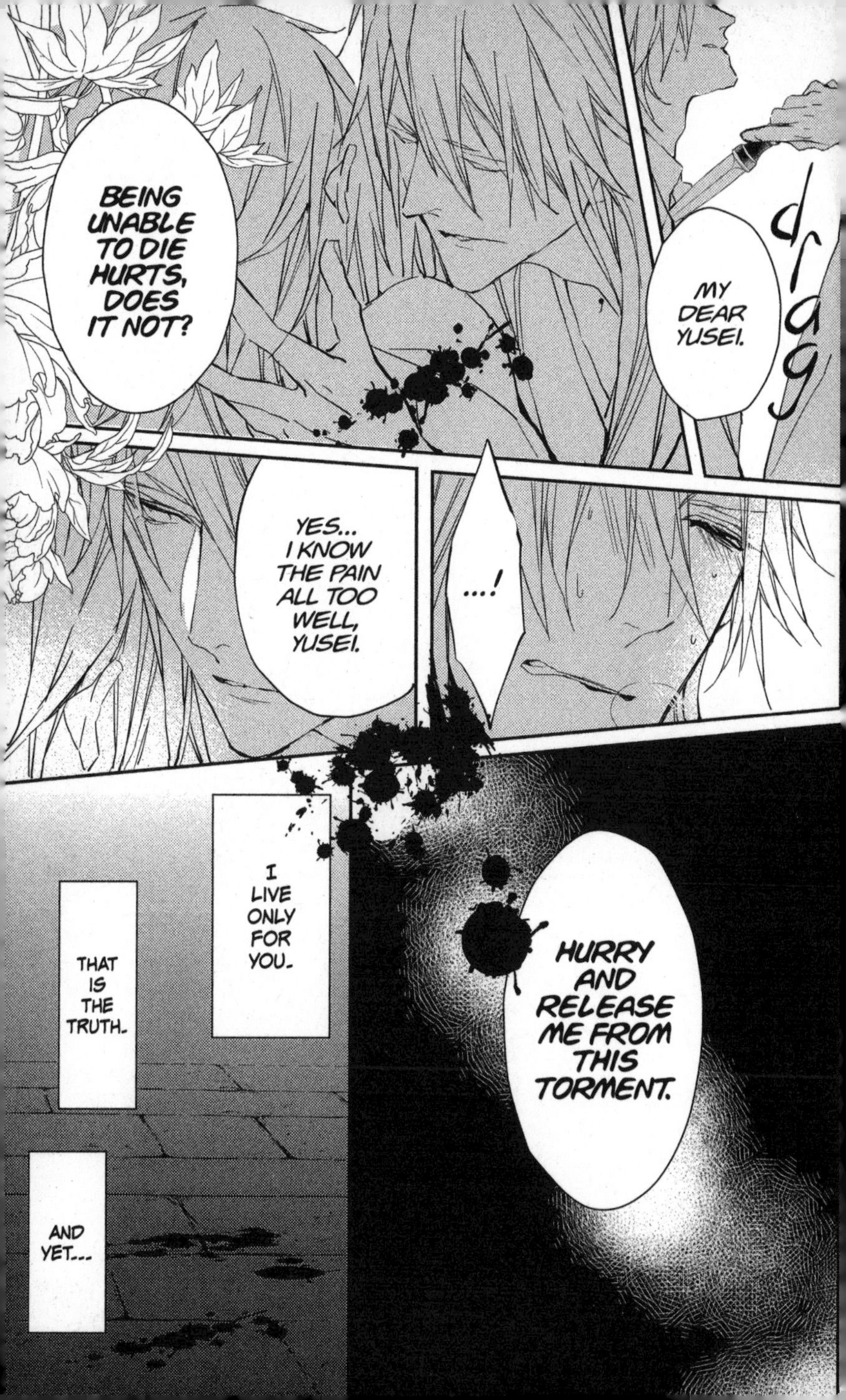
drag
MY DEAR YUSEI.
BEING UNABLE TO DIE HURTS, DOES IT NOT?
...!
YES... I KNOW THE PAIN ALL TOO WELL, YUSEI.
HURRY AND RELEASE ME FROM THIS TORMENT.
I LIVE ONLY FOR YOU.
THAT IS THE TRUTH.
AND YET...

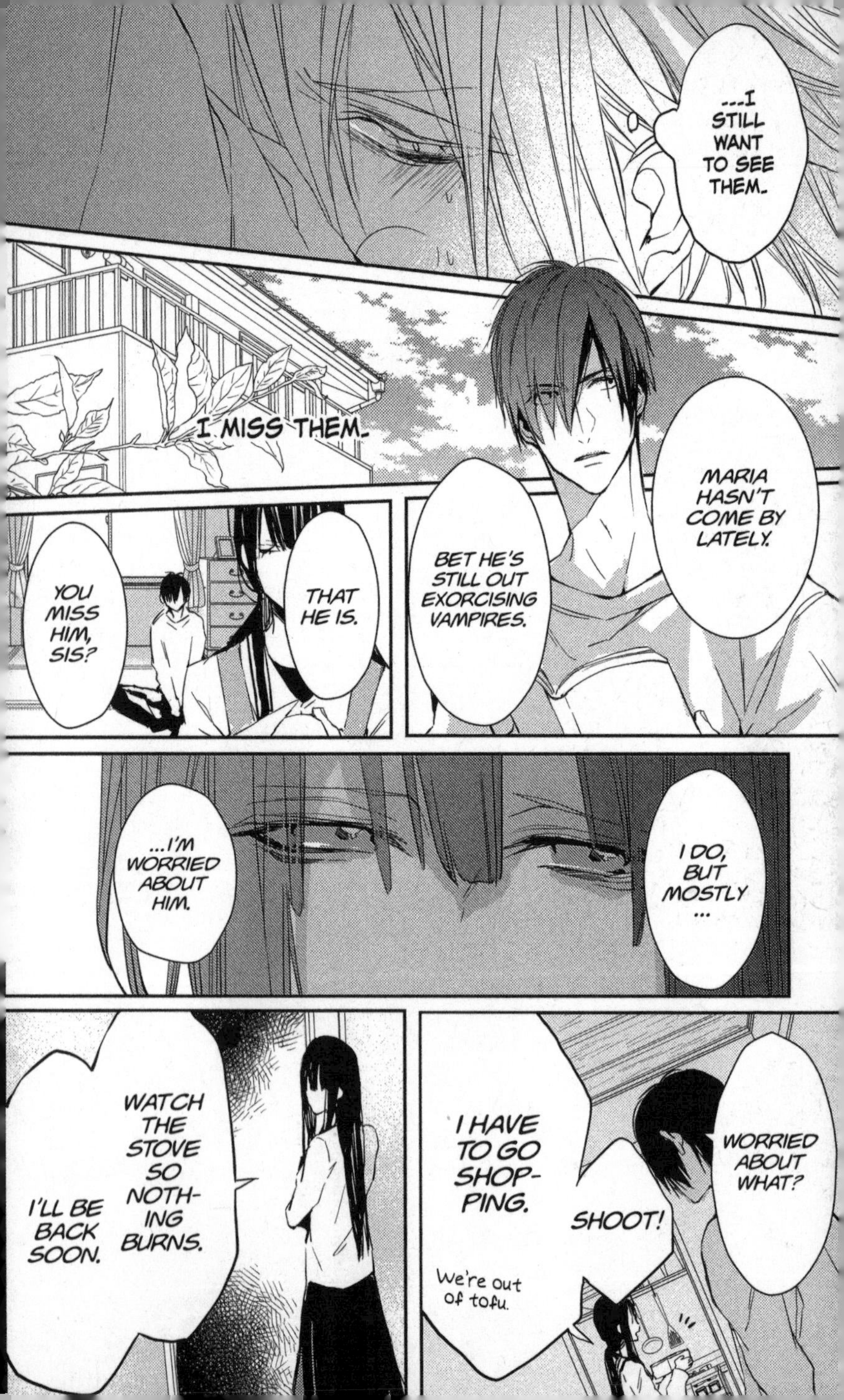

...I STILL WANT TO SEE THEM...
I MISS THEM...
MARIA HASN'T COME BY LATELY.
BET HE'S STILL OUT EXORCISING VAMPIRES.
THAT HE IS.
YOU MISS HIM, SIS?
I DO, BUT MOSTLY...
...I'M WORRIED ABOUT HIM.
WORRIED ABOUT WHAT?
SHOOT!
I HAVE TO GO SHOPPING.
We're out of tofu.
WATCH THE STOVE SO NOTHING BURNS.
I'LL BE BACK SOON.

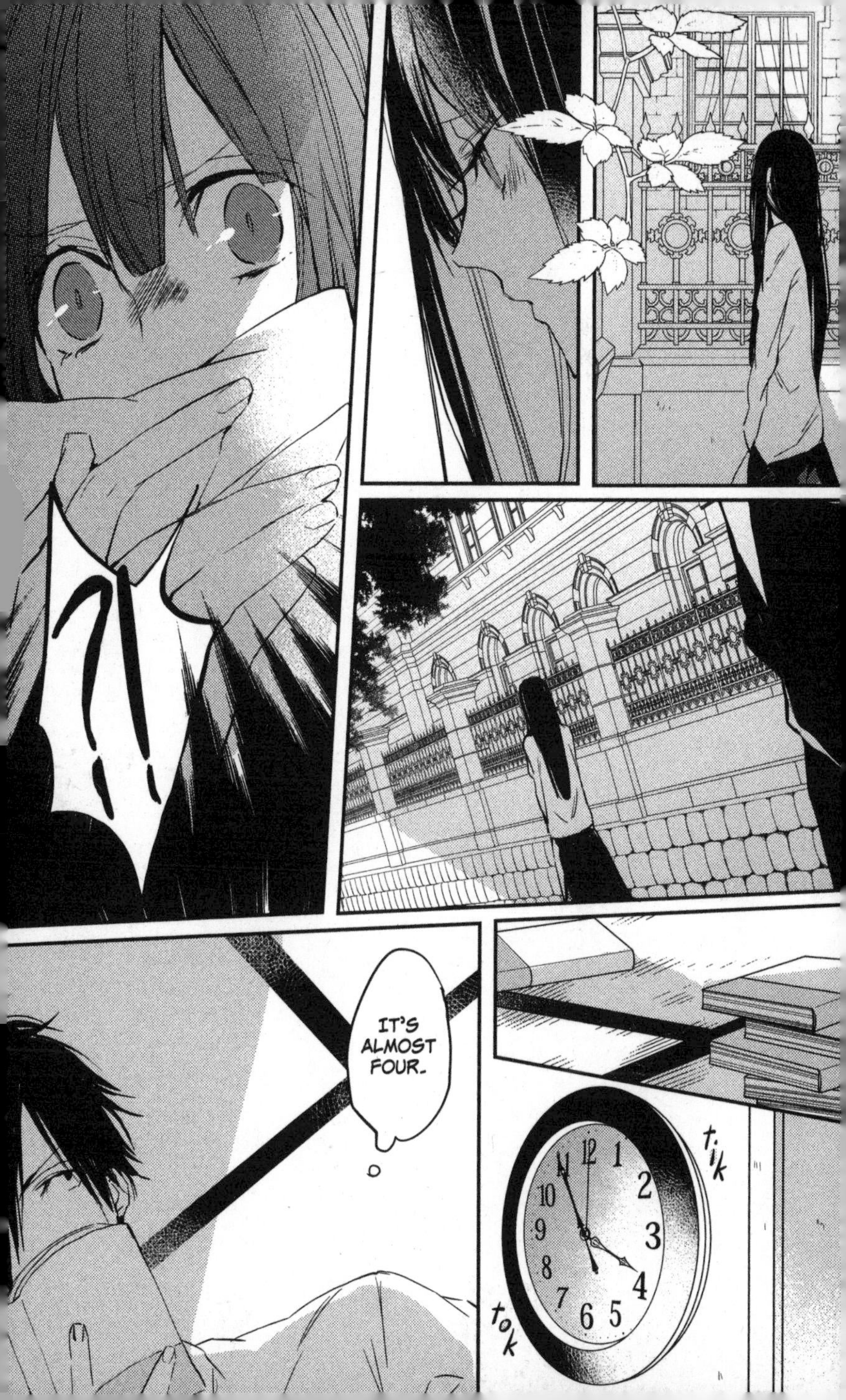
tik
tok
IT'S ALMOST FOUR.

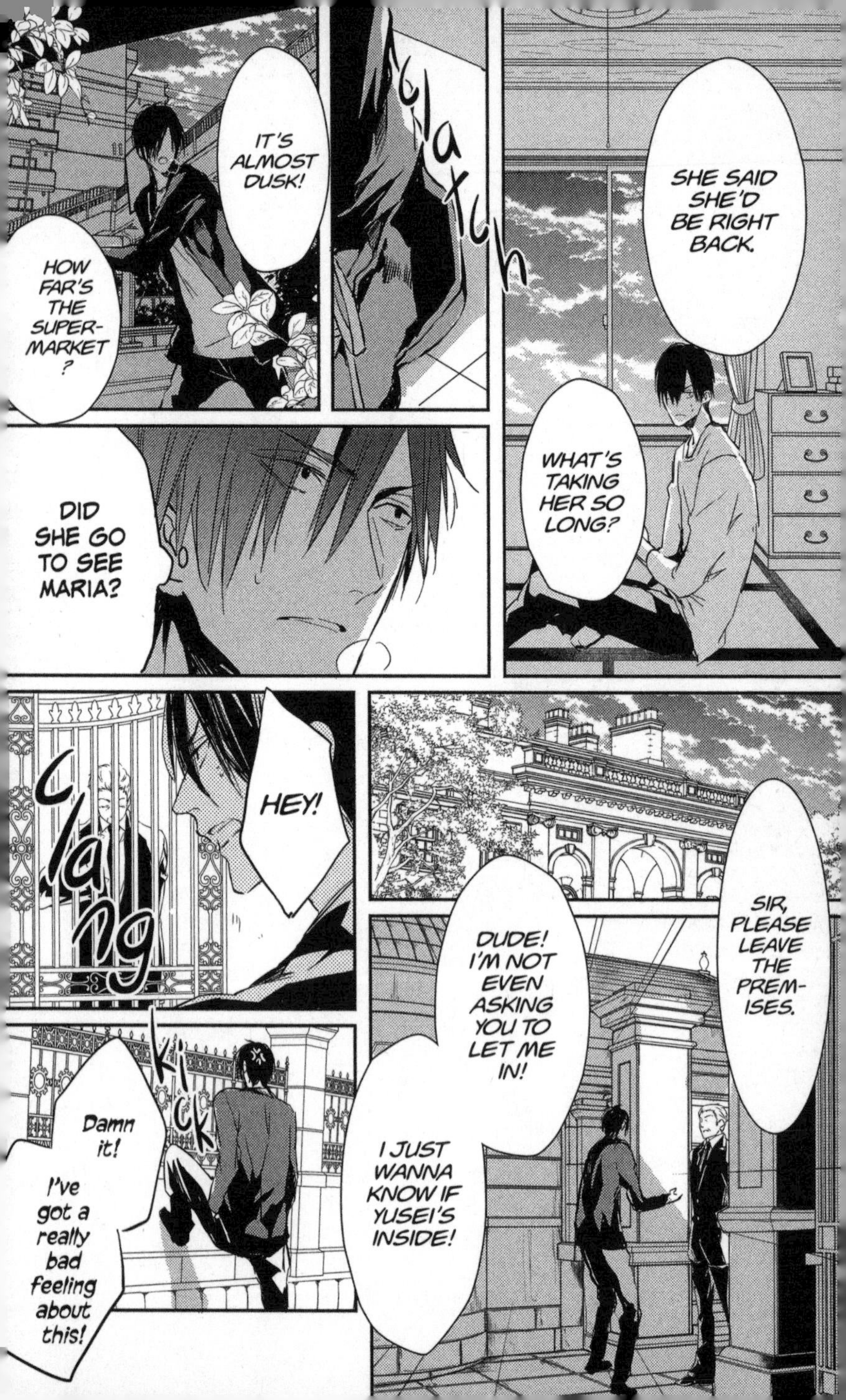
SHE SAID SHE'D BE RIGHT BACK.
WHAT'S TAKING HER SO LONG?
IT'S ALMOST DUSK!
HOW FAR'S THE SUPER-MARKET?
DID SHE GO TO SEE MARIA?
SIR, PLEASE LEAVE THE PREM-ISES.
DUDE! I'M NOT EVEN ASKING YOU TO LET ME IN!
I JUST WANNA KNOW IF YUSEI'S INSIDE!
HEY!
Clang
Kick
Damn it!
I've got a really bad feeling about this!

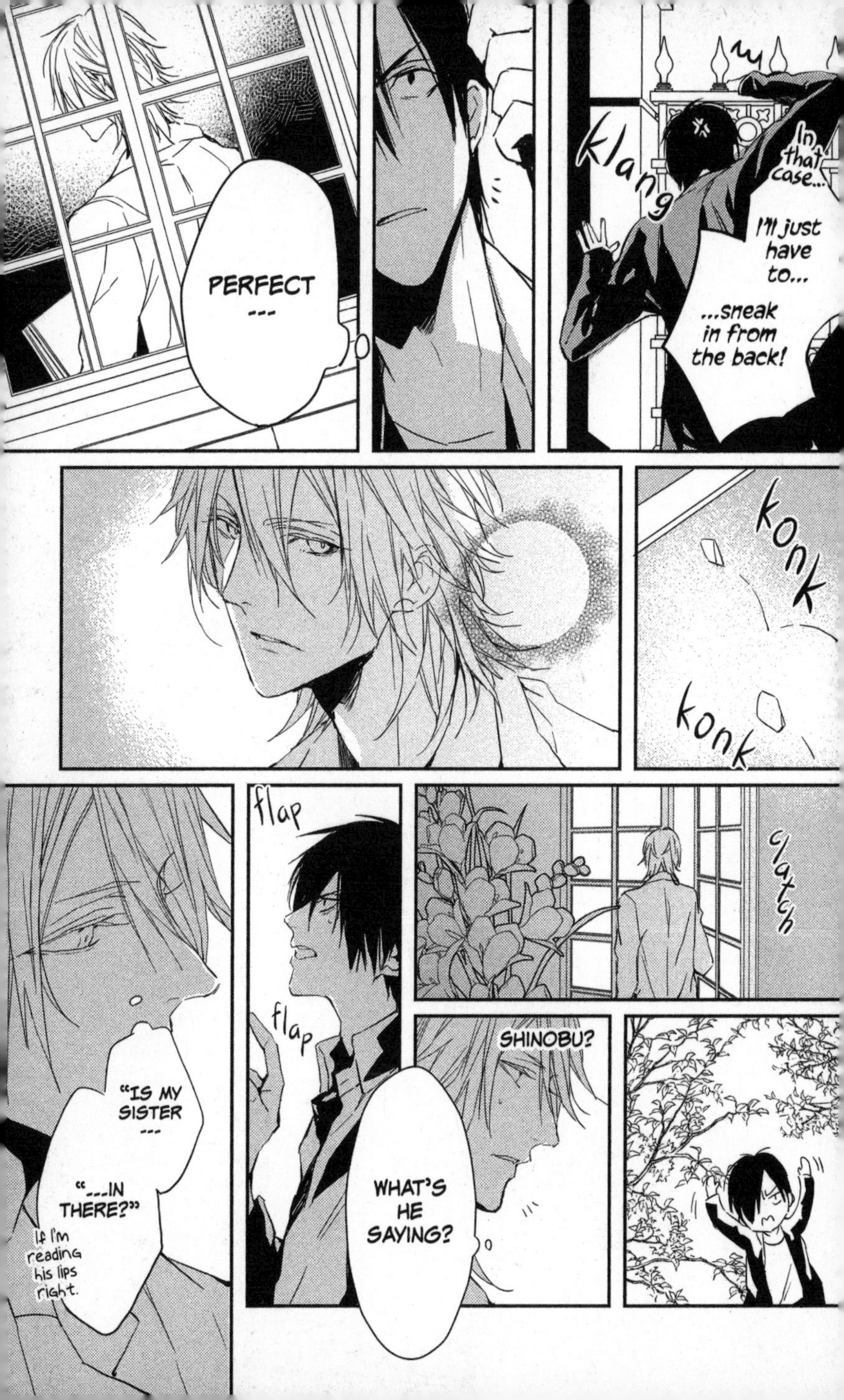
klang
In that case...
I'll just have to...
...sneak in from the back!
PERFECT ---
konk
konk
clatch
SHINOBU?
WHAT'S HE SAYING?
flap
flap
"IS MY SISTER ---
"---IN THERE?"
If I'm reading his lips right.

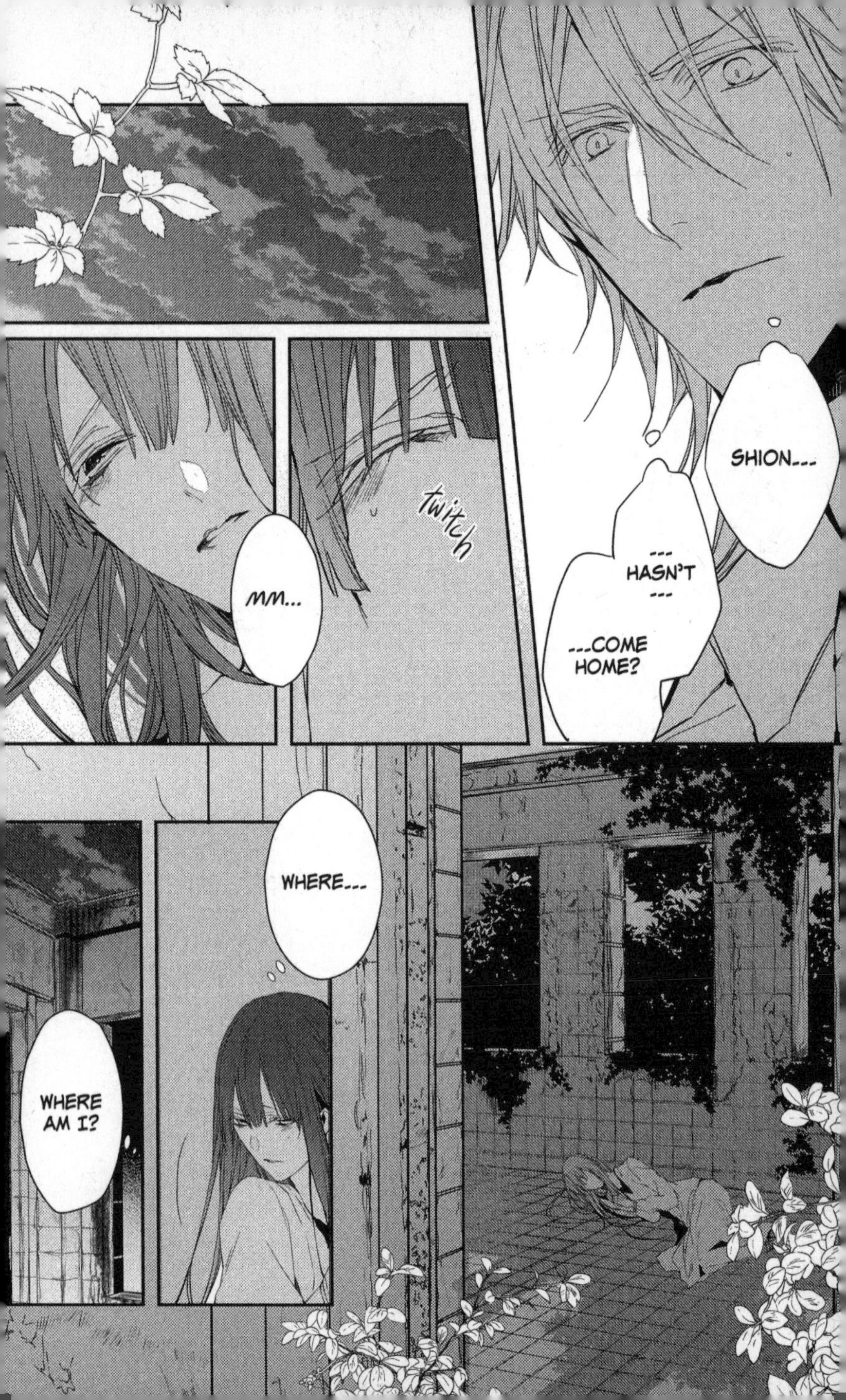
SHION...
...HASN'T...
...COME HOME?
twitch
MM...
WHERE...
WHERE AM I?

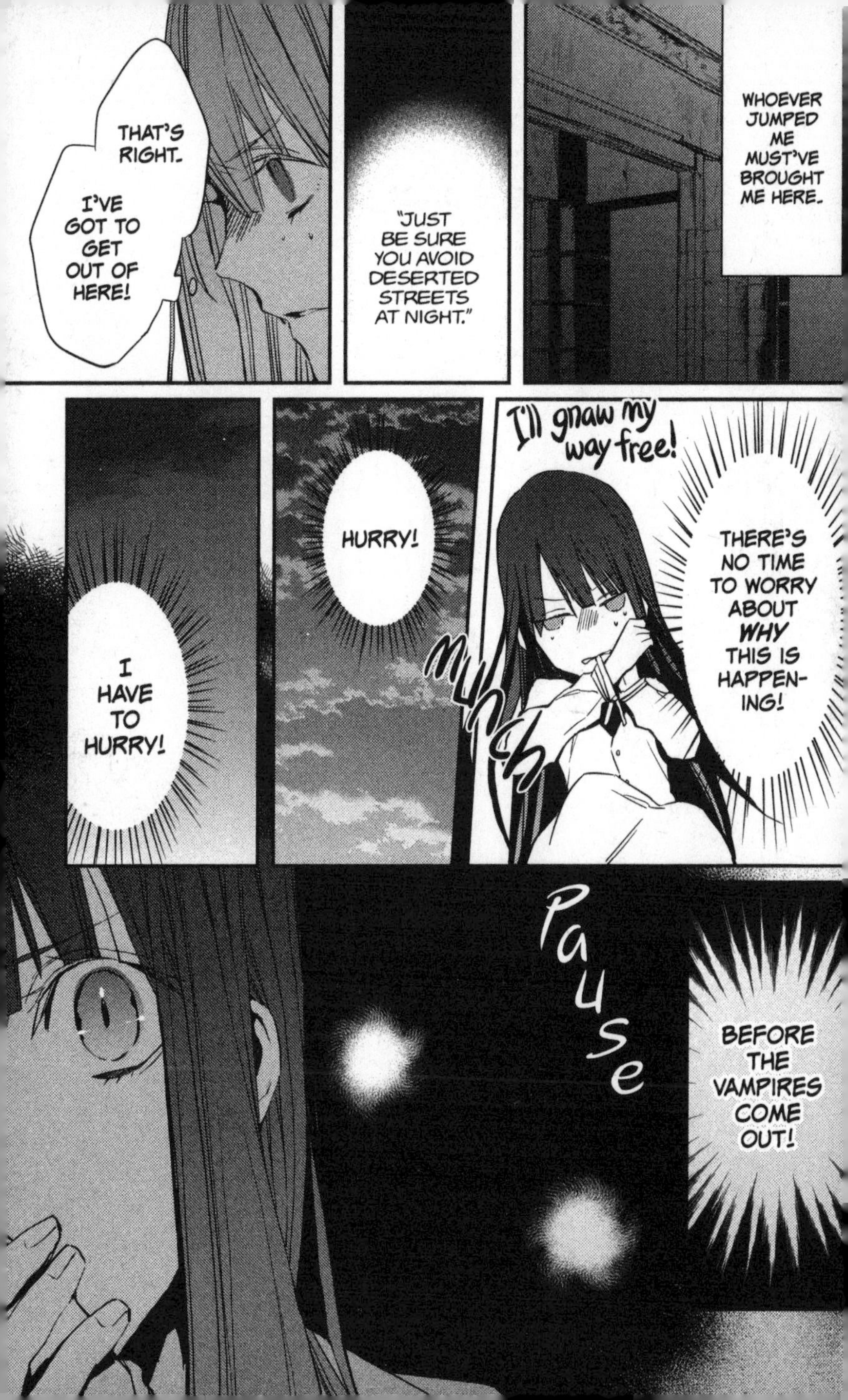
WHOEVER JUMPED ME MUST'VE BROUGHT ME HERE.
"JUST BE SURE YOU AVOID DESERTED STREETS AT NIGHT."
THAT'S RIGHT.
I'VE GOT TO GET OUT OF HERE!
I'll gnaw my way free!
THERE'S NO TIME TO WORRY ABOUT WHY THIS IS HAPPEN-ING!
MUNCH
HURRY!
I HAVE TO HURRY!
BEFORE THE VAMPIRES COME OUT!
Pause

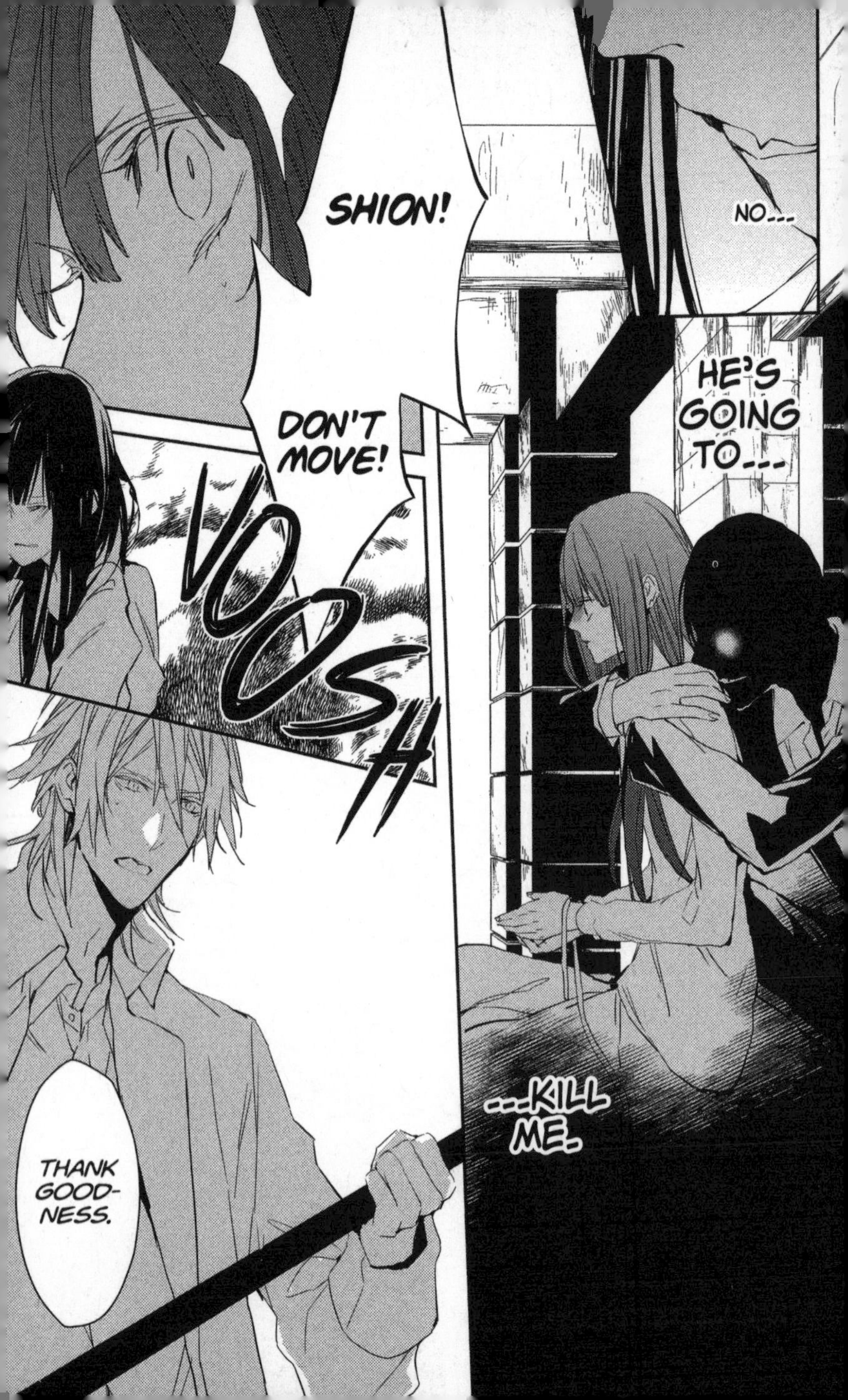
NO...
HE'S GOING TO...
...KILL ME.
SHION!
DON'T MOVE!
VOOSH
THANK GOOD-NESS.

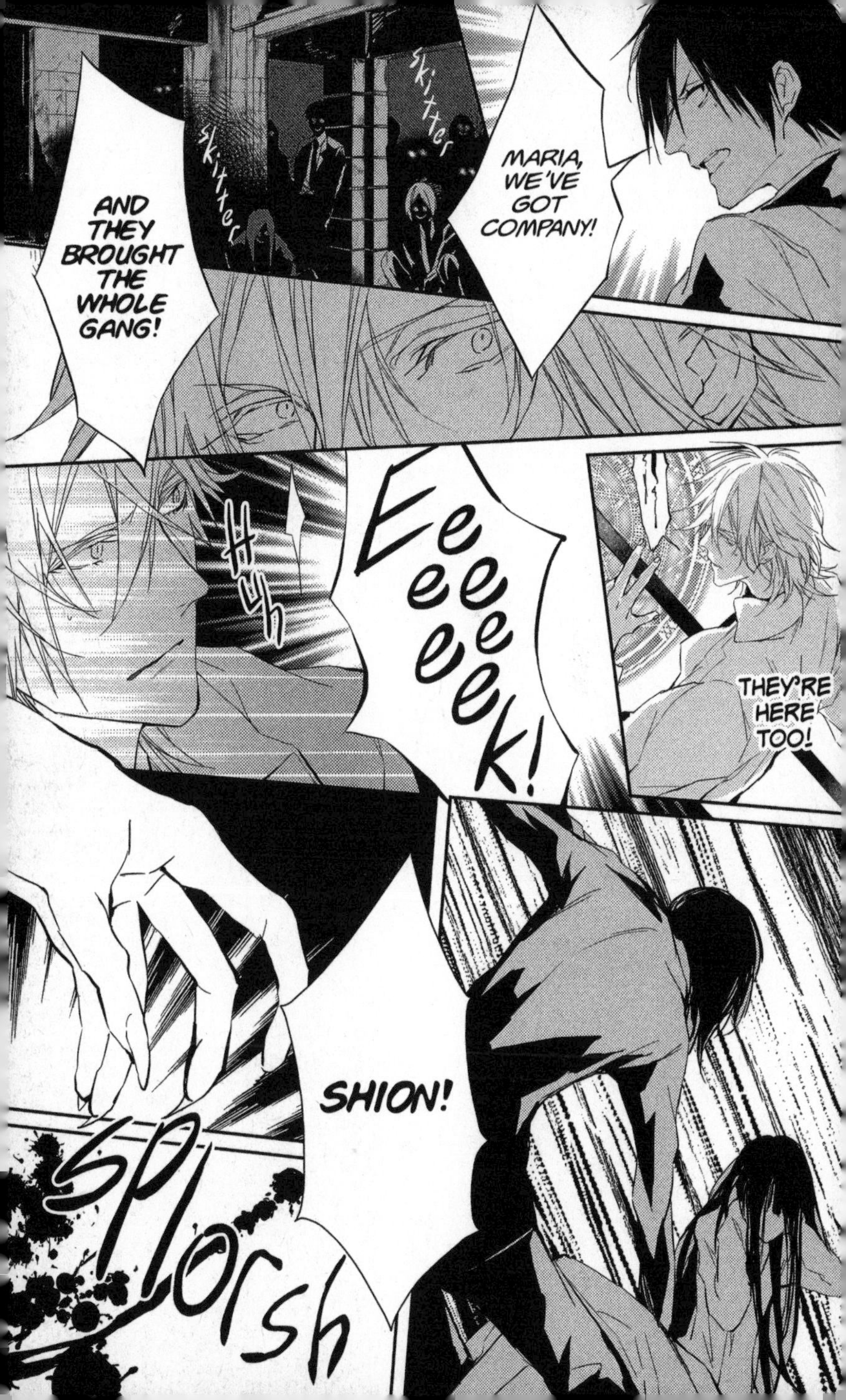
MARIA, WE'VE GOT COMPANY!
skitter
skitter
AND THEY BROUGHT THE WHOLE GANG!
THEY'RE HERE TOO!
Eeeeeeek!
Huh
SHION!
Splorsh

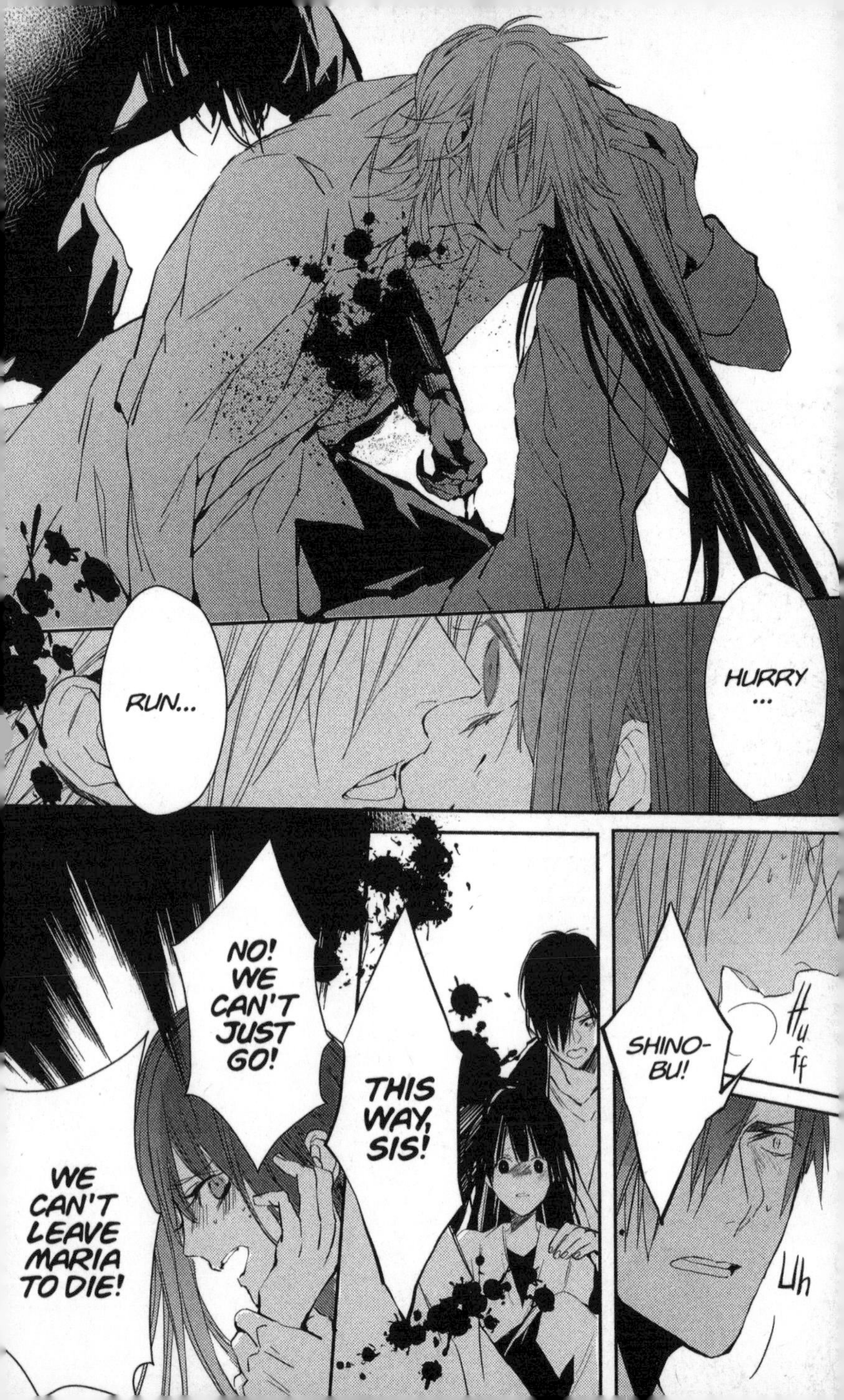

HURRY ...
RUN...
Huff
SHINO-BU!
Uh
THIS WAY, SIS!
NO! WE CAN'T JUST GO!
WE CAN'T LEAVE MARIA TO DIE!

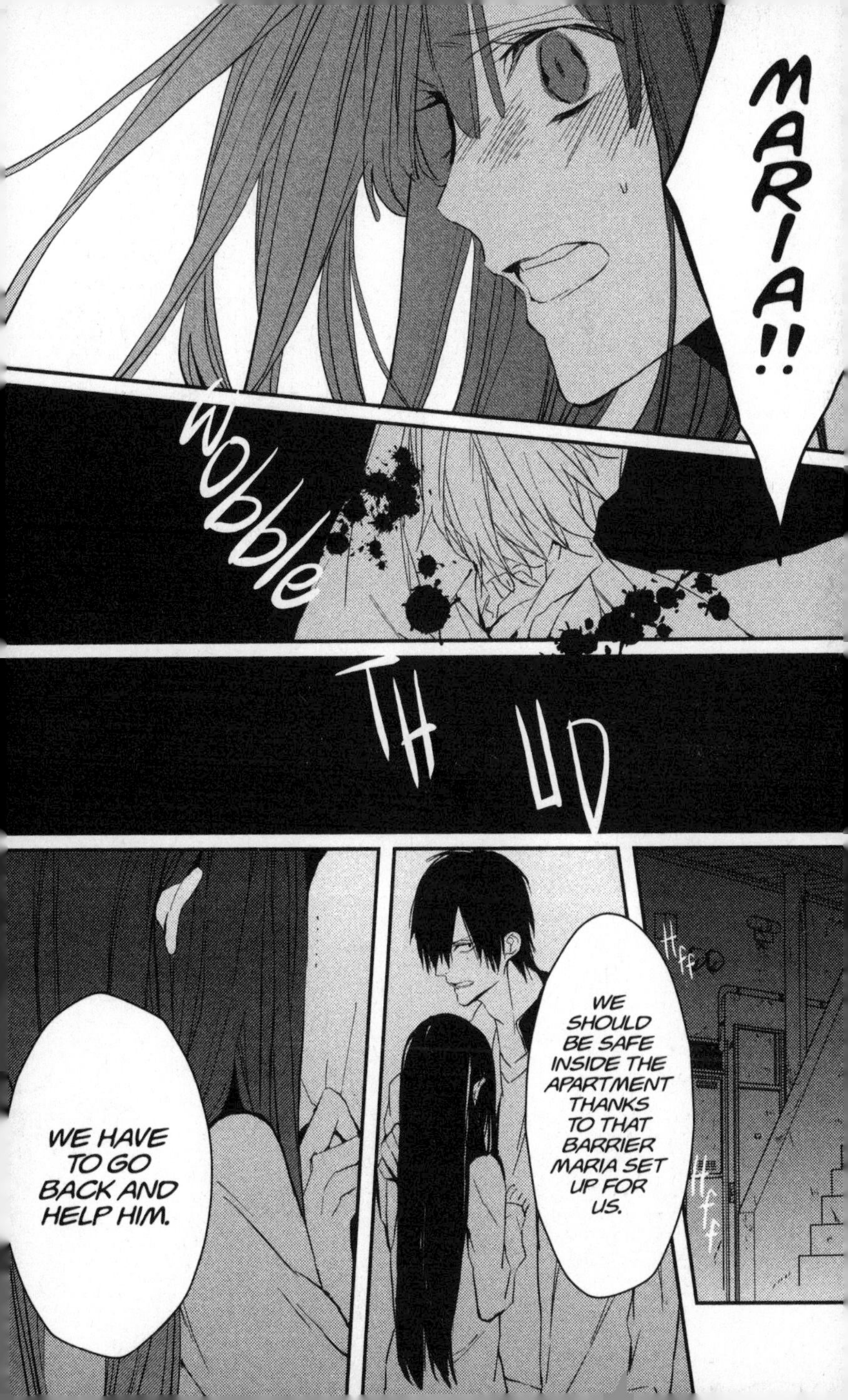
MARIA!!
wobble
THUD
Hff
Hff
WE SHOULD BE SAFE INSIDE THE APARTMENT THANKS TO THAT BARRIER MARIA SET UP FOR US.
WE HAVE TO GO BACK AND HELP HIM.

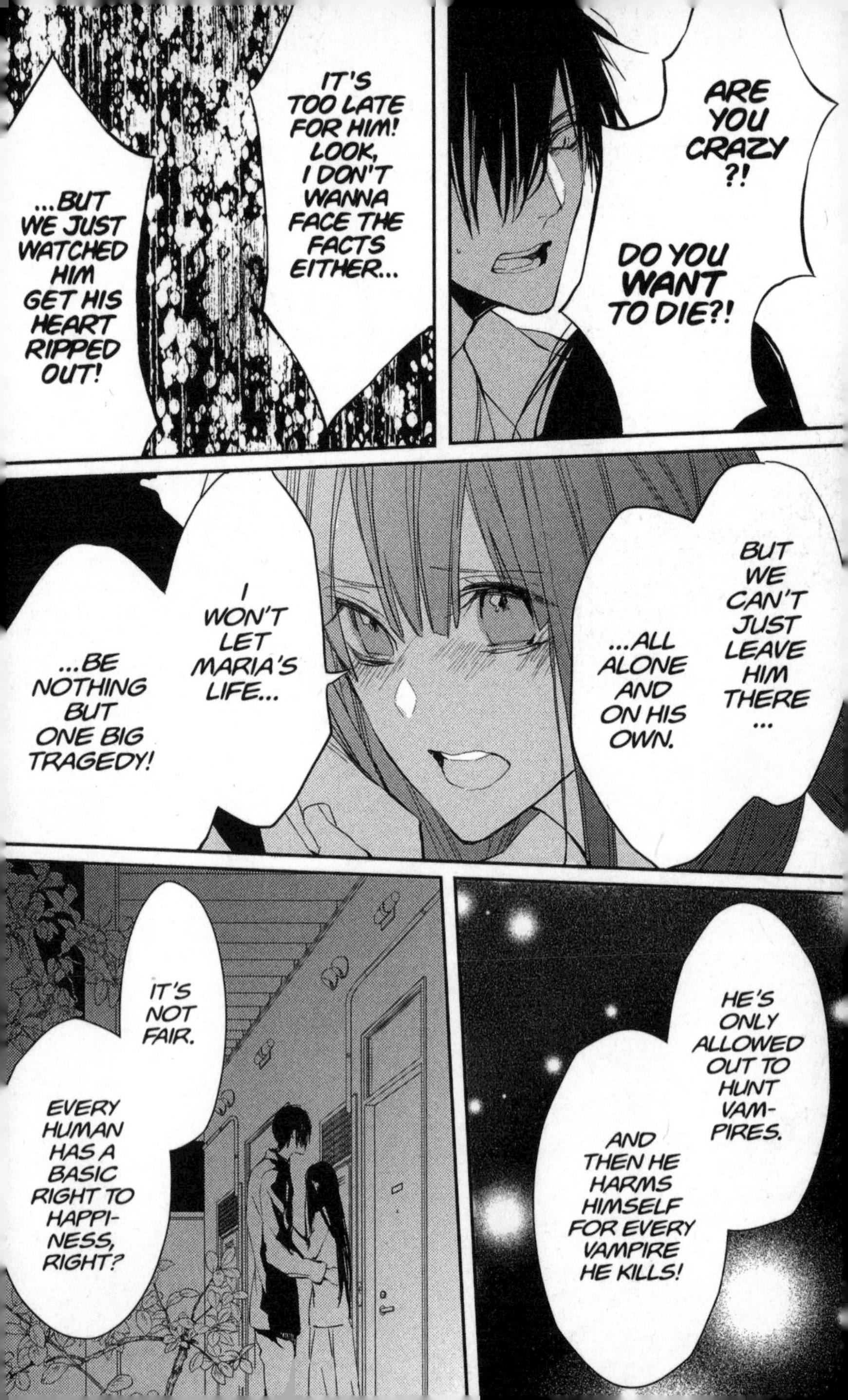
ARE YOU CRAZY?!
DO YOU WANT TO DIE?!
IT'S TOO LATE FOR HIM! LOOK, I DON'T WANNA FACE THE FACTS EITHER...
...BUT WE JUST WATCHED HIM GET HIS HEART RIPPED OUT!
BUT WE CAN'T JUST LEAVE HIM THERE...
...ALL ALONE AND ON HIS OWN.
I WON'T LET MARIA'S LIFE...
...BE NOTHING BUT ONE BIG TRAGEDY!
HE'S ONLY ALLOWED OUT TO HUNT VAM-PIRES.
AND THEN HE HARMS HIMSELF FOR EVERY VAMPIRE HE KILLS!
IT'S NOT FAIR.
EVERY HUMAN HAS A BASIC RIGHT TO HAPPI-NESS, RIGHT?

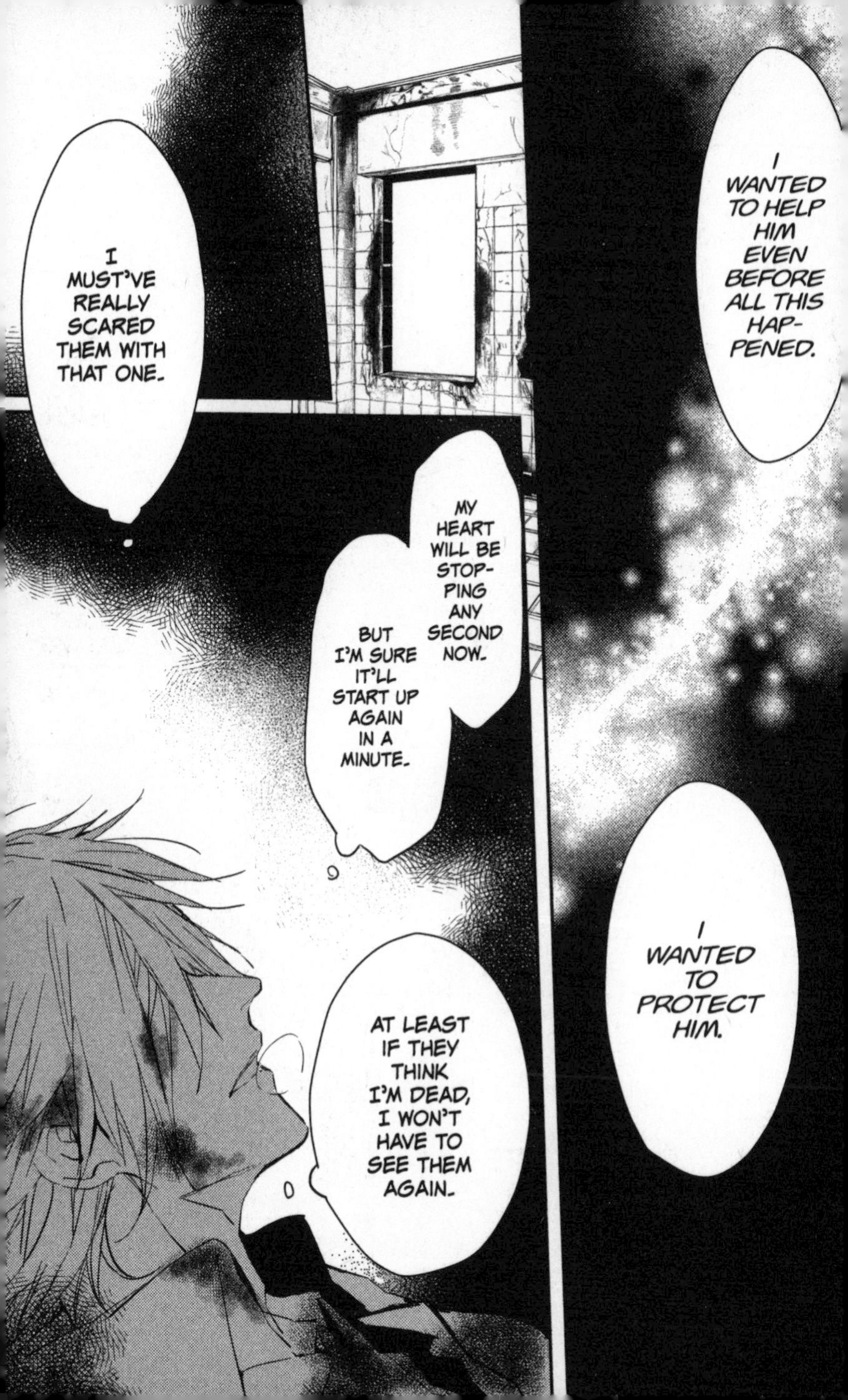
I WANTED TO HELP HIM EVEN BEFORE ALL THIS HAP-PENED.
I WANTED TO PROTECT HIM.
I MUST'VE REALLY SCARED THEM WITH THAT ONE.
MY HEART WILL BE STOP-PING ANY SECOND NOW.
BUT I'M SURE IT'LL START UP AGAIN IN A MINUTE.
AT LEAST IF THEY THINK I'M DEAD, I WON'T HAVE TO SEE THEM AGAIN.

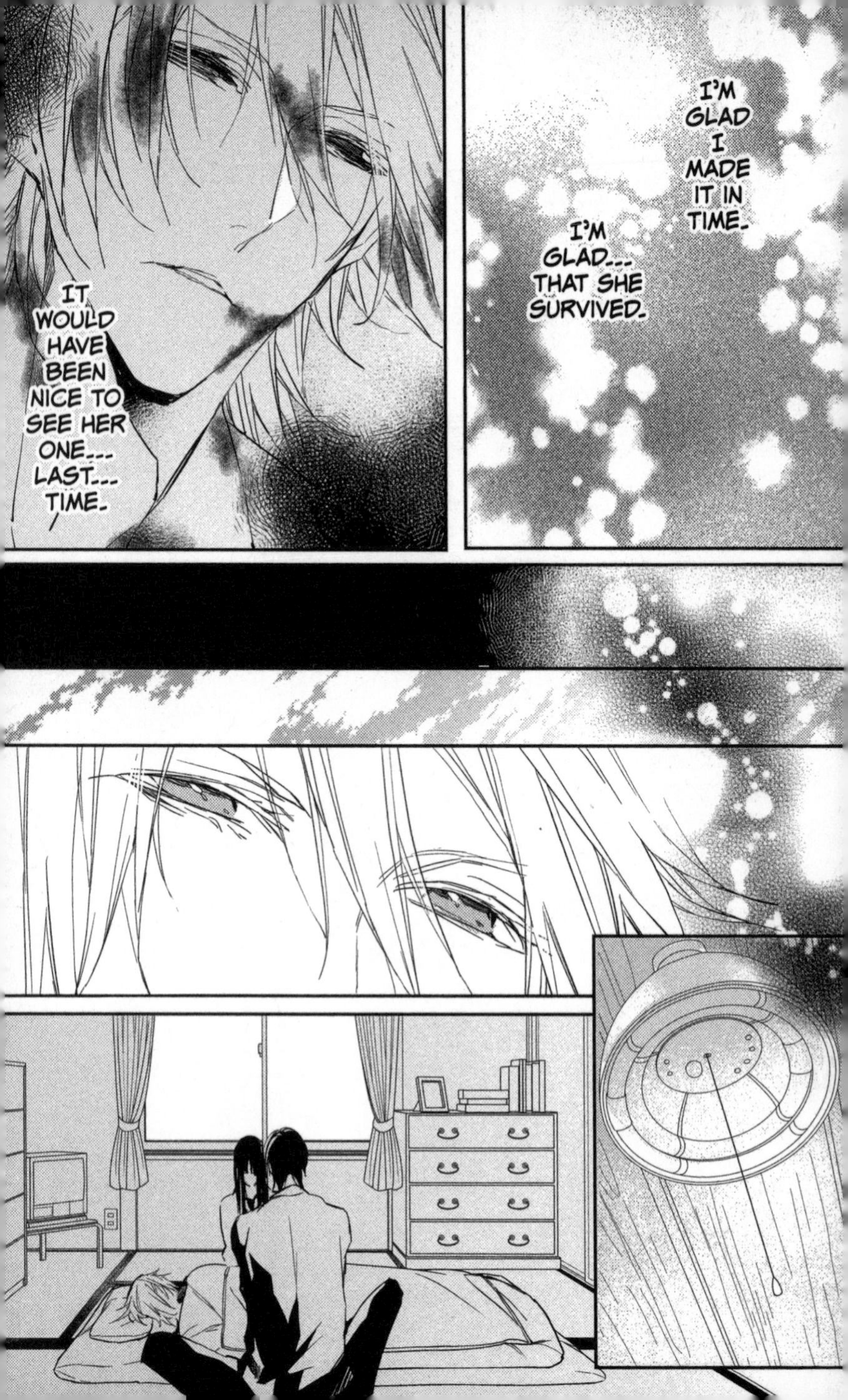
I'M GLAD I MADE IT IN TIME.
I'M GLAD... THAT SHE SURVIVED.
IT WOULD HAVE BEEN NICE TO SEE HER ONE... LAST... TIME.

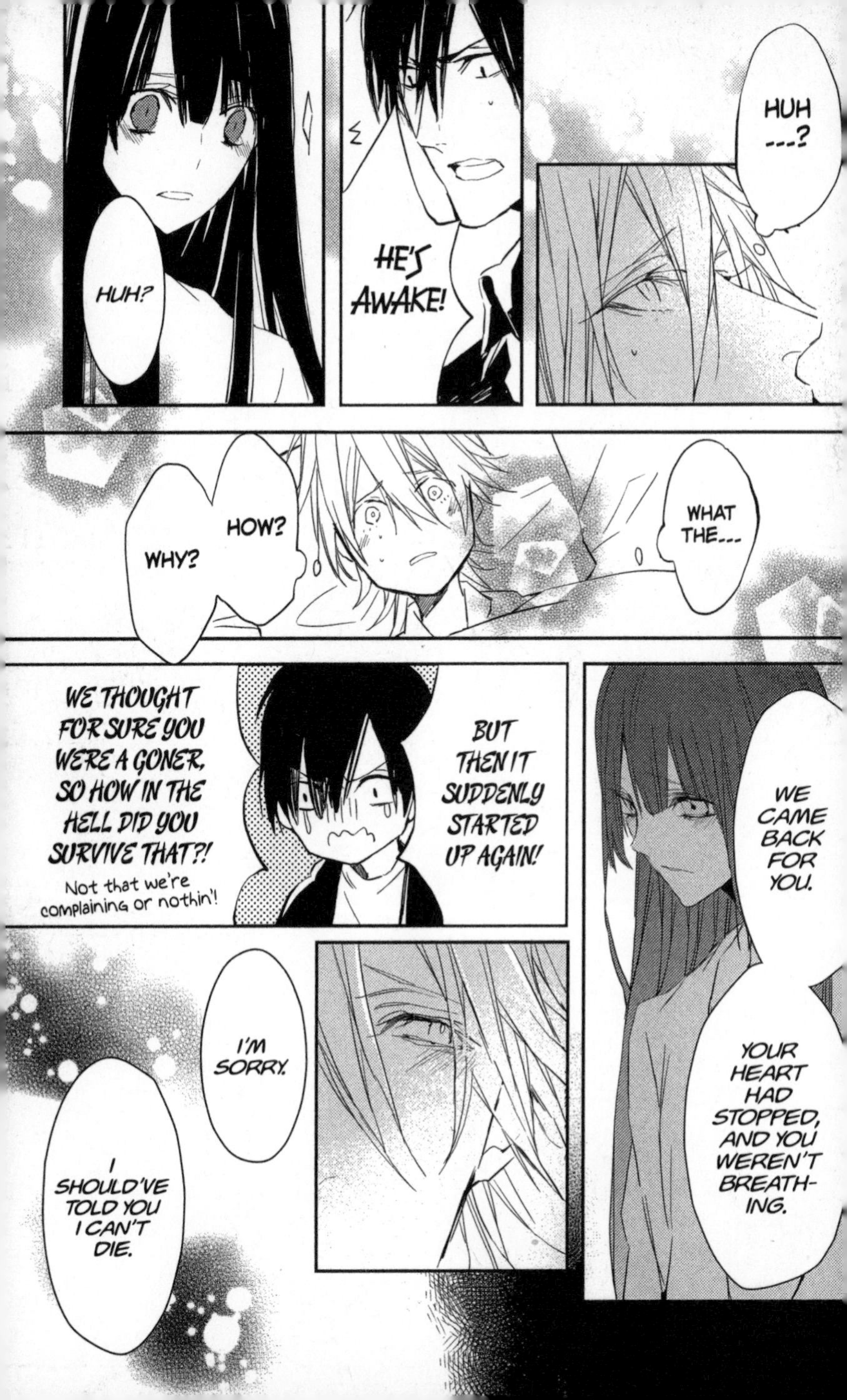
HUH---?
HE'S AWAKE!
HUH?
WHAT THE...
HOW?
WHY?
WE CAME BACK FOR YOU.
YOUR HEART HAD STOPPED, AND YOU WEREN'T BREATH-ING.
BUT THEN IT SUDDENLY STARTED UP AGAIN!
WE THOUGHT FOR SURE YOU WERE A GONER, SO HOW IN THE HELL DID YOU SURVIVE THAT?!
Not that we're complaining or nothin'!
I'M SORRY.
I SHOULD'VE TOLD YOU I CAN'T DIE.

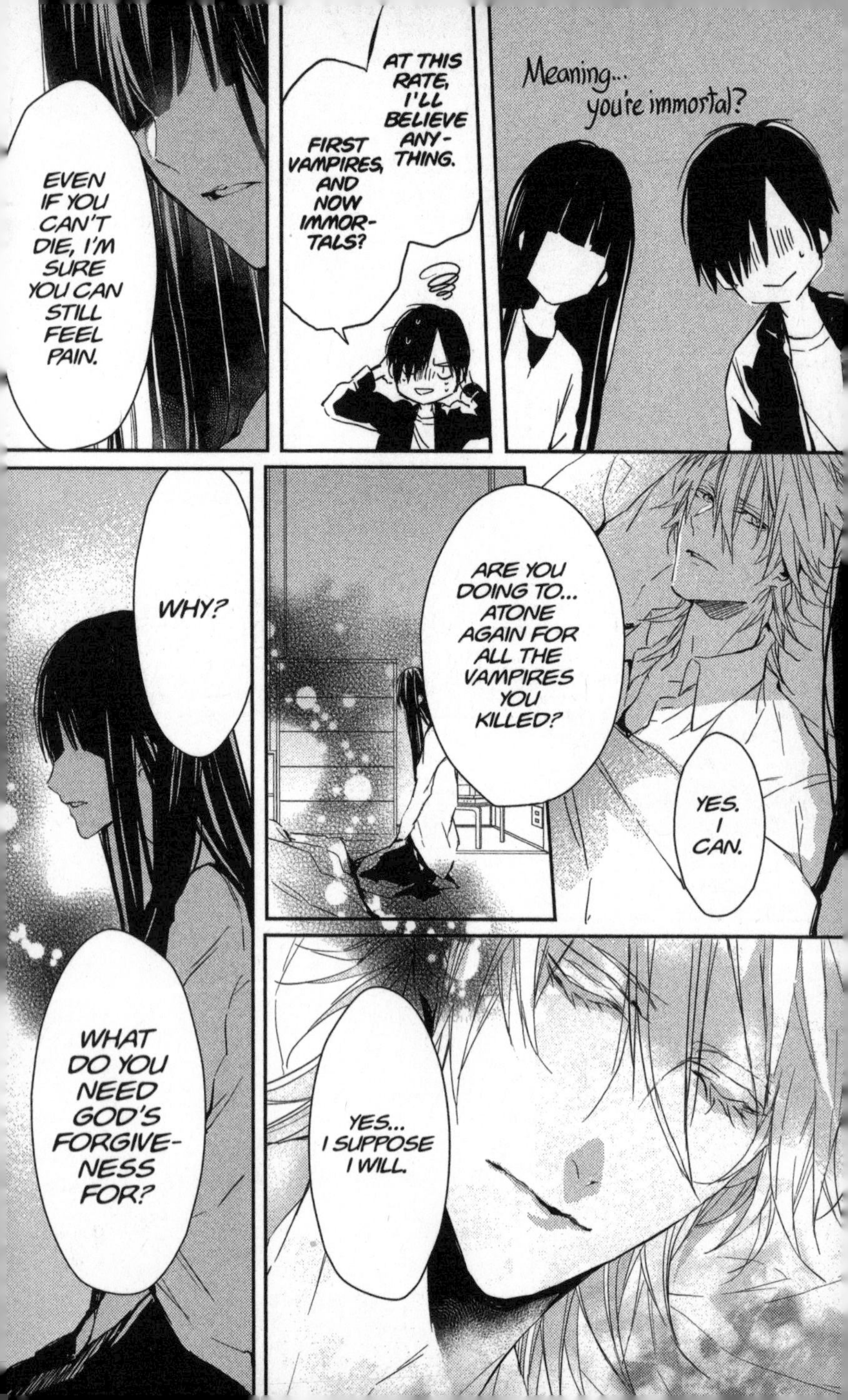
Meaning... you're immortal?
AT THIS RATE, I'LL BELIEVE ANYTHING.
FIRST VAMPIRES, AND NOW IMMORTALS?
EVEN IF YOU CAN'T DIE, I'M SURE YOU CAN STILL FEEL PAIN.
YES. I CAN.
ARE YOU DOING TO... ATONE AGAIN FOR ALL THE VAMPIRES YOU KILLED?
YES... I SUPPOSE I WILL.
WHY?
WHAT DO YOU NEED GOD'S FORGIVENESS FOR?

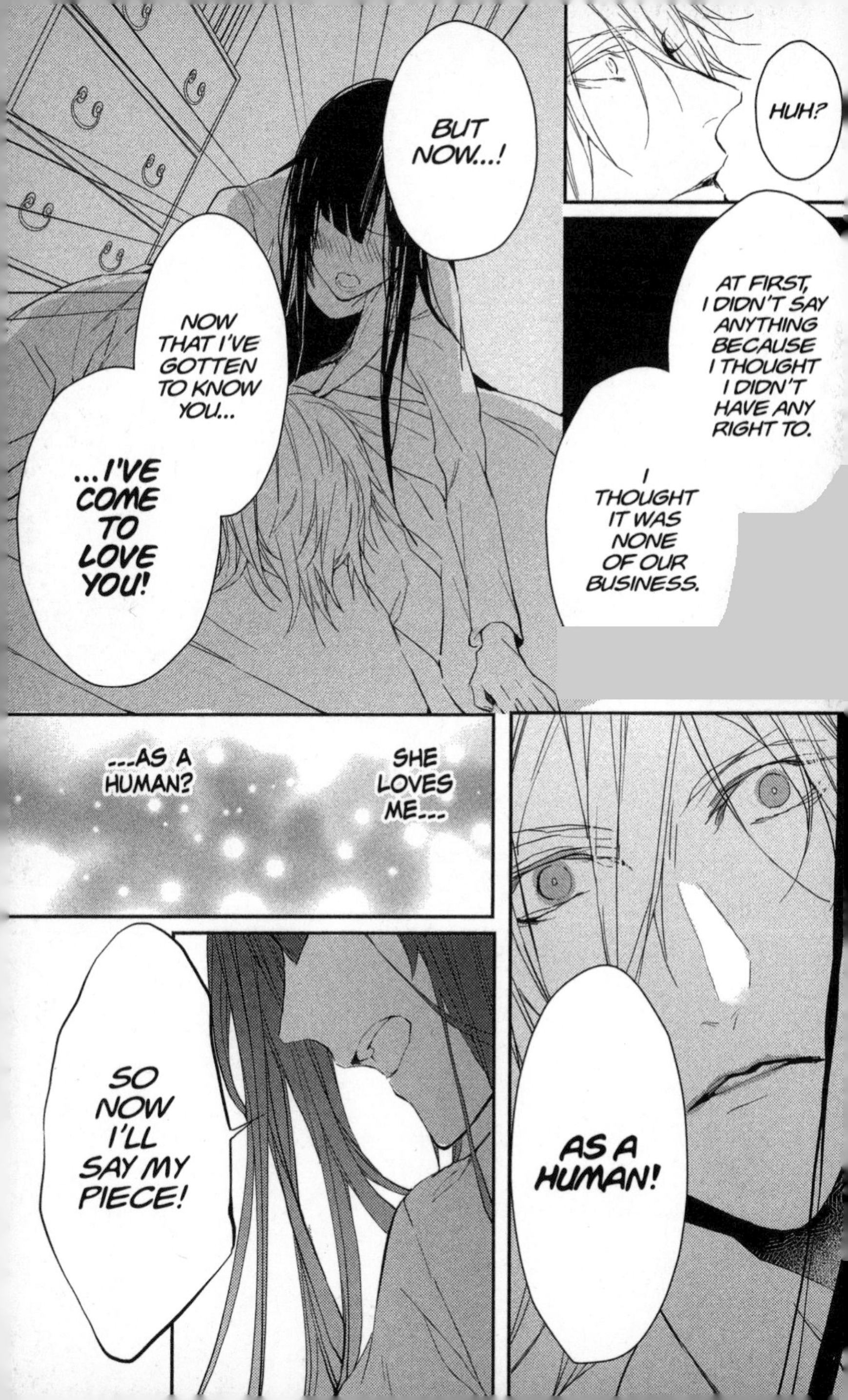
HUH?
AT FIRST, I DIDN'T SAY ANYTHING BECAUSE I THOUGHT I DIDN'T HAVE ANY RIGHT TO.
I THOUGHT IT WAS NONE OF OUR BUSINESS.
BUT NOW...!
NOW THAT I'VE GOTTEN TO KNOW YOU...
...I'VE COME TO LOVE YOU!
AS A HUMAN!
SHE LOVES ME...
...AS A HUMAN?
SO NOW I'LL SAY MY PIECE!

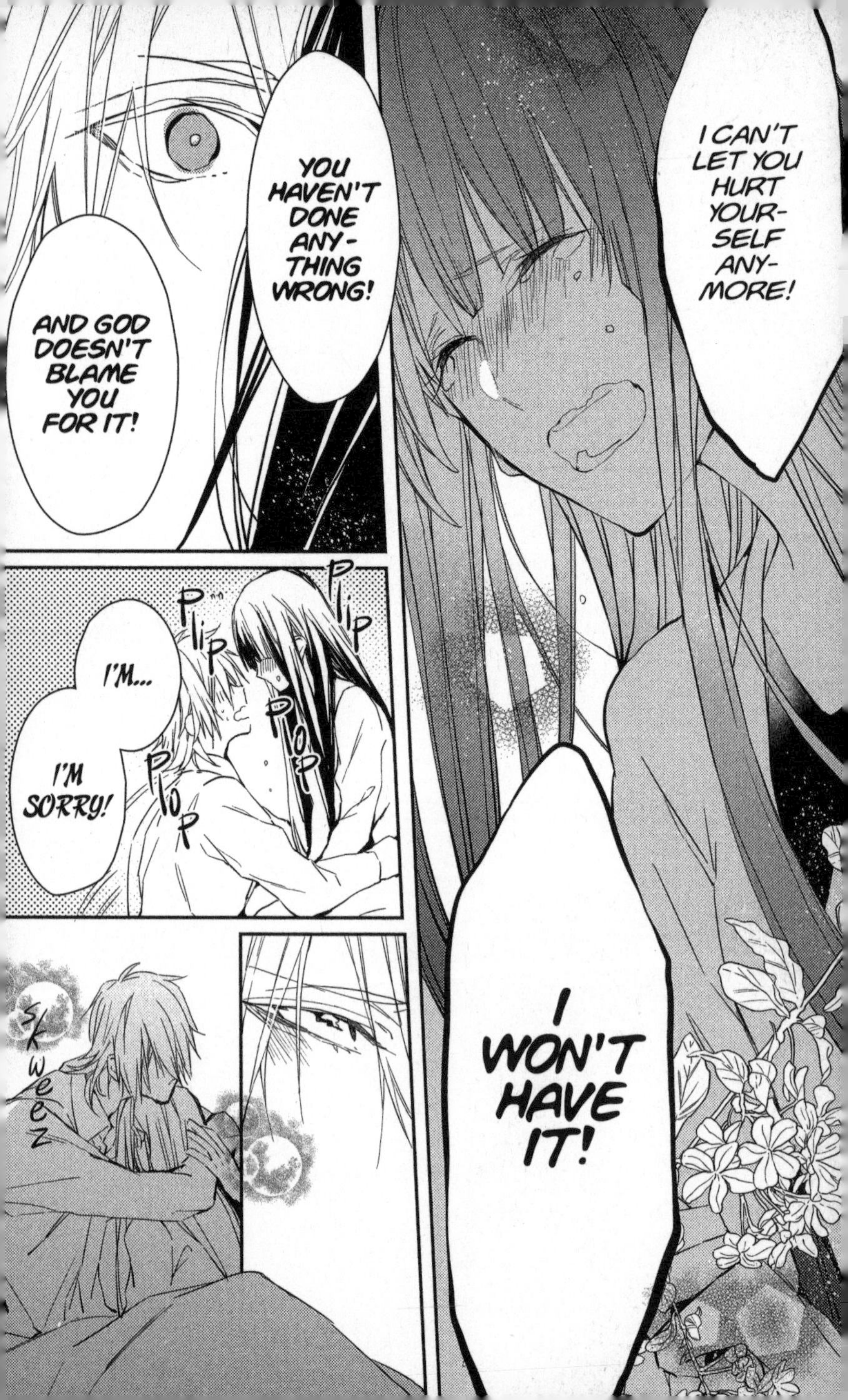
I CAN'T LET YOU HURT YOUR-SELF ANY-MORE!
I WON'T HAVE IT!
YOU HAVEN'T DONE ANY-THING WRONG!
AND GOD DOESN'T BLAME YOU FOR IT!
Plip
Plip
I'M...
I'M SORRY!
Plop
Plop
SKWEEZ

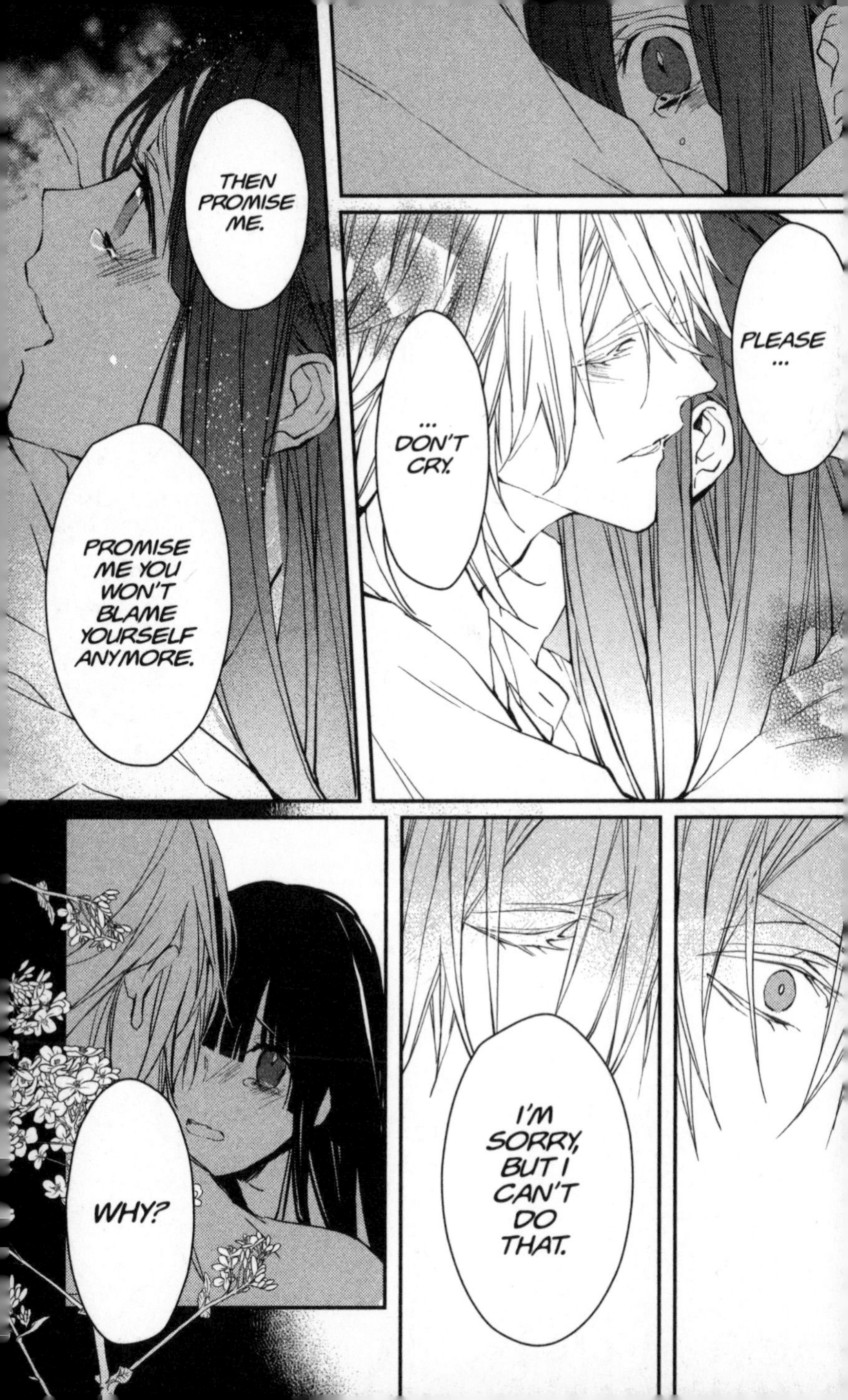
PLEASE...
...DON'T CRY.
THEN PROMISE ME.
PROMISE ME YOU WON'T BLAME YOURSELF ANYMORE.
I'M SORRY, BUT I CAN'T DO THAT.
WHY?

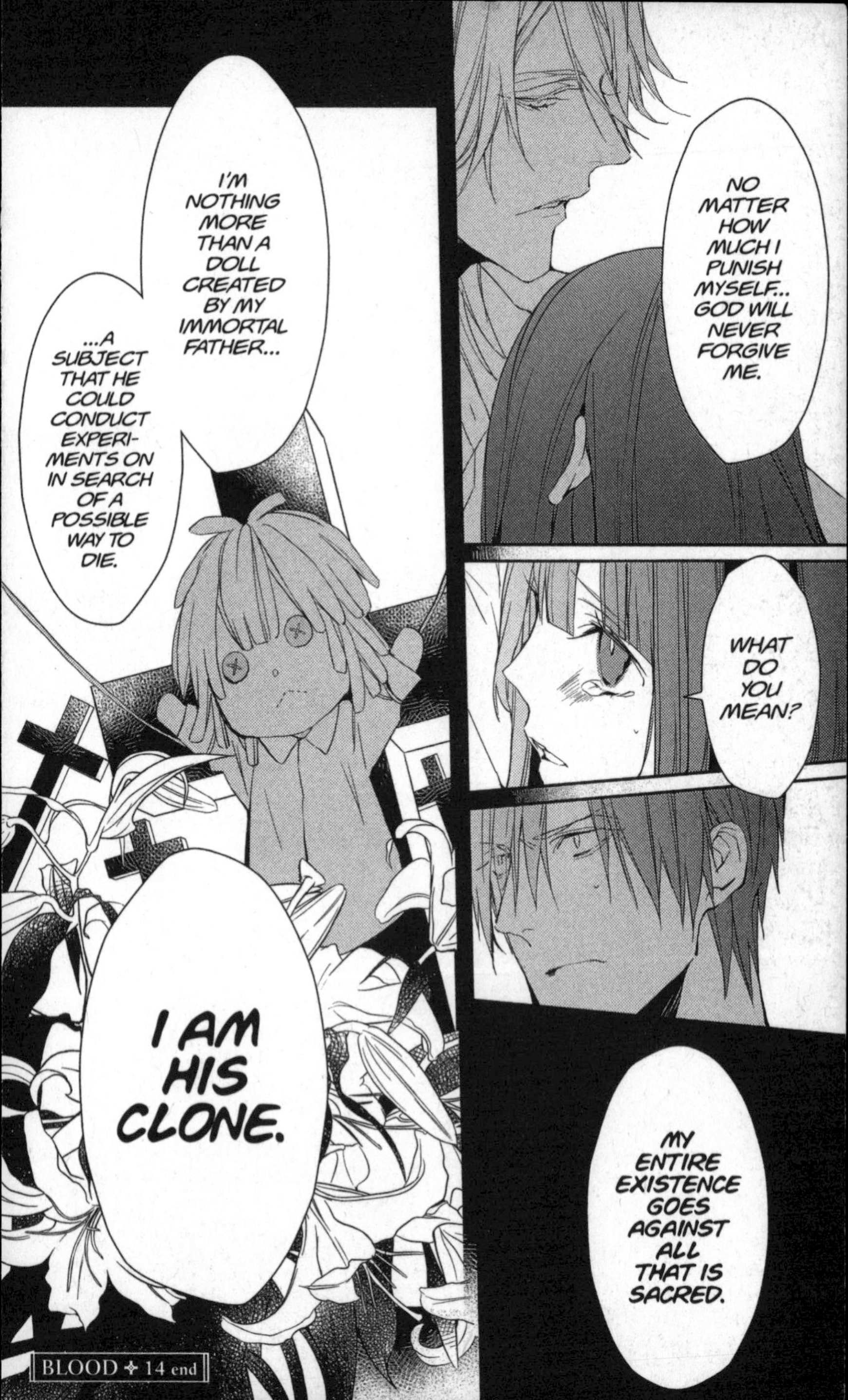
NO MATTER HOW MUCH I PUNISH MYSELF... GOD WILL NEVER FORGIVE ME.
WHAT DO YOU MEAN?
MY ENTIRE EXISTENCE GOES AGAINST ALL THAT IS SACRED.
I'M NOTHING MORE THAN A DOLL CREATED BY MY IMMORTAL FATHER...
...A SUBJECT THAT HE COULD CONDUCT EXPERI-MENTS ON IN SEARCH OF A POSSIBLE WAY TO DIE.
I AM HIS CLONE.
BLOOD ✦ 14 end

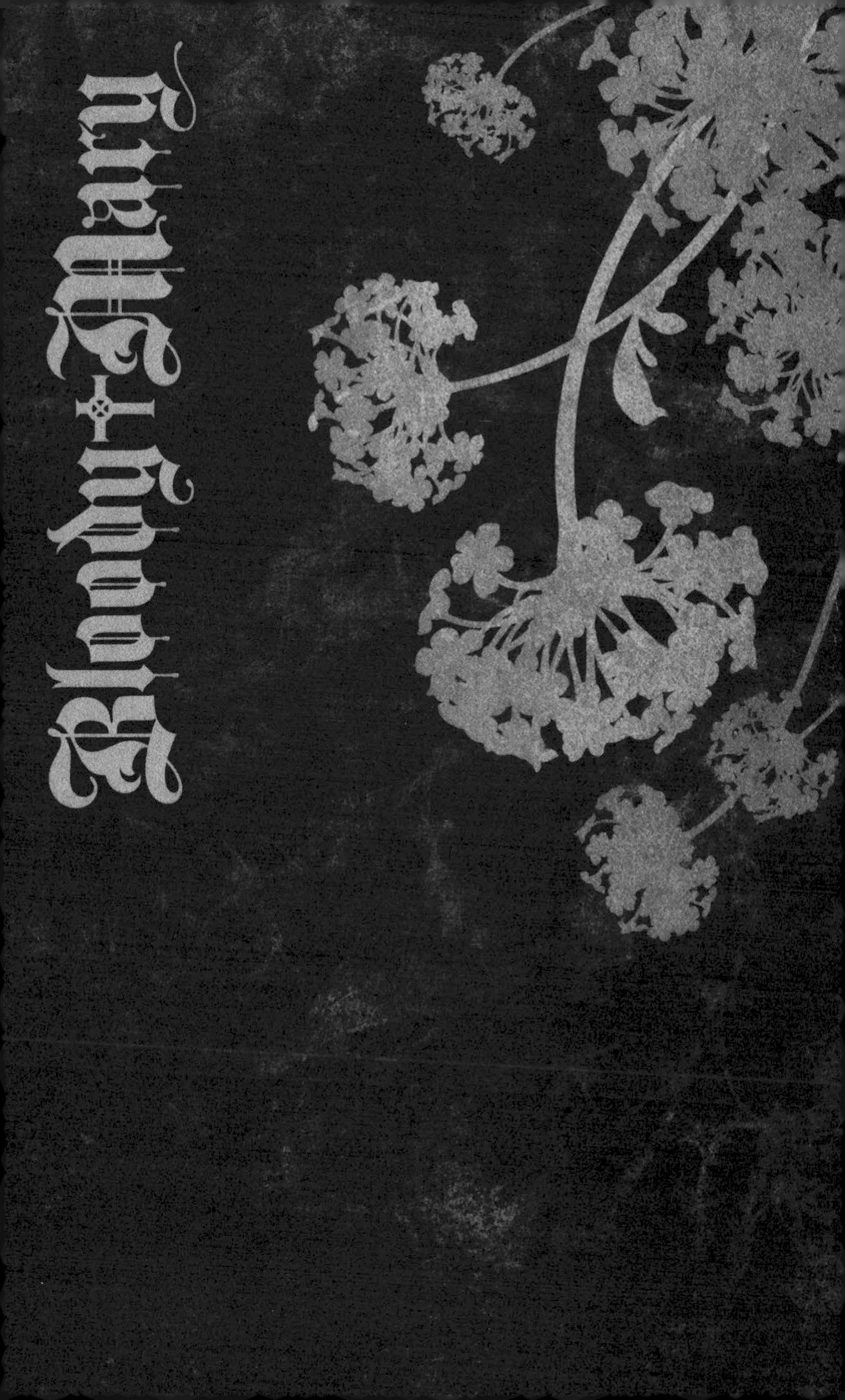
Bloody Mary

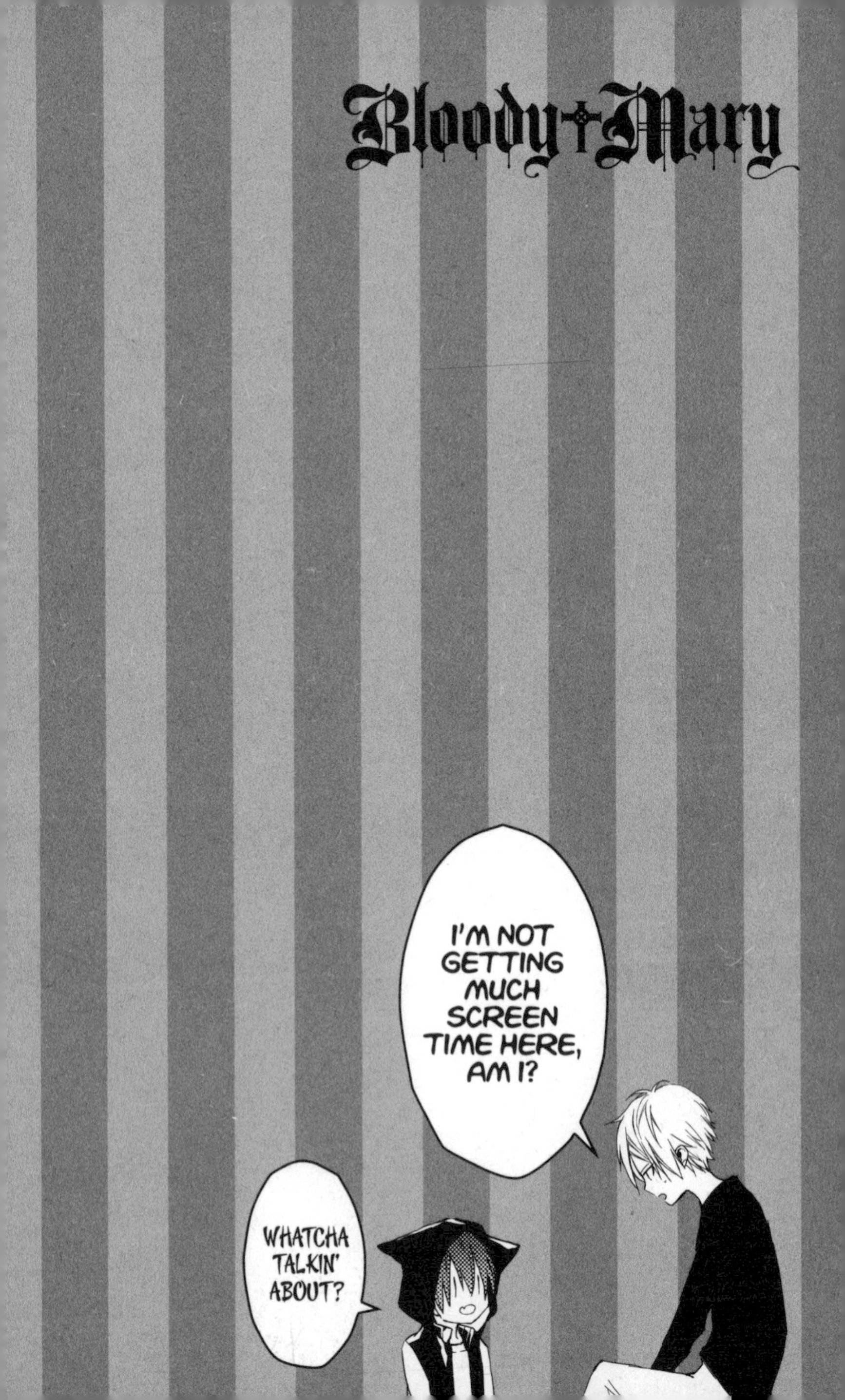
Bloody+Mary
I'M NOT GETTING MUCH SCREEN TIME HERE, AM I?
WHATCHA TALKIN' ABOUT?

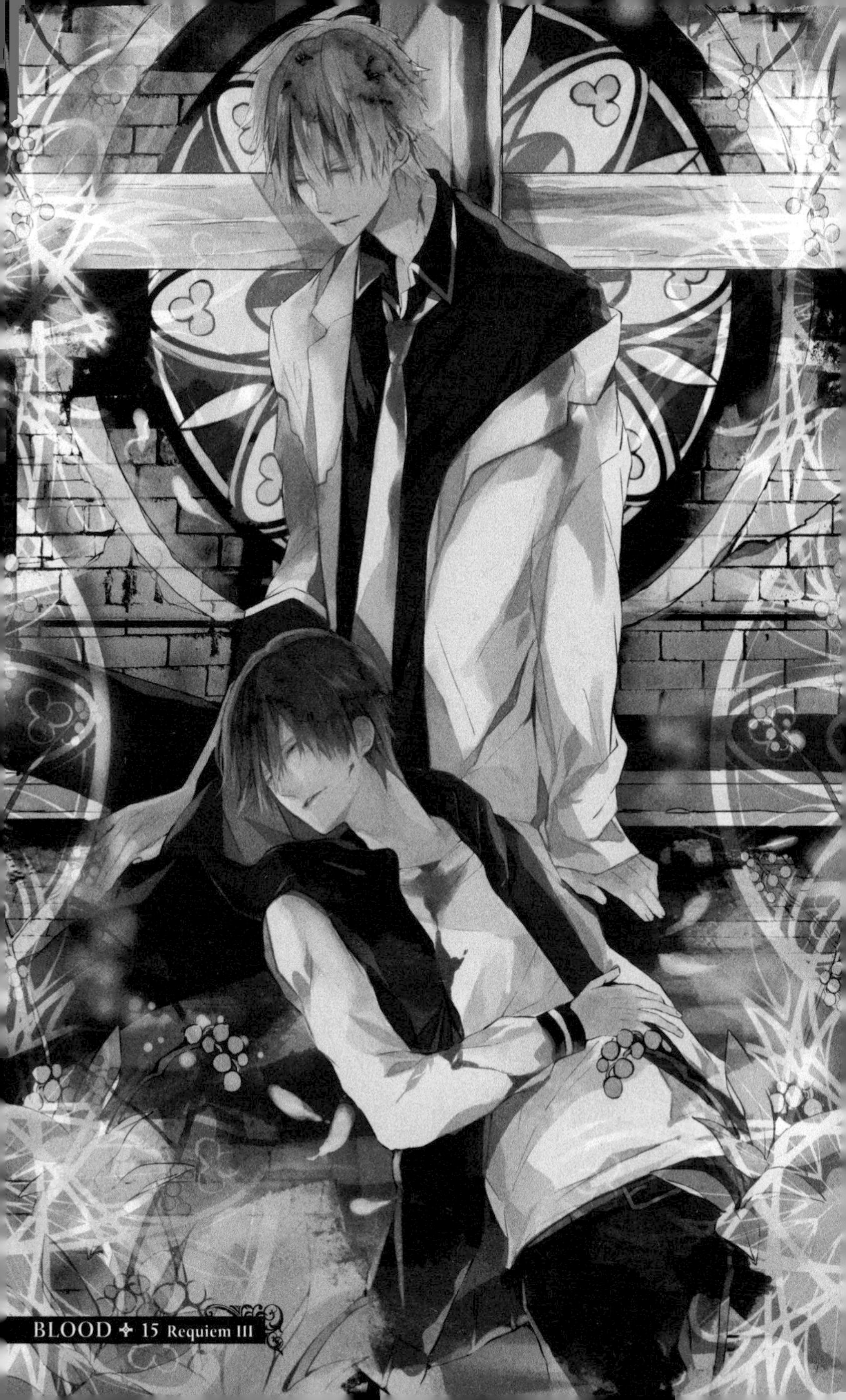

BLOOD ✣ 15 Requiem III

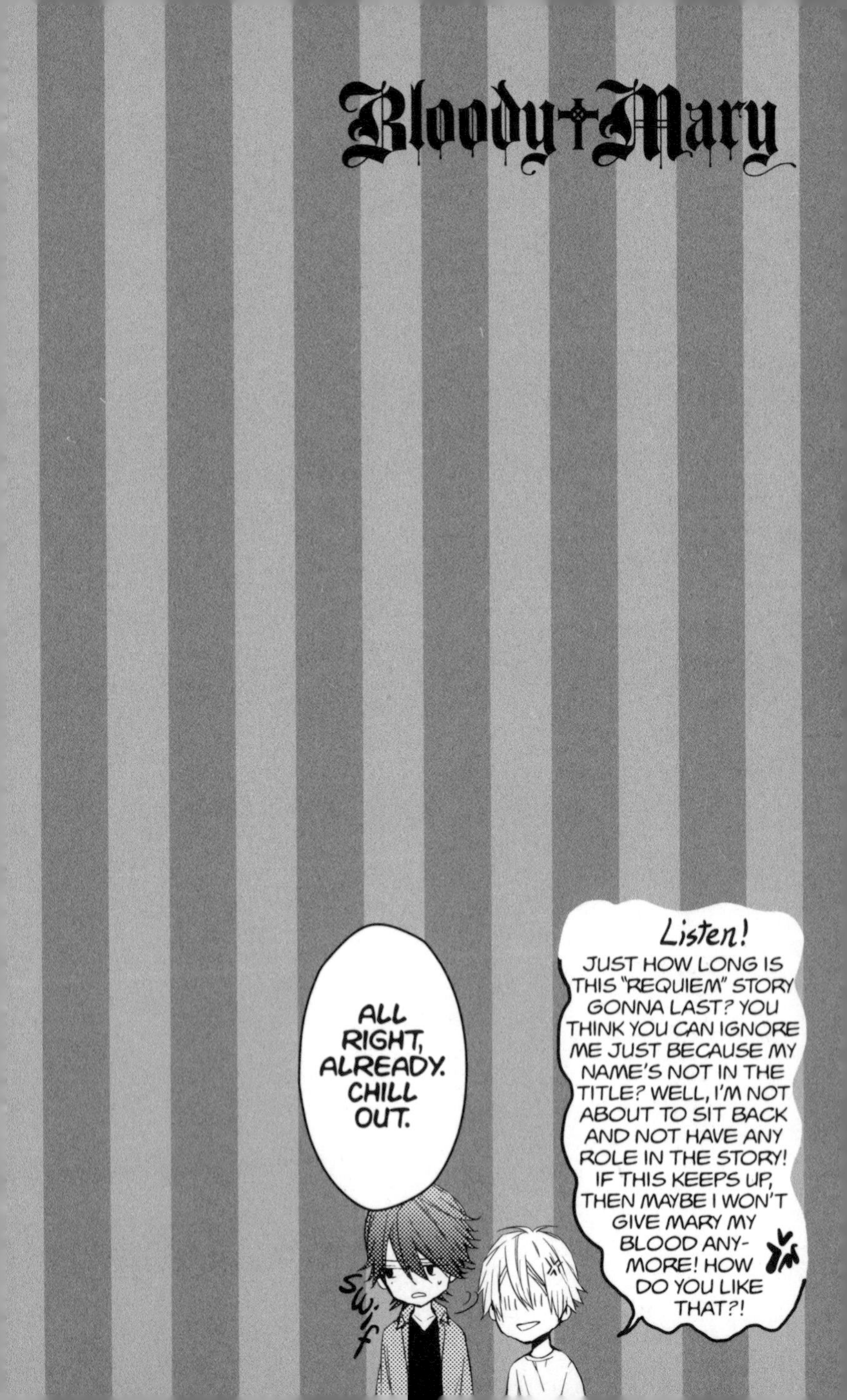
Bloody+Mary
Listen! JUST HOW LONG IS THIS "REQUIEM" STORY GONNA LAST? YOU THINK YOU CAN IGNORE ME JUST BECAUSE MY NAME'S NOT IN THE TITLE? WELL, I'M NOT ABOUT TO SIT BACK AND NOT HAVE ANY ROLE IN THE STORY! IF THIS KEEPS UP, THEN MAYBE I WON'T GIVE MARY MY BLOOD ANY-MORE! HOW DO YOU LIKE THAT?!
ALL RIGHT, ALREADY. CHILL OUT.
SWIF

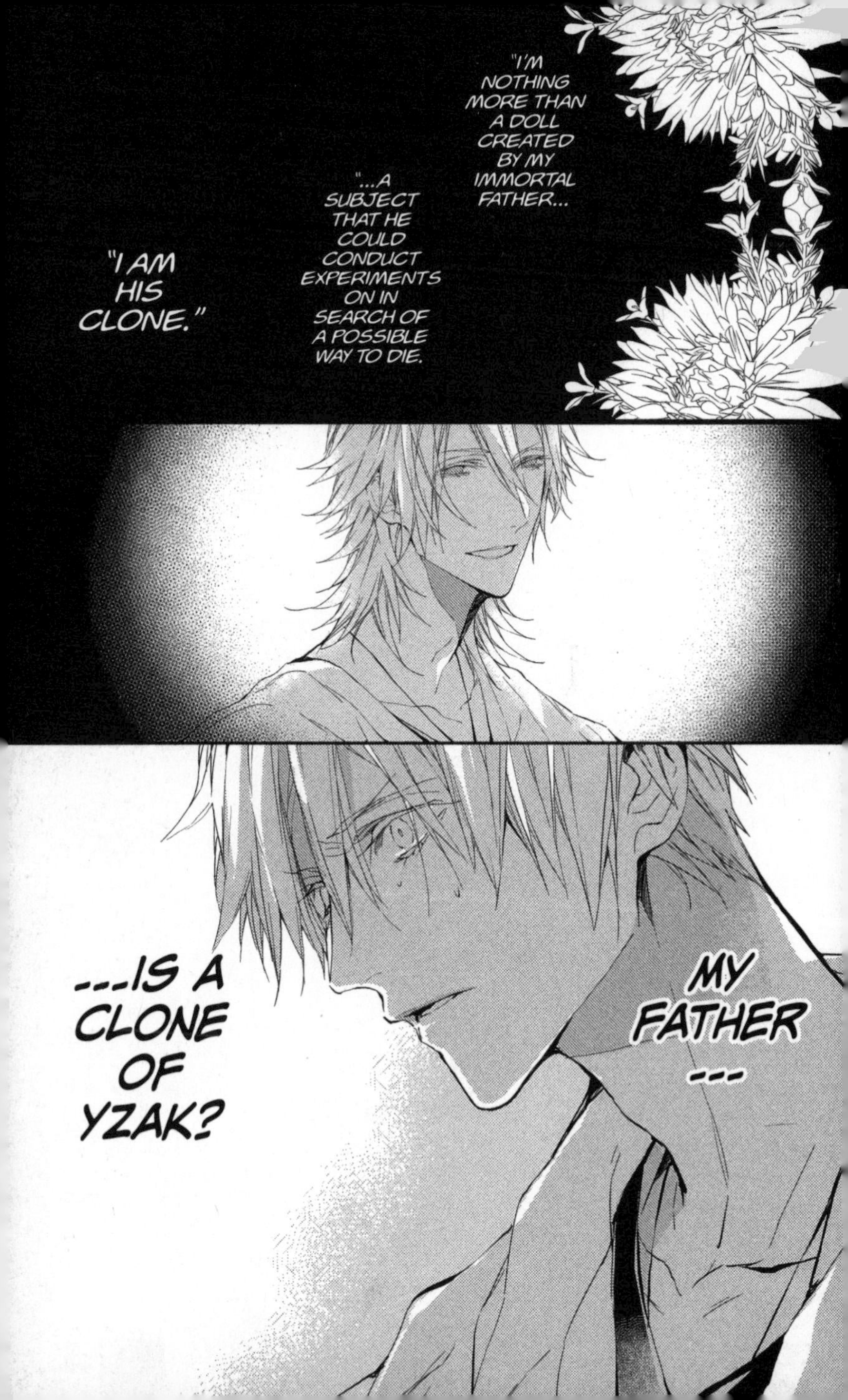
"I'M NOTHING MORE THAN A DOLL CREATED BY MY IMMORTAL FATHER...
"...A SUBJECT THAT HE COULD CONDUCT EXPERIMENTS ON IN SEARCH OF A POSSIBLE WAY TO DIE.
"I AM HIS CLONE."
MY FATHER---
---IS A CLONE OF YZAK?

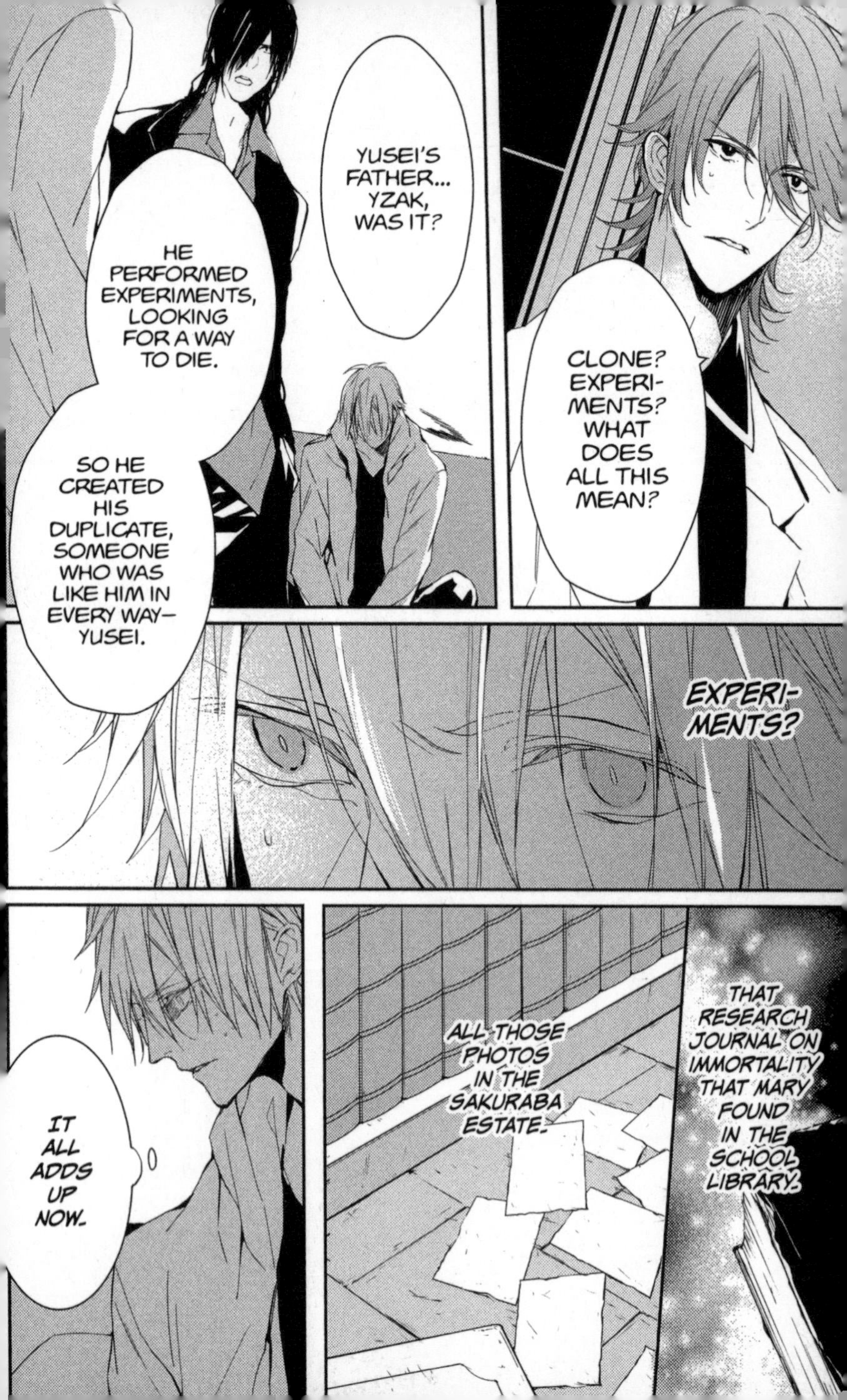
CLONE? EXPERI-MENTS? WHAT DOES ALL THIS MEAN?
YUSEI'S FATHER... YZAK, WAS IT?
HE PERFORMED EXPERIMENTS, LOOKING FOR A WAY TO DIE.
SO HE CREATED HIS DUPLICATE, SOMEONE WHO WAS LIKE HIM IN EVERY WAY—YUSEI.
EXPERI-MENTS?
THAT RESEARCH JOURNAL ON IMMORTALITY THAT MARY FOUND IN THE SCHOOL LIBRARY...
ALL THOSE PHOTOS IN THE SAKURABA ESTATE...
IT ALL ADDS UP NOW...

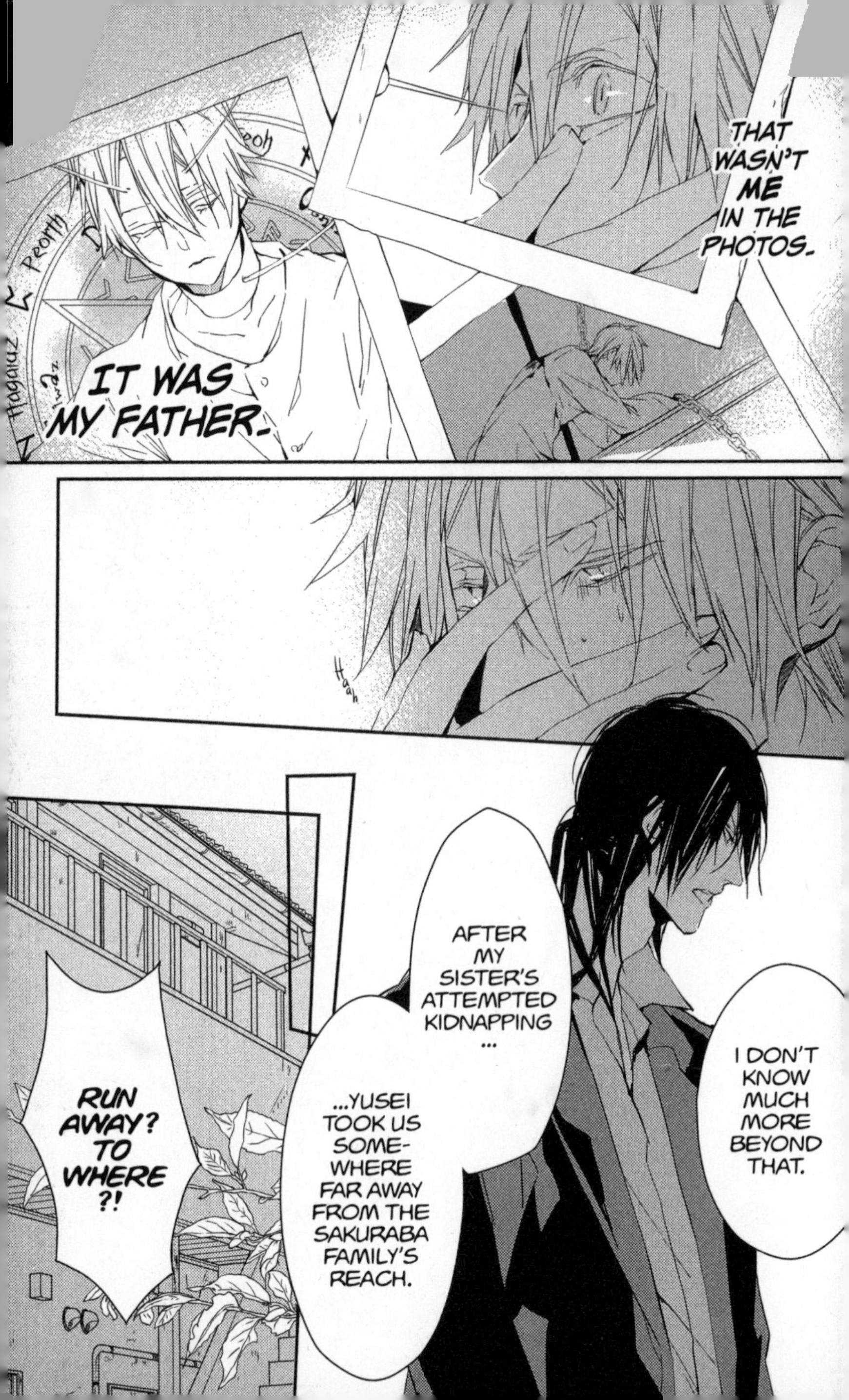
THAT WASN'T ME IN THE PHOTOS.
IT WAS MY FATHER.
Haah
AFTER MY SISTER'S ATTEMPTED KIDNAPPING...
...YUSEI TOOK US SOME-WHERE FAR AWAY FROM THE SAKURABA FAMILY'S REACH.
I DON'T KNOW MUCH MORE BEYOND THAT.
RUN AWAY? TO WHERE?!

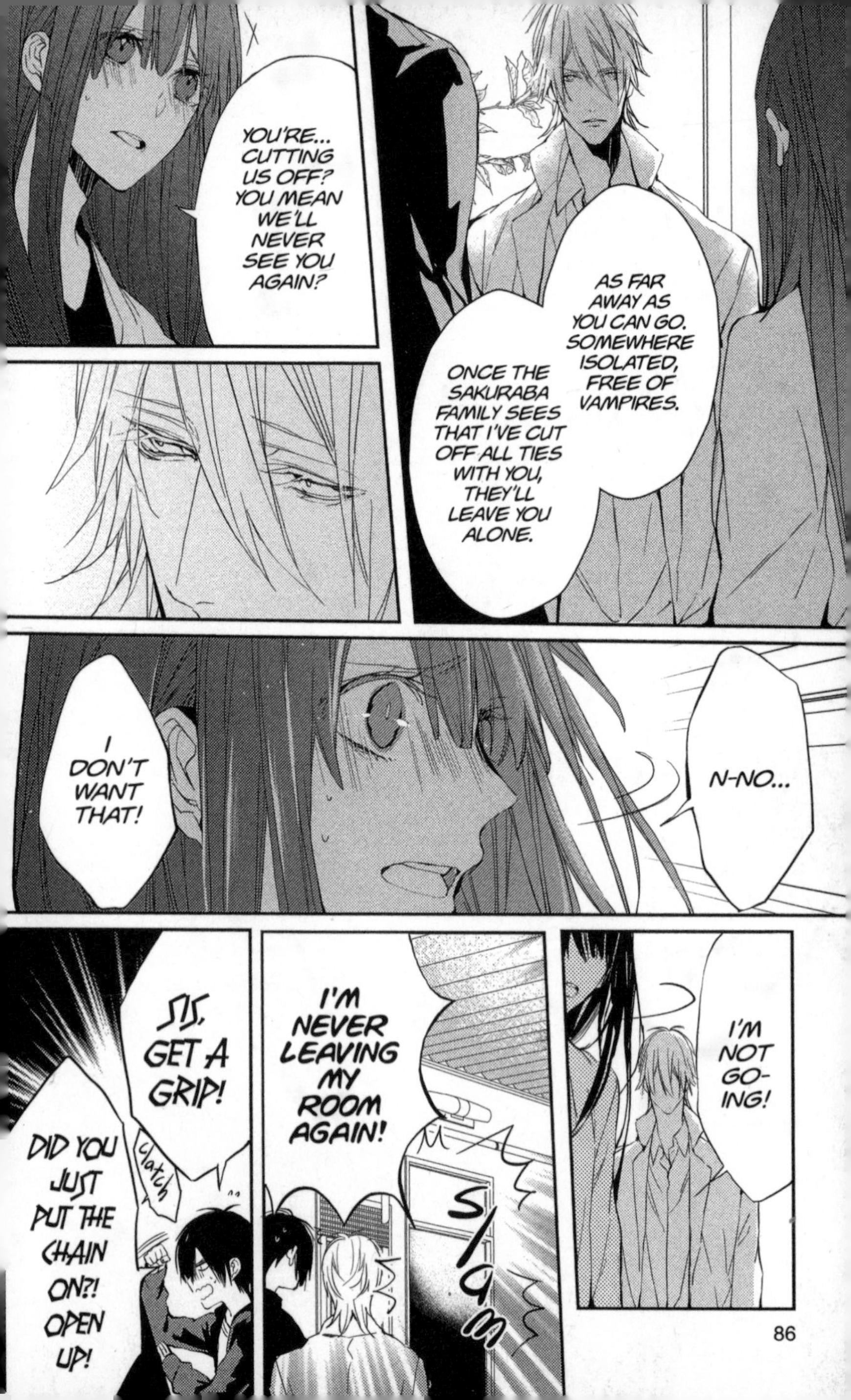
AS FAR AWAY AS YOU CAN GO. SOMEWHERE ISOLATED, FREE OF VAMPIRES.
ONCE THE SAKURABA FAMILY SEES THAT I'VE CUT OFF ALL TIES WITH YOU, THEY'LL LEAVE YOU ALONE.
YOU'RE... CUTTING US OFF? YOU MEAN WE'LL NEVER SEE YOU AGAIN?
N-NO...
I DON'T WANT THAT!
I'M NOT GO-ING!
I'M NEVER LEAVING MY ROOM AGAIN!
SLAM
SIS, GET A GRIP!
clatch
DID YOU JUST PUT THE CHAIN ON?! OPEN UP!

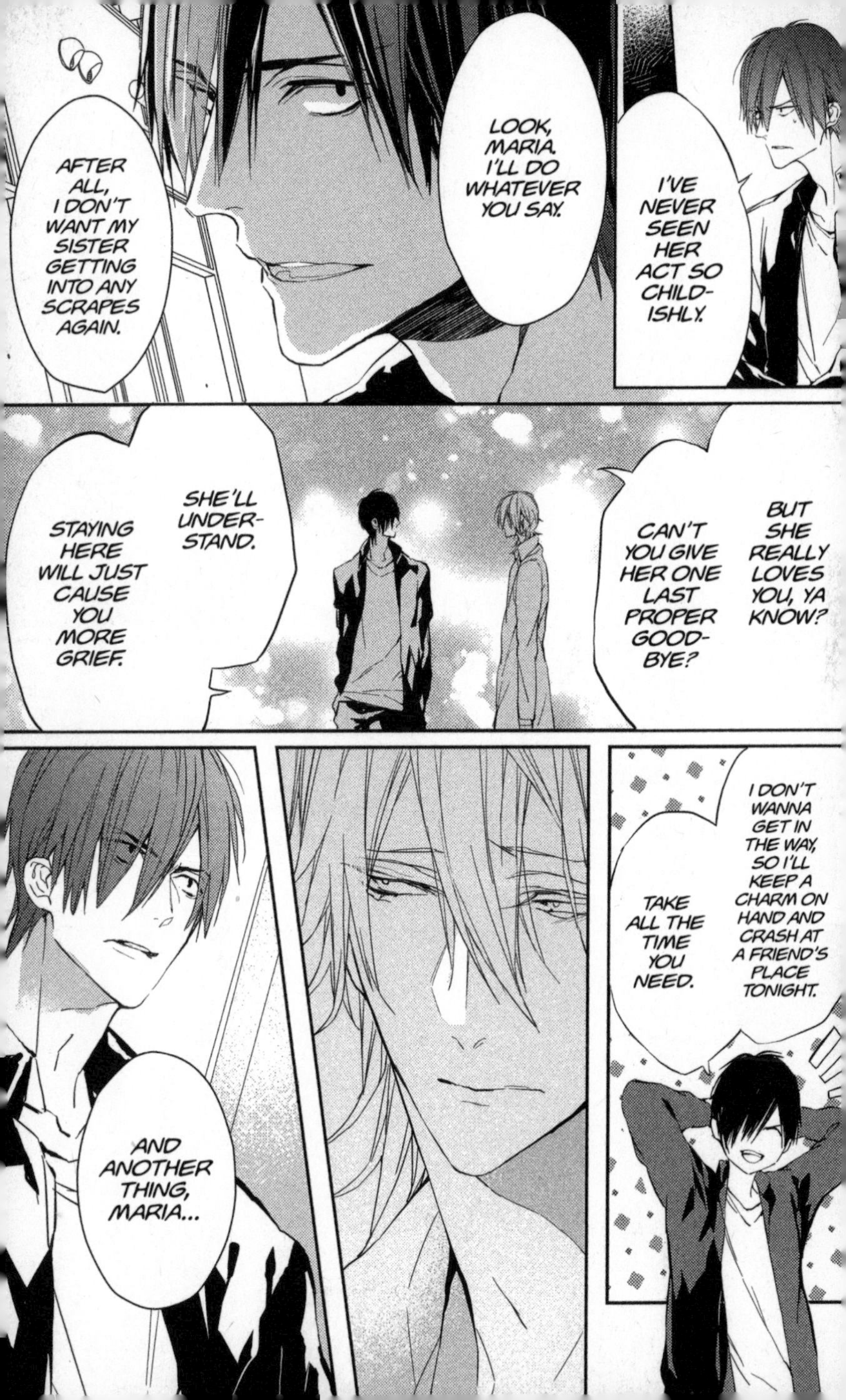
I'VE NEVER SEEN HER ACT SO CHILD-ISHLY.
LOOK, MARIA. I'LL DO WHATEVER YOU SAY.
AFTER ALL, I DON'T WANT MY SISTER GETTING INTO ANY SCRAPES AGAIN.
BUT SHE REALLY LOVES YOU, YA KNOW?
CAN'T YOU GIVE HER ONE LAST PROPER GOOD-BYE?
SHE'LL UNDER-STAND.
STAYING HERE WILL JUST CAUSE YOU MORE GRIEF.
I DON'T WANNA GET IN THE WAY, SO I'LL KEEP A CHARM ON HAND AND CRASH AT A FRIEND'S PLACE TONIGHT.
TAKE ALL THE TIME YOU NEED.
AND ANOTHER THING, MARIA...

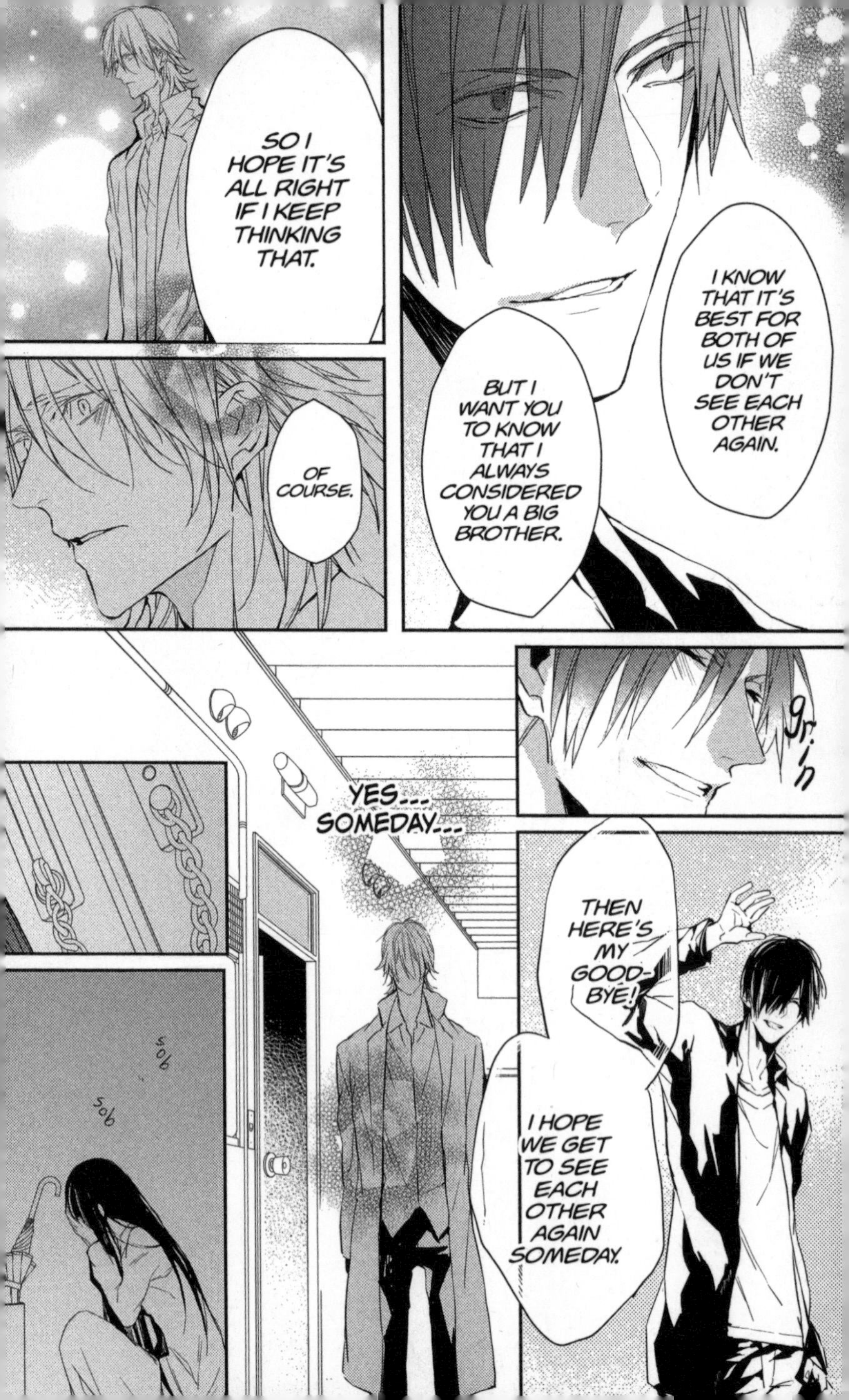
I KNOW THAT IT'S BEST FOR BOTH OF US IF WE DON'T SEE EACH OTHER AGAIN.
BUT I WANT YOU TO KNOW THAT I ALWAYS CONSIDERED YOU A BIG BROTHER.
SO I HOPE IT'S ALL RIGHT IF I KEEP THINKING THAT.
OF COURSE.
grin
THEN HERE'S MY GOOD-BYE!
I HOPE WE GET TO SEE EACH OTHER AGAIN SOMEDAY.
YES... SOMEDAY...
sob
sob

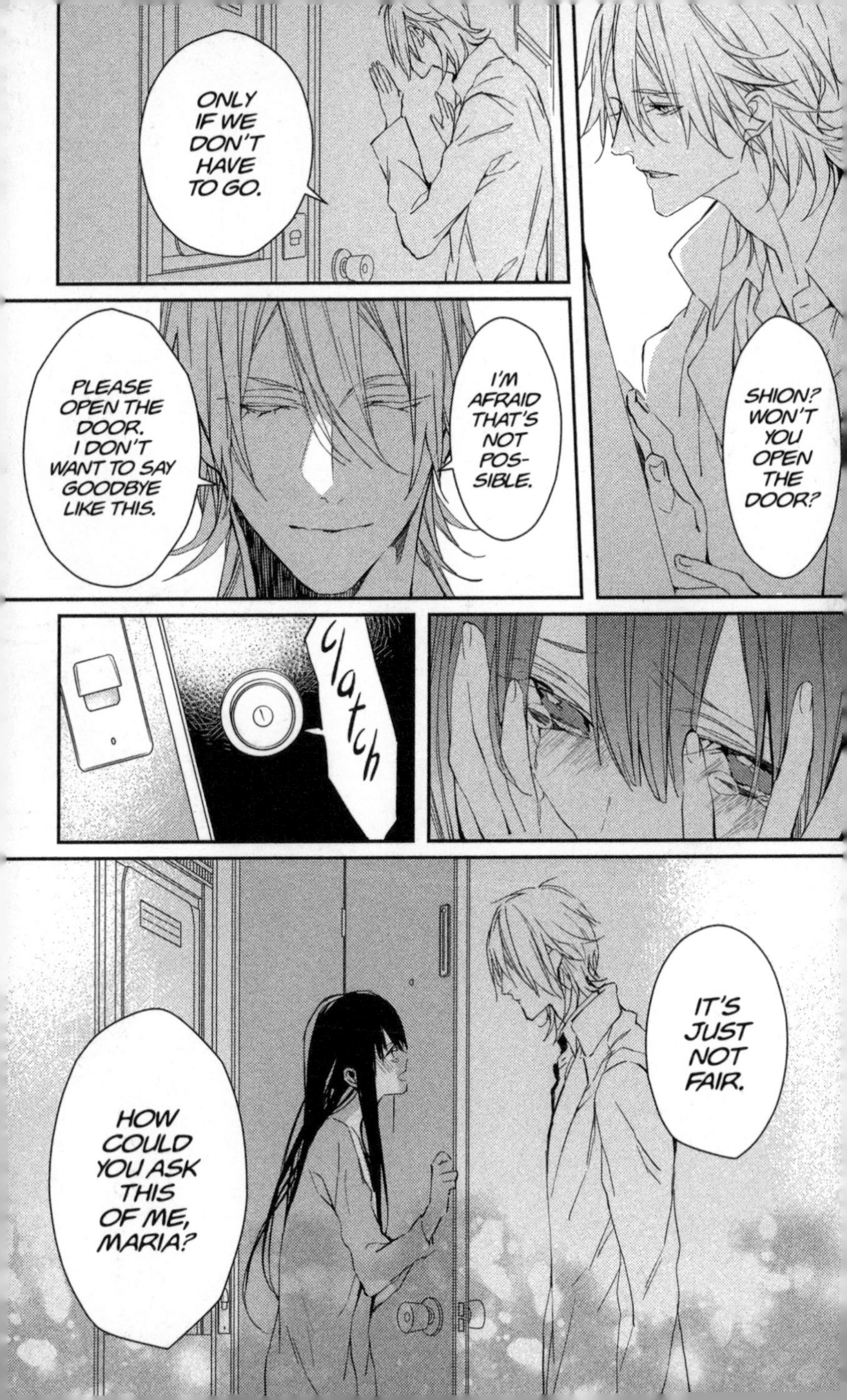
SHION? WON'T YOU OPEN THE DOOR?
ONLY IF WE DON'T HAVE TO GO.
I'M AFRAID THAT'S NOT POS-SIBLE.
PLEASE OPEN THE DOOR. I DON'T WANT TO SAY GOODBYE LIKE THIS.
clatch
IT'S JUST NOT FAIR.
HOW COULD YOU ASK THIS OF ME, MARIA?

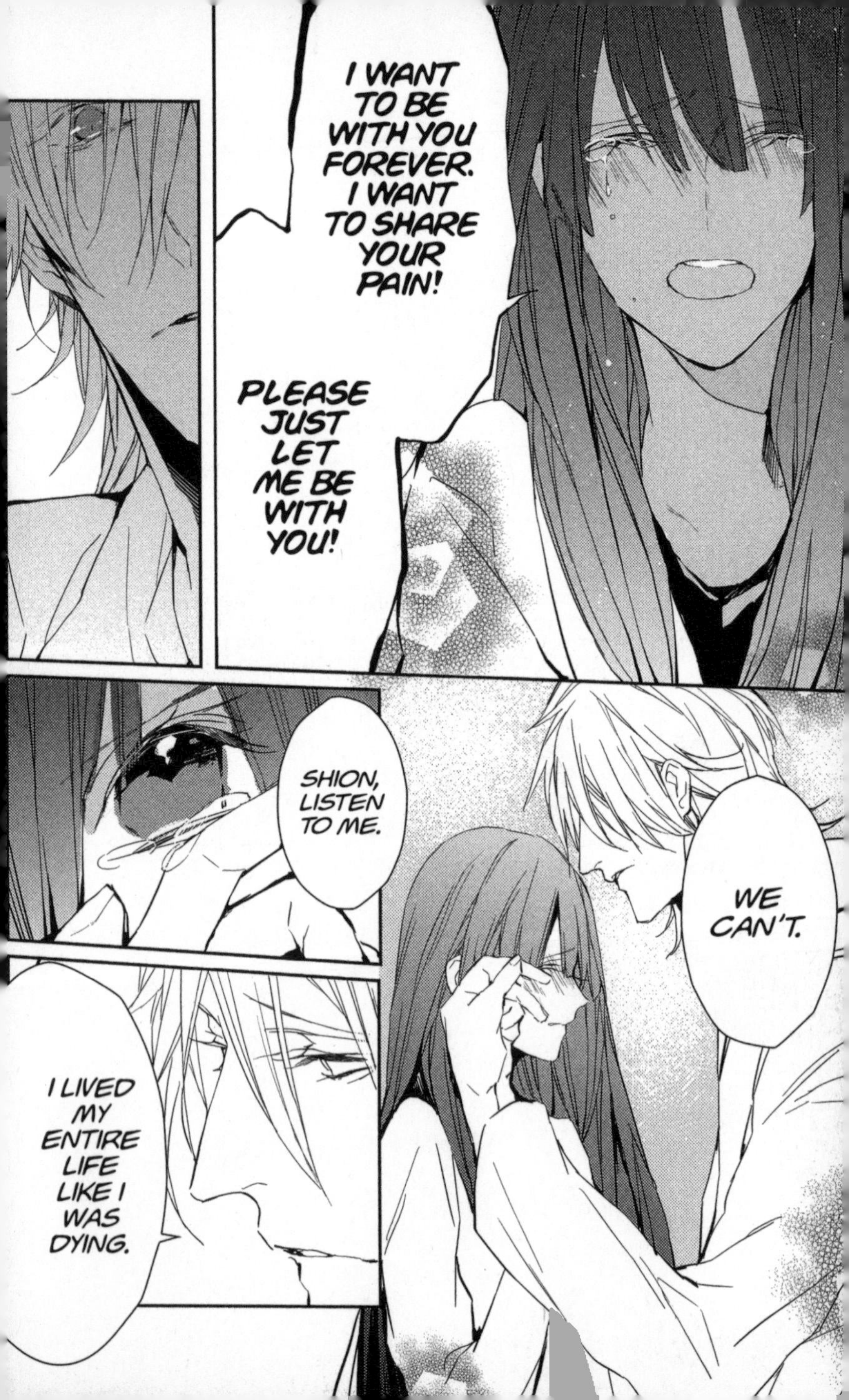
I WANT TO BE WITH YOU FOREVER. I WANT TO SHARE YOUR PAIN!
PLEASE JUST LET ME BE WITH YOU!
WE CAN'T.
SHION, LISTEN TO ME.
I LIVED MY ENTIRE LIFE LIKE I WAS DYING.

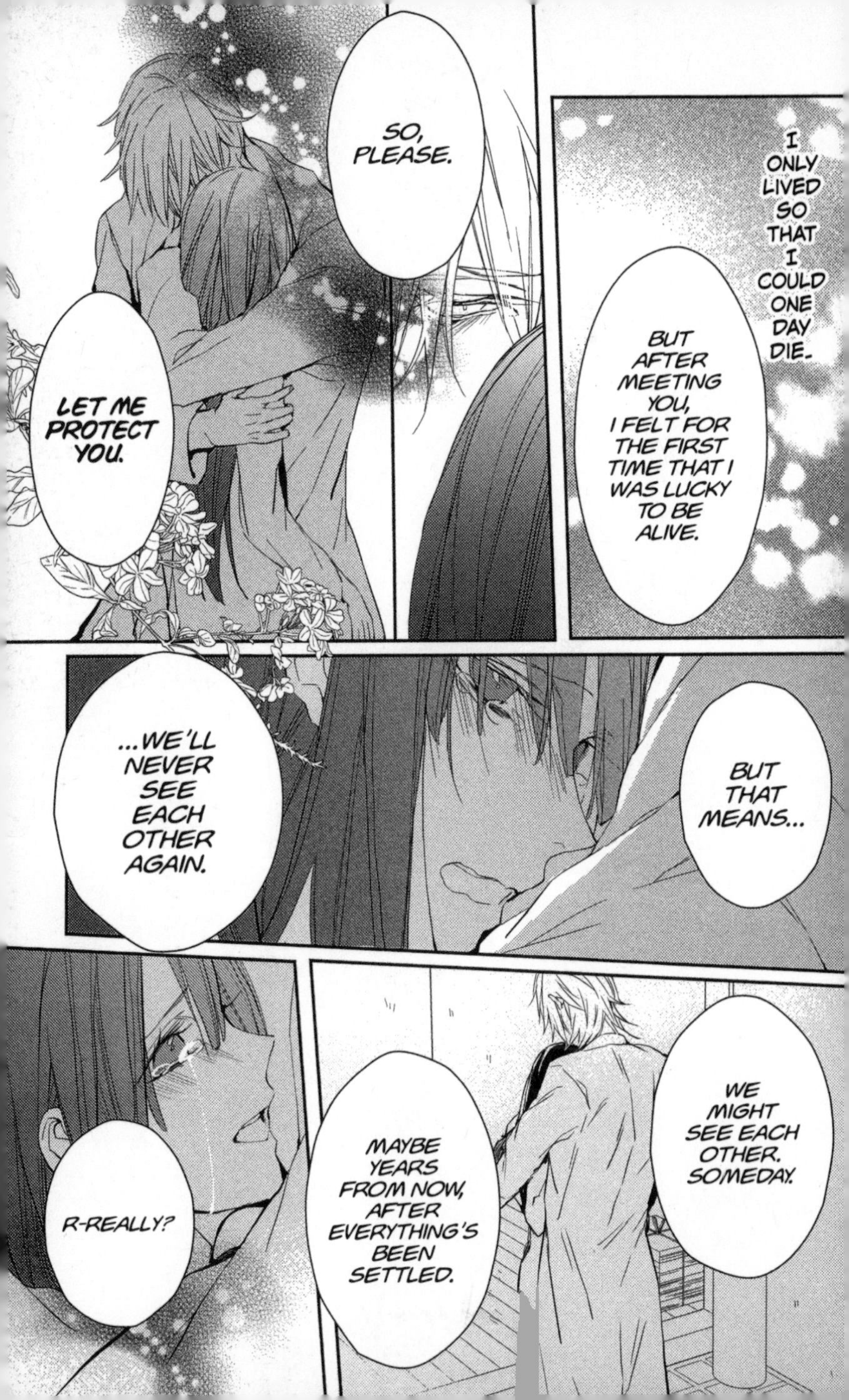
I ONLY LIVED SO THAT I COULD ONE DAY DIE.
BUT AFTER MEETING YOU, I FELT FOR THE FIRST TIME THAT I WAS LUCKY TO BE ALIVE.
SO, PLEASE.
LET ME PROTECT YOU.
BUT THAT MEANS...
...WE'LL NEVER SEE EACH OTHER AGAIN.
WE MIGHT SEE EACH OTHER. SOMEDAY.
MAYBE YEARS FROM NOW, AFTER EVERYTHING'S BEEN SETTLED.
R-REALLY?

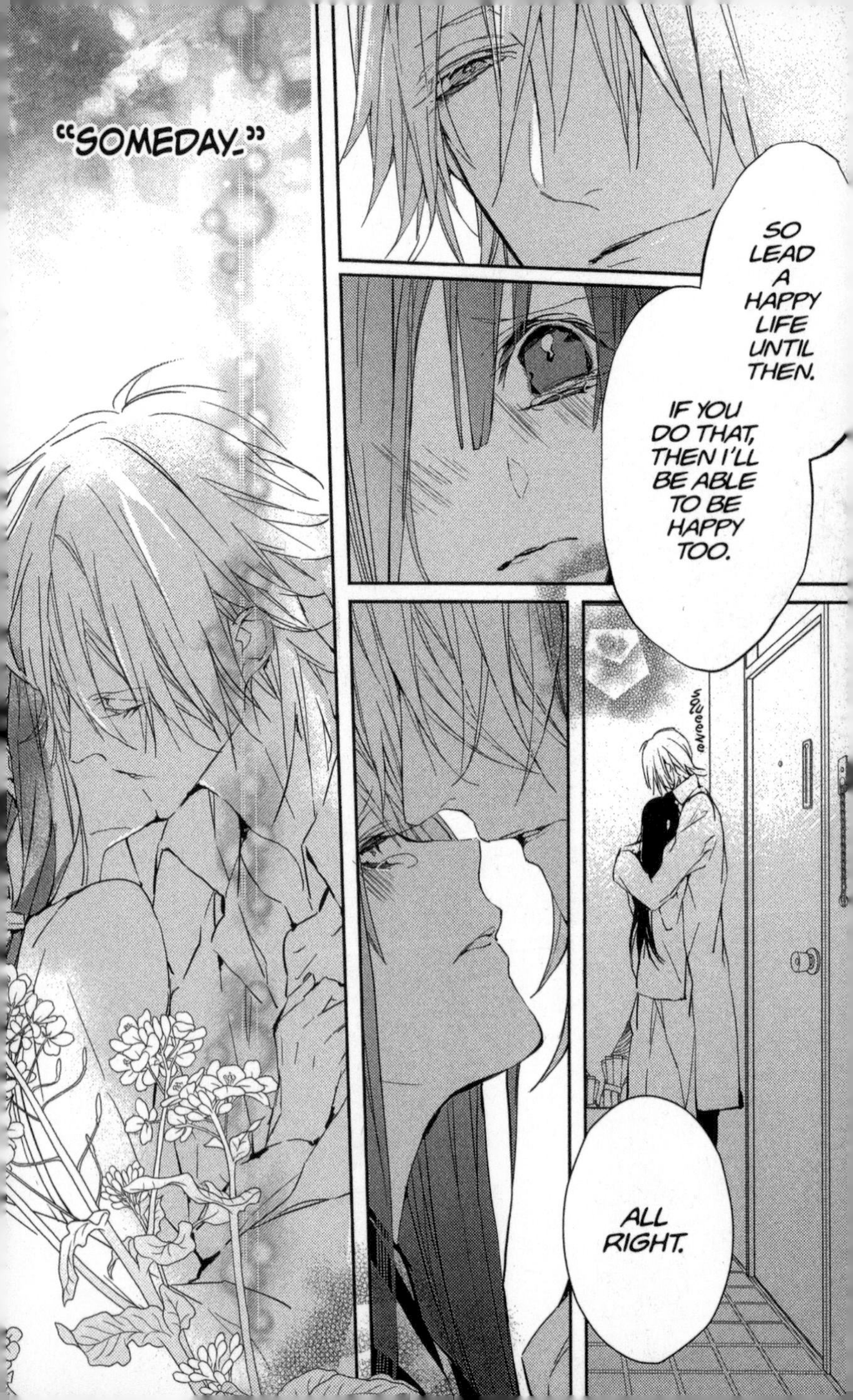
SO LEAD A HAPPY LIFE UNTIL THEN.
IF YOU DO THAT, THEN I'LL BE ABLE TO BE HAPPY TOO.
squeeze
ALL RIGHT.
"SOMEDAY..."

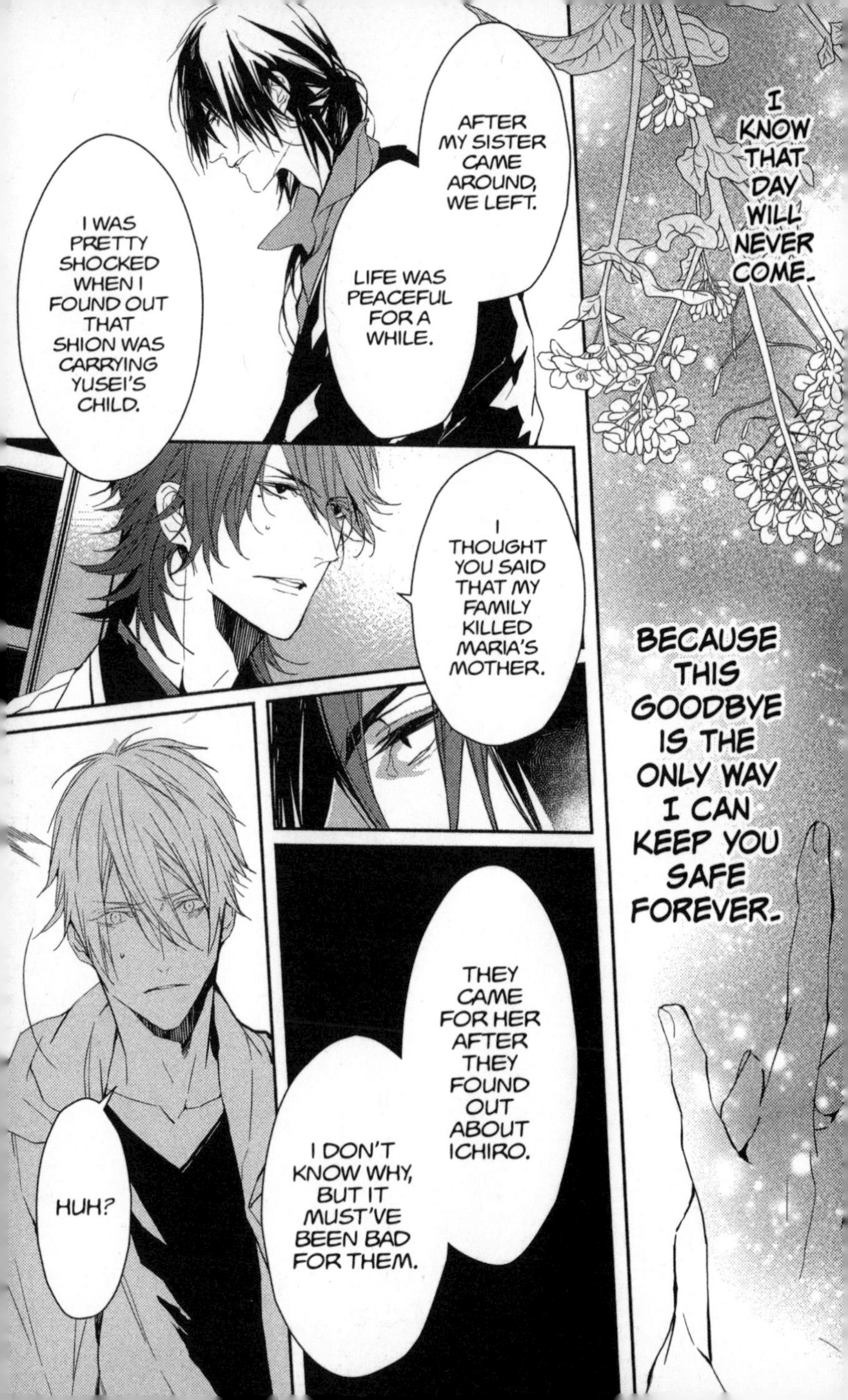
I KNOW THAT DAY WILL NEVER COME.
BECAUSE THIS GOODBYE IS THE ONLY WAY I CAN KEEP YOU SAFE FOREVER.
AFTER MY SISTER CAME AROUND, WE LEFT.
LIFE WAS PEACEFUL FOR A WHILE.
I WAS PRETTY SHOCKED WHEN I FOUND OUT THAT SHION WAS CARRYING YUSEI'S CHILD.
I THOUGHT YOU SAID THAT MY FAMILY KILLED MARIA'S MOTHER.
THEY CAME FOR HER AFTER THEY FOUND OUT ABOUT ICHIRO.
I DON'T KNOW WHY, BUT IT MUST'VE BEEN BAD FOR THEM.
HUH?

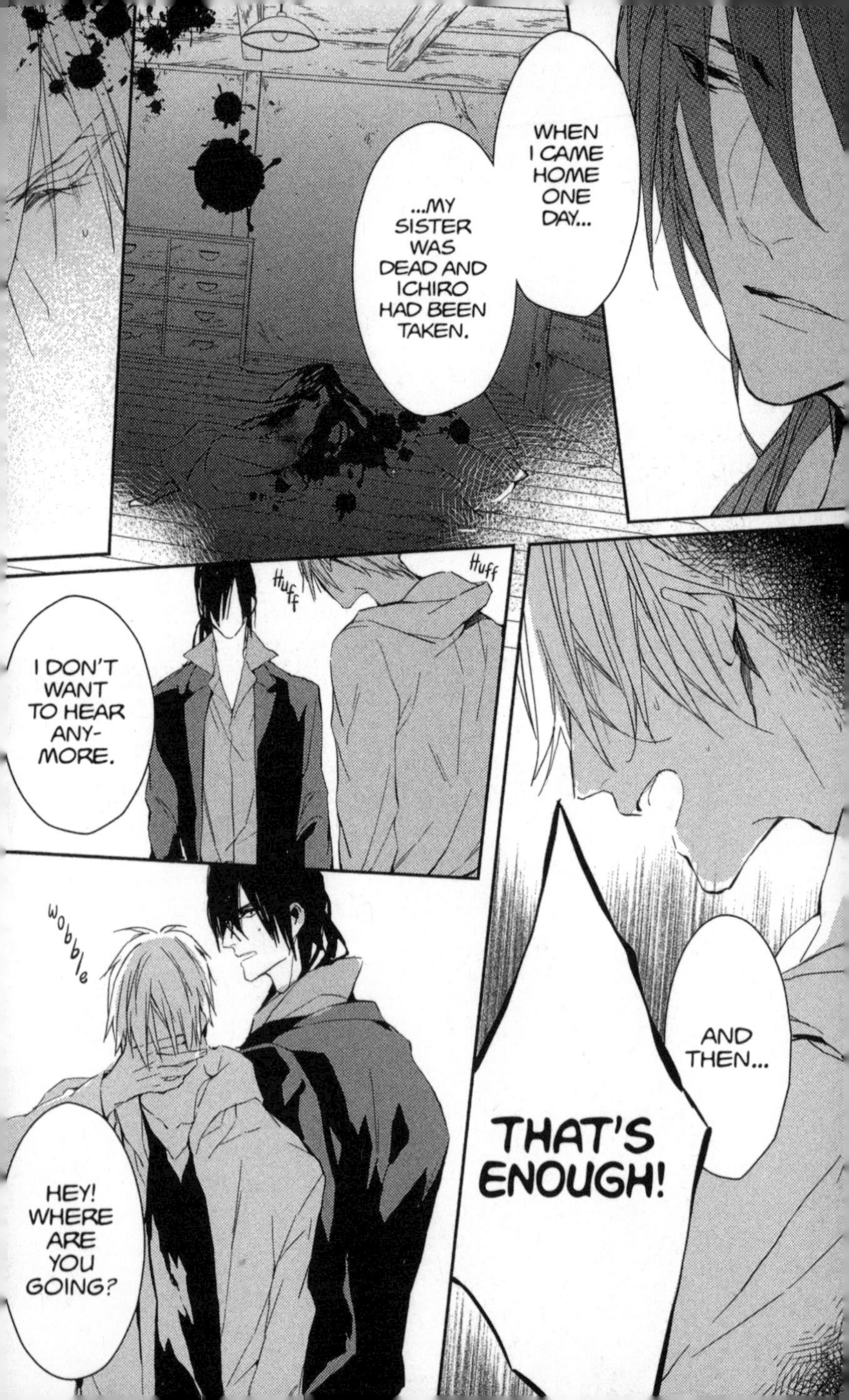
WHEN I CAME HOME ONE DAY...
...MY SISTER WAS DEAD AND ICHIRO HAD BEEN TAKEN.
AND THEN...
THAT'S ENOUGH!
Huff
Huff
I DON'T WANT TO HEAR ANY-MORE.
wobble
HEY! WHERE ARE YOU GOING?

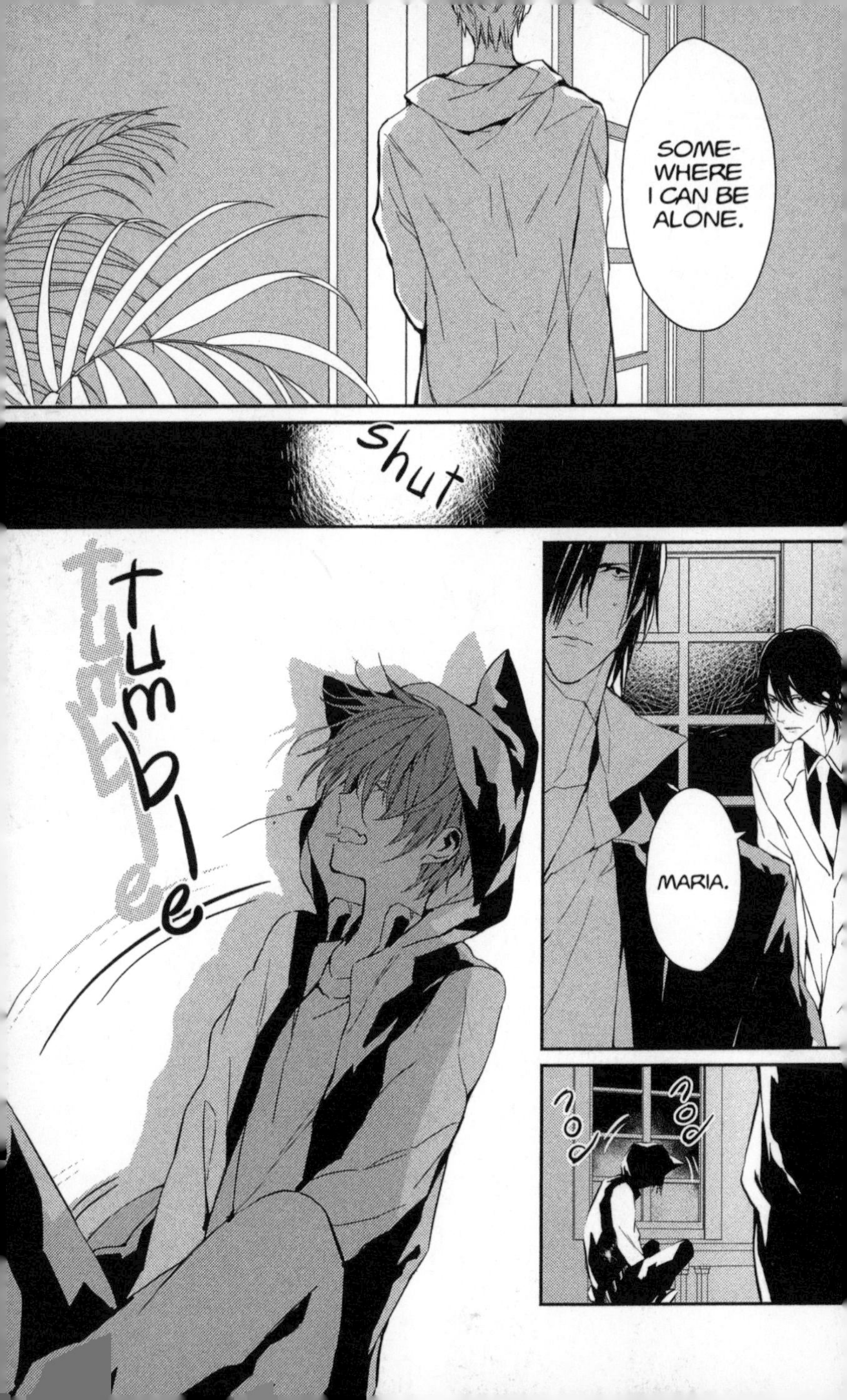
SOME-
WHERE
I CAN BE
ALONE.
Shut
MARIA.
pop
pop
tumble
tumble

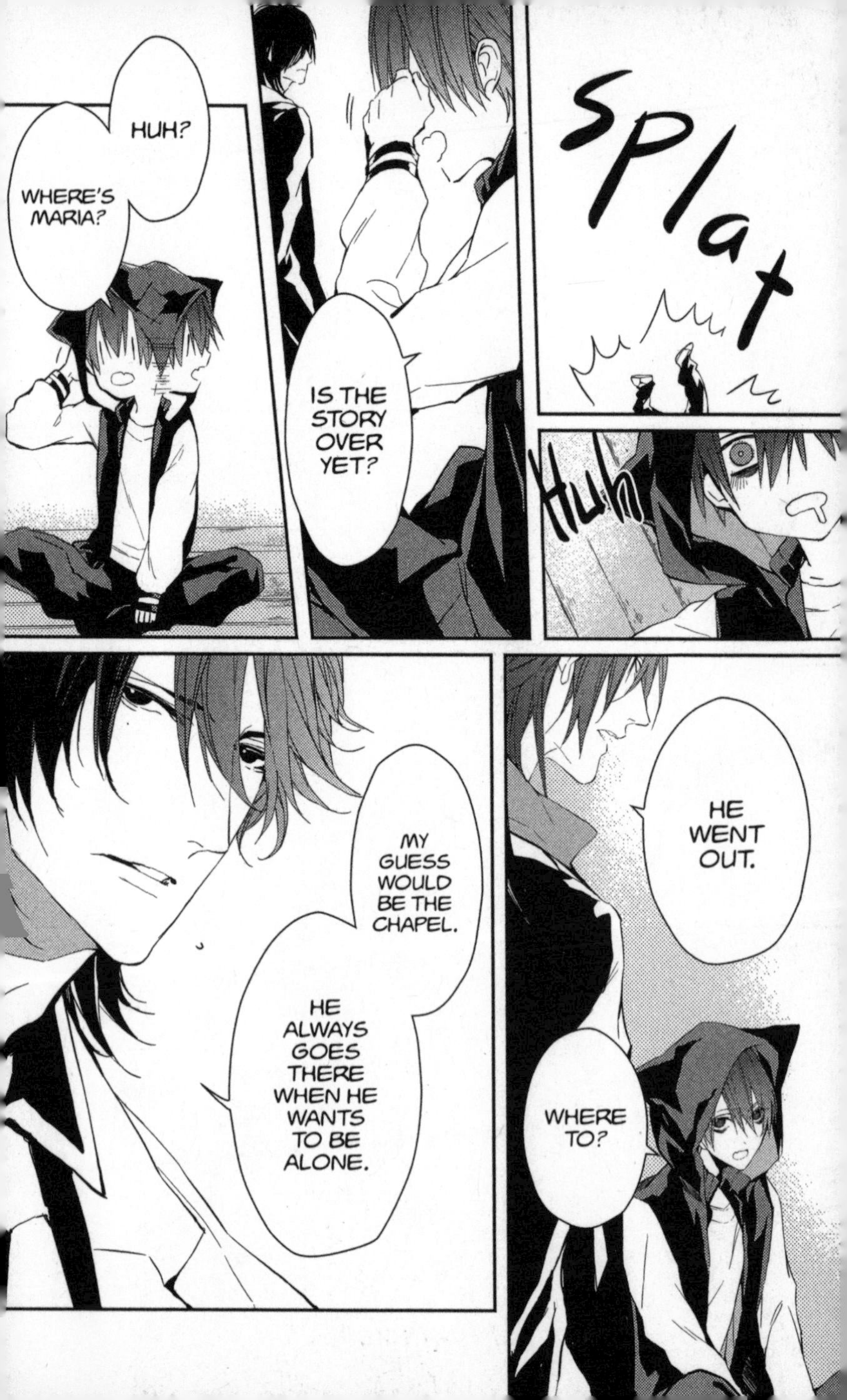
Splat
Huh
IS THE STORY OVER YET?
HUH?
WHERE'S MARIA?
HE WENT OUT.
WHERE TO?
MY GUESS WOULD BE THE CHAPEL.
HE ALWAYS GOES THERE WHEN HE WANTS TO BE ALONE.

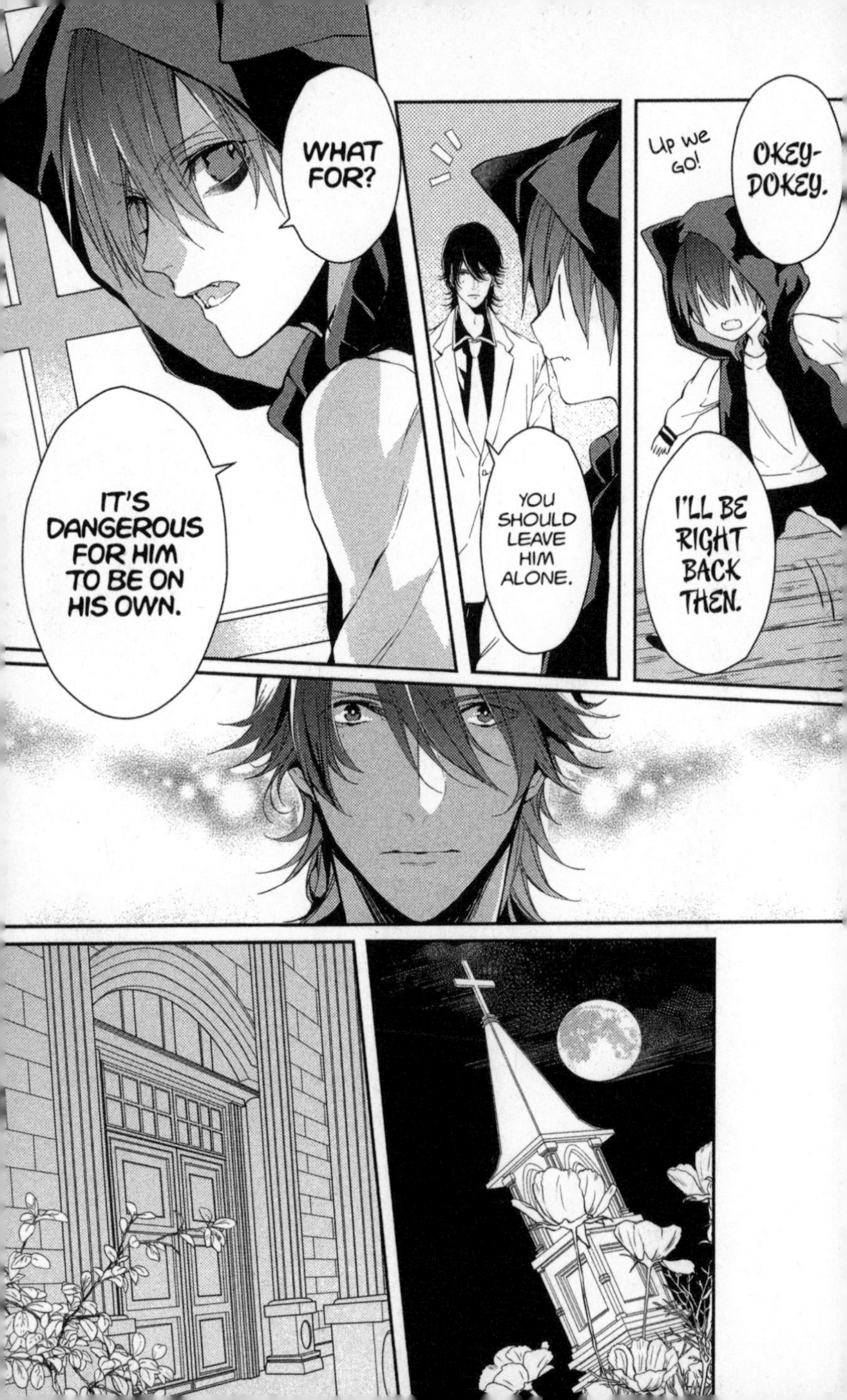
OKEY-DOKEY.
Up we go!
I'LL BE RIGHT BACK THEN.
YOU SHOULD LEAVE HIM ALONE.
WHAT FOR?
IT'S DANGEROUS FOR HIM TO BE ON HIS OWN.

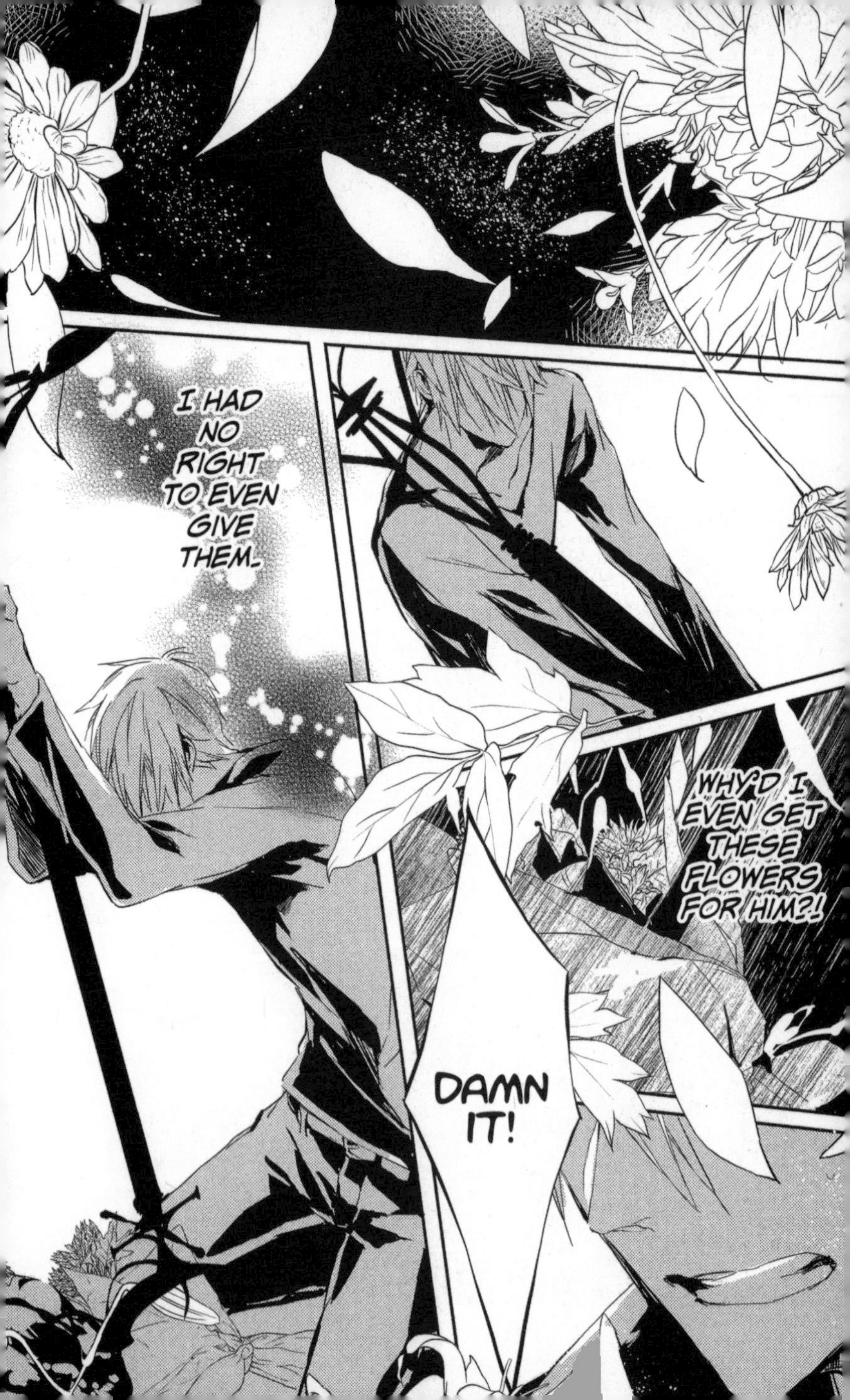
WHY'D I EVEN GET THESE FLOWERS FOR HIM?!
DAMN IT!
I HAD NO RIGHT TO EVEN GIVE THEM...

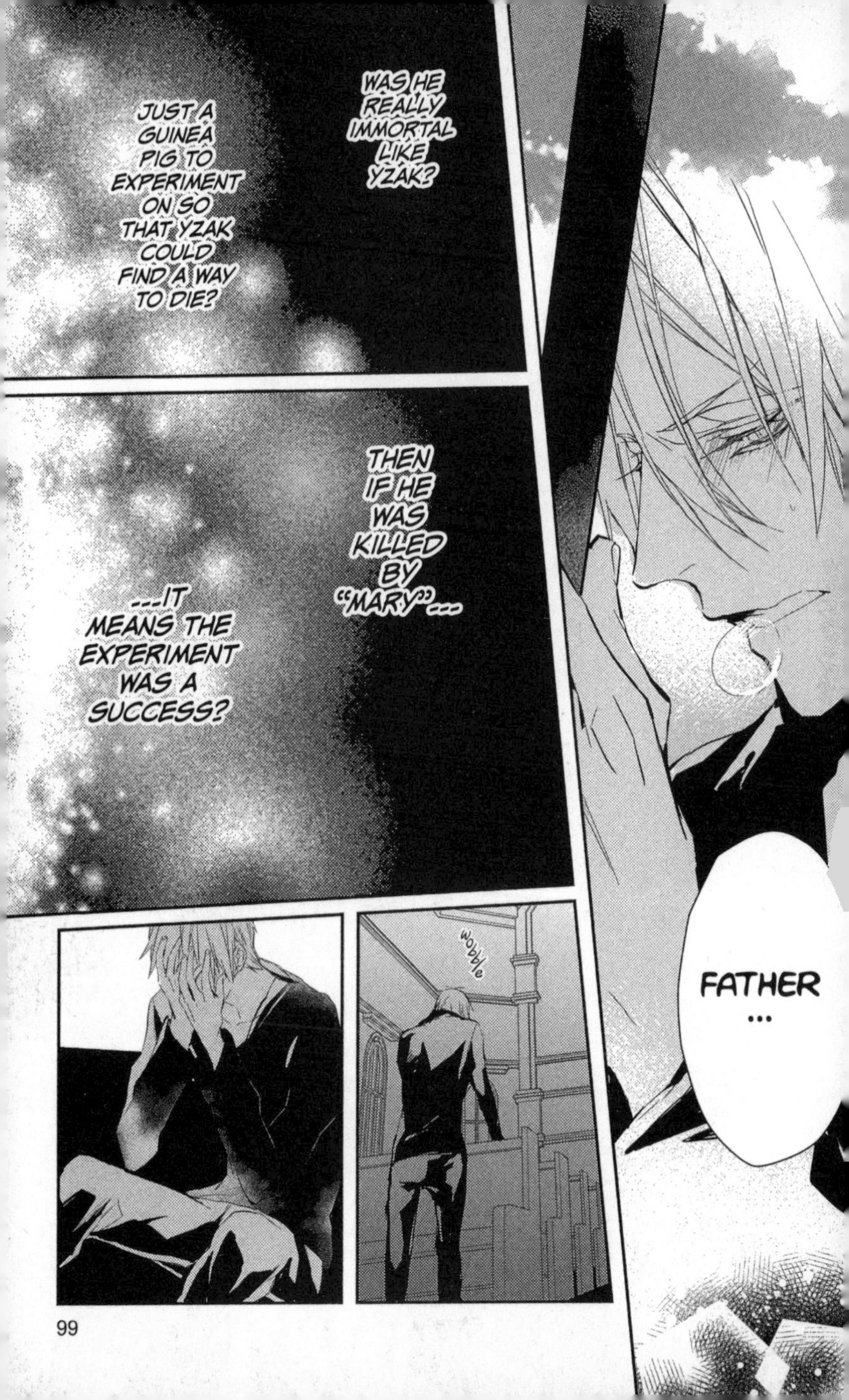
FATHER...
WAS HE REALLY IMMORTAL LIKE YZAK?
JUST A GUINEA PIG TO EXPERIMENT ON SO THAT YZAK COULD FIND A WAY TO DIE?
THEN IF HE WAS KILLED BY "MARY"...
...IT MEANS THE EXPERIMENT WAS A SUCCESS?
wobble

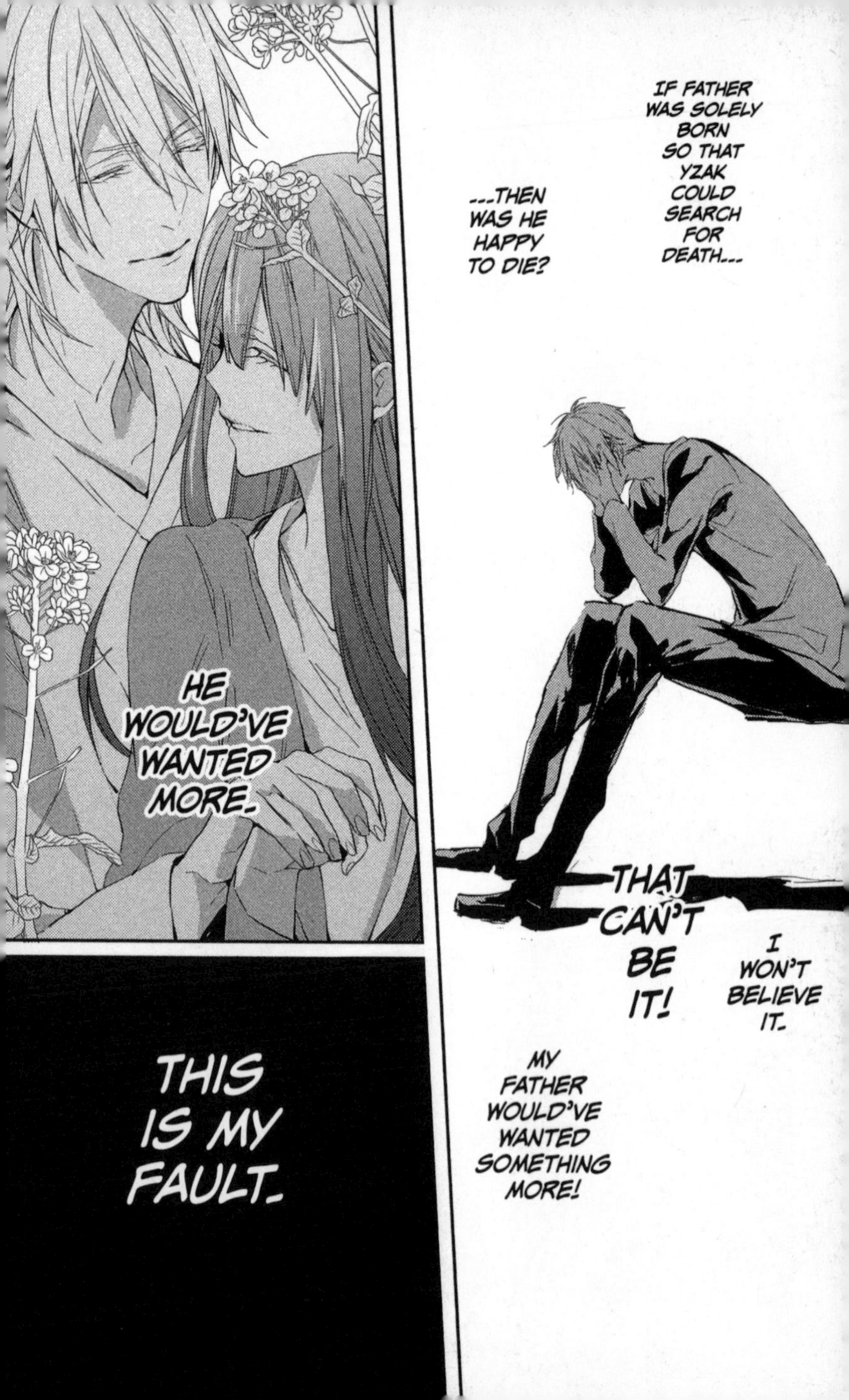
IF FATHER WAS SOLELY BORN SO THAT YZAK COULD SEARCH FOR DEATH...
...THEN WAS HE HAPPY TO DIE?
THAT CAN'T BE IT!
I WON'T BELIEVE IT.
MY FATHER WOULD'VE WANTED SOMETHING MORE!
HE WOULD'VE WANTED MORE.
THIS IS MY FAULT.

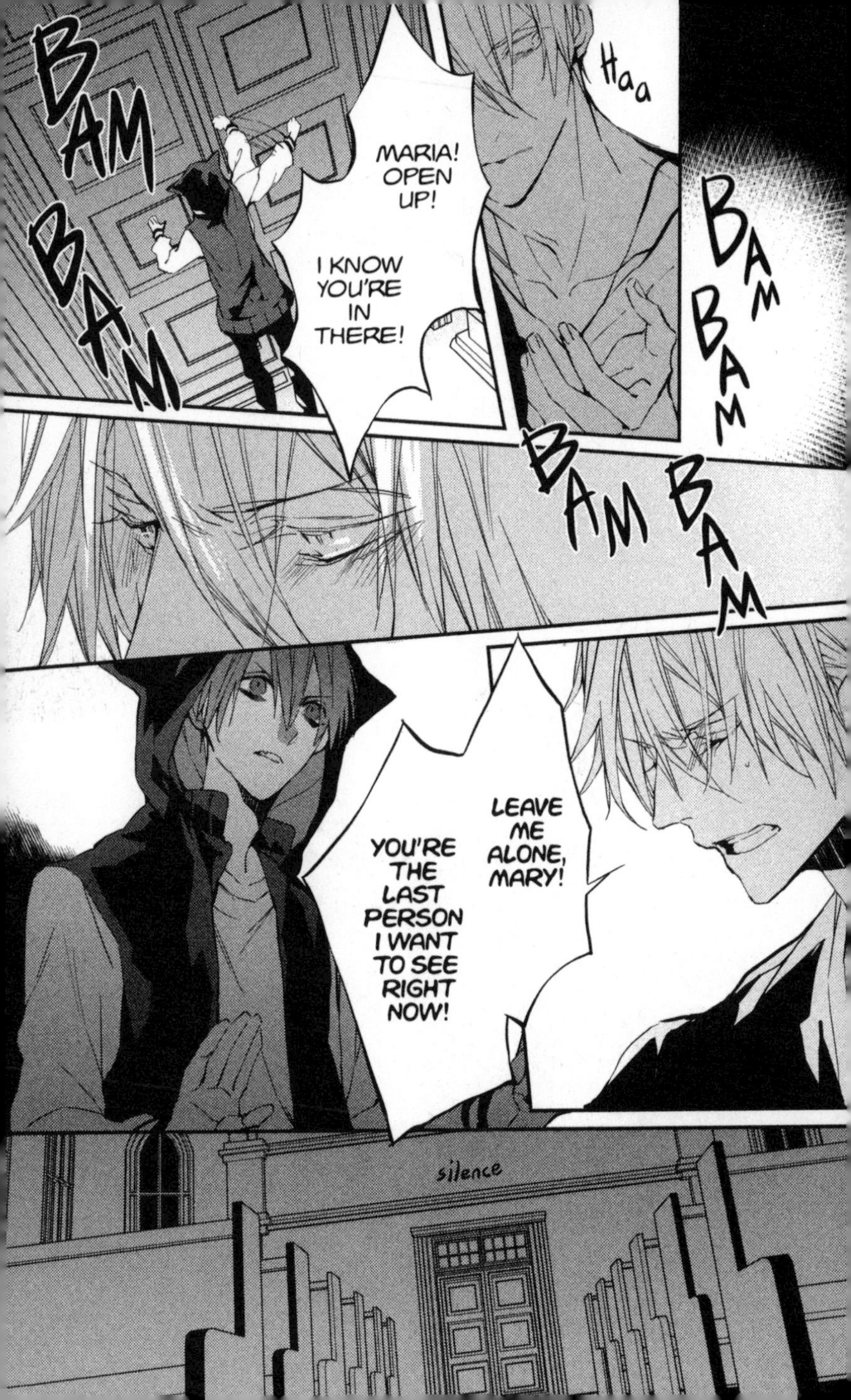
Haa
BAM BAM BAM
BAM BAM
MARIA! OPEN UP!
I KNOW YOU'RE IN THERE!
BAM BAM
LEAVE ME ALONE, MARY!
YOU'RE THE LAST PERSON I WANT TO SEE RIGHT NOW!
silence

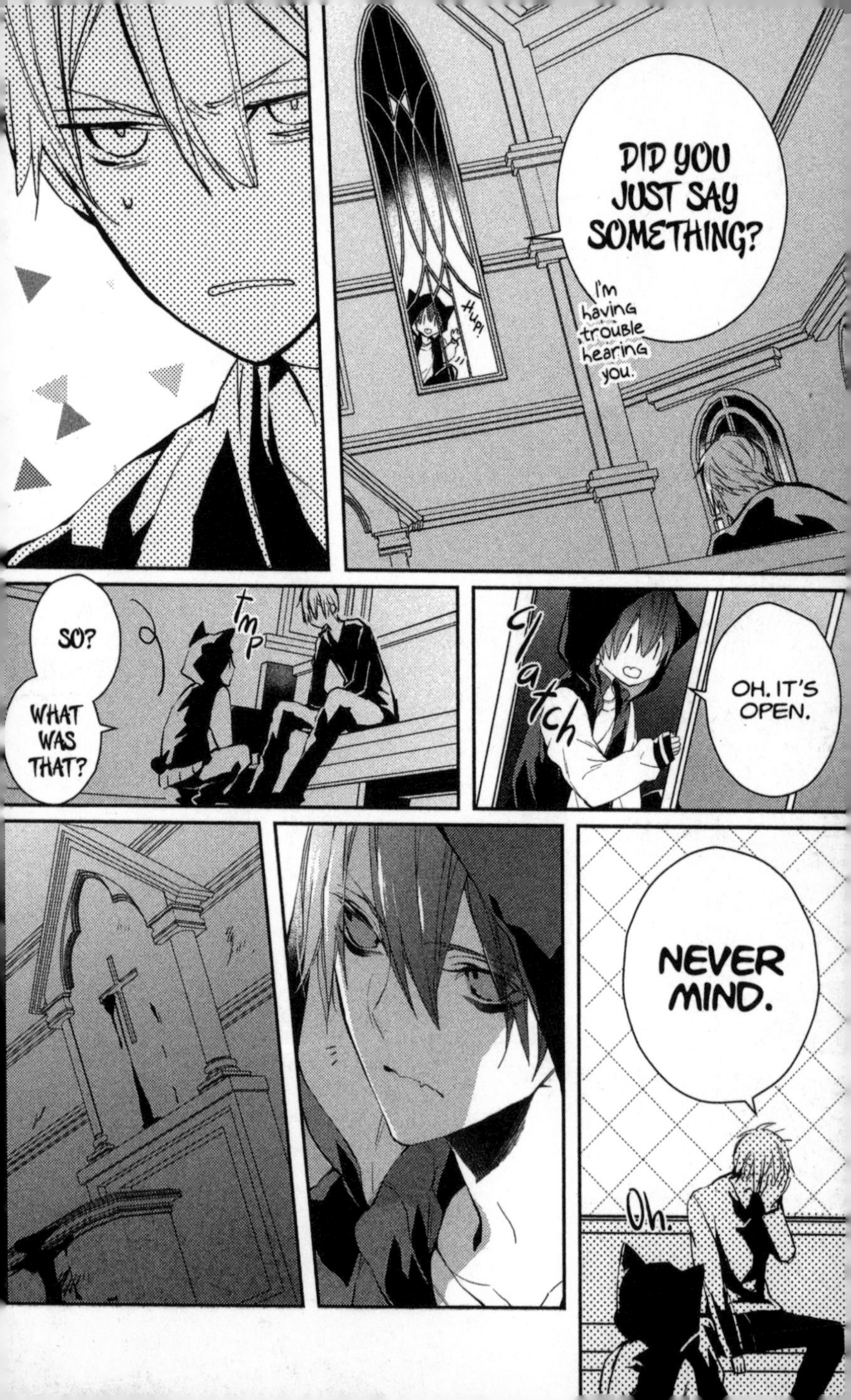
DID YOU JUST SAY SOMETHING?
I'm having trouble hearing you.
Hup!
OH. IT'S OPEN.
clatch
SO?
WHAT WAS THAT?
tmp
NEVER MIND.
Oh.

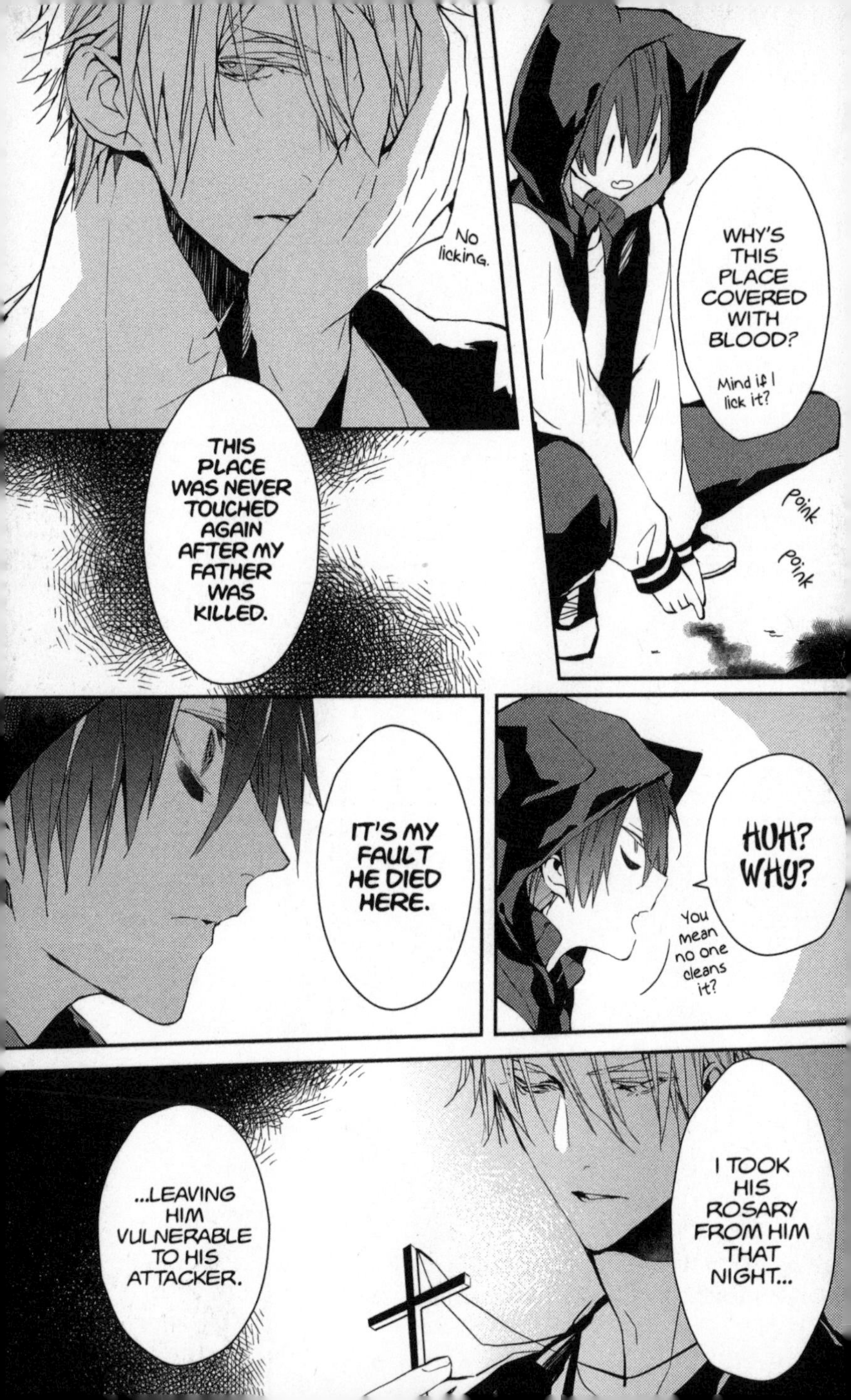
WHY'S THIS PLACE COVERED WITH BLOOD?
Mind if I lick it?
Poink
Poink
No licking.
THIS PLACE WAS NEVER TOUCHED AGAIN AFTER MY FATHER WAS KILLED.
HUH? WHY?
You mean no one cleans it?
IT'S MY FAULT HE DIED HERE.
I TOOK HIS ROSARY FROM HIM THAT NIGHT...
...LEAVING HIM VULNERABLE TO HIS ATTACKER.

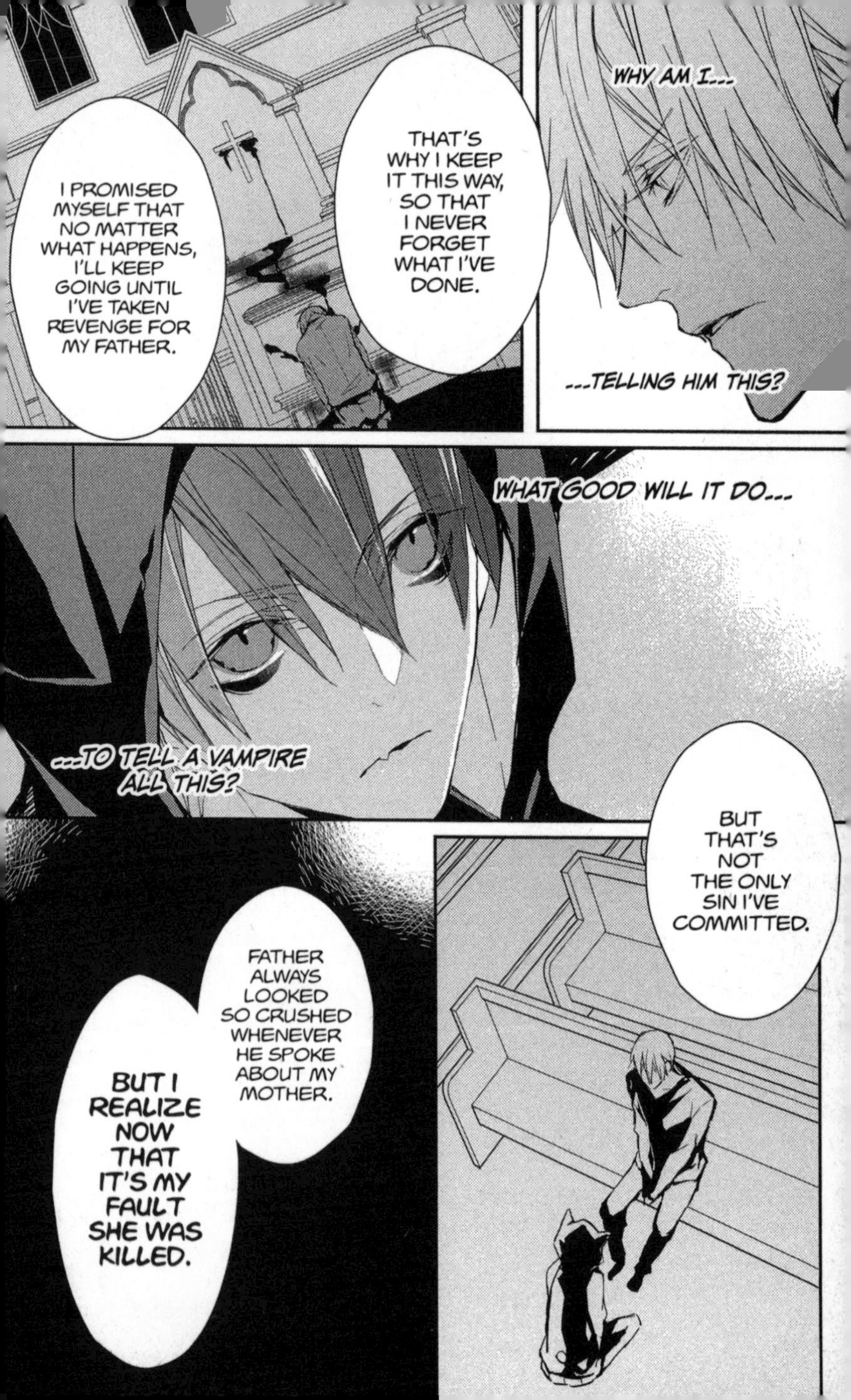
WHY AM I...
...TELLING HIM THIS?
THAT'S WHY I KEEP IT THIS WAY, SO THAT I NEVER FORGET WHAT I'VE DONE.
I PROMISED MYSELF THAT NO MATTER WHAT HAPPENS, I'LL KEEP GOING UNTIL I'VE TAKEN REVENGE FOR MY FATHER.
WHAT GOOD WILL IT DO...
...TO TELL A VAMPIRE ALL THIS?
BUT THAT'S NOT THE ONLY SIN I'VE COMMITTED.
FATHER ALWAYS LOOKED SO CRUSHED WHENEVER HE SPOKE ABOUT MY MOTHER.
BUT I REALIZE NOW THAT IT'S MY FAULT SHE WAS KILLED.

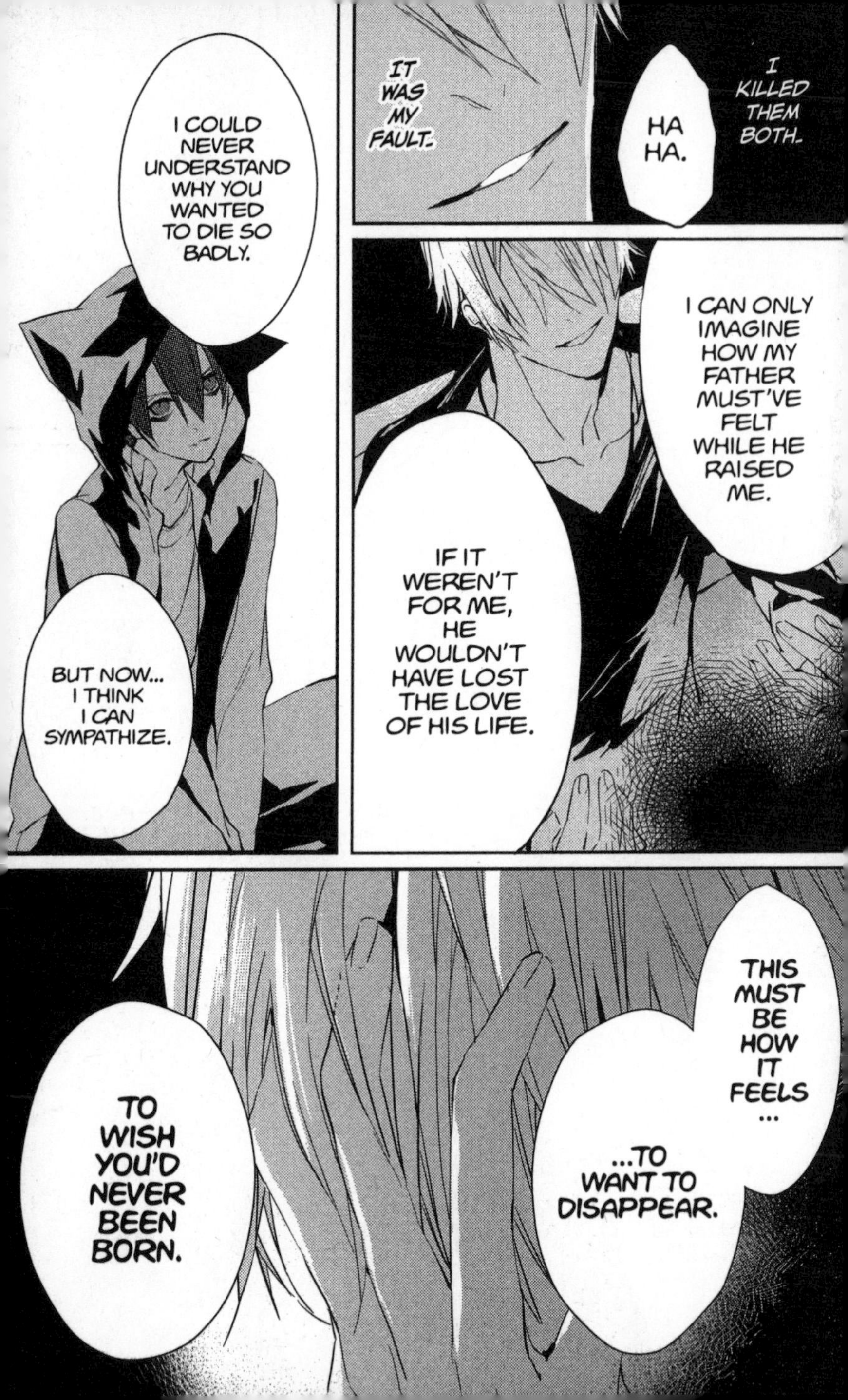
I KILLED THEM BOTH.
HA HA.
IT WAS MY FAULT.
I CAN ONLY IMAGINE HOW MY FATHER MUST'VE FELT WHILE HE RAISED ME.
IF IT WEREN'T FOR ME, HE WOULDN'T HAVE LOST THE LOVE OF HIS LIFE.
I COULD NEVER UNDERSTAND WHY YOU WANTED TO DIE SO BADLY.
BUT NOW... I THINK I CAN SYMPATHIZE.
THIS MUST BE HOW IT FEELS...
...TO WANT TO DISAPPEAR.
TO WISH YOU'D NEVER BEEN BORN.

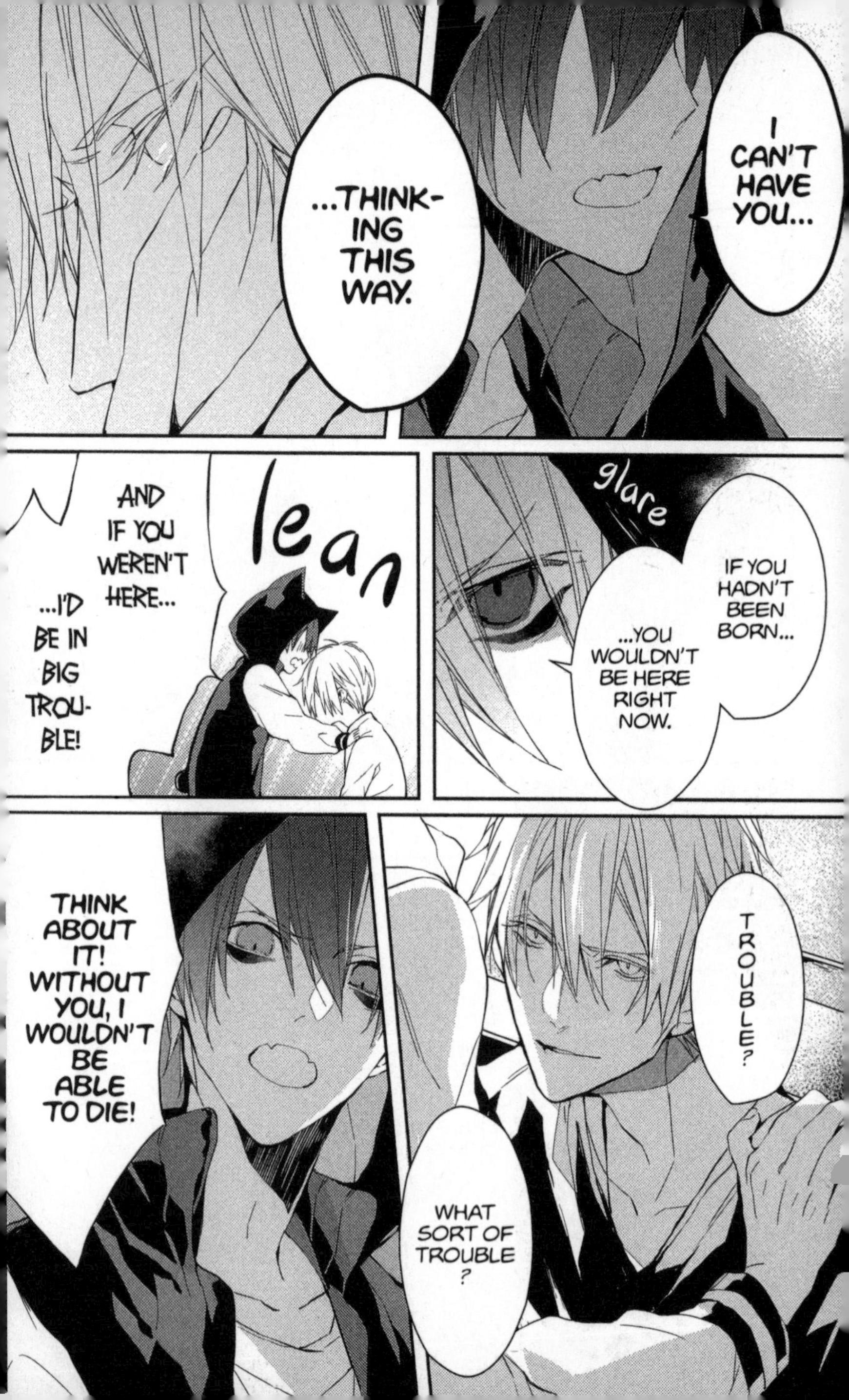
I CAN'T HAVE YOU...
...THINKING THIS WAY.
glare
IF YOU HADN'T BEEN BORN...
...YOU WOULDN'T BE HERE RIGHT NOW.
lean
AND IF YOU WEREN'T HERE...
...I'D BE IN BIG TROUBLE!
TROUBLE?
WHAT SORT OF TROUBLE?
THINK ABOUT IT! WITHOUT YOU, I WOULDN'T BE ABLE TO DIE!

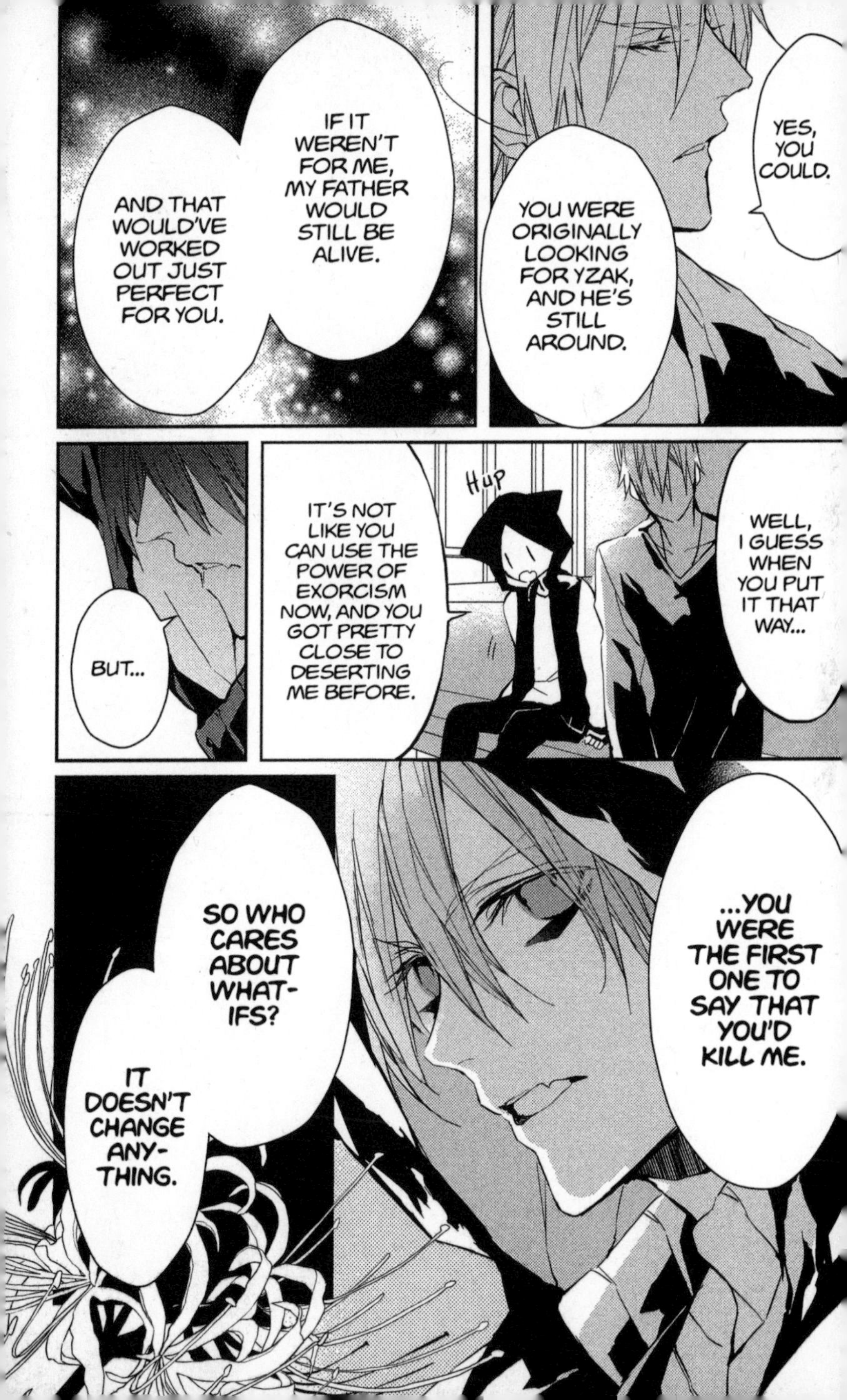
YES, YOU COULD.
YOU WERE ORIGINALLY LOOKING FOR YZAK, AND HE'S STILL AROUND.
IF IT WEREN'T FOR ME, MY FATHER WOULD STILL BE ALIVE.
AND THAT WOULD'VE WORKED OUT JUST PERFECT FOR YOU.
WELL, I GUESS WHEN YOU PUT IT THAT WAY...
Hup
IT'S NOT LIKE YOU CAN USE THE POWER OF EXORCISM NOW, AND YOU GOT PRETTY CLOSE TO DESERTING ME BEFORE.
BUT...
...YOU WERE THE FIRST ONE TO SAY THAT YOU'D KILL ME.
SO WHO CARES ABOUT WHAT-IFS?
IT DOESN'T CHANGE ANY-THING.

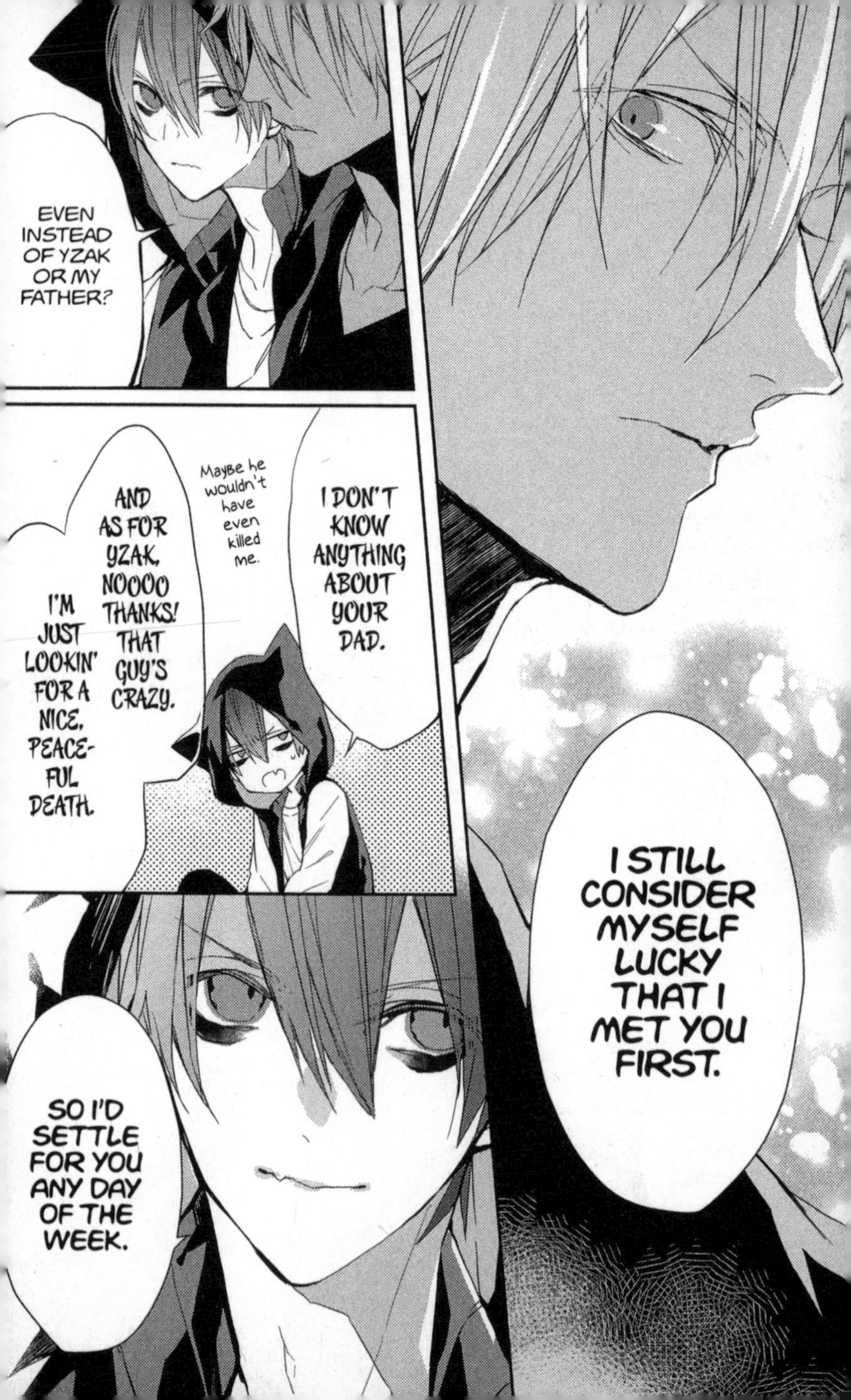
I STILL CONSIDER MYSELF LUCKY THAT I MET YOU FIRST.
EVEN INSTEAD OF YZAK OR MY FATHER?
I DON'T KNOW ANYTHING ABOUT YOUR DAD.
Maybe he wouldn't have even killed me.
AND AS FOR YZAK, NOOOO THANKS! THAT GUY'S CRAZY.
I'M JUST LOOKIN' FOR A NICE, PEACE-FUL DEATH.
SO I'D SETTLE FOR YOU ANY DAY OF THE WEEK.

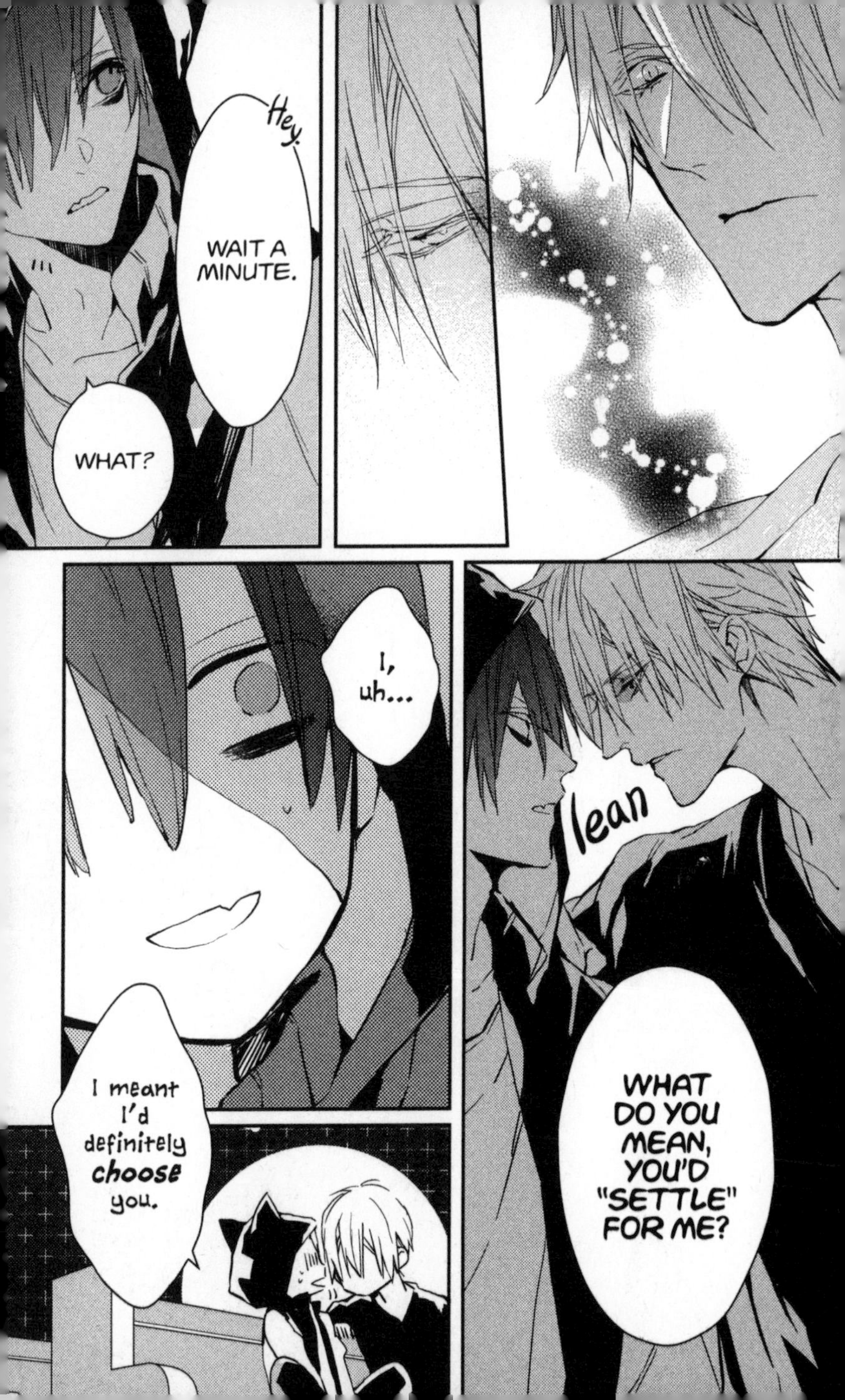
Hey.
WAIT A MINUTE.
WHAT?
lean
WHAT DO YOU MEAN, YOU'D "SETTLE" FOR ME?
I, uh...
I meant I'd definitely **choose** you.

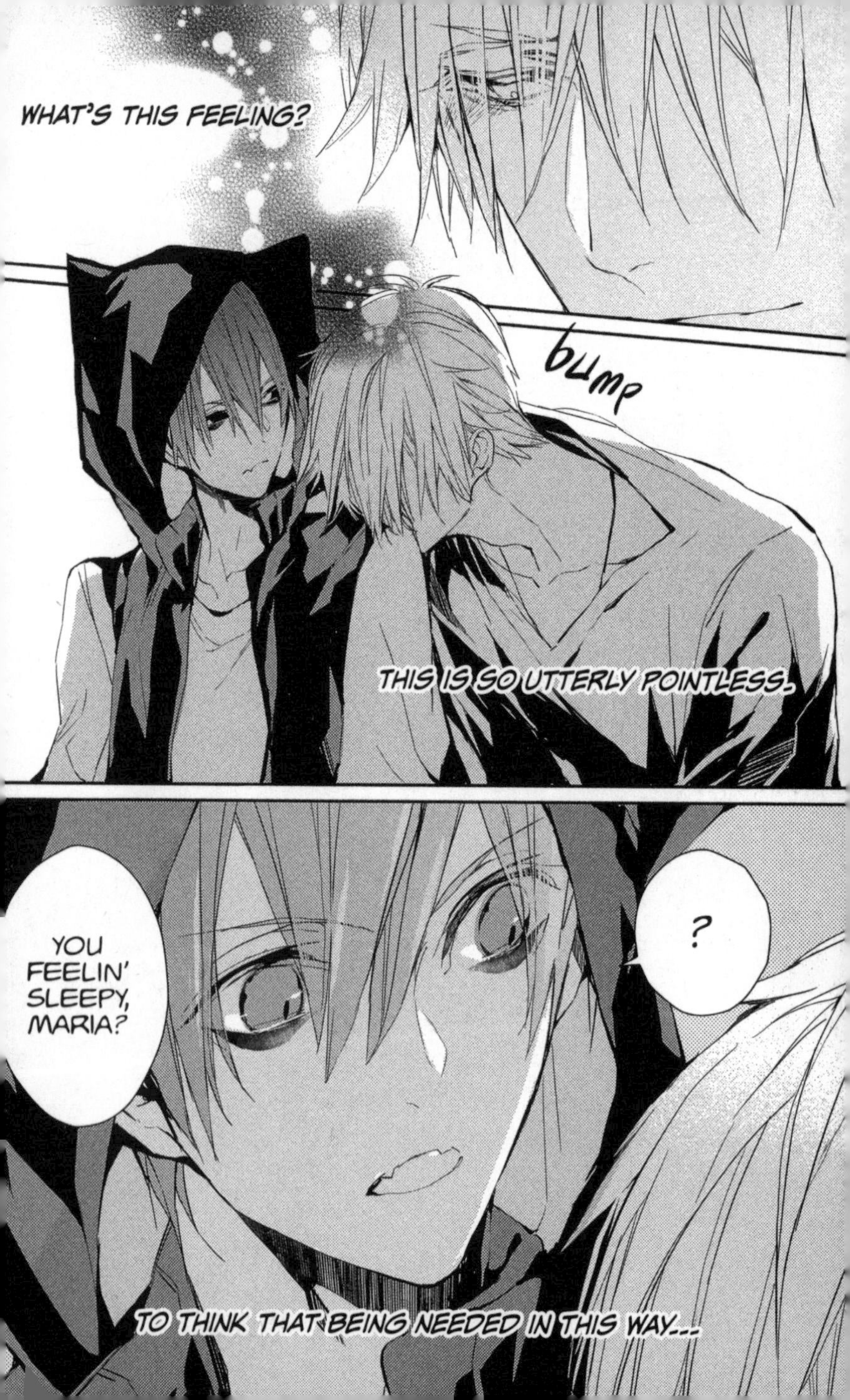
WHAT'S THIS FEELING?
bump
THIS IS SO UTTERLY POINTLESS.
YOU FEELIN' SLEEPY, MARIA?
?
TO THINK THAT BEING NEEDED IN THIS WAY...

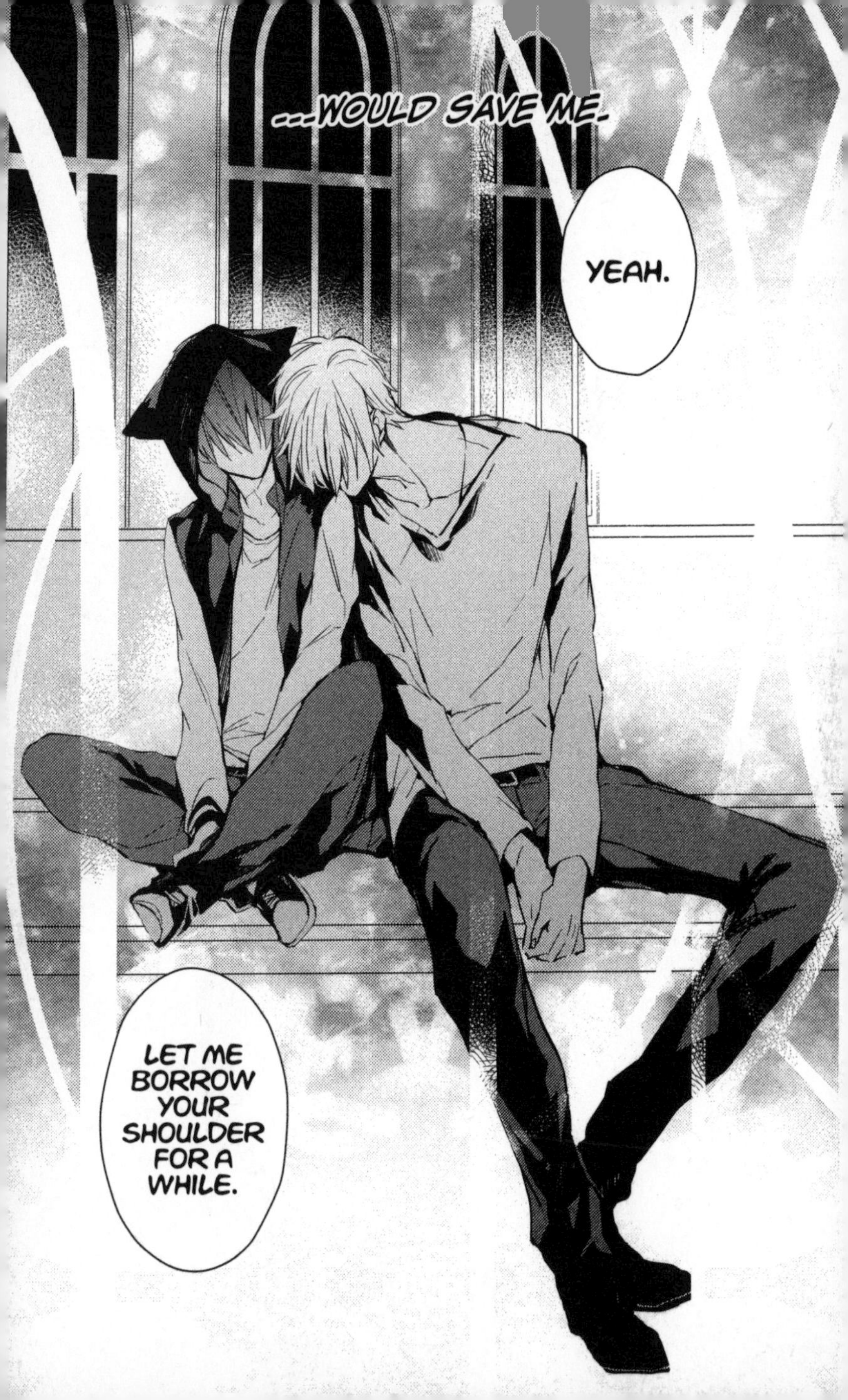
...WOULD SAVE ME.
YEAH.
LET ME BORROW YOUR SHOULDER FOR A WHILE.

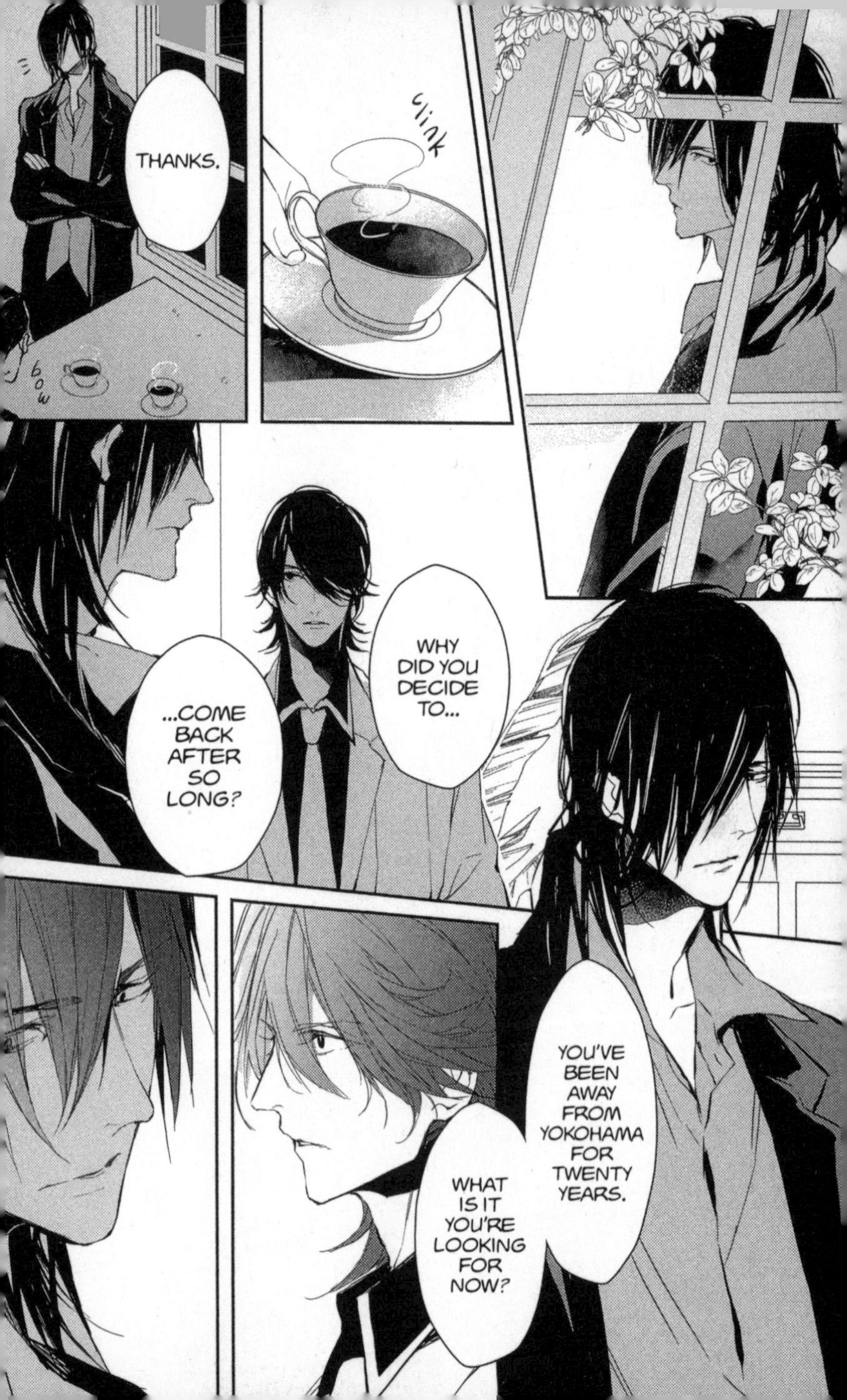
clink
THANKS.
bow
WHY DID YOU DECIDE TO...
...COME BACK AFTER SO LONG?
YOU'VE BEEN AWAY FROM YOKOHAMA FOR TWENTY YEARS.
WHAT IS IT YOU'RE LOOKING FOR NOW?

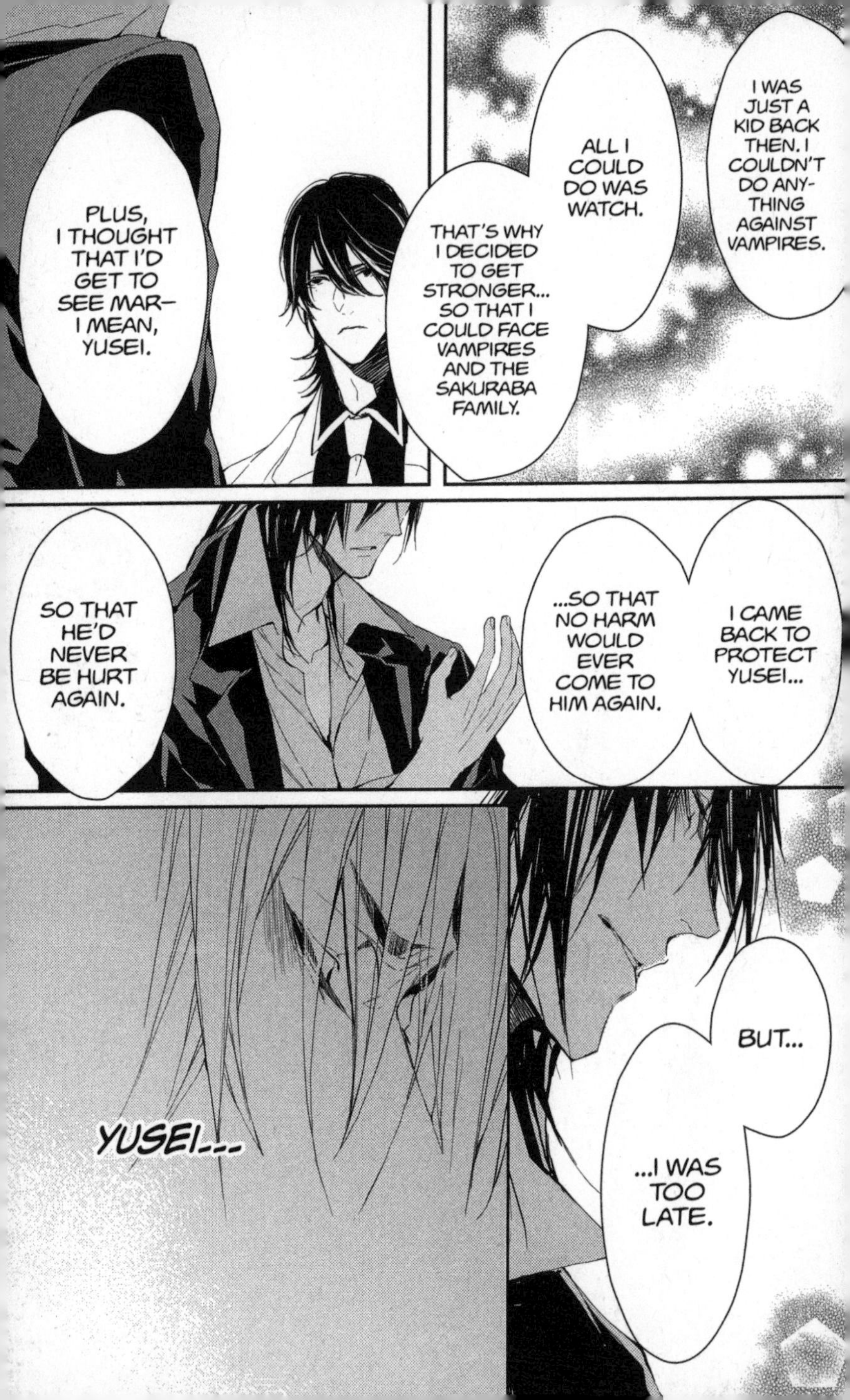
I WAS JUST A KID BACK THEN. I COULDN'T DO ANY-THING AGAINST VAMPIRES.
ALL I COULD DO WAS WATCH.
THAT'S WHY I DECIDED TO GET STRONGER... SO THAT I COULD FACE VAMPIRES AND THE SAKURABA FAMILY.
PLUS, I THOUGHT THAT I'D GET TO SEE MAR— I MEAN, YUSEI.
I CAME BACK TO PROTECT YUSEI...
...SO THAT NO HARM WOULD EVER COME TO HIM AGAIN.
SO THAT HE'D NEVER BE HURT AGAIN.
BUT...
...I WAS TOO LATE.
YUSEI...

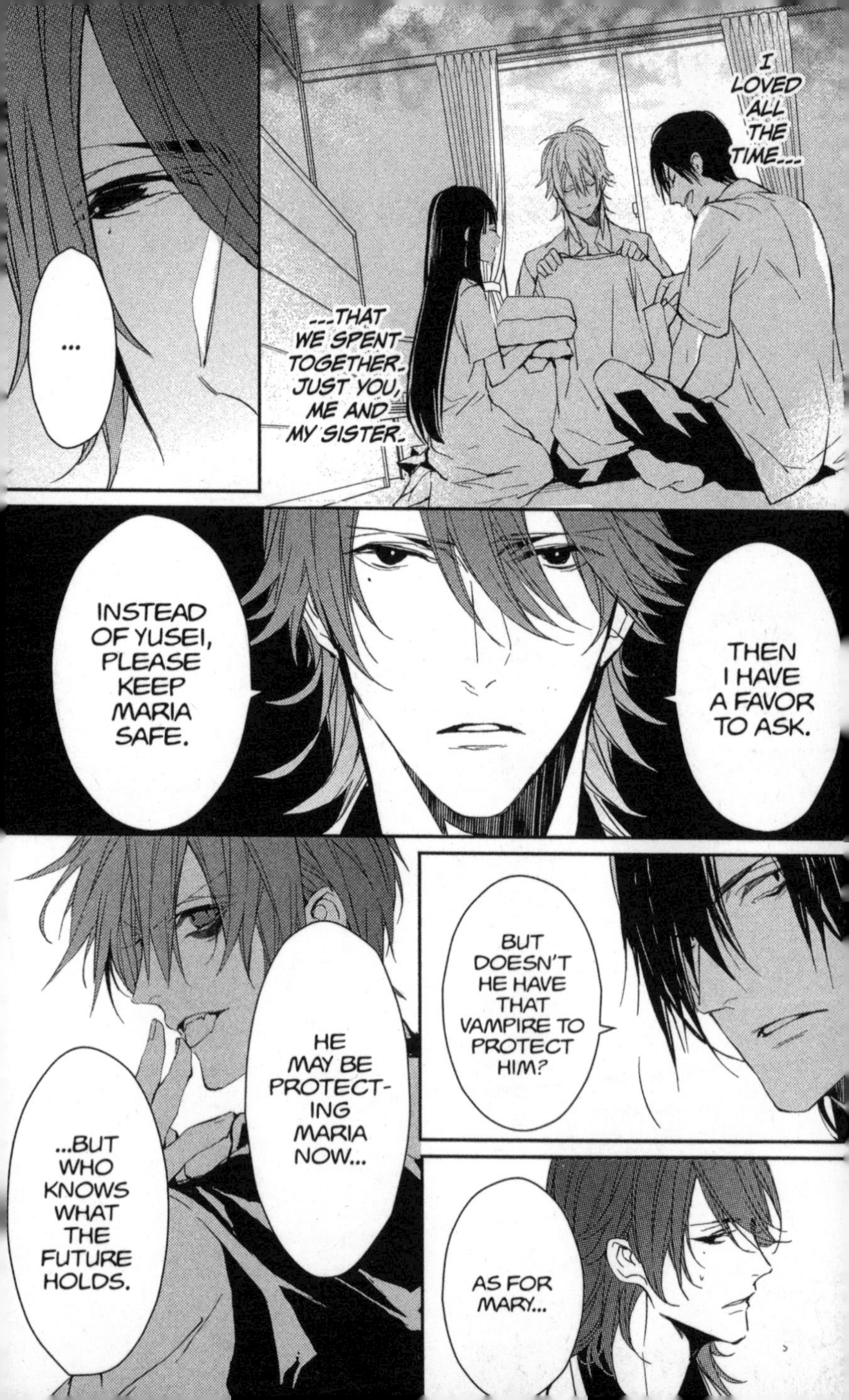
I LOVED ALL THE TIME...
...THAT WE SPENT TOGETHER. JUST YOU, ME AND MY SISTER.
...
THEN I HAVE A FAVOR TO ASK.
INSTEAD OF YUSEI, PLEASE KEEP MARIA SAFE.
BUT DOESN'T HE HAVE THAT VAMPIRE TO PROTECT HIM?
AS FOR MARY...
HE MAY BE PROTECTING MARIA NOW...
...BUT WHO KNOWS WHAT THE FUTURE HOLDS.

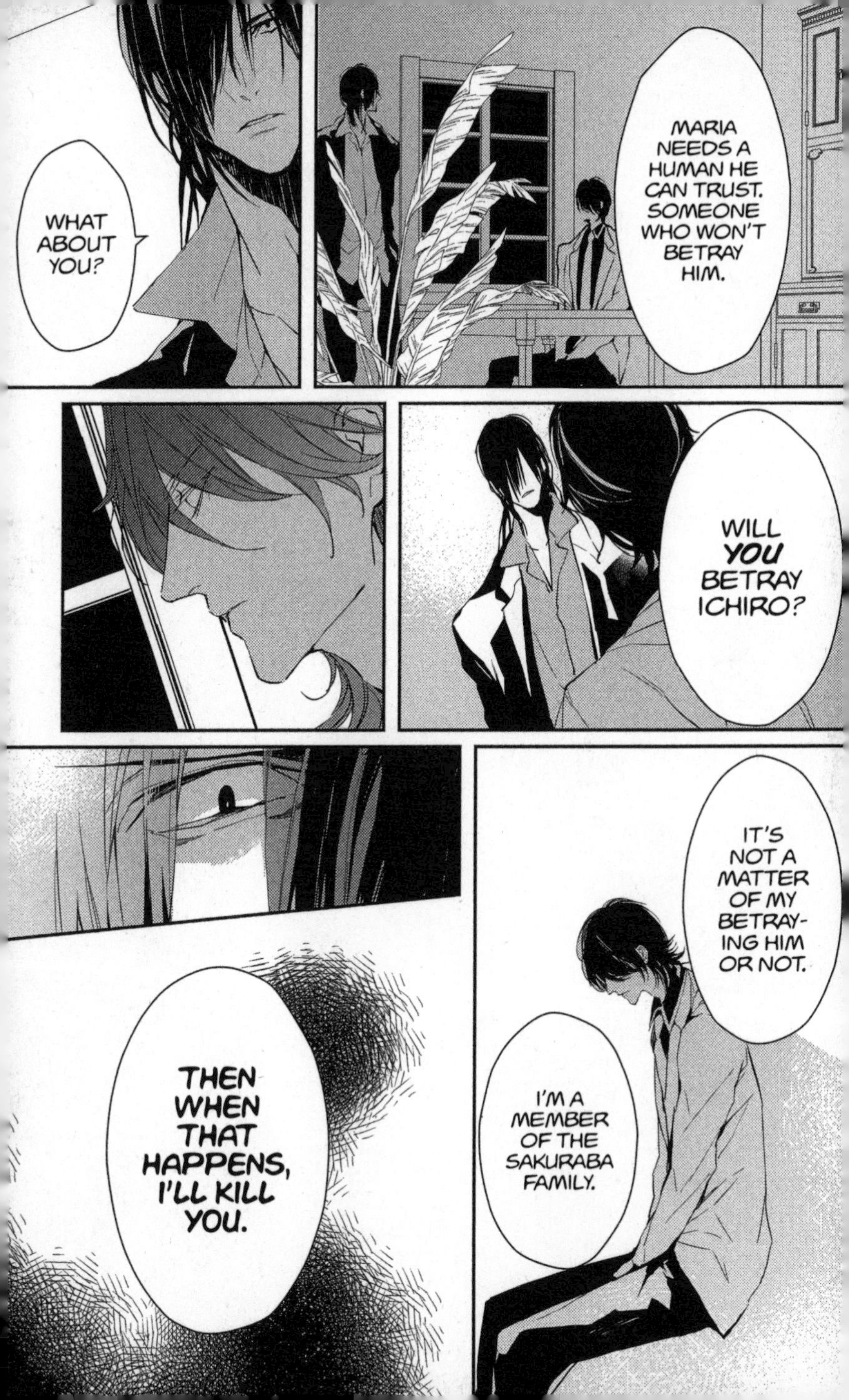
MARIA NEEDS A HUMAN HE CAN TRUST. SOMEONE WHO WON'T BETRAY HIM.
WHAT ABOUT YOU?
WILL YOU BETRAY ICHIRO?
IT'S NOT A MATTER OF MY BETRAY-ING HIM OR NOT.
I'M A MEMBER OF THE SAKURABA FAMILY.
THEN WHEN THAT HAPPENS, I'LL KILL YOU.

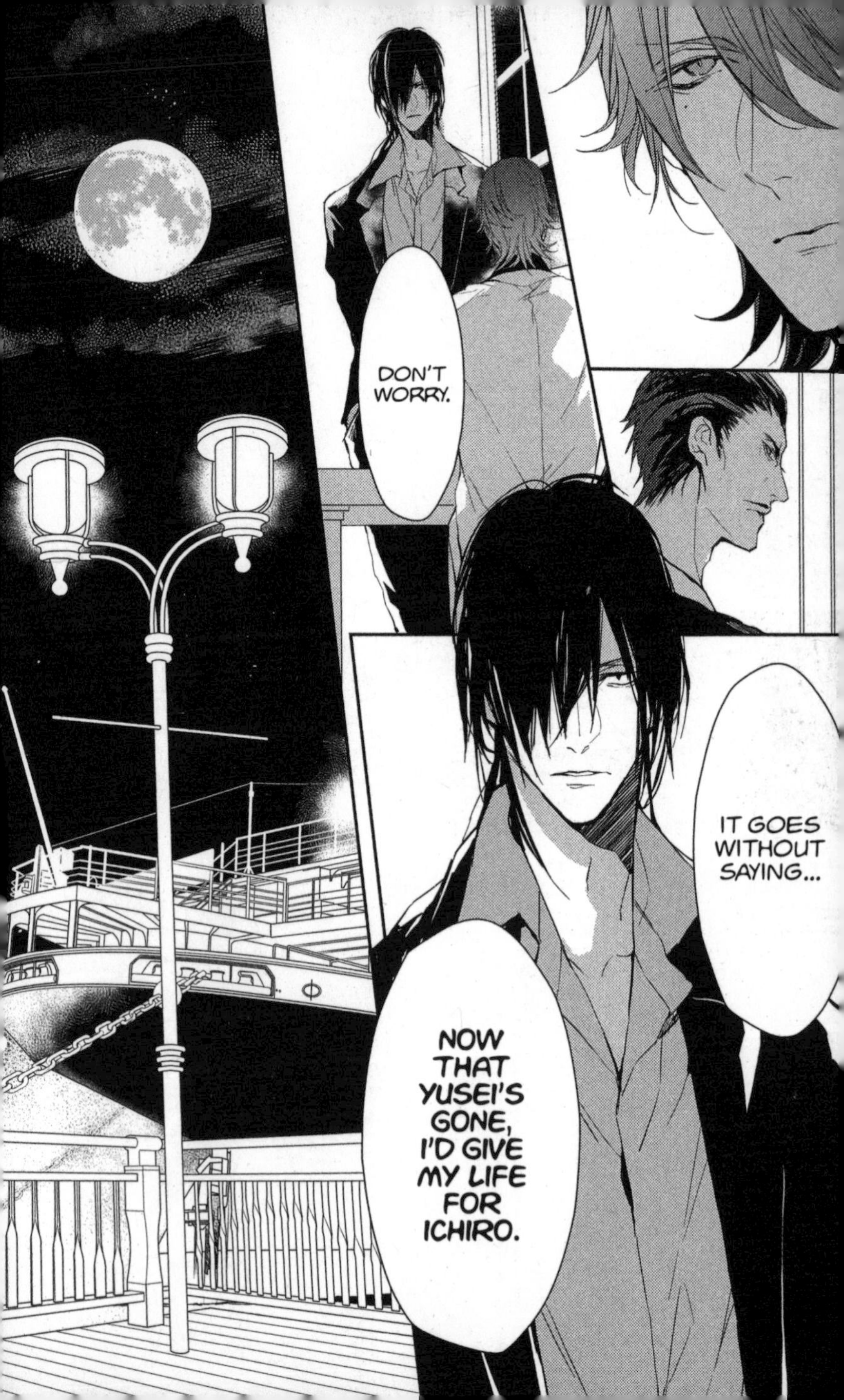
DON'T WORRY.
IT GOES WITHOUT SAYING...
NOW THAT YUSEI'S GONE, I'D GIVE MY LIFE FOR ICHIRO.

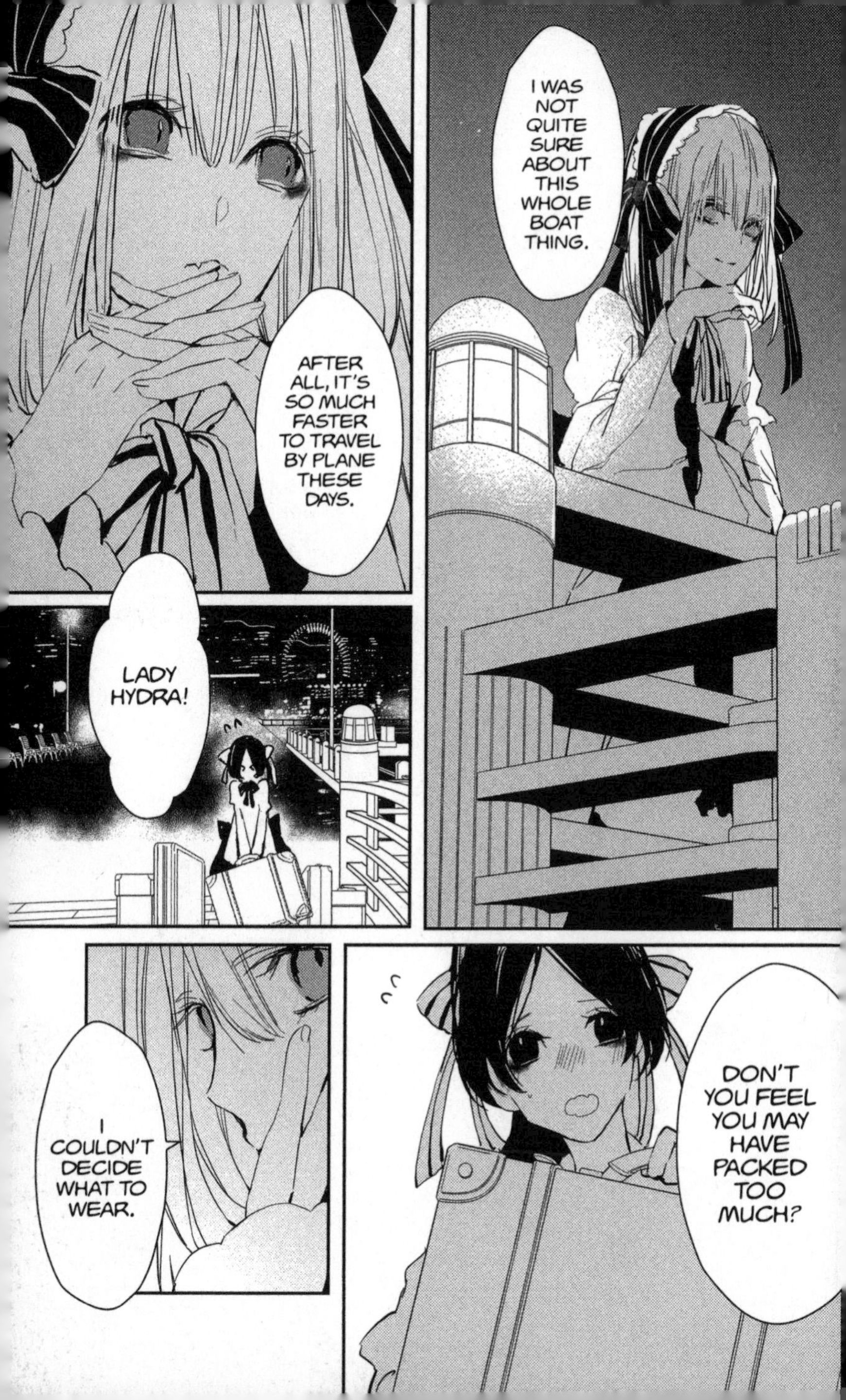
I WAS NOT QUITE SURE ABOUT THIS WHOLE BOAT THING.
AFTER ALL, IT'S SO MUCH FASTER TO TRAVEL BY PLANE THESE DAYS.
LADY HYDRA!
DON'T YOU FEEL YOU MAY HAVE PACKED TOO MUCH?
I COULDN'T DECIDE WHAT TO WEAR.

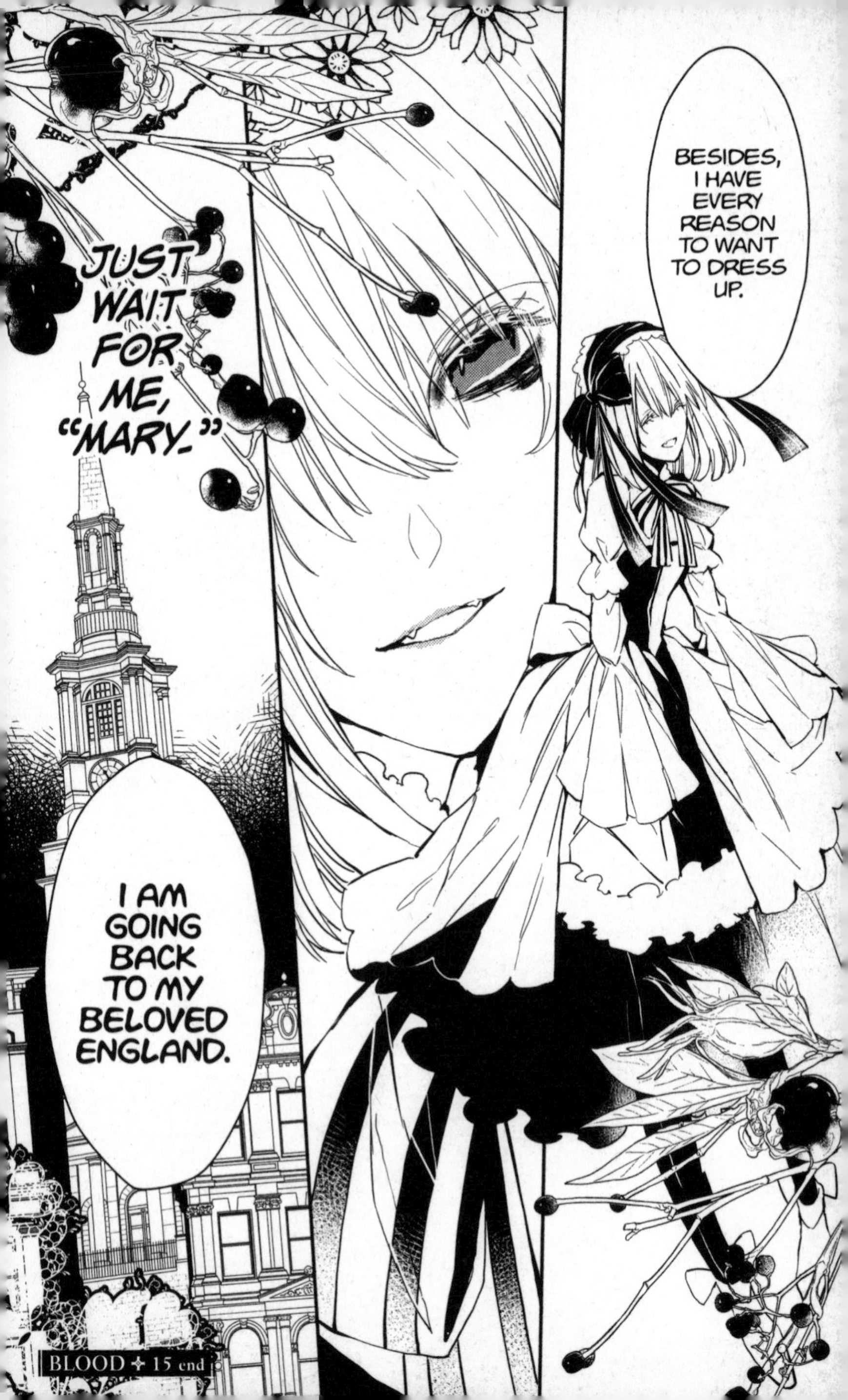
BESIDES, I HAVE EVERY REASON TO WANT TO DRESS UP.
JUST WAIT FOR ME, "MARY_"
I AM GOING BACK TO MY BELOVED ENGLAND.
BLOOD ✦ 15 end

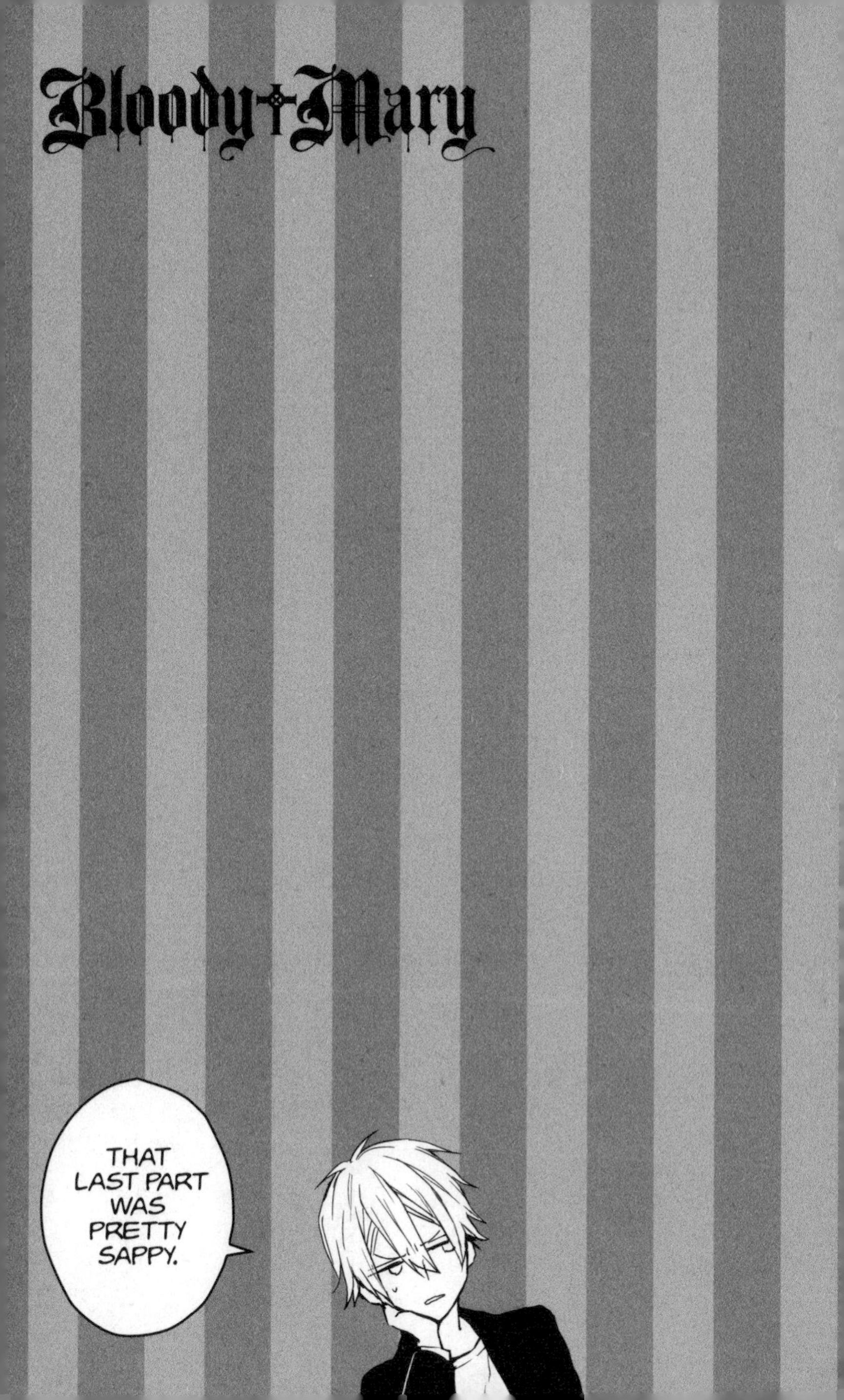
Bloody+Mary
THAT LAST PART WAS PRETTY SAPPY.

Bloody+Mary

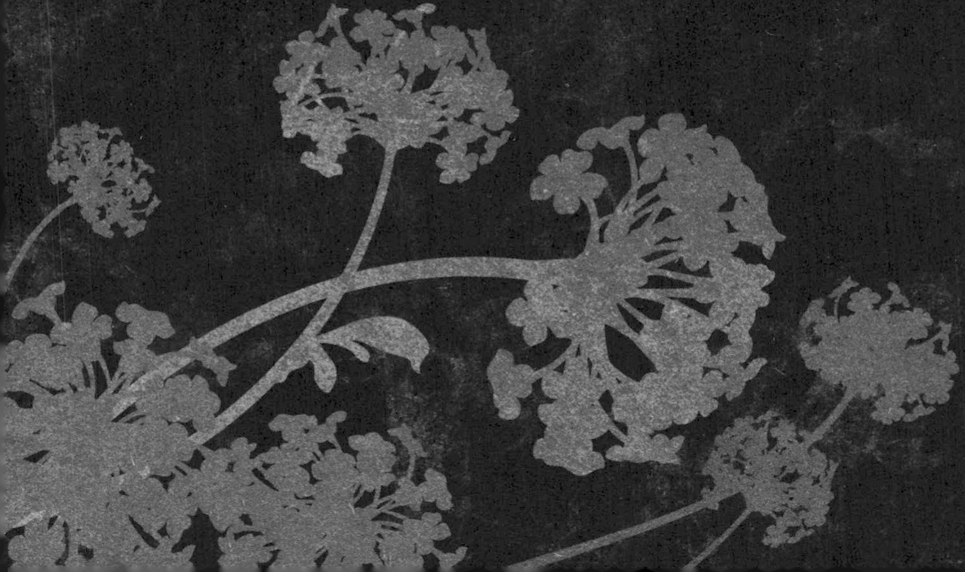

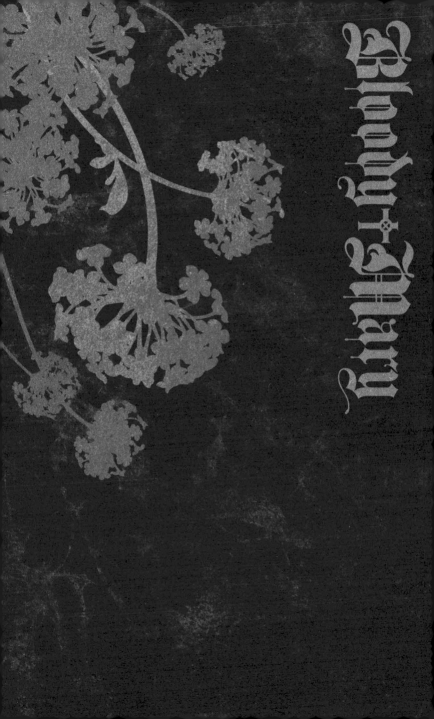

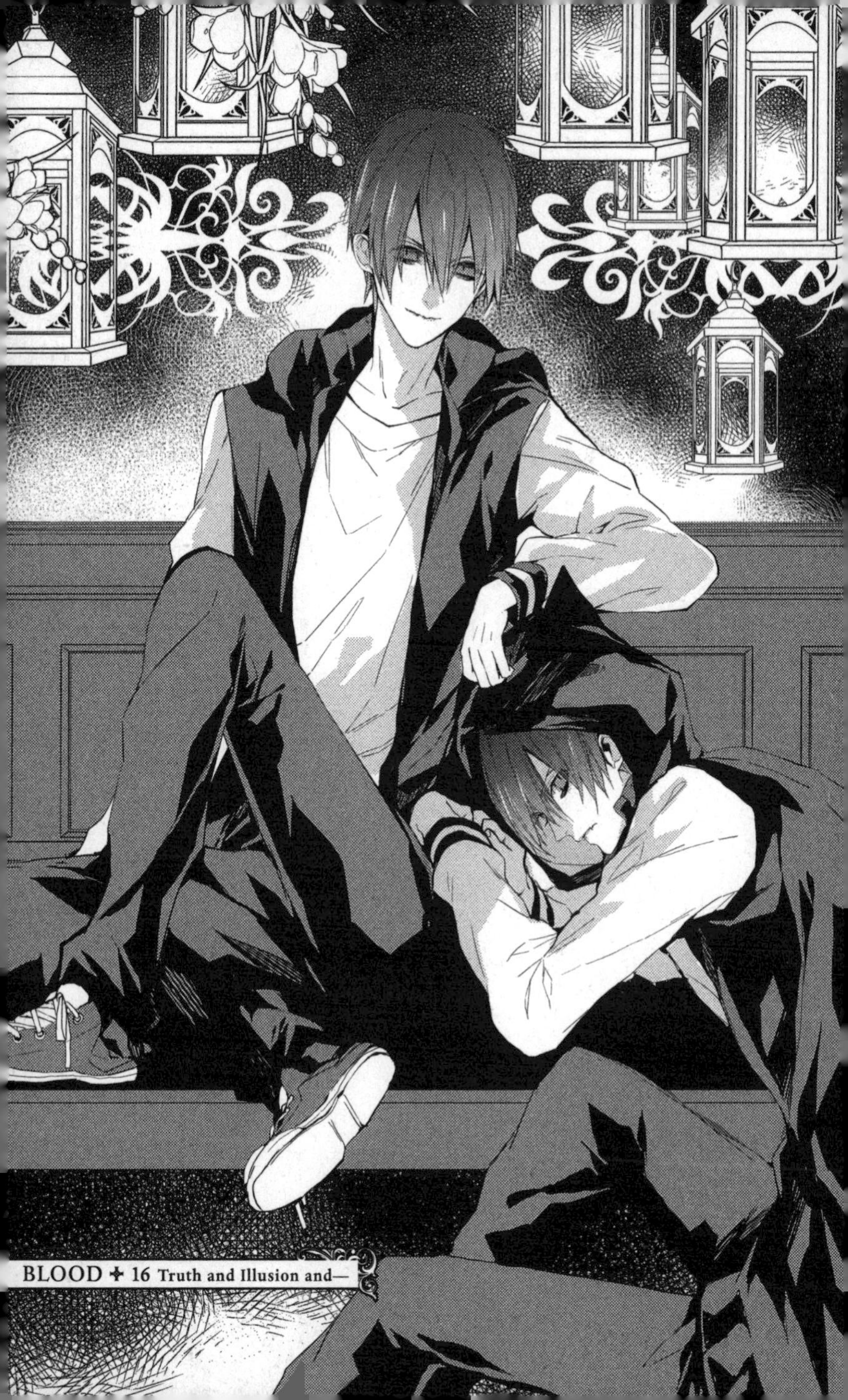
BLOOD ✣ 16 Truth and Illusion and—

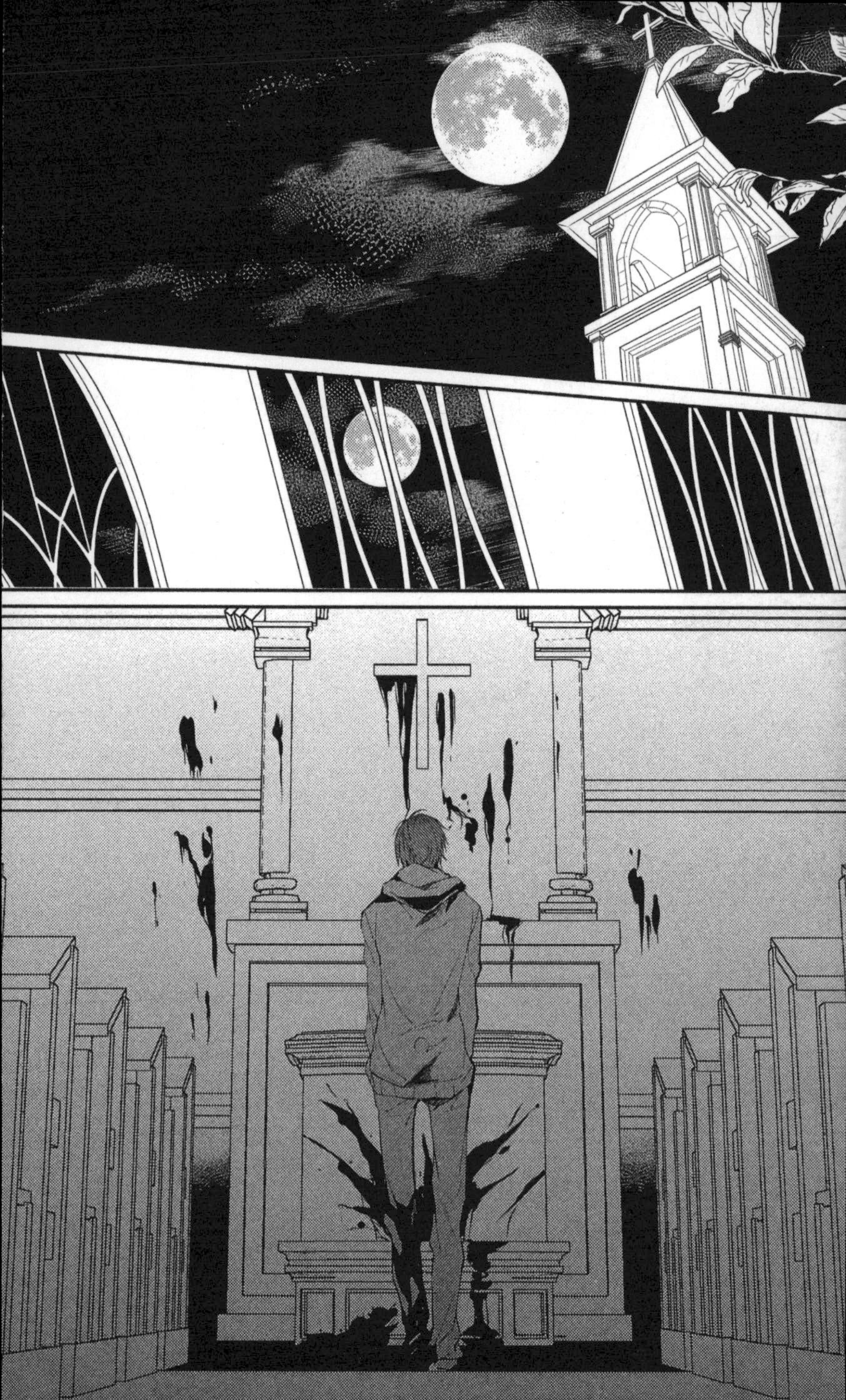

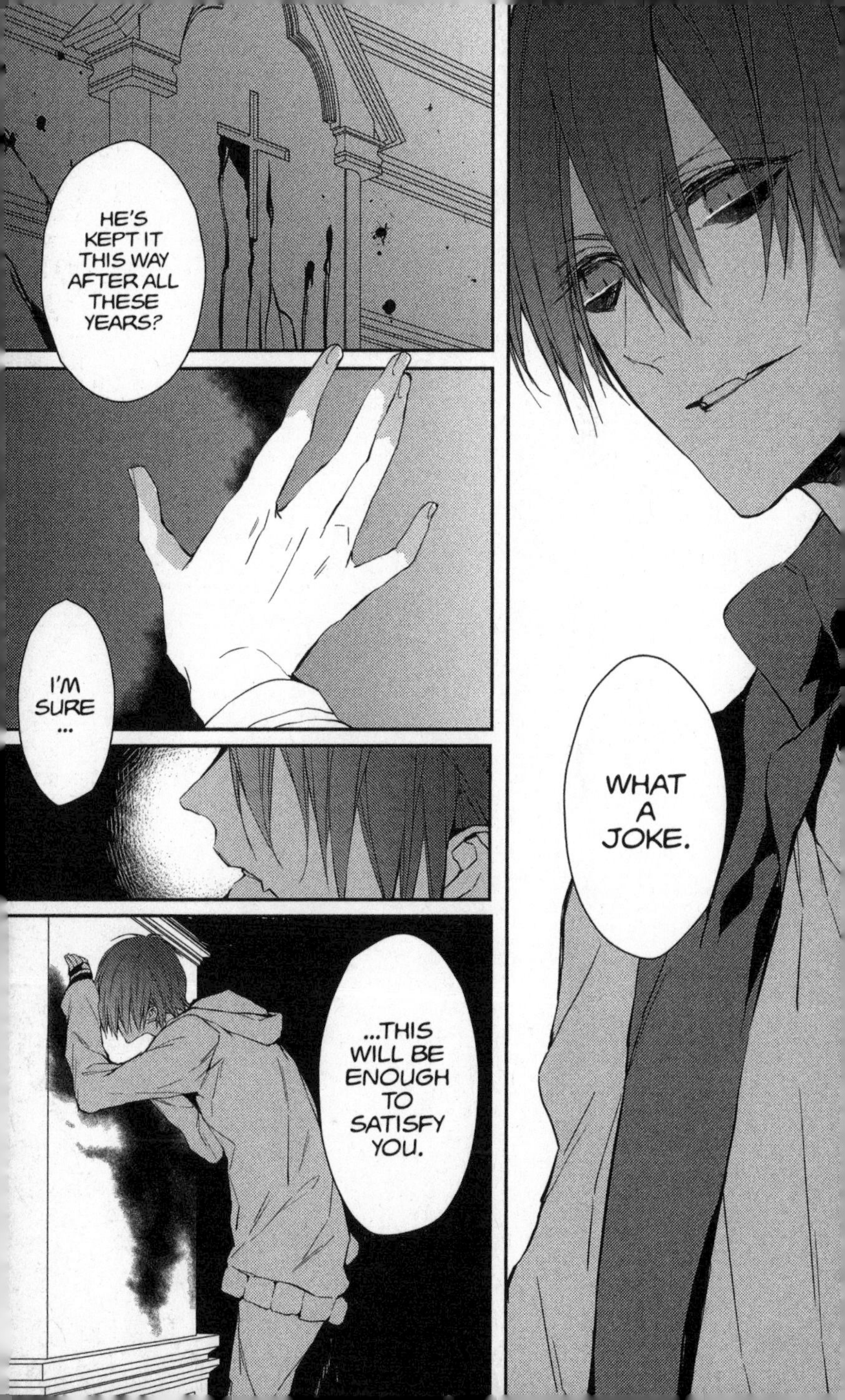
WHAT A JOKE.
HE'S KEPT IT THIS WAY AFTER ALL THESE YEARS?
I'M SURE ...
...THIS WILL BE ENOUGH TO SATISFY YOU.

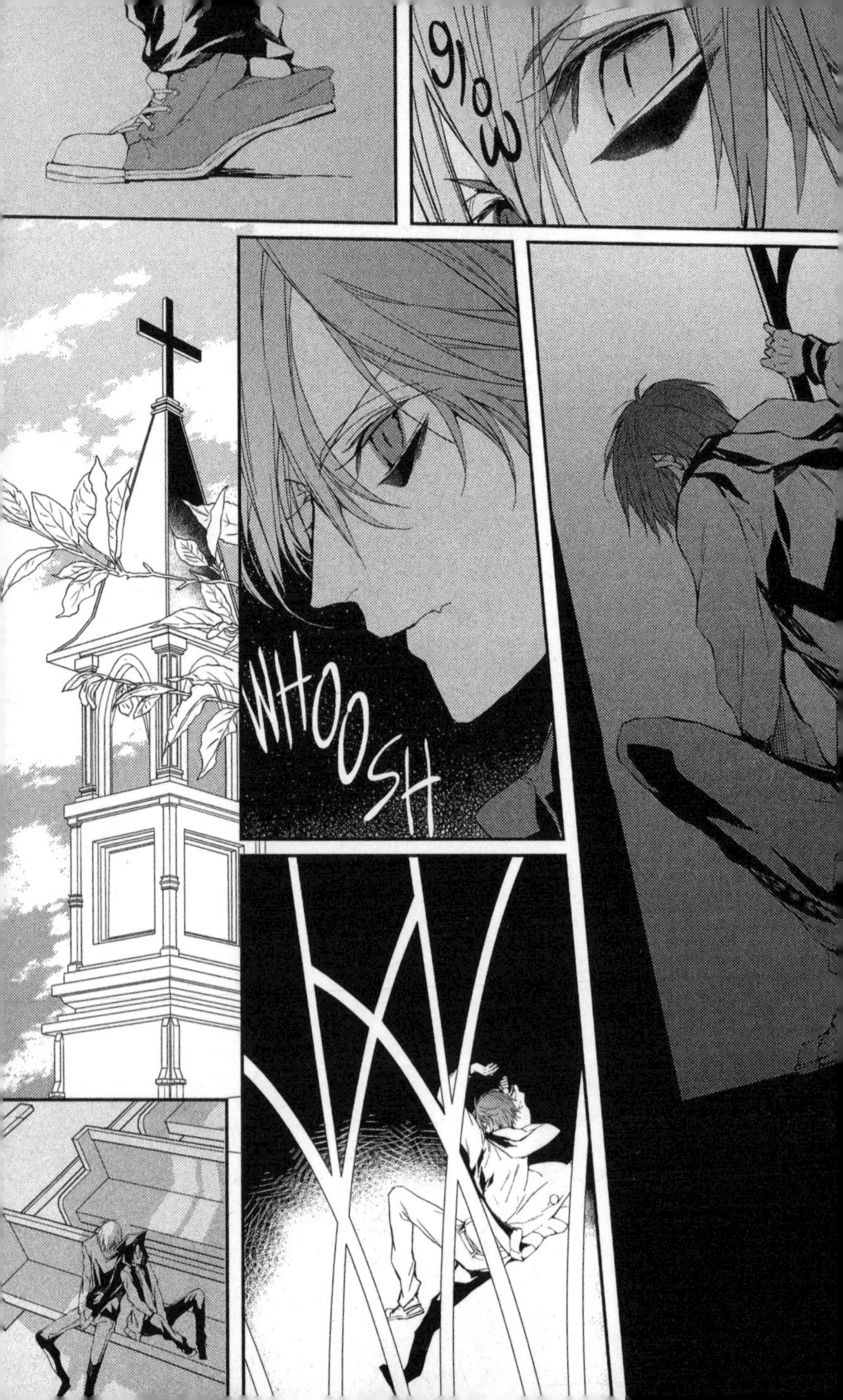
WHOOSH

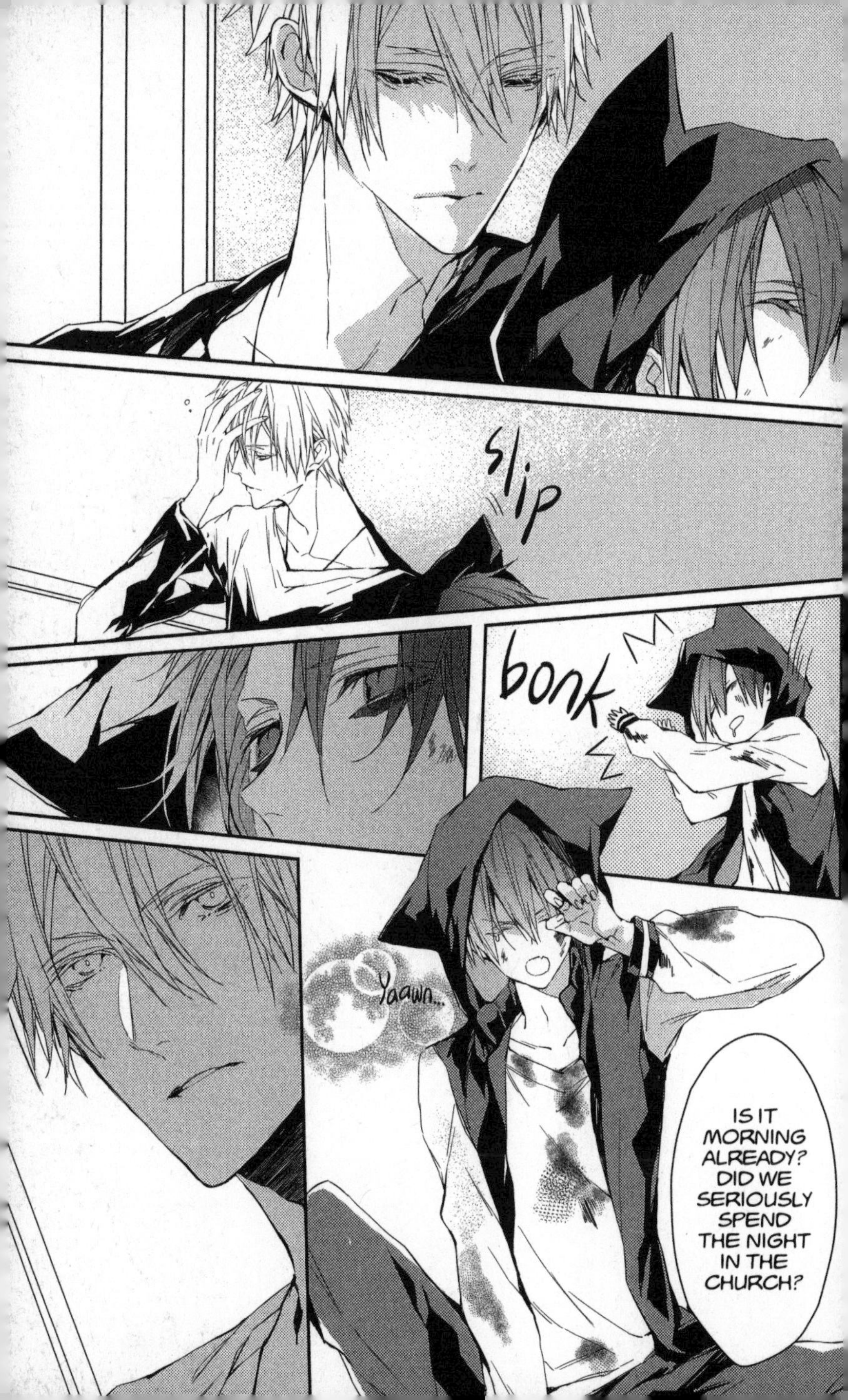
slip
bonk
Yaawn...
IS IT MORNING ALREADY? DID WE SERIOUSLY SPEND THE NIGHT IN THE CHURCH?

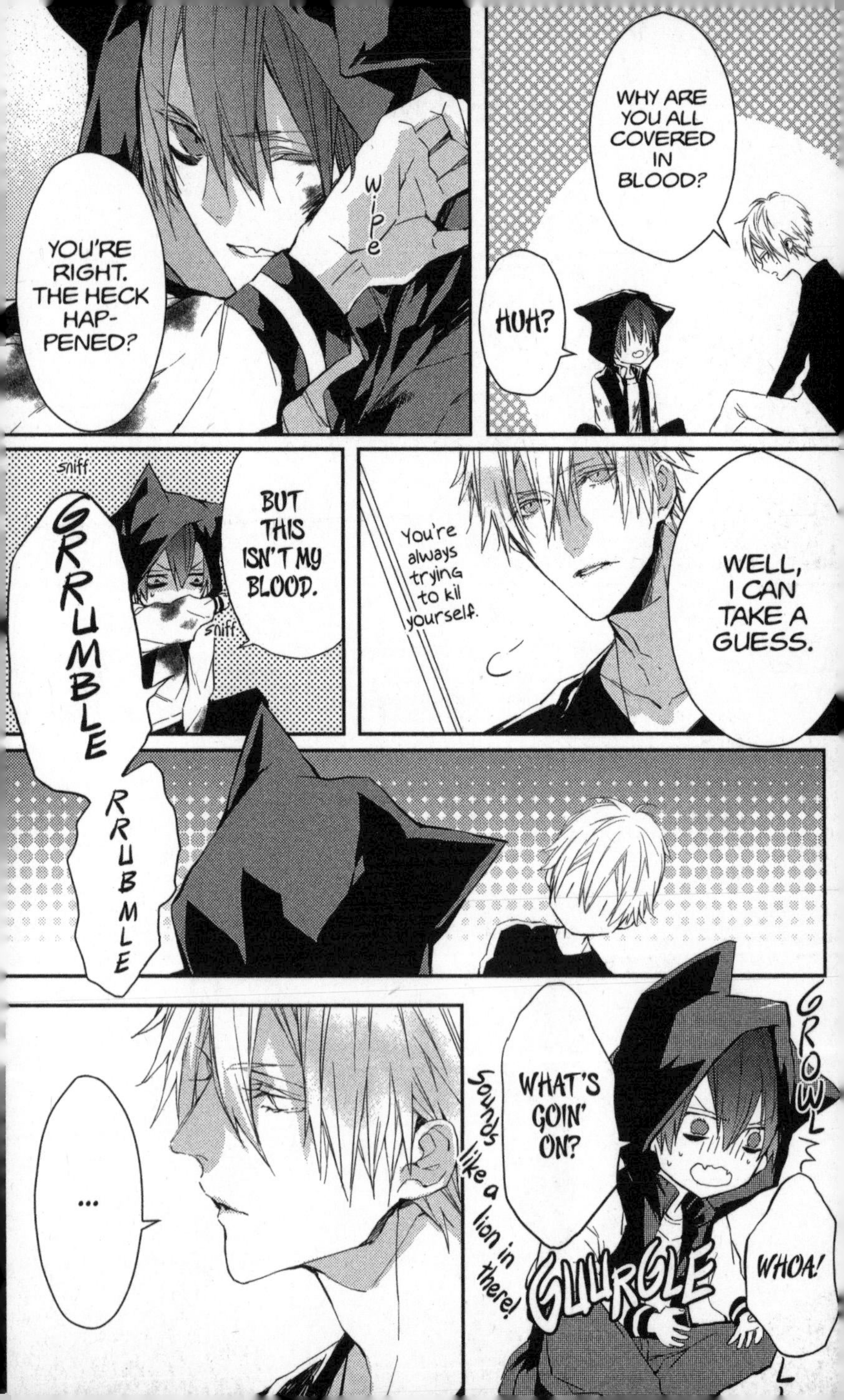
WHY ARE YOU ALL COVERED IN BLOOD?
HUH?
wipe
YOU'RE RIGHT. THE HECK HAP-PENED?
WELL, I CAN TAKE A GUESS.
You're always trying to kil yourself.
sniff
BUT THIS ISN'T MY BLOOD.
sniff
GRRUMBLE
RRUBMLE
GROWL
WHAT'S GOIN' ON?
WHOA!
GLURGLE
Sounds like a lion in there!
...

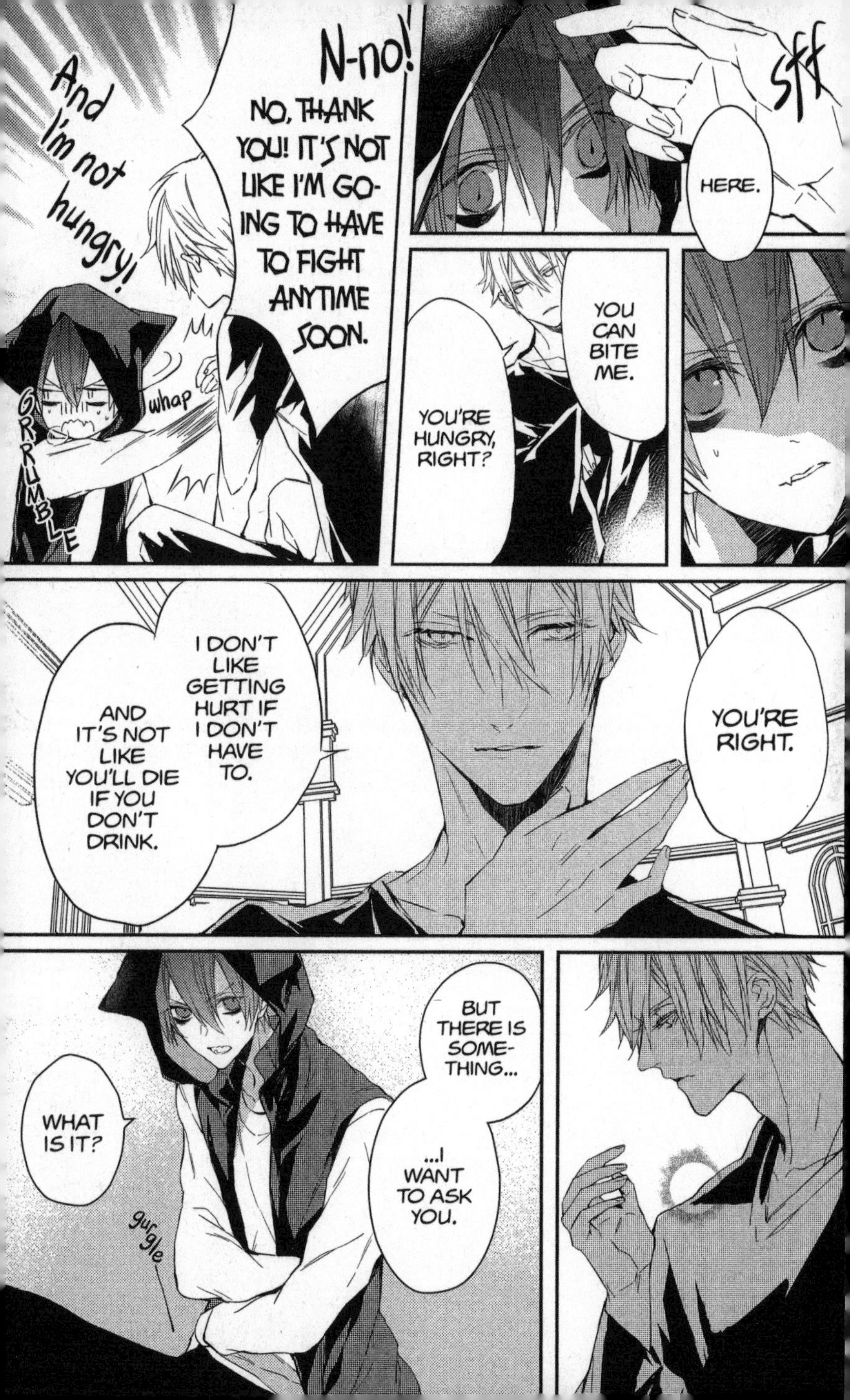
sff
HERE.
YOU CAN BITE ME.
YOU'RE HUNGRY, RIGHT?
N-no!
NO, THANK YOU! IT'S NOT LIKE I'M GOING TO HAVE TO FIGHT ANYTIME SOON.
And I'm not hungry!
whap
GRRUMBLE
YOU'RE RIGHT.
I DON'T LIKE GETTING HURT IF I DON'T HAVE TO.
AND IT'S NOT LIKE YOU'LL DIE IF YOU DON'T DRINK.
BUT THERE IS SOMETHING...
...I WANT TO ASK YOU.
WHAT IS IT?
gurgle

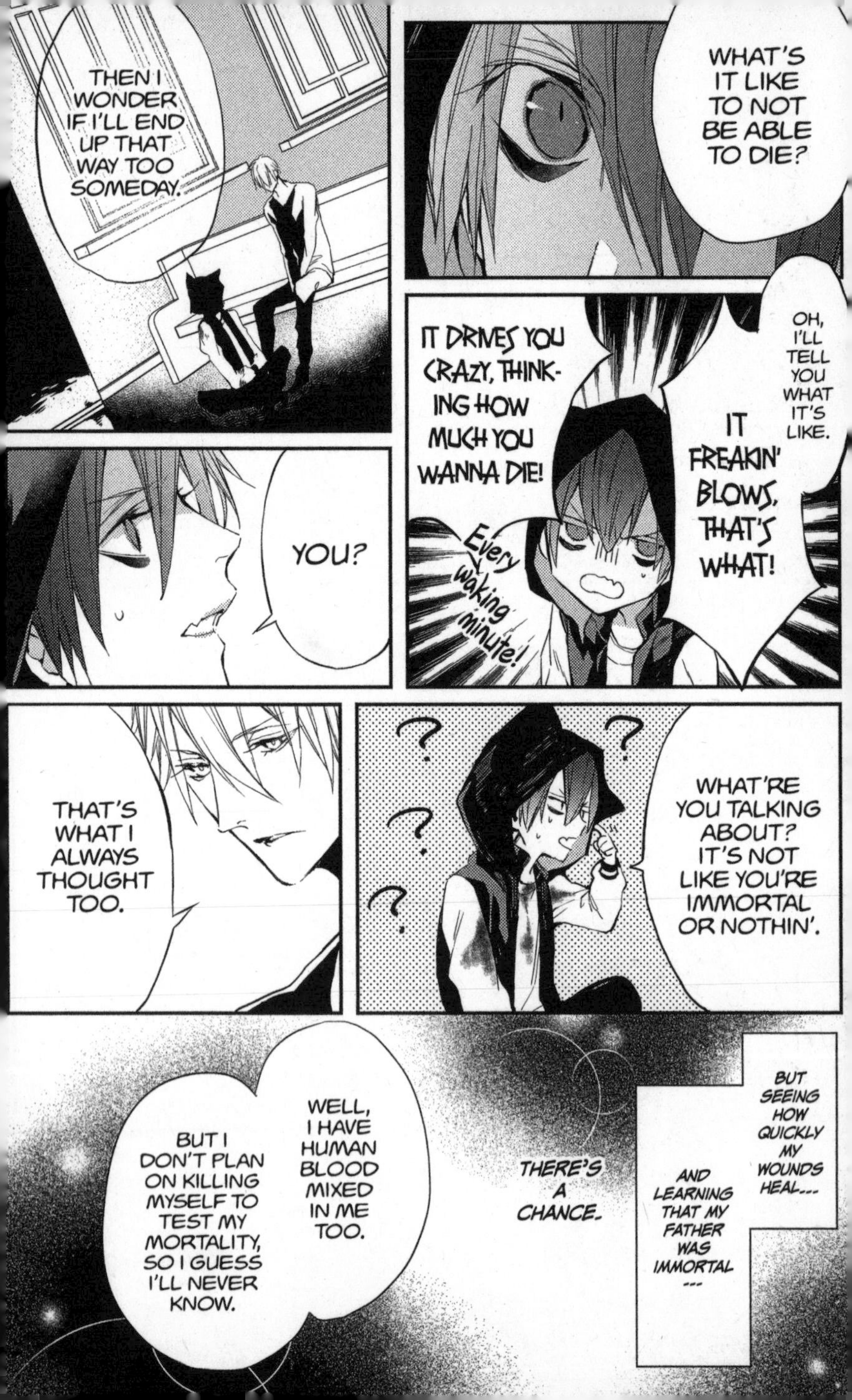
WHAT'S IT LIKE TO NOT BE ABLE TO DIE?
THEN I WONDER IF I'LL END UP THAT WAY TOO SOMEDAY.
OH, I'LL TELL YOU WHAT IT'S LIKE.
IT FREAKIN' BLOWS, THAT'S WHAT!
IT DRIVES YOU CRAZY, THINKING HOW MUCH YOU WANNA DIE!
Every waking minute!
YOU?
WHAT'RE YOU TALKING ABOUT? IT'S NOT LIKE YOU'RE IMMORTAL OR NOTHIN'.
THAT'S WHAT I ALWAYS THOUGHT TOO.
BUT SEEING HOW QUICKLY MY WOUNDS HEAL...
AND LEARNING THAT MY FATHER WAS IMMORTAL...
THERE'S A CHANCE.
WELL, I HAVE HUMAN BLOOD MIXED IN ME TOO.
BUT I DON'T PLAN ON KILLING MYSELF TO TEST MY MORTALITY, SO I GUESS I'LL NEVER KNOW.

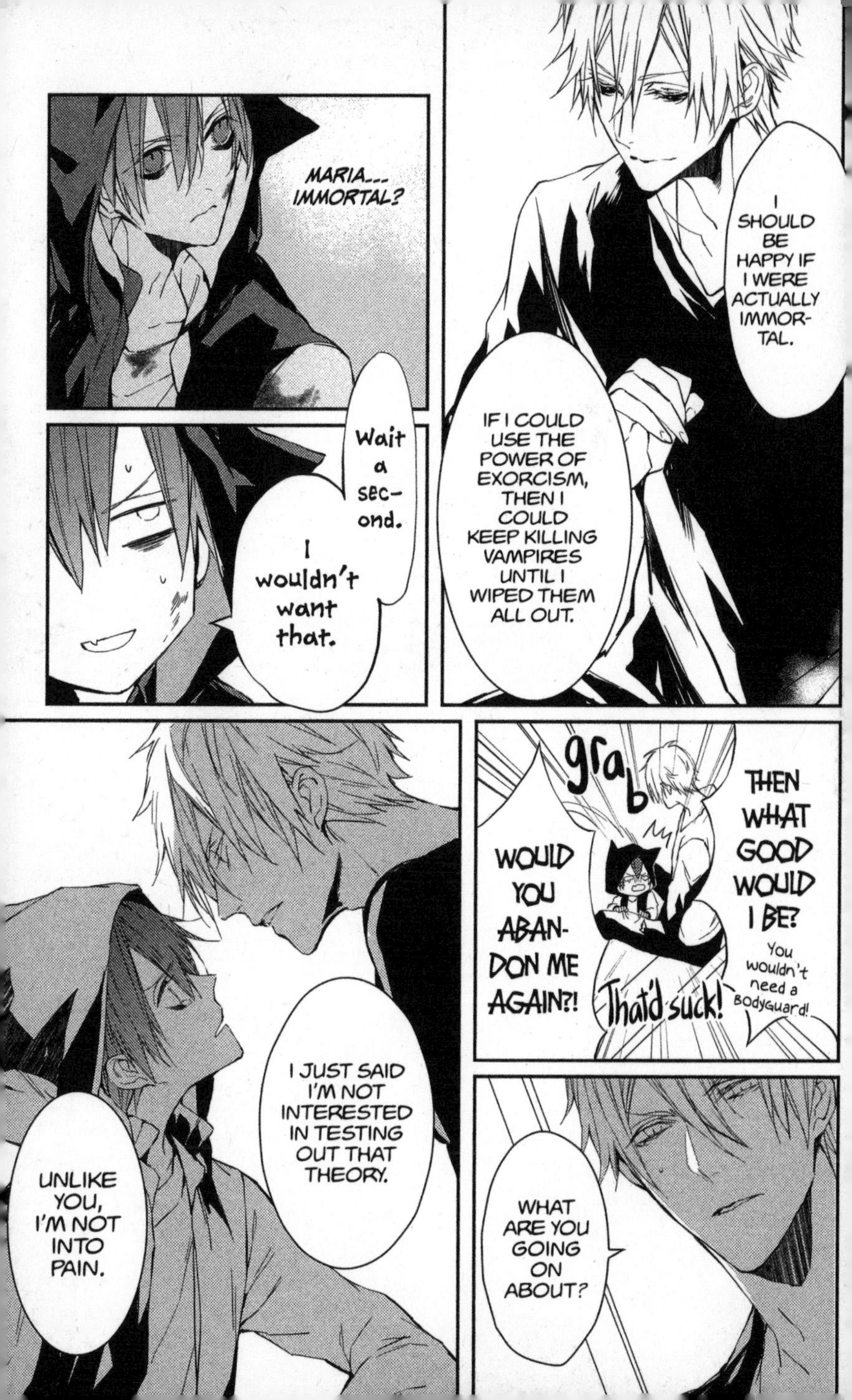
I SHOULD BE HAPPY IF I WERE ACTUALLY IMMORTAL.
IF I COULD USE THE POWER OF EXORCISM, THEN I COULD KEEP KILLING VAMPIRES UNTIL I WIPED THEM ALL OUT.
MARIA... IMMORTAL?
Wait a second.
I wouldn't want that.
grab
THEN WHAT GOOD WOULD I BE?
You wouldn't need a BodyGuard!
WOULD YOU ABANDON ME AGAIN?!
That'd suck!
WHAT ARE YOU GOING ON ABOUT?
I JUST SAID I'M NOT INTERESTED IN TESTING OUT THAT THEORY.
UNLIKE YOU, I'M NOT INTO PAIN.

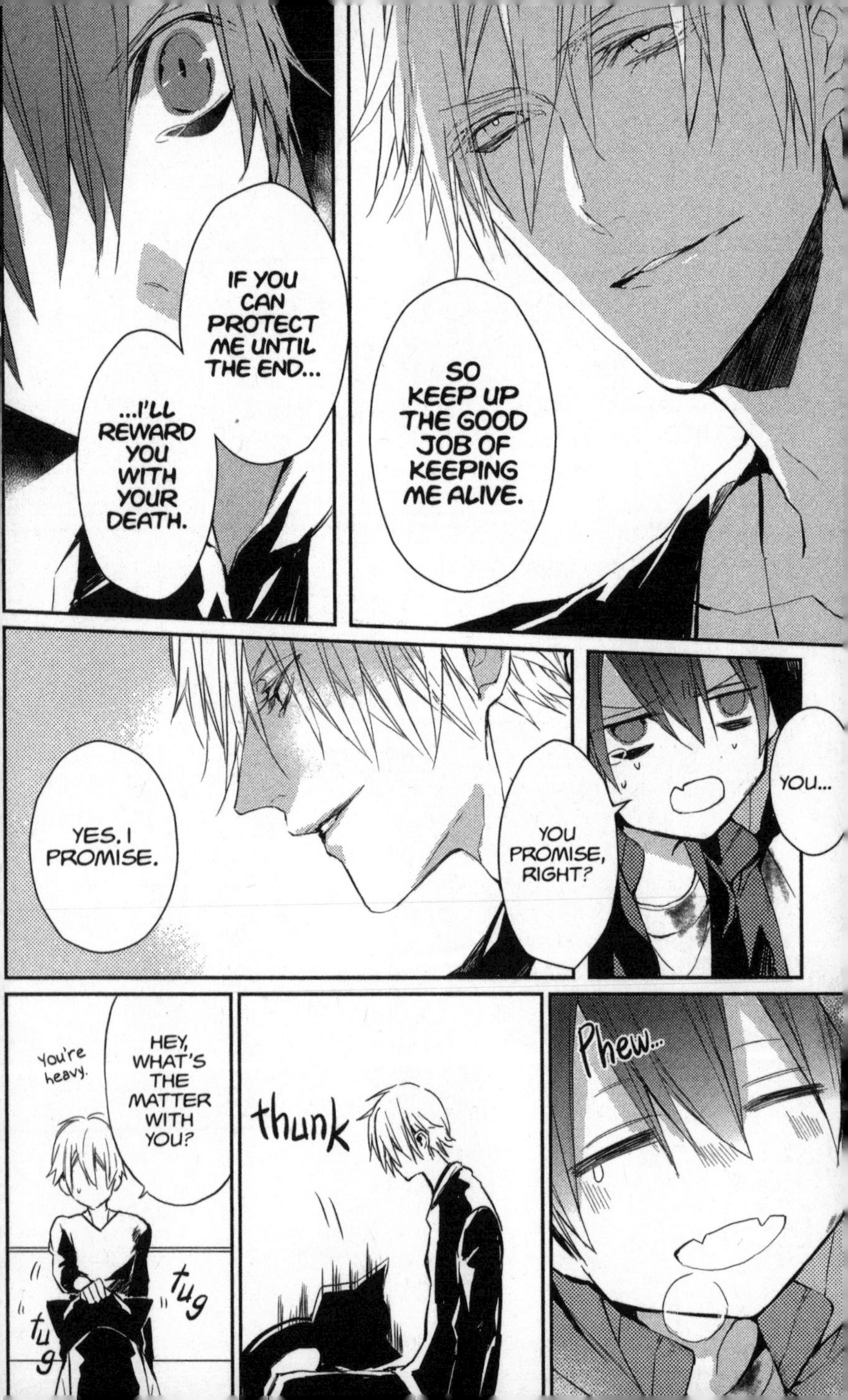
SO KEEP UP THE GOOD JOB OF KEEPING ME ALIVE.
IF YOU CAN PROTECT ME UNTIL THE END...
...I'LL REWARD YOU WITH YOUR DEATH.
YOU...
YOU PROMISE, RIGHT?
YES. I PROMISE.
Phew...
thunk
HEY, WHAT'S THE MATTER WITH YOU?
You're heavy.
tug
tug

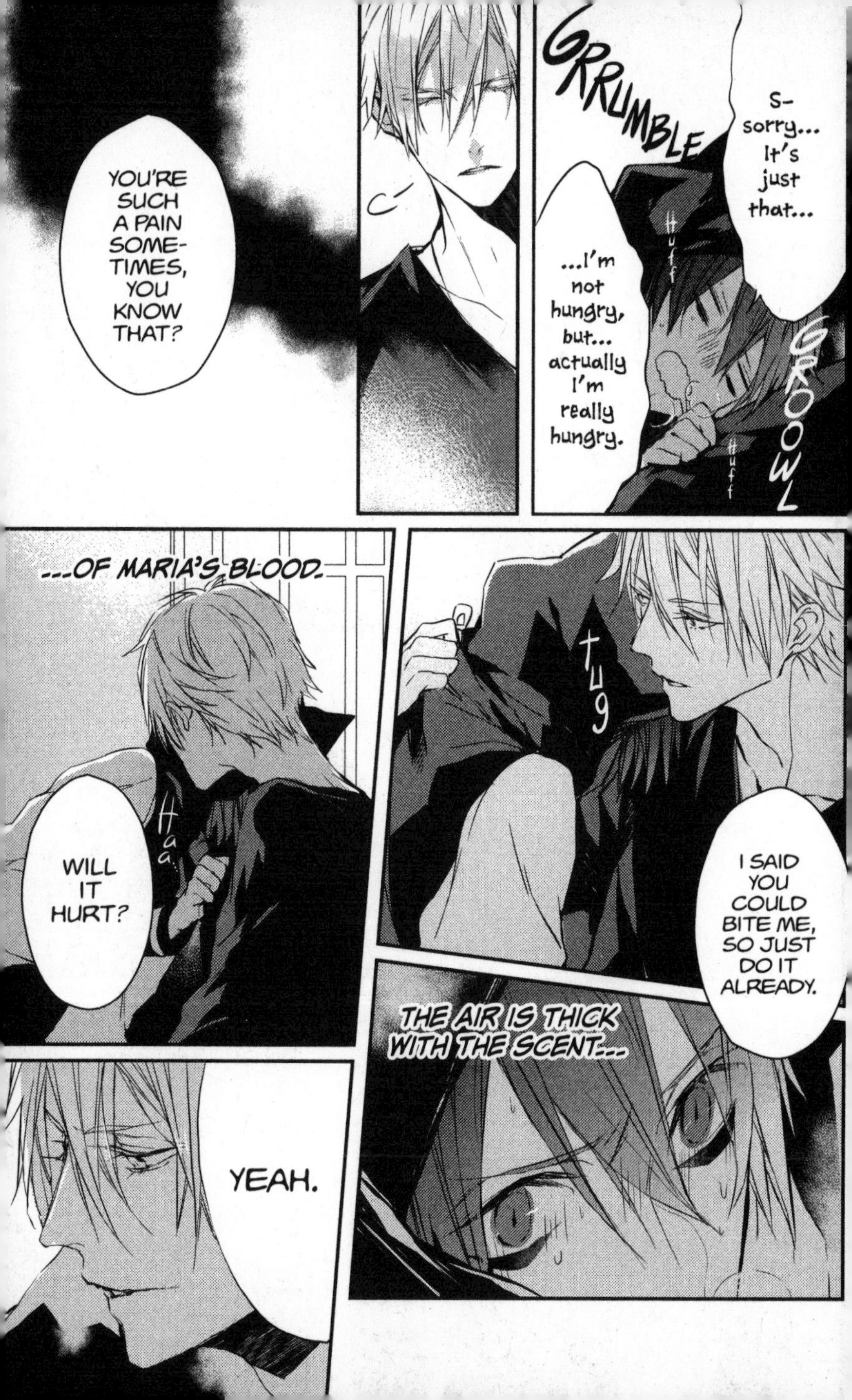
GRRUMBLE
S-sorry... It's just that...
...I'm not hungry, but... actually I'm really hungry.
Huff
GROOWL
Huff
YOU'RE SUCH A PAIN SOMETIMES, YOU KNOW THAT?
tug
I SAID YOU COULD BITE ME, SO JUST DO IT ALREADY.
THE AIR IS THICK WITH THE SCENT...
...OF MARIA'S BLOOD.
Haa...
WILL IT HURT?
YEAH.

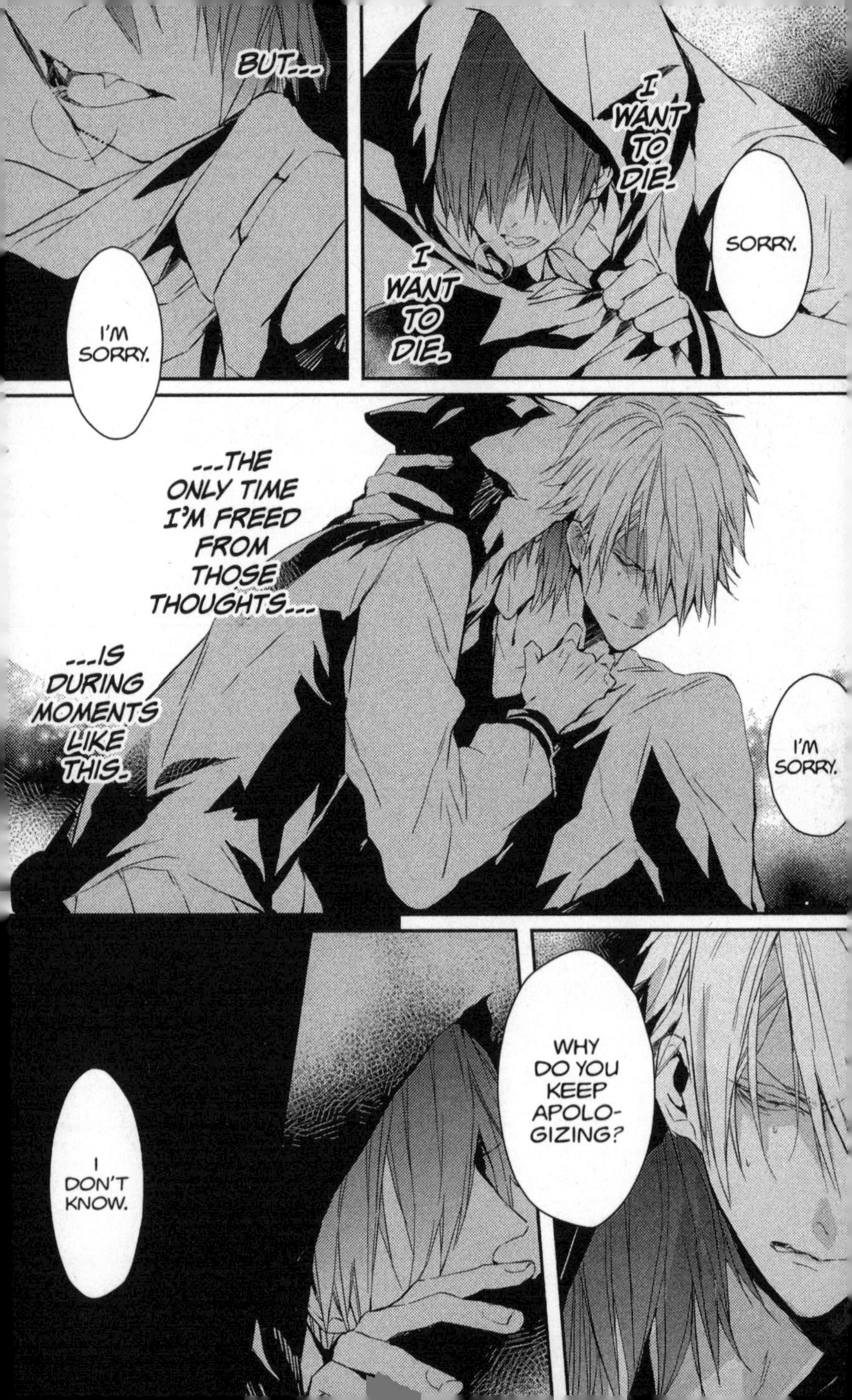
I WANT TO DIE.
SORRY.
I WANT TO DIE.
BUT...
I'M SORRY.
...THE ONLY TIME I'M FREED FROM THOSE THOUGHTS...
...IS DURING MOMENTS LIKE THIS.
I'M SORRY.
WHY DO YOU KEEP APOLO-GIZING?
I DON'T KNOW.

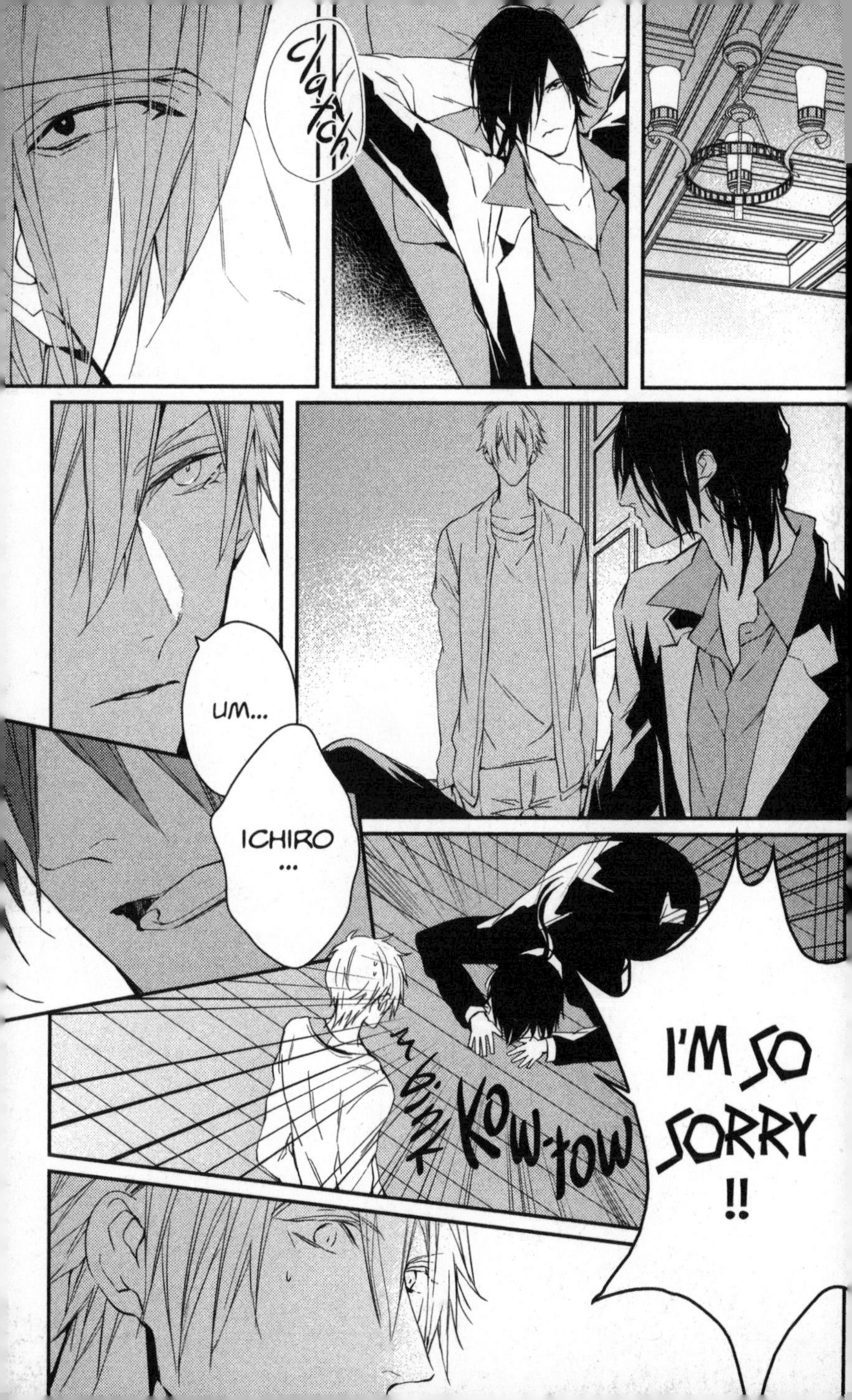
clatch
UM...
ICHIRO ...
I'M SO SORRY !!
KOW-TOW
bink

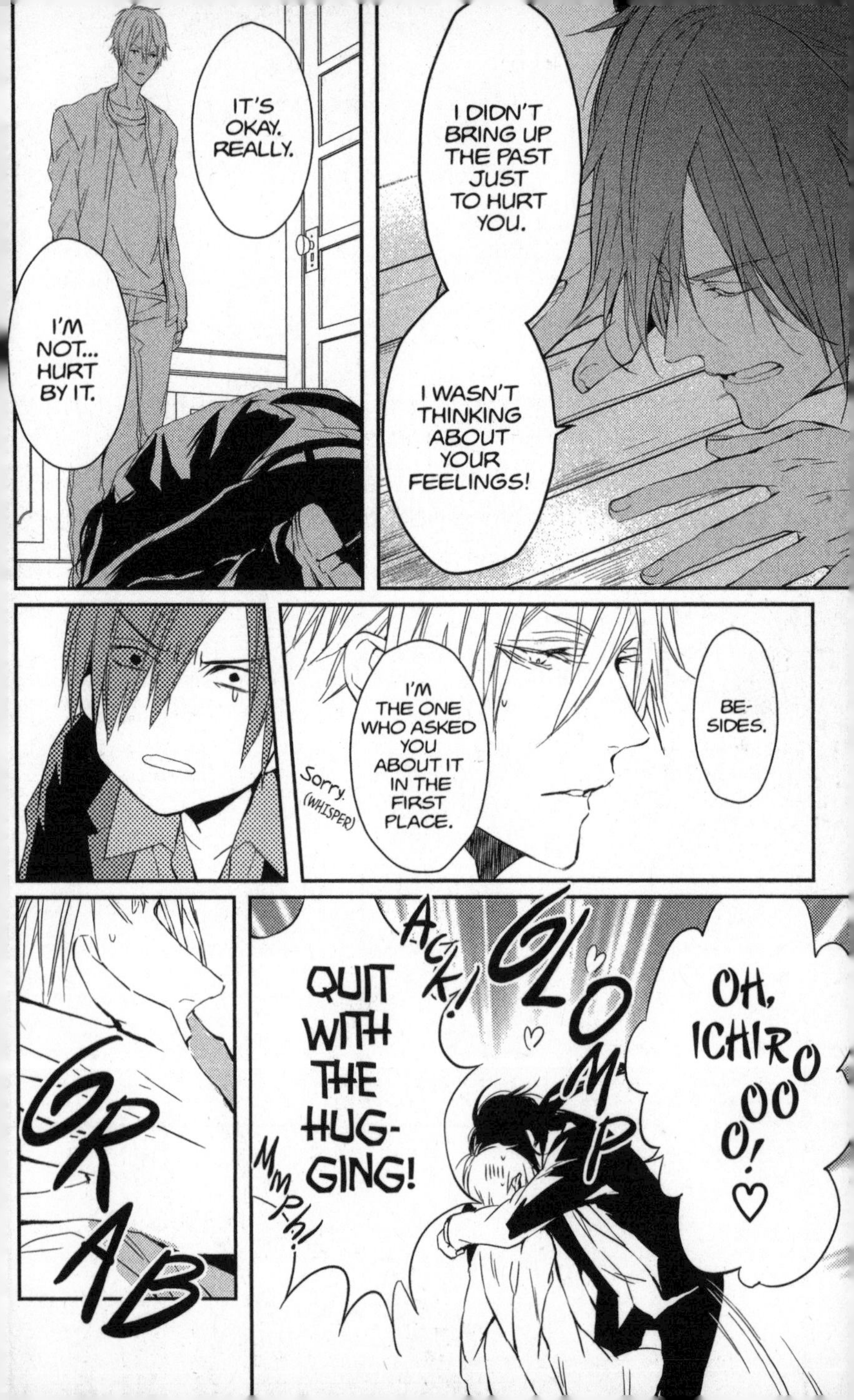
I DIDN'T BRING UP THE PAST JUST TO HURT YOU.
I WASN'T THINKING ABOUT YOUR FEELINGS!
IT'S OKAY. REALLY.
I'M NOT... HURT BY IT.
BE-SIDES.
I'M THE ONE WHO ASKED YOU ABOUT IT IN THE FIRST PLACE.
Sorry. (WHISPER)
OH, ICHIROOOOO! ♥
GLOMP
ACK!
QUIT WITH THE HUG-GING!
MMPH!
GRAB

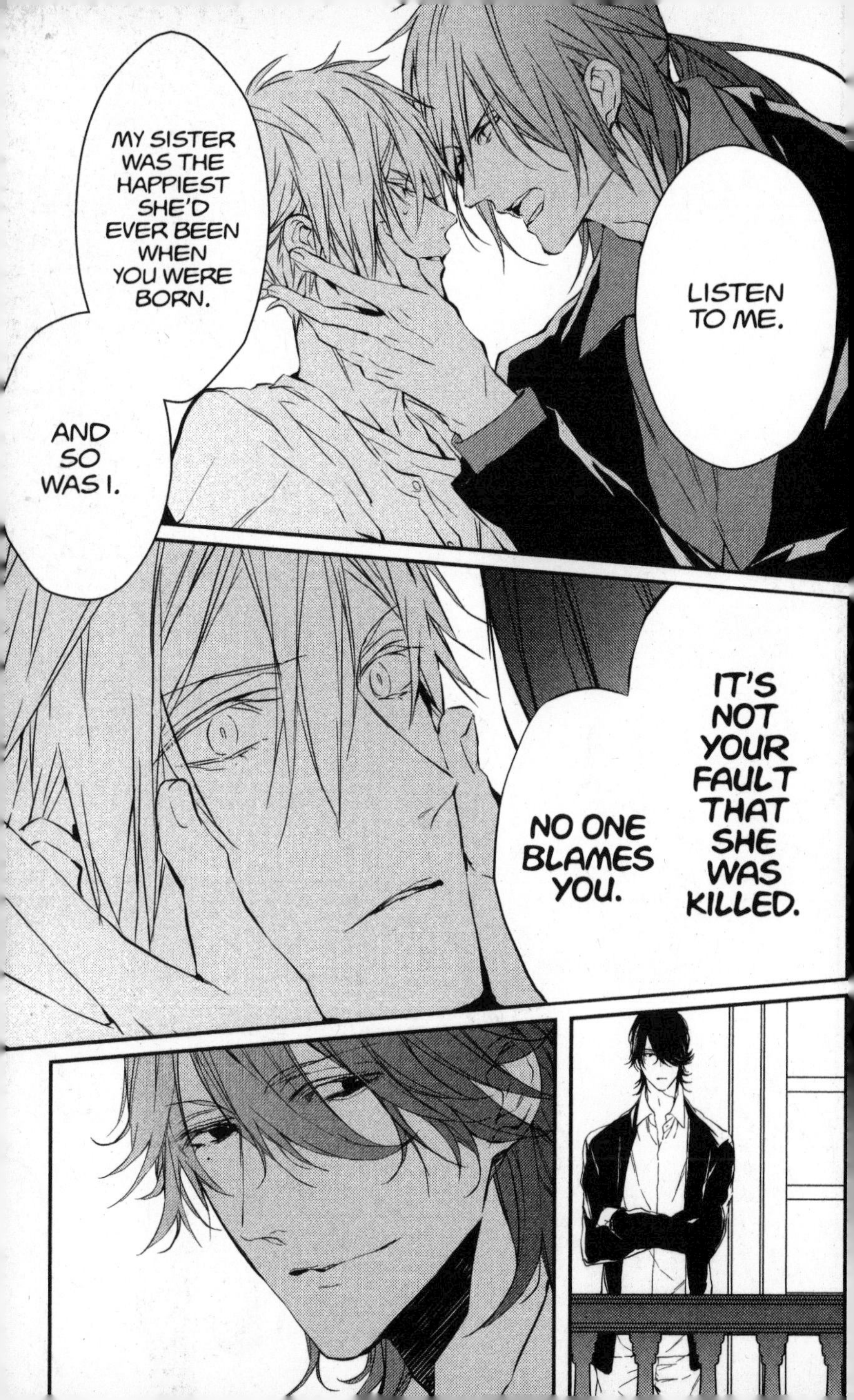
LISTEN TO ME.
MY SISTER WAS THE HAPPIEST SHE'D EVER BEEN WHEN YOU WERE BORN.
AND SO WAS I.
IT'S NOT YOUR FAULT THAT SHE WAS KILLED.
NO ONE BLAMES YOU.

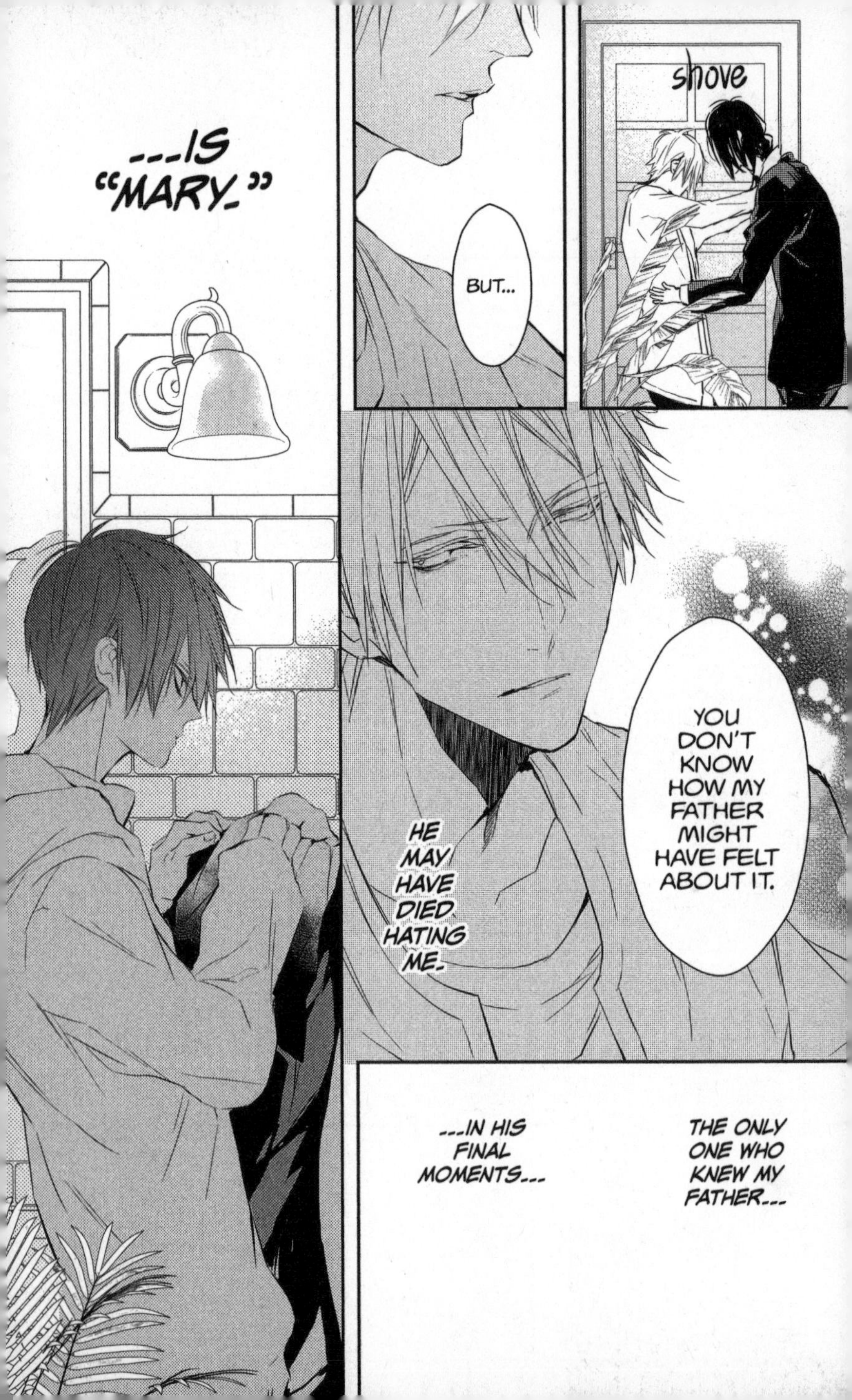
shove
BUT...
YOU DON'T KNOW HOW MY FATHER MIGHT HAVE FELT ABOUT IT.
HE MAY HAVE DIED HATING ME.
THE ONLY ONE WHO KNEW MY FATHER...
...IN HIS FINAL MOMENTS...
...IS "MARY."

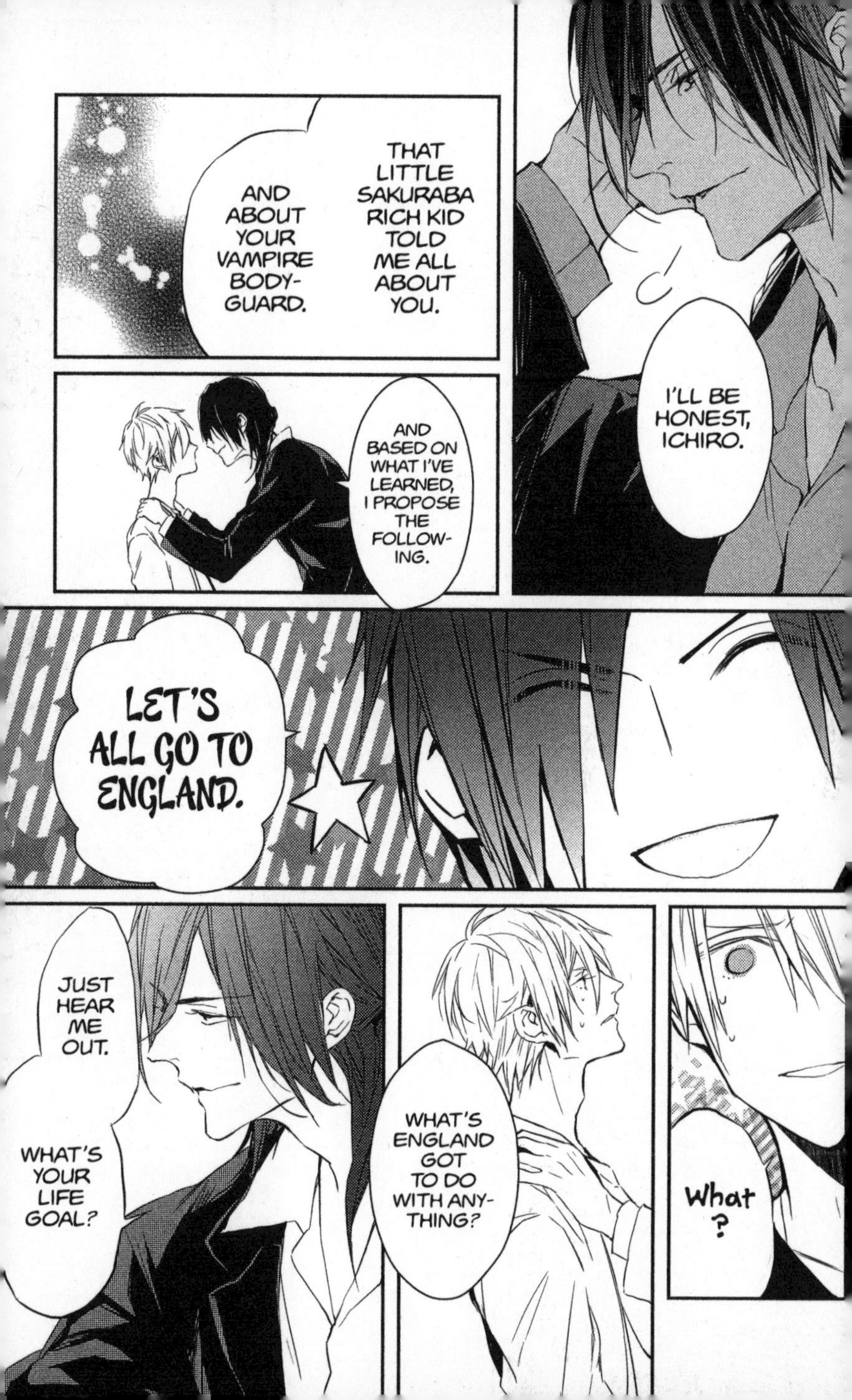
I'LL BE HONEST, ICHIRO.
THAT LITTLE SAKURABA RICH KID TOLD ME ALL ABOUT YOU.
AND ABOUT YOUR VAMPIRE BODY-GUARD.
AND BASED ON WHAT I'VE LEARNED, I PROPOSE THE FOLLOWING.
LET'S ALL GO TO ENGLAND.
What?
WHAT'S ENGLAND GOT TO DO WITH ANY-THING?
JUST HEAR ME OUT.
WHAT'S YOUR LIFE GOAL?

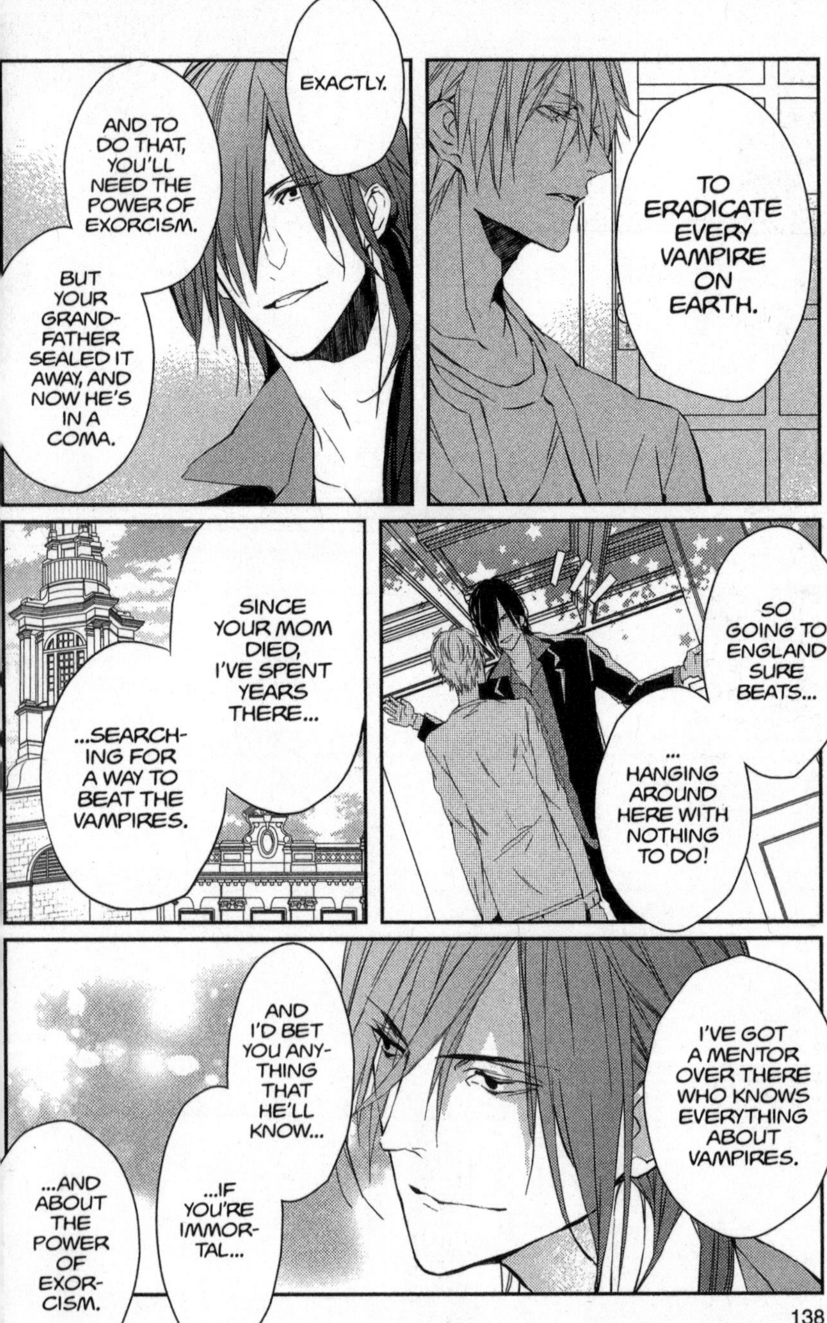
TO ERADICATE EVERY VAMPIRE ON EARTH.
EXACTLY.
AND TO DO THAT, YOU'LL NEED THE POWER OF EXORCISM.
BUT YOUR GRAND-FATHER SEALED IT AWAY, AND NOW HE'S IN A COMA.
SO GOING TO ENGLAND SURE BEATS...
...HANGING AROUND HERE WITH NOTHING TO DO!
SINCE YOUR MOM DIED, I'VE SPENT YEARS THERE...
...SEARCH-ING FOR A WAY TO BEAT THE VAMPIRES.
I'VE GOT A MENTOR OVER THERE WHO KNOWS EVERYTHING ABOUT VAMPIRES.
AND I'D BET YOU ANY-THING THAT HE'LL KNOW...
...IF YOU'RE IMMOR-TAL...
...AND ABOUT THE POWER OF EXOR-CISM.

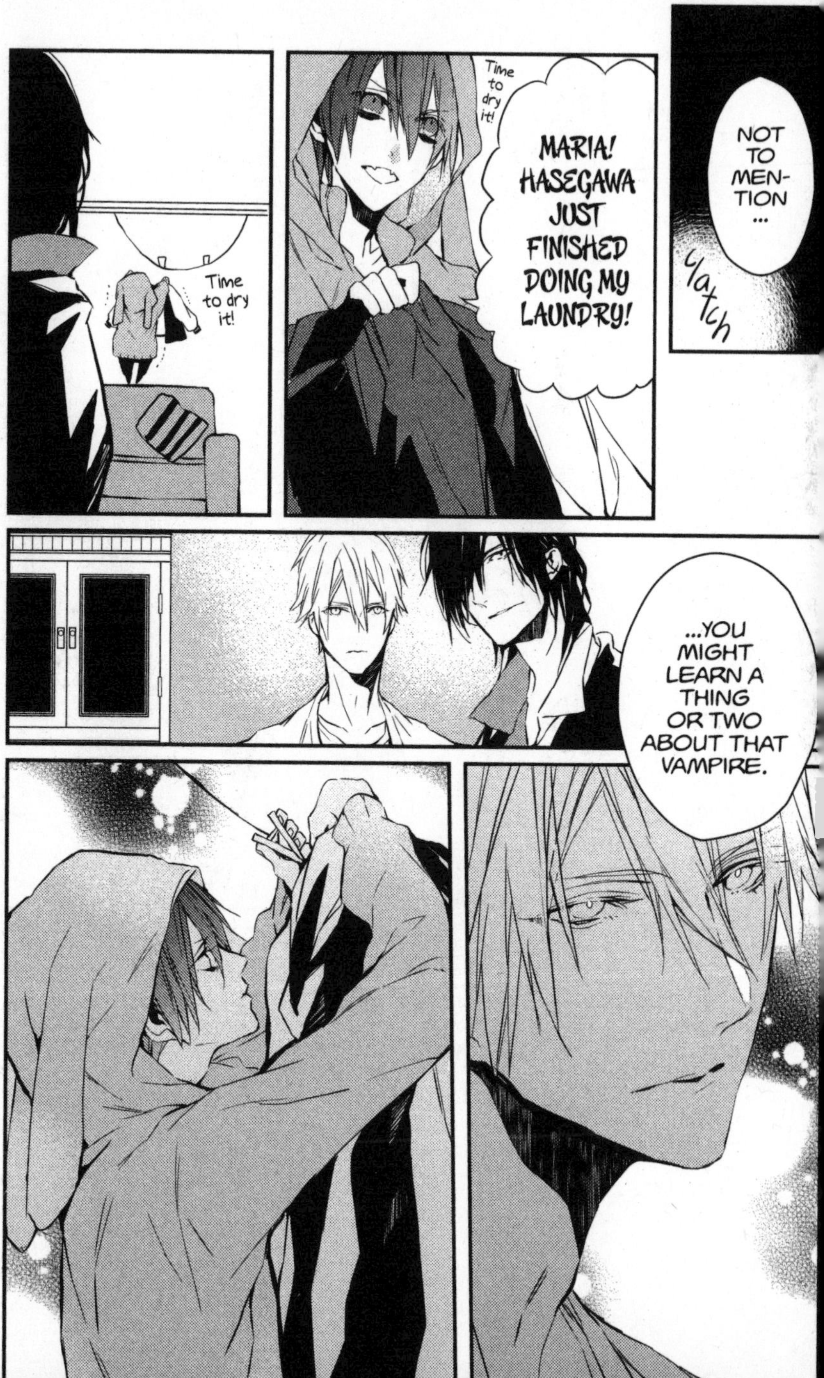
NOT TO MEN-TION...
clatch
Time to dry it!
MARIA! HASEGAWA JUST FINISHED DOING MY LAUNDRY!
Time to dry it!
...YOU MIGHT LEARN A THING OR TWO ABOUT THAT VAMPIRE.

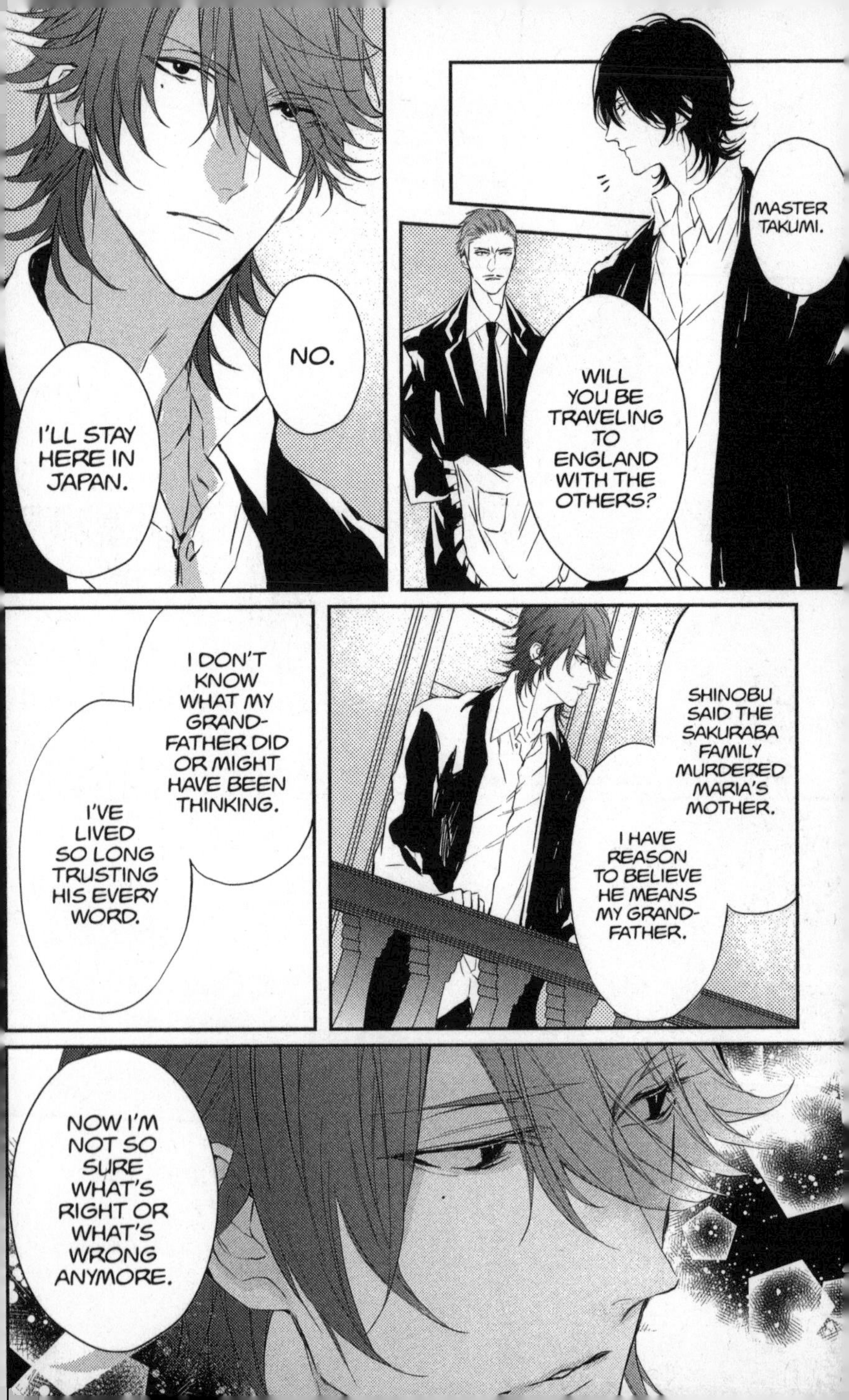
MASTER TAKUMI.
WILL YOU BE TRAVELING TO ENGLAND WITH THE OTHERS?
NO.
I'LL STAY HERE IN JAPAN.
SHINOBU SAID THE SAKURABA FAMILY MURDERED MARIA'S MOTHER.
I HAVE REASON TO BELIEVE HE MEANS MY GRAND-FATHER.
I DON'T KNOW WHAT MY GRAND-FATHER DID OR MIGHT HAVE BEEN THINKING.
I'VE LIVED SO LONG TRUSTING HIS EVERY WORD.
NOW I'M NOT SO SURE WHAT'S RIGHT OR WHAT'S WRONG ANYMORE.

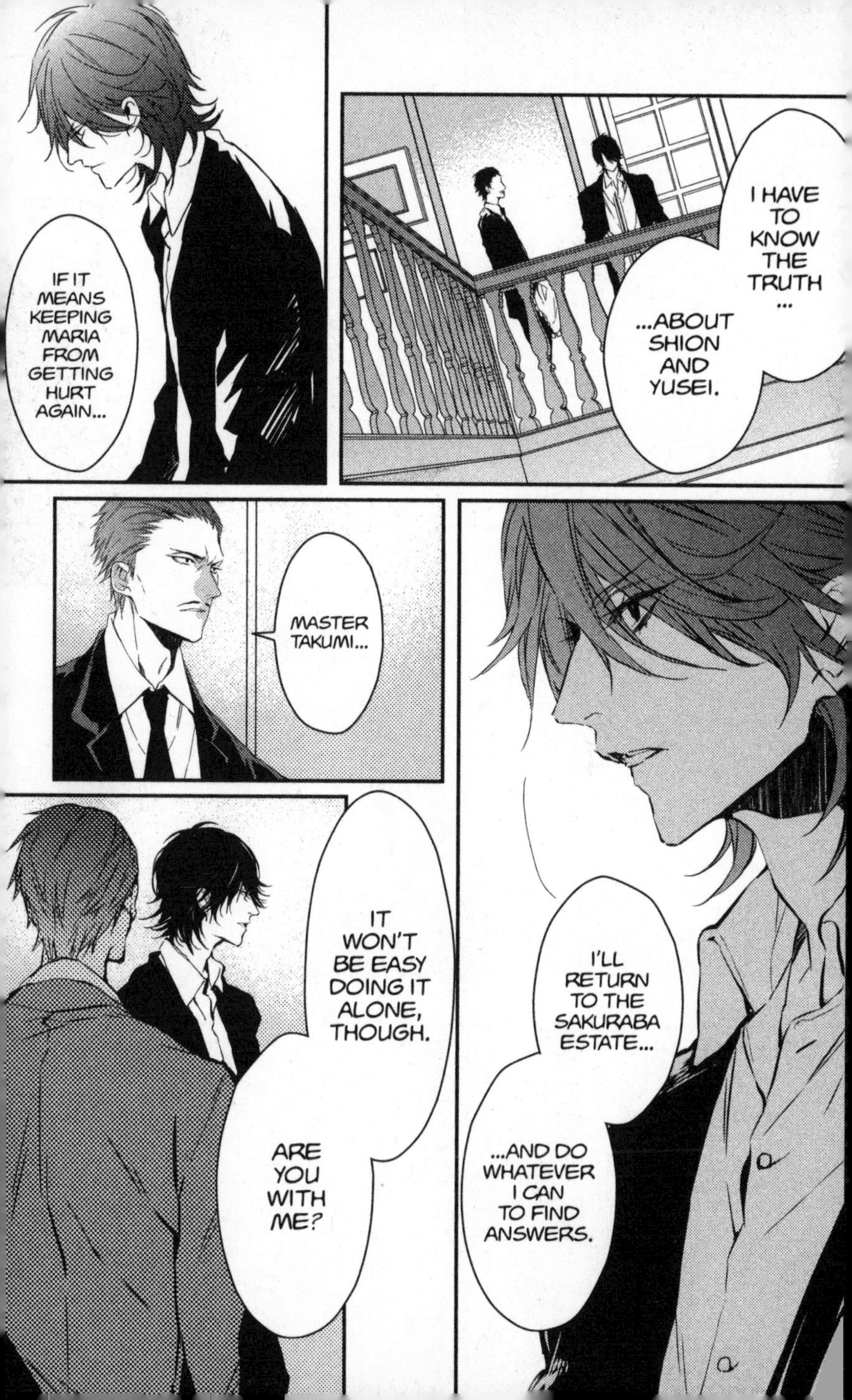
I HAVE TO KNOW THE TRUTH...
...ABOUT SHION AND YUSEI.
IF IT MEANS KEEPING MARIA FROM GETTING HURT AGAIN...
I'LL RETURN TO THE SAKURABA ESTATE...
...AND DO WHATEVER I CAN TO FIND ANSWERS.
MASTER TAKUMI...
IT WON'T BE EASY DOING IT ALONE, THOUGH.
ARE YOU WITH ME?

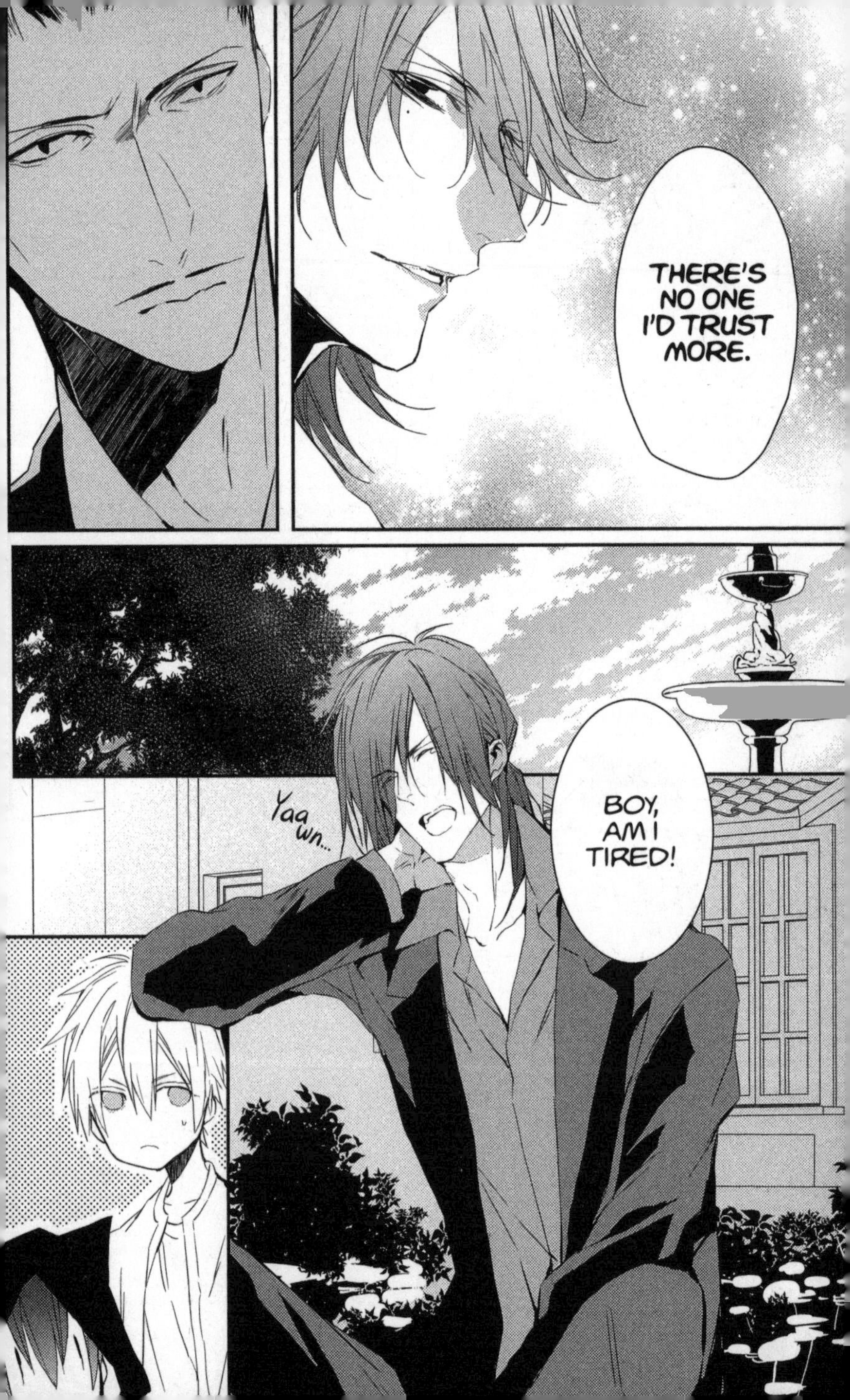
THERE'S NO ONE I'D TRUST MORE.
BOY, AM I TIRED!
Yaawn...

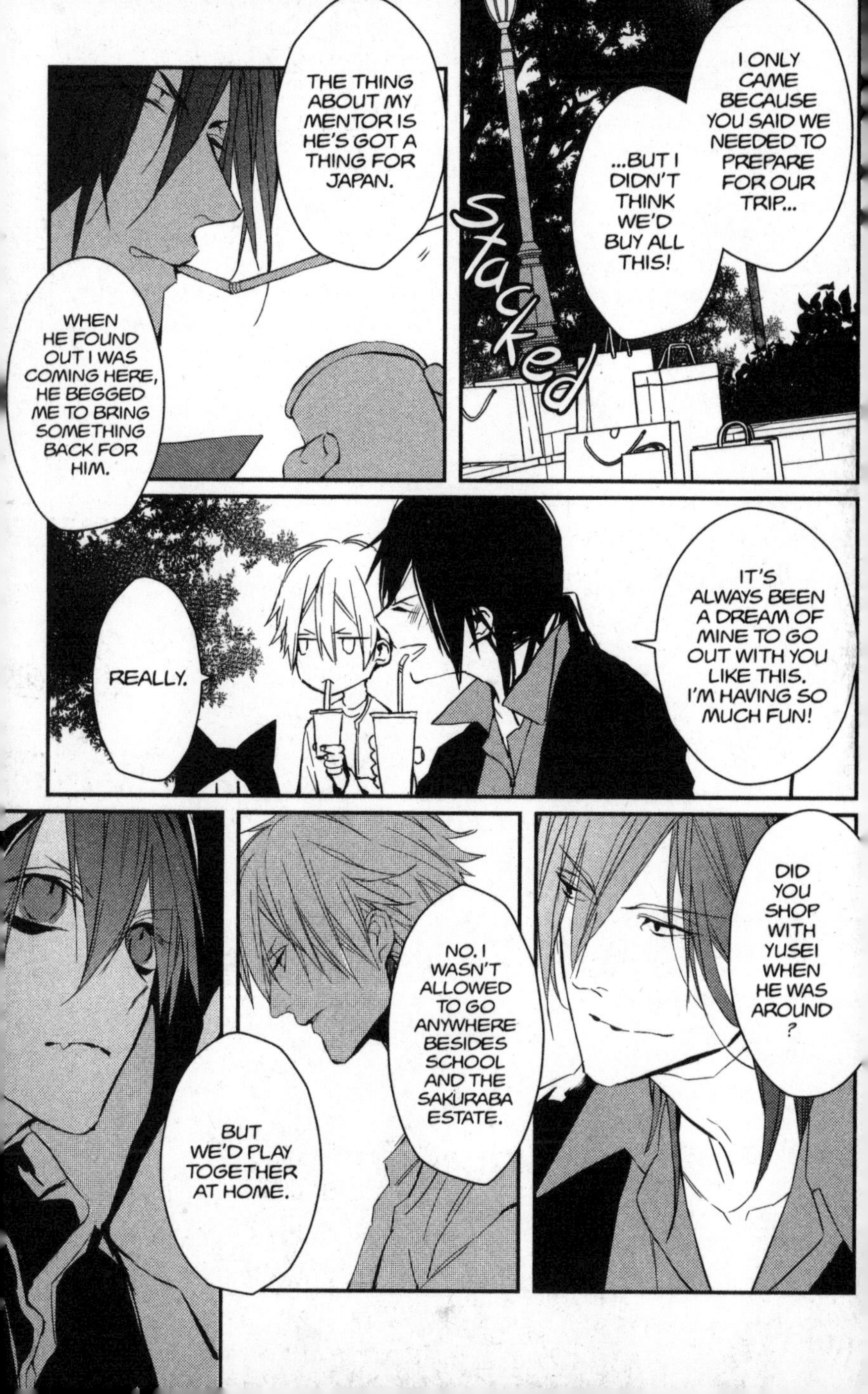
I ONLY CAME BECAUSE YOU SAID WE NEEDED TO PREPARE FOR OUR TRIP...
...BUT I DIDN'T THINK WE'D BUY ALL THIS!
Stacked
THE THING ABOUT MY MENTOR IS HE'S GOT A THING FOR JAPAN.
WHEN HE FOUND OUT I WAS COMING HERE, HE BEGGED ME TO BRING SOMETHING BACK FOR HIM.
IT'S ALWAYS BEEN A DREAM OF MINE TO GO OUT WITH YOU LIKE THIS. I'M HAVING SO MUCH FUN!
REALLY.
DID YOU SHOP WITH YUSEI WHEN HE WAS AROUND?
NO. I WASN'T ALLOWED TO GO ANYWHERE BESIDES SCHOOL AND THE SAKURABA ESTATE.
BUT WE'D PLAY TOGETHER AT HOME.

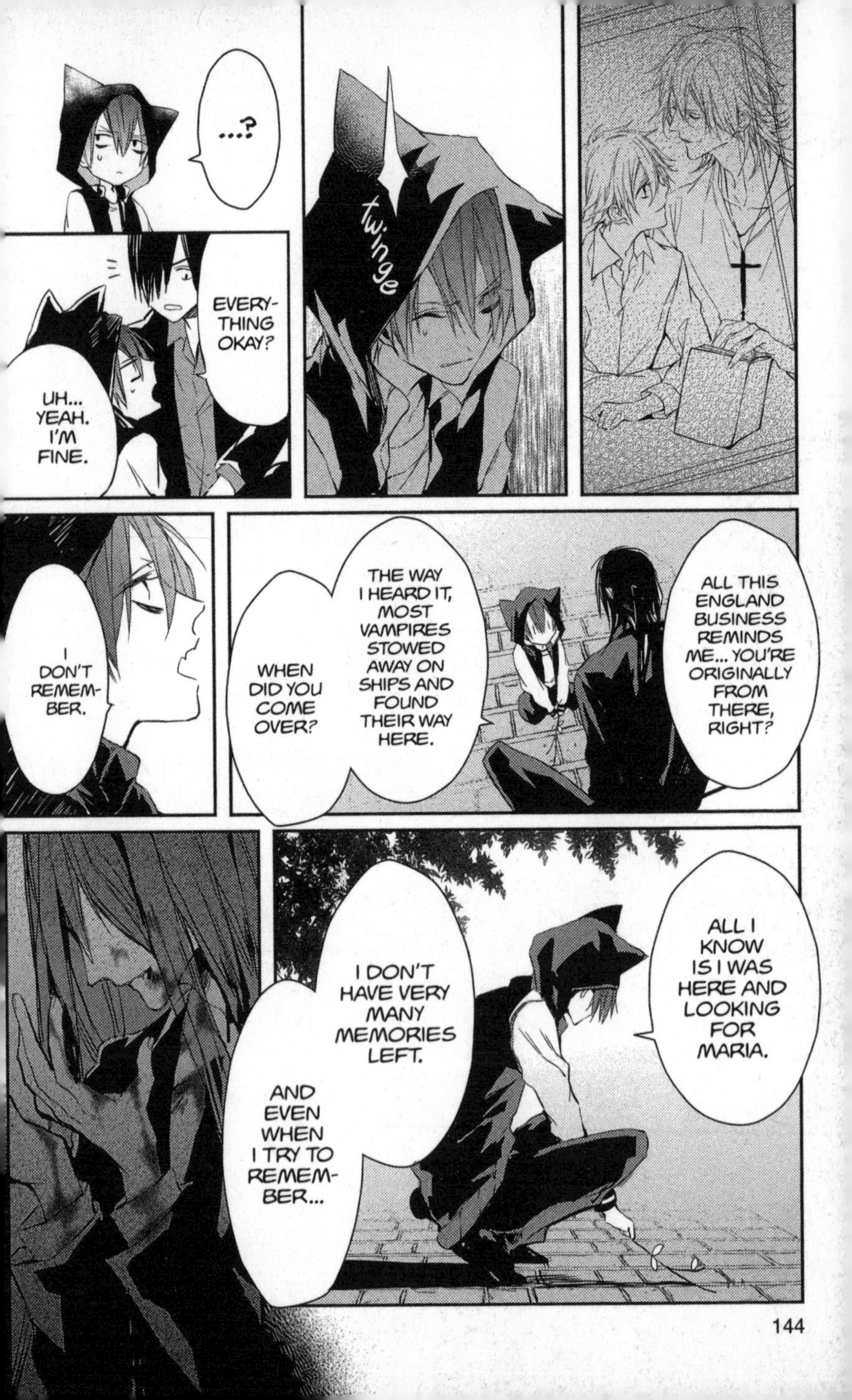
twinge
...?
EVERY-THING OKAY?
UH... YEAH. I'M FINE.
ALL THIS ENGLAND BUSINESS REMINDS ME... YOU'RE ORIGINALLY FROM THERE, RIGHT?
THE WAY I HEARD IT, MOST VAMPIRES STOWED AWAY ON SHIPS AND FOUND THEIR WAY HERE.
WHEN DID YOU COME OVER?
I DON'T REMEM-BER.
ALL I KNOW IS I WAS HERE AND LOOKING FOR MARIA.
I DON'T HAVE VERY MANY MEMORIES LEFT.
AND EVEN WHEN I TRY TO REMEM-BER...

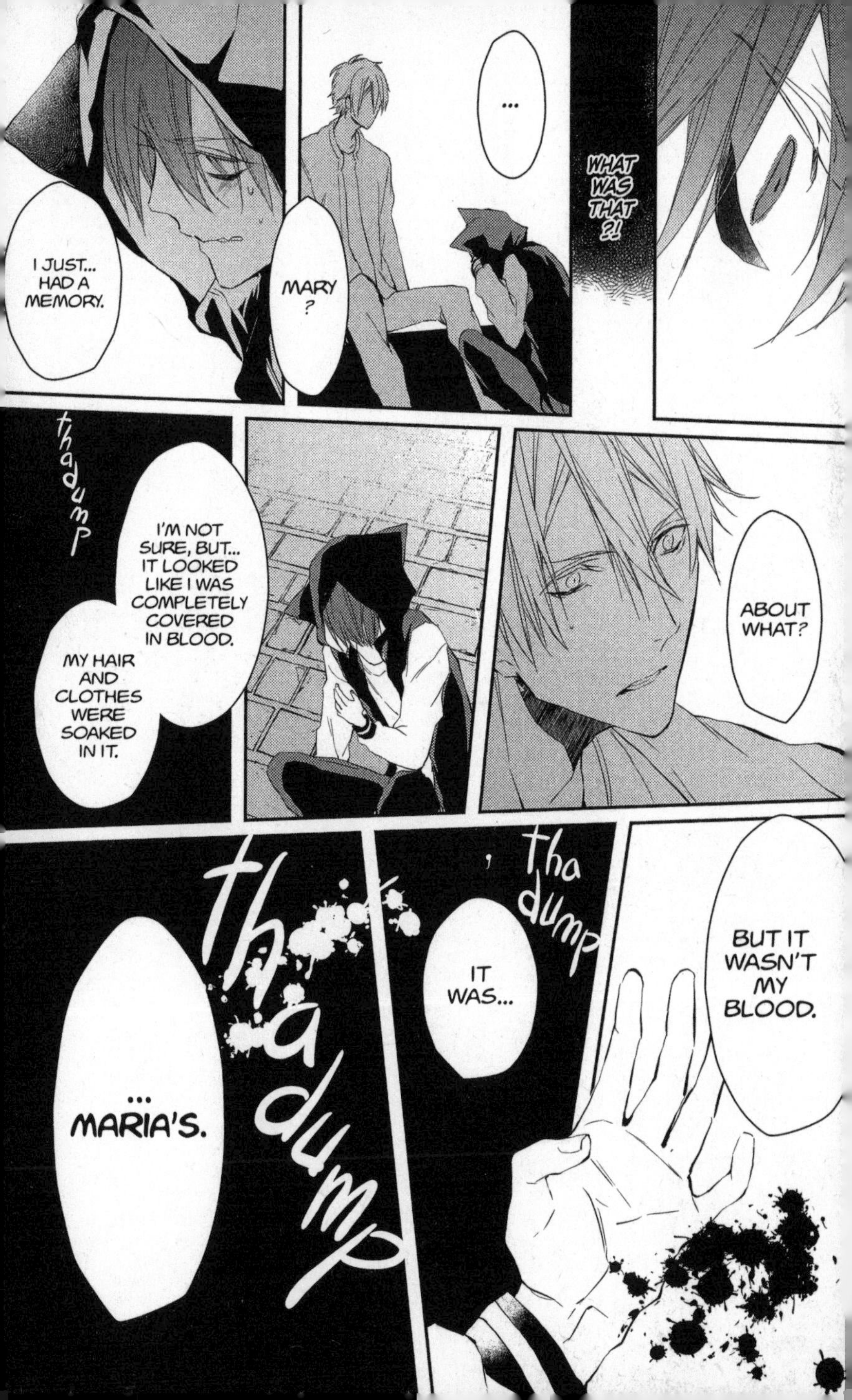
WHAT WAS THAT?!
...
MARY?
I JUST... HAD A MEMORY.
ABOUT WHAT?
I'M NOT SURE, BUT... IT LOOKED LIKE I WAS COMPLETELY COVERED IN BLOOD.
MY HAIR AND CLOTHES WERE SOAKED IN IT.
thadump
BUT IT WASN'T MY BLOOD.
tha dump
IT WAS...
tha dump
... MARIA'S.

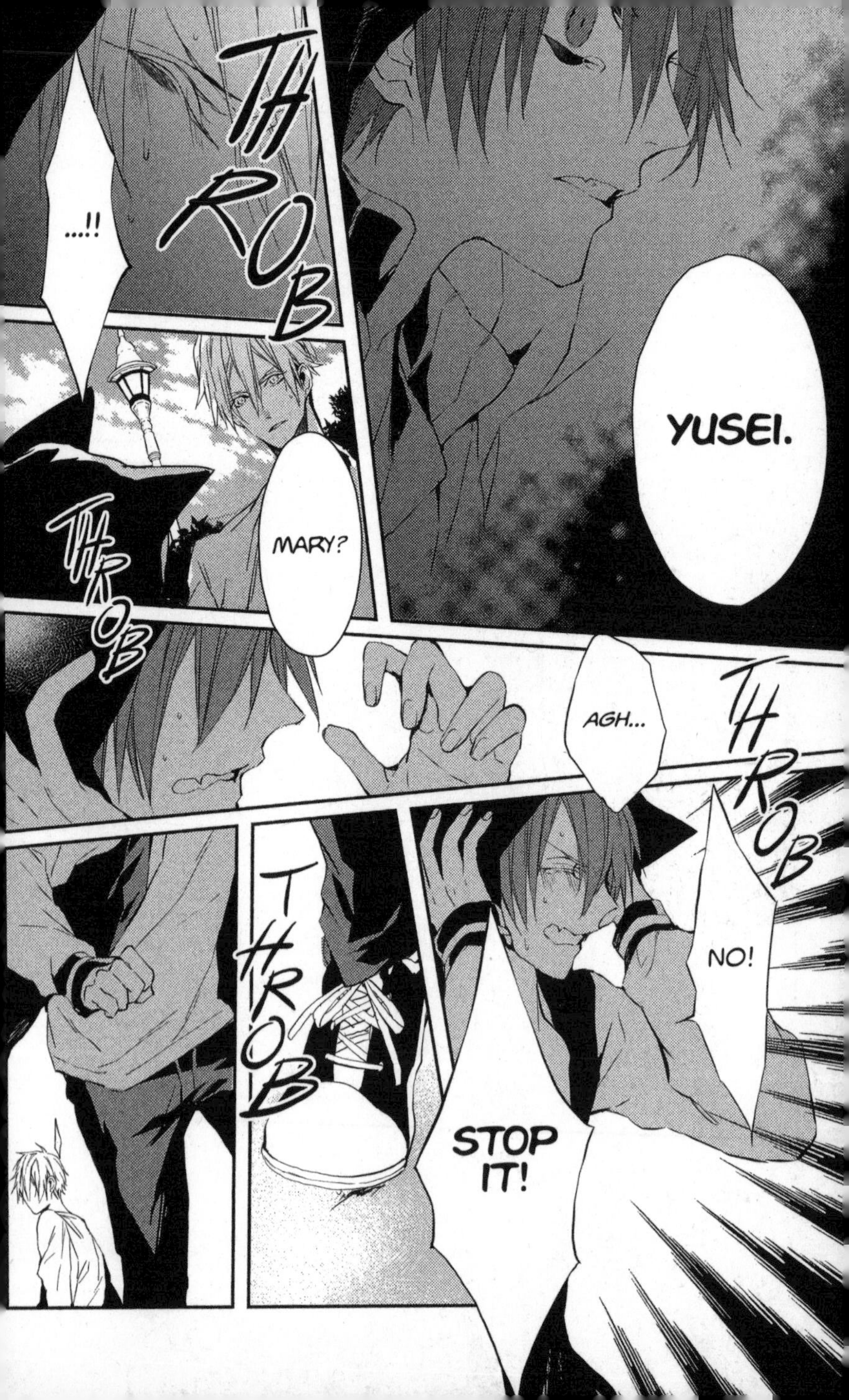
YUSEI.
THROB
...!!
MARY?
THROB
THROB
AGH...
NO!
STOP IT!
THROB

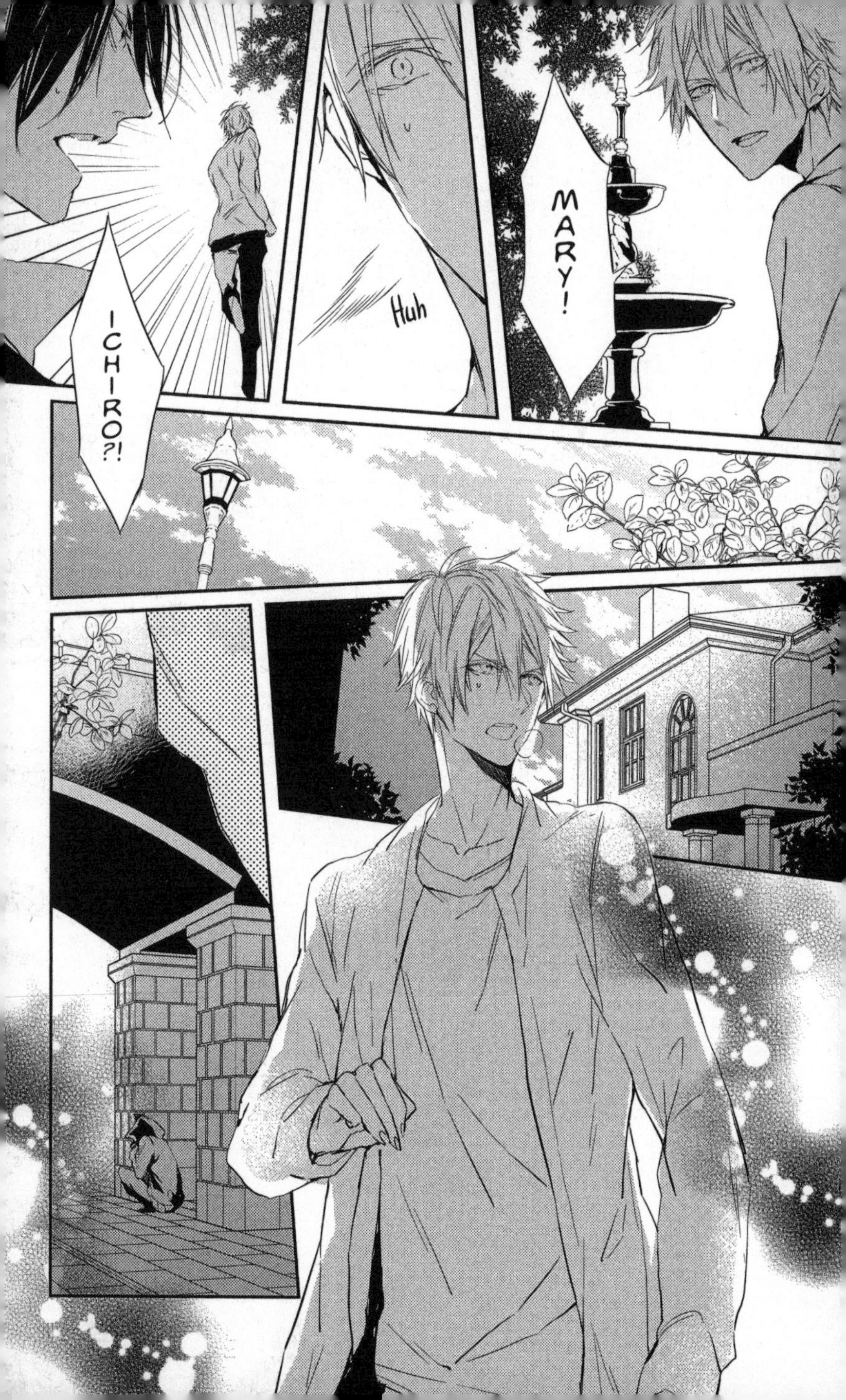
MARY!
Huh
ICHIRO?!

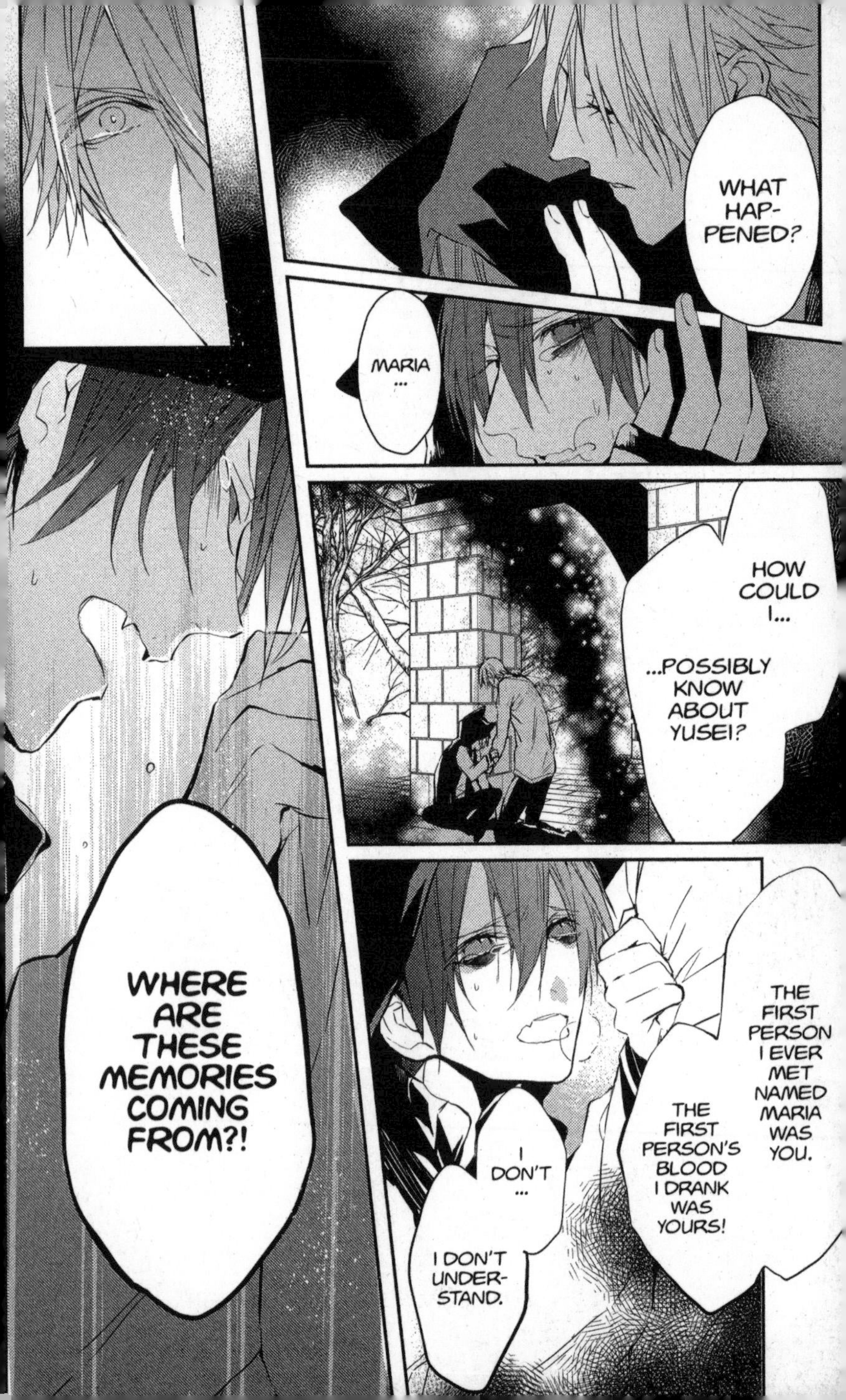
WHAT HAP-PENED?
MARIA ...
HOW COULD I...
...POSSIBLY KNOW ABOUT YUSEI?
THE FIRST PERSON I EVER MET NAMED MARIA WAS YOU.
THE FIRST PERSON'S BLOOD I DRANK WAS YOURS!
I DON'T ...
I DON'T UNDER-STAND.
WHERE ARE THESE MEMORIES COMING FROM?!

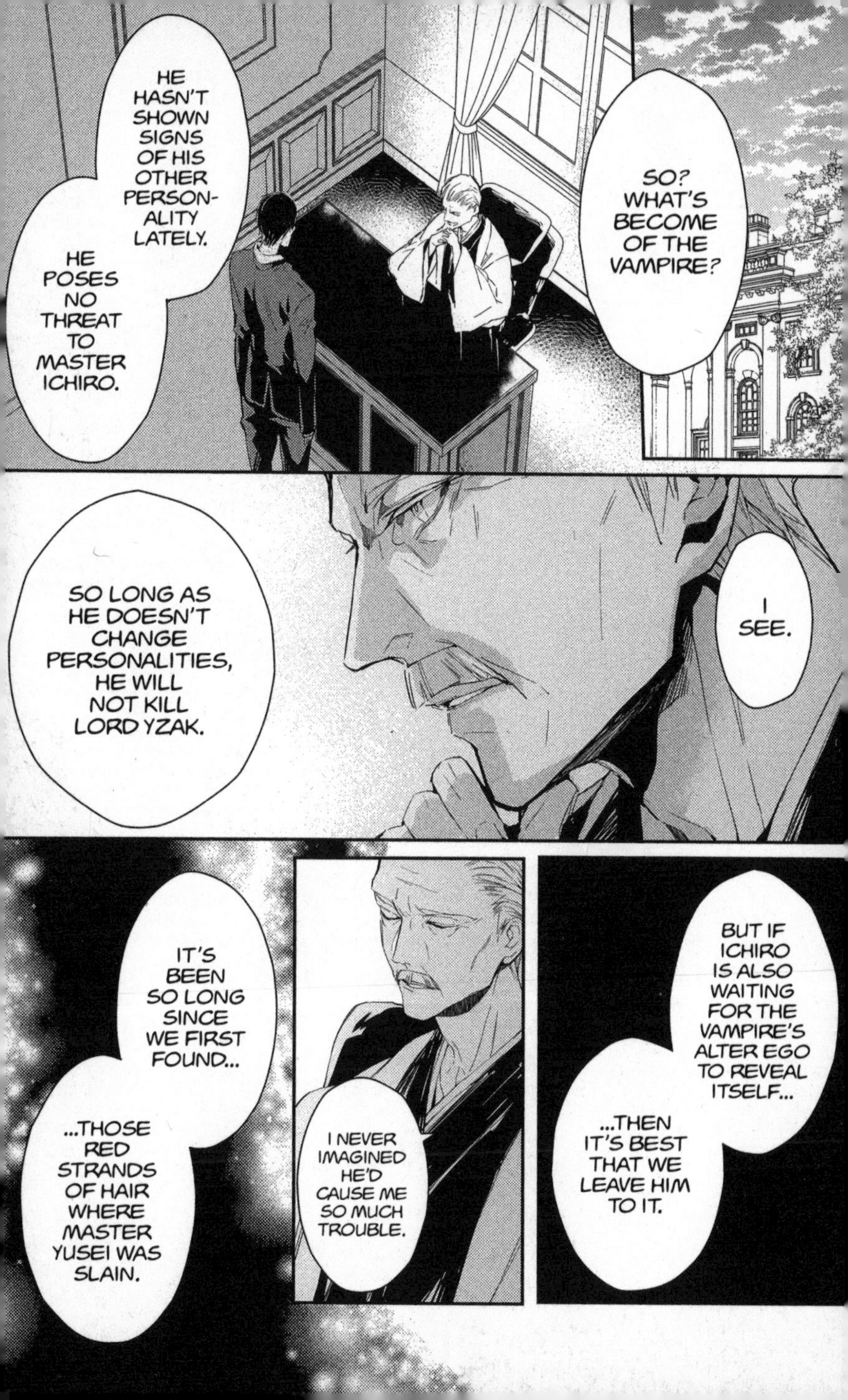
SO? WHAT'S BECOME OF THE VAMPIRE?
HE HASN'T SHOWN SIGNS OF HIS OTHER PERSON-ALITY LATELY.
HE POSES NO THREAT TO MASTER ICHIRO.
I SEE.
SO LONG AS HE DOESN'T CHANGE PERSONALITIES, HE WILL NOT KILL LORD YZAK.
BUT IF ICHIRO IS ALSO WAITING FOR THE VAMPIRE'S ALTER EGO TO REVEAL ITSELF...
...THEN IT'S BEST THAT WE LEAVE HIM TO IT.
I NEVER IMAGINED HE'D CAUSE ME SO MUCH TROUBLE.
IT'S BEEN SO LONG SINCE WE FIRST FOUND...
...THOSE RED STRANDS OF HAIR WHERE MASTER YUSEI WAS SLAIN.

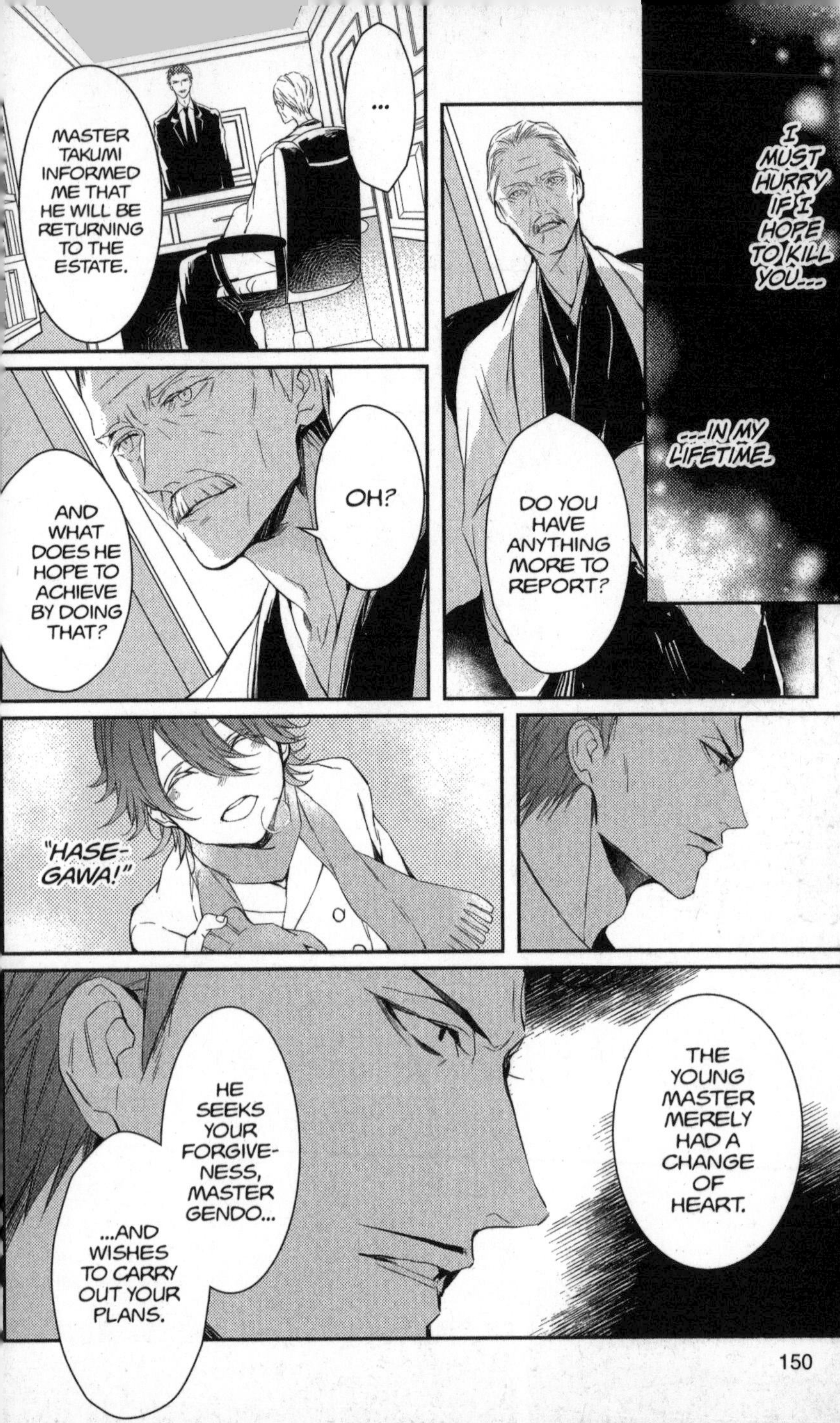
I MUST HURRY IF I HOPE TO KILL YOU...
...IN MY LIFETIME.
DO YOU HAVE ANYTHING MORE TO REPORT?
...
MASTER TAKUMI INFORMED ME THAT HE WILL BE RETURNING TO THE ESTATE.
OH?
AND WHAT DOES HE HOPE TO ACHIEVE BY DOING THAT?
"HASE-GAWA!"
THE YOUNG MASTER MERELY HAD A CHANGE OF HEART.
HE SEEKS YOUR FORGIVE-NESS, MASTER GENDO...
...AND WISHES TO CARRY OUT YOUR PLANS.

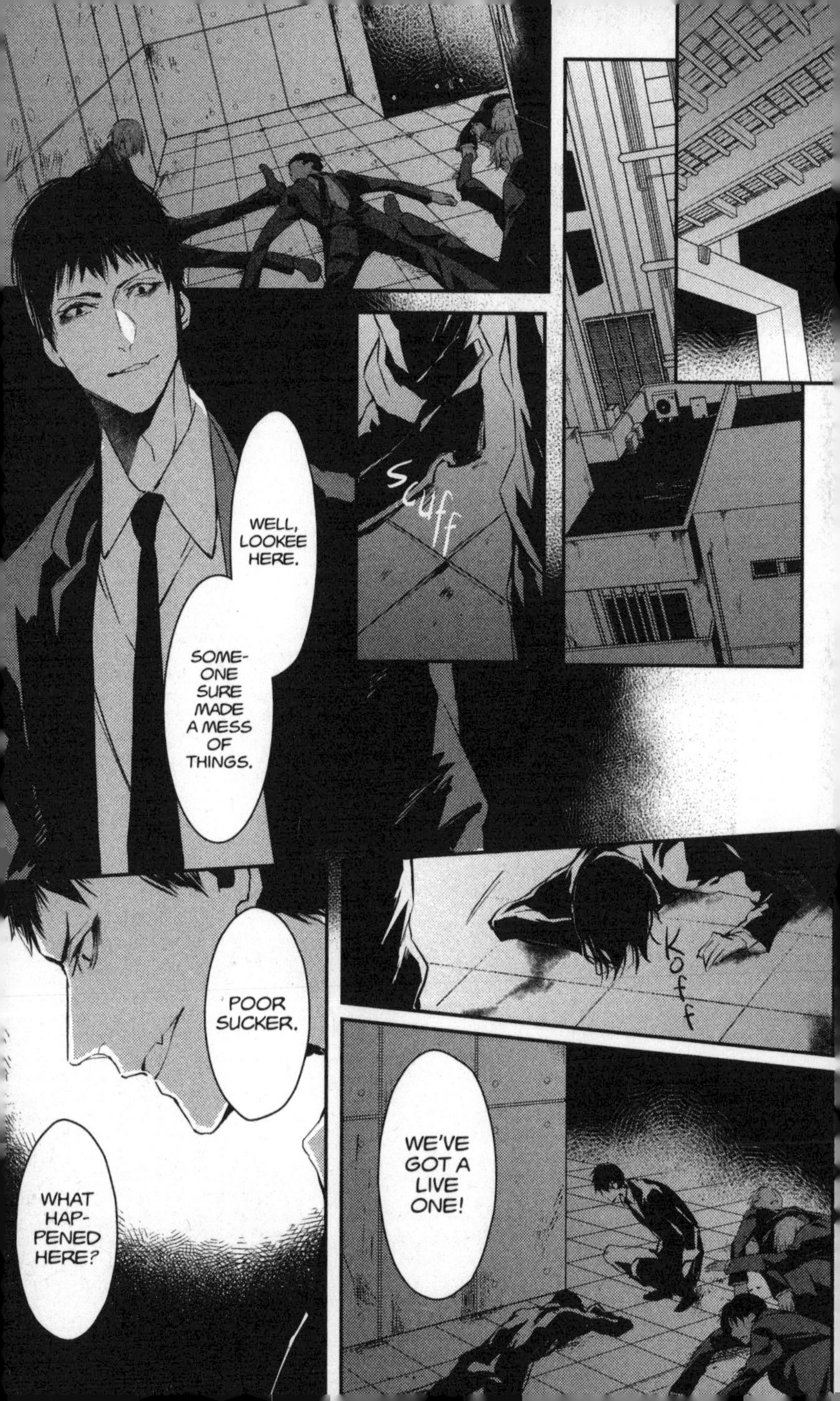
SCUFF
WELL, LOOKEE HERE.
SOME-ONE SURE MADE A MESS OF THINGS.
KOFF
POOR SUCKER.
WHAT HAP-PENED HERE?
WE'VE GOT A LIVE ONE!

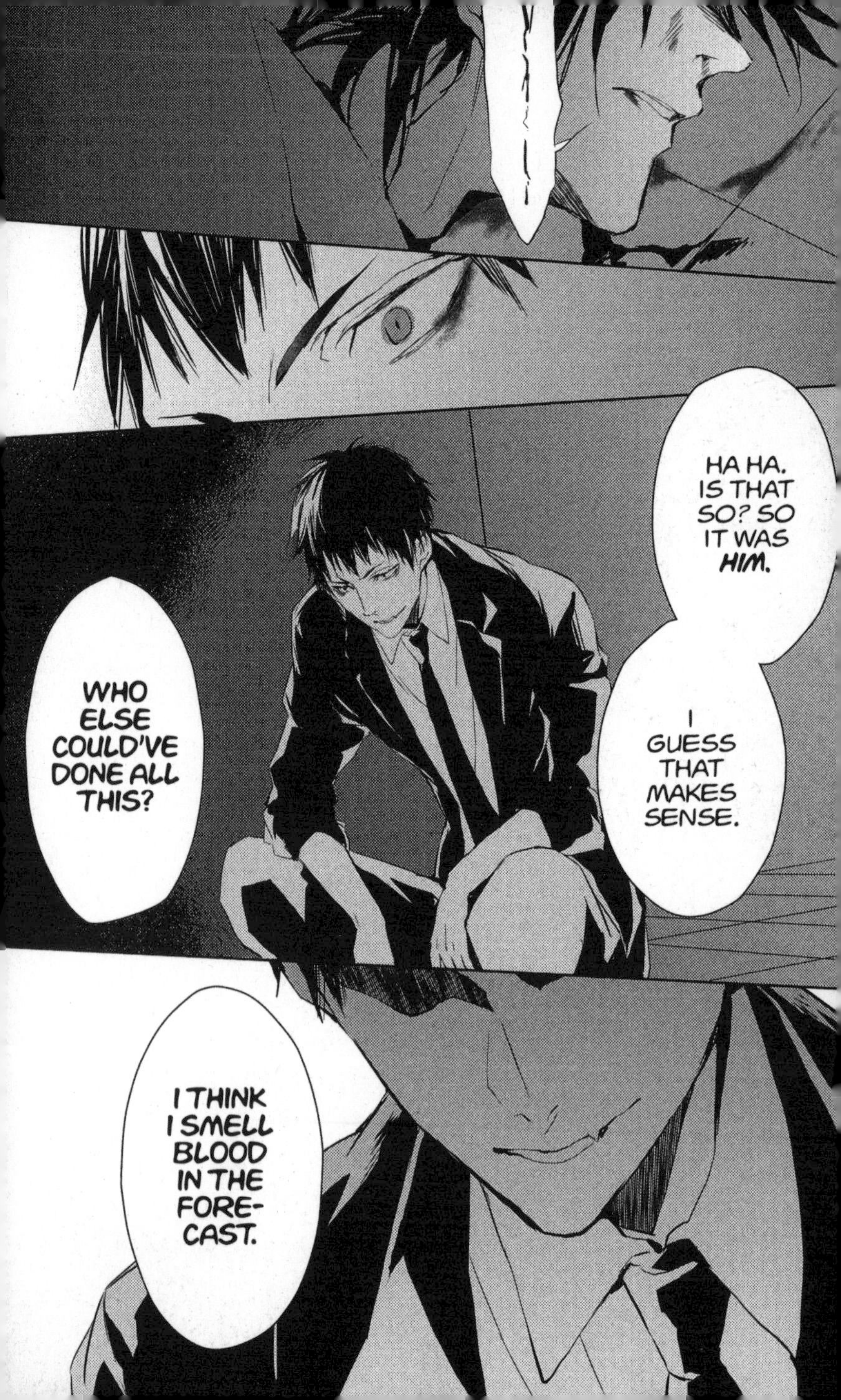
HA HA. IS THAT SO? SO IT WAS *HIM*.
I GUESS THAT MAKES SENSE.
WHO ELSE COULD'VE DONE ALL THIS?
I THINK I SMELL BLOOD IN THE FORE-CAST.

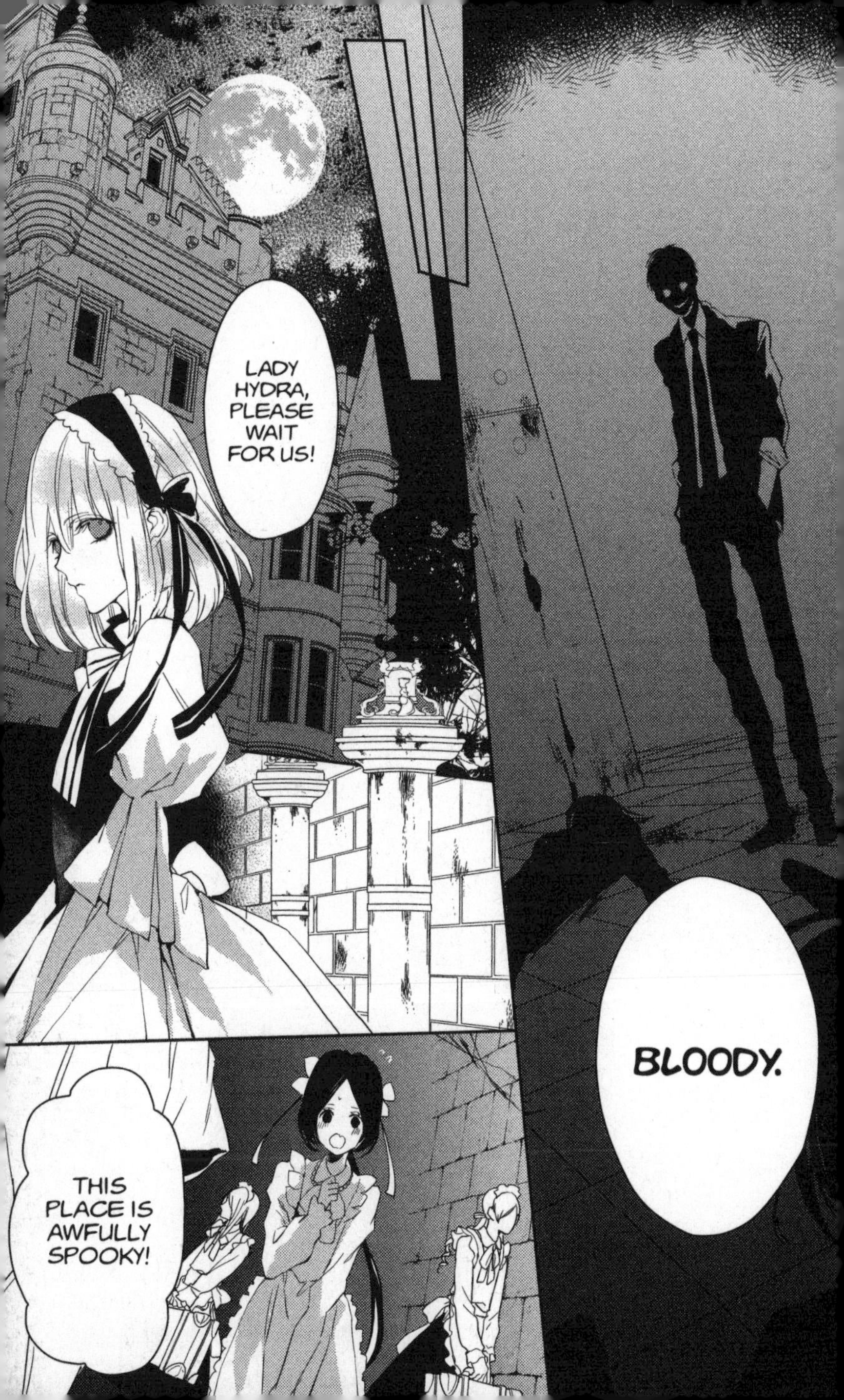
BLOODY.
LADY HYDRA, PLEASE WAIT FOR US!
THIS PLACE IS AWFULLY SPOOKY!

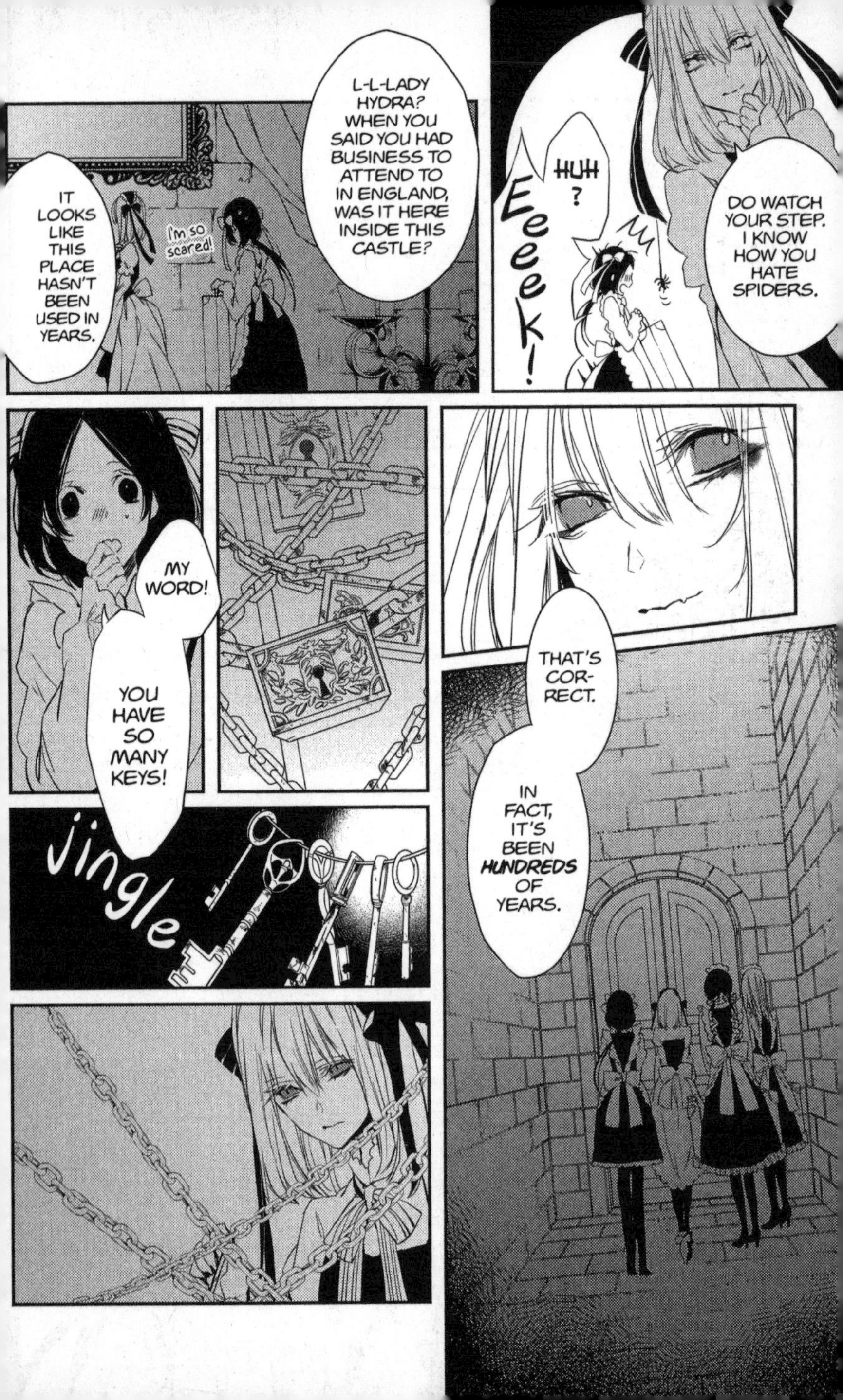
DO WATCH YOUR STEP. I KNOW HOW YOU HATE SPIDERS.
HUH?
Eeeek!
L-L-LADY HYDRA? WHEN YOU SAID YOU HAD BUSINESS TO ATTEND TO IN ENGLAND, WAS IT HERE INSIDE THIS CASTLE?
I'm so scared!
IT LOOKS LIKE THIS PLACE HASN'T BEEN USED IN YEARS.
THAT'S COR-RECT.
MY WORD!
YOU HAVE SO MANY KEYS!
IN FACT, IT'S BEEN **HUNDREDS** OF YEARS.
jingle

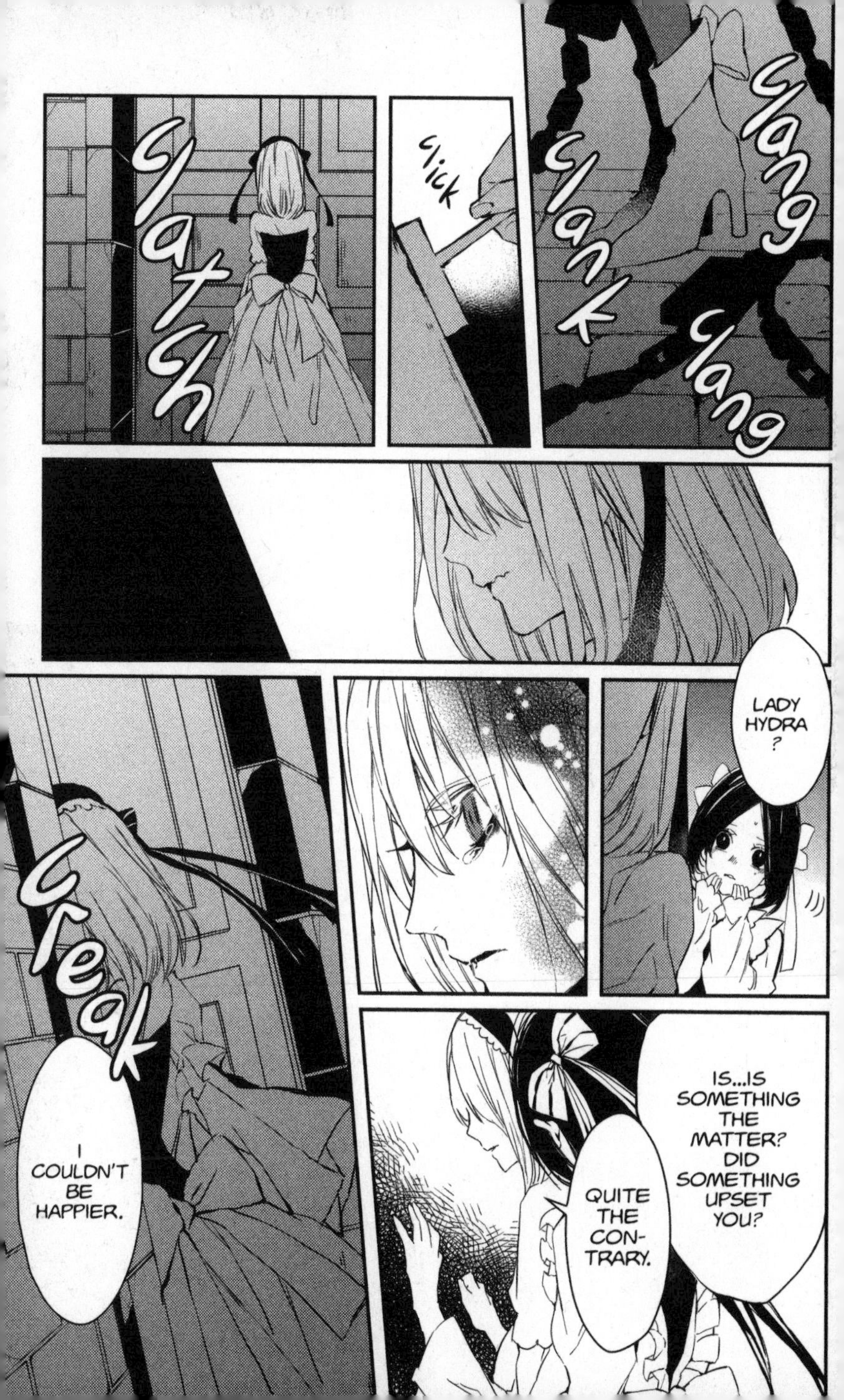

clang
clank
clang
click
clatch
LADY HYDRA?
IS...IS SOMETHING THE MATTER? DID SOMETHING UPSET YOU?
QUITE THE CON-TRARY.
creak
I COULDN'T BE HAPPIER.

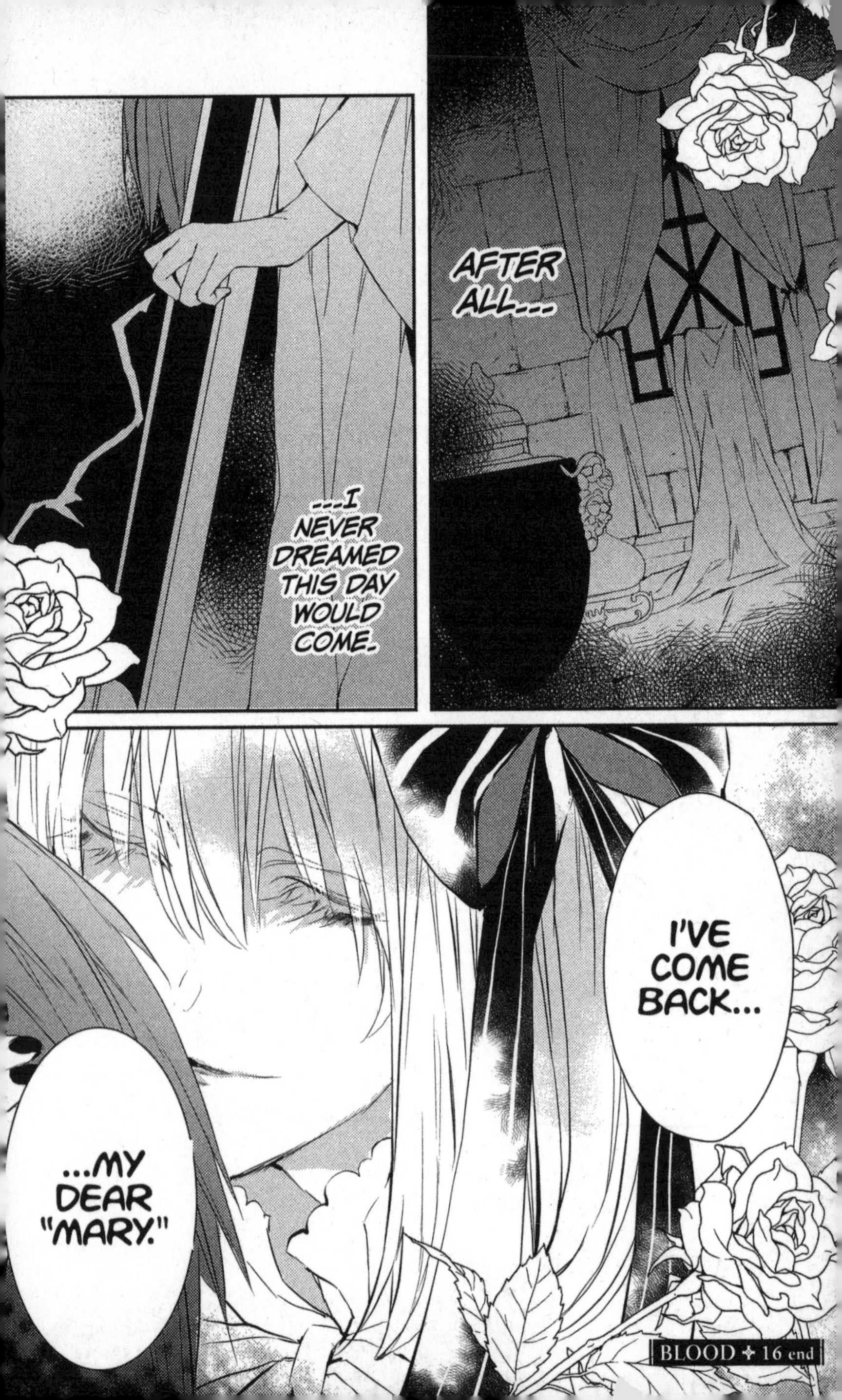
AFTER ALL...
...I NEVER DREAMED THIS DAY WOULD COME.
I'VE COME BACK...
...MY DEAR "MARY."

BLOOD ✦ 16 end

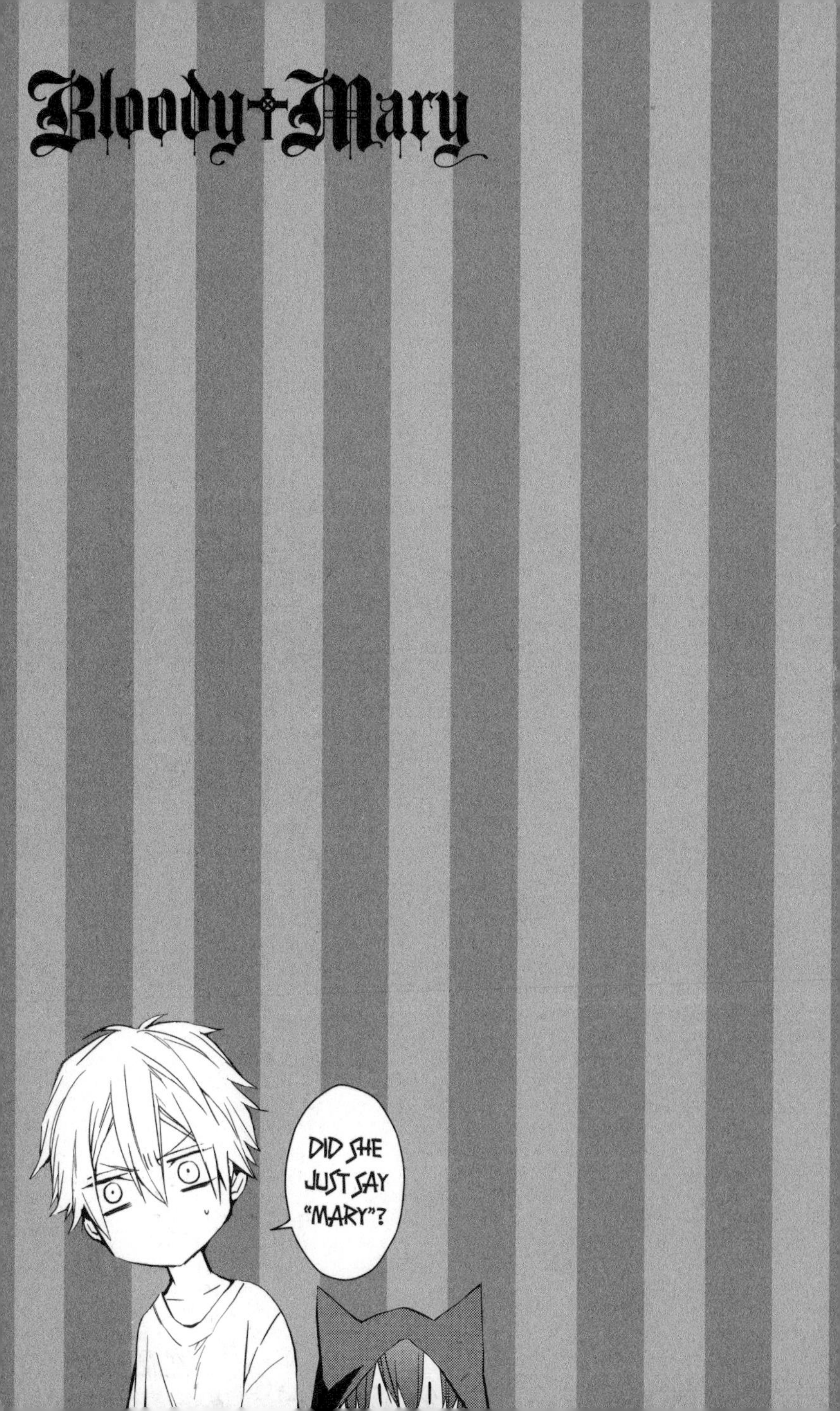
Bloody+Mary
DID SHE JUST SAY "MARY"?

Bloody+Mary

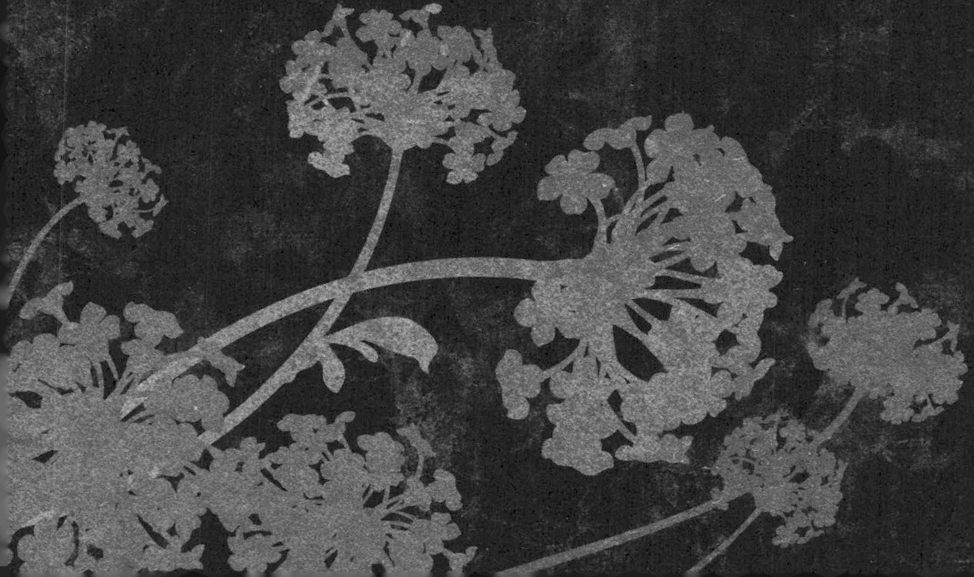

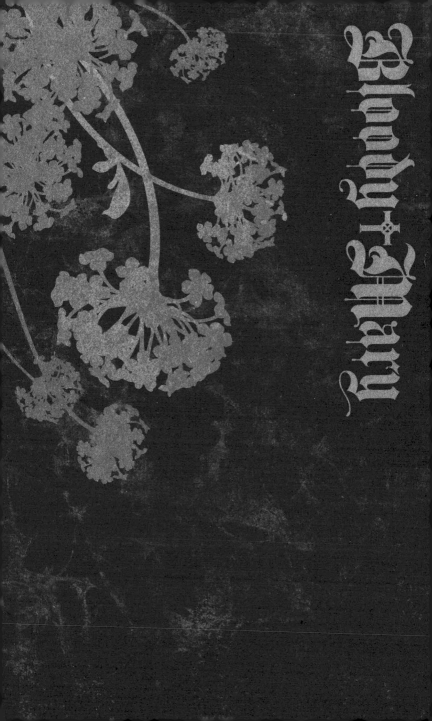

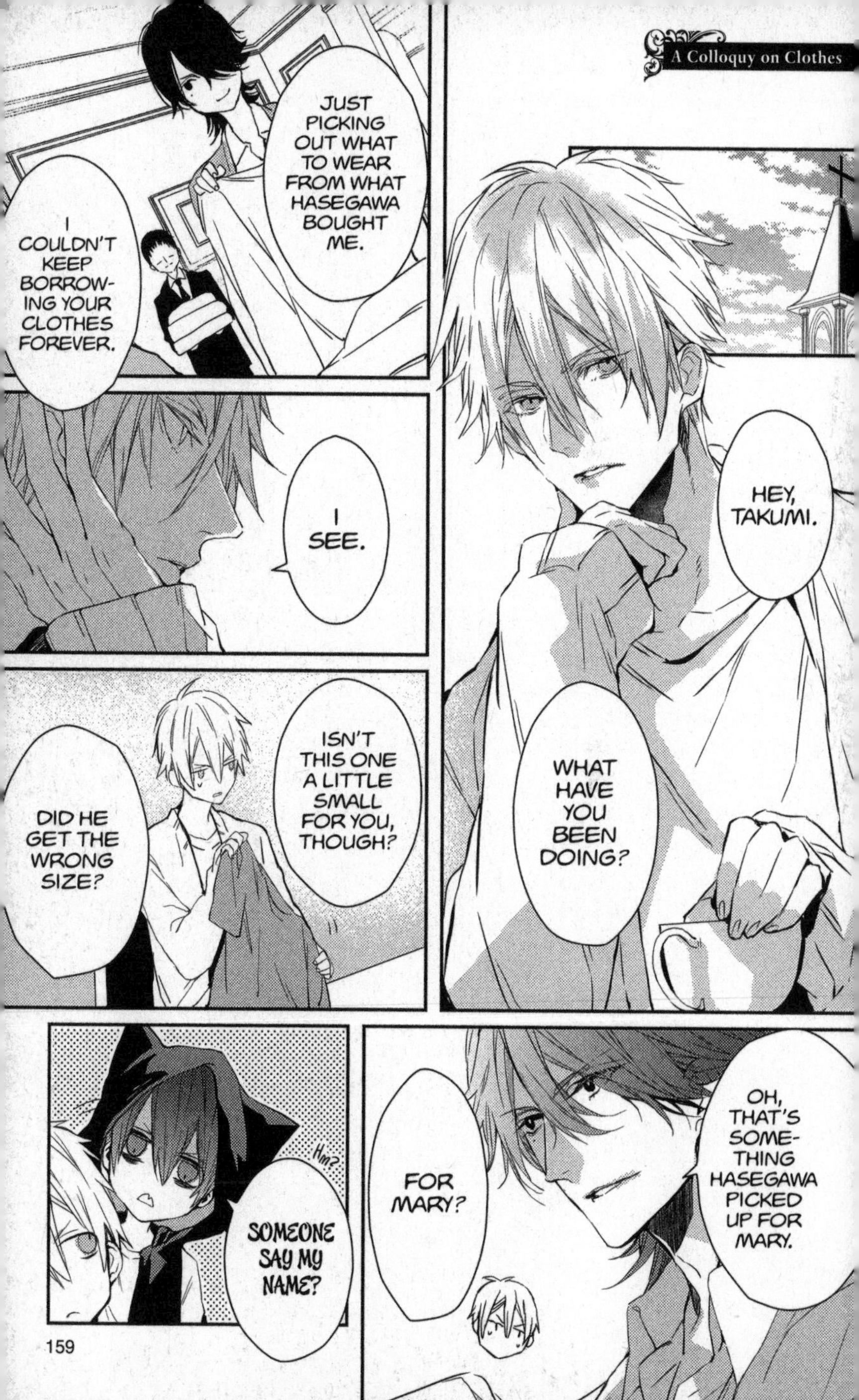
HEY, TAKUMI.
WHAT HAVE YOU BEEN DOING?
JUST PICKING OUT WHAT TO WEAR FROM WHAT HASEGAWA BOUGHT ME.
I COULDN'T KEEP BORROW-ING YOUR CLOTHES FOREVER.
I SEE.
ISN'T THIS ONE A LITTLE SMALL FOR YOU, THOUGH?
DID HE GET THE WRONG SIZE?
OH, THAT'S SOME-THING HASEGAWA PICKED UP FOR MARY.
FOR MARY?
Hm?
SOMEONE SAY MY NAME?

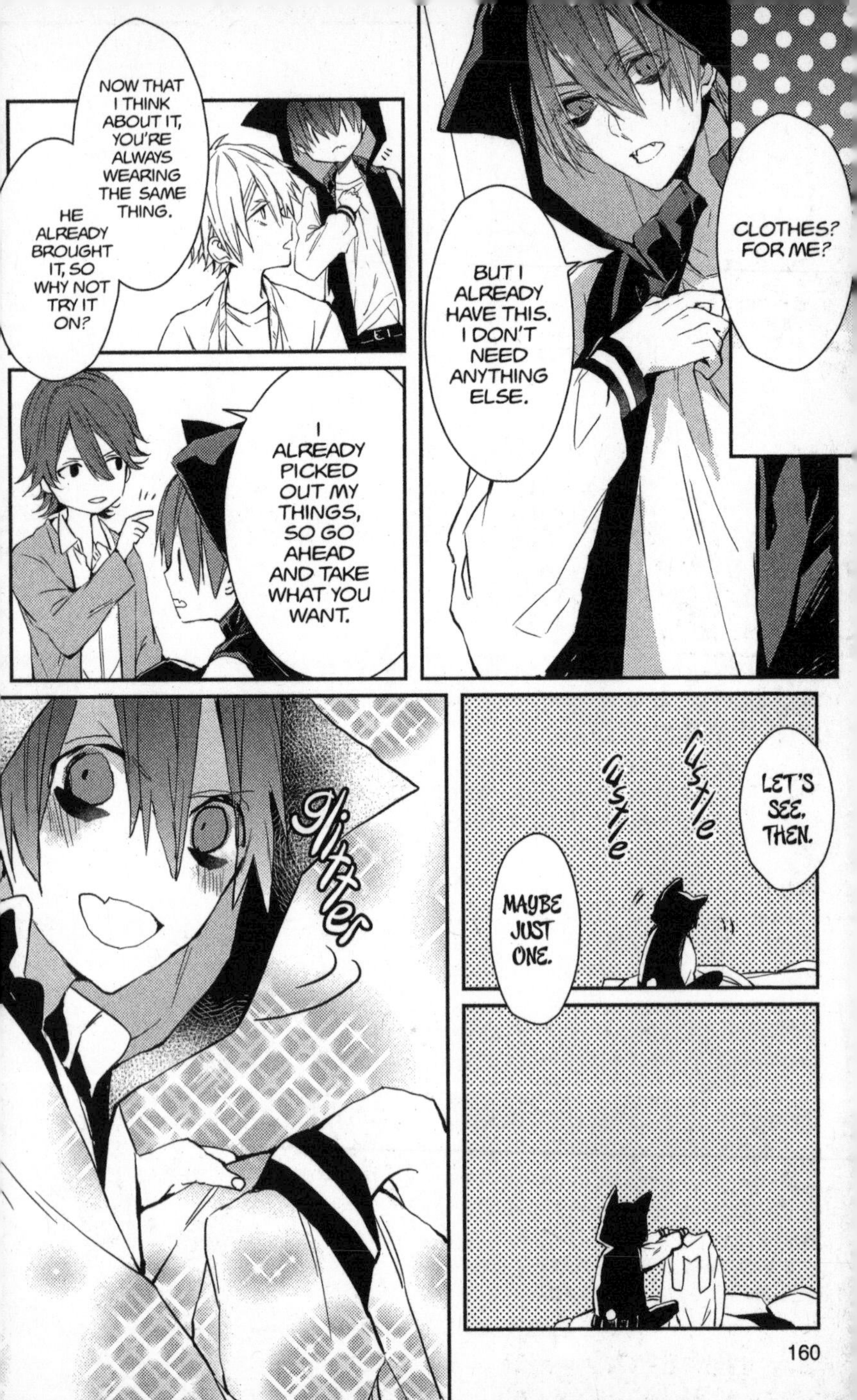
CLOTHES? FOR ME?
BUT I ALREADY HAVE THIS. I DON'T NEED ANYTHING ELSE.
NOW THAT I THINK ABOUT IT, YOU'RE ALWAYS WEARING THE SAME THING.
HE ALREADY BROUGHT IT, SO WHY NOT TRY IT ON?
I ALREADY PICKED OUT MY THINGS, SO GO AHEAD AND TAKE WHAT YOU WANT.
LET'S SEE, THEN.
rustle
rustle
MAYBE JUST ONE.
glitter

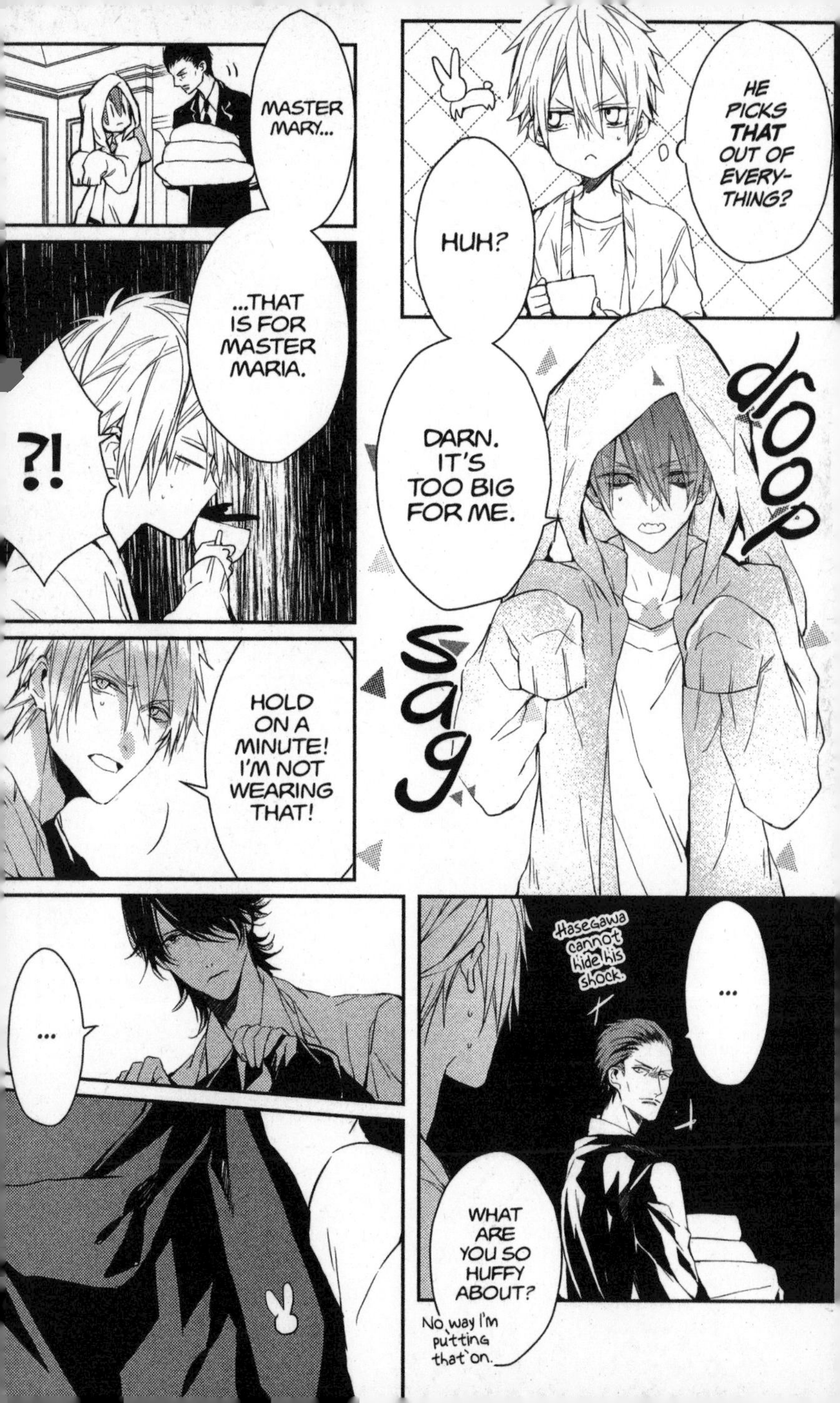
HE PICKS THAT OUT OF EVERYTHING?
HUH?
DARN. IT'S TOO BIG FOR ME.
droop
sag
MASTER MARY...
...THAT IS FOR MASTER MARIA.
?!
HOLD ON A MINUTE! I'M NOT WEARING THAT!
...
Hasegawa cannot hide his shock.
WHAT ARE YOU SO HUFFY ABOUT?
No way I'm putting that on.
...

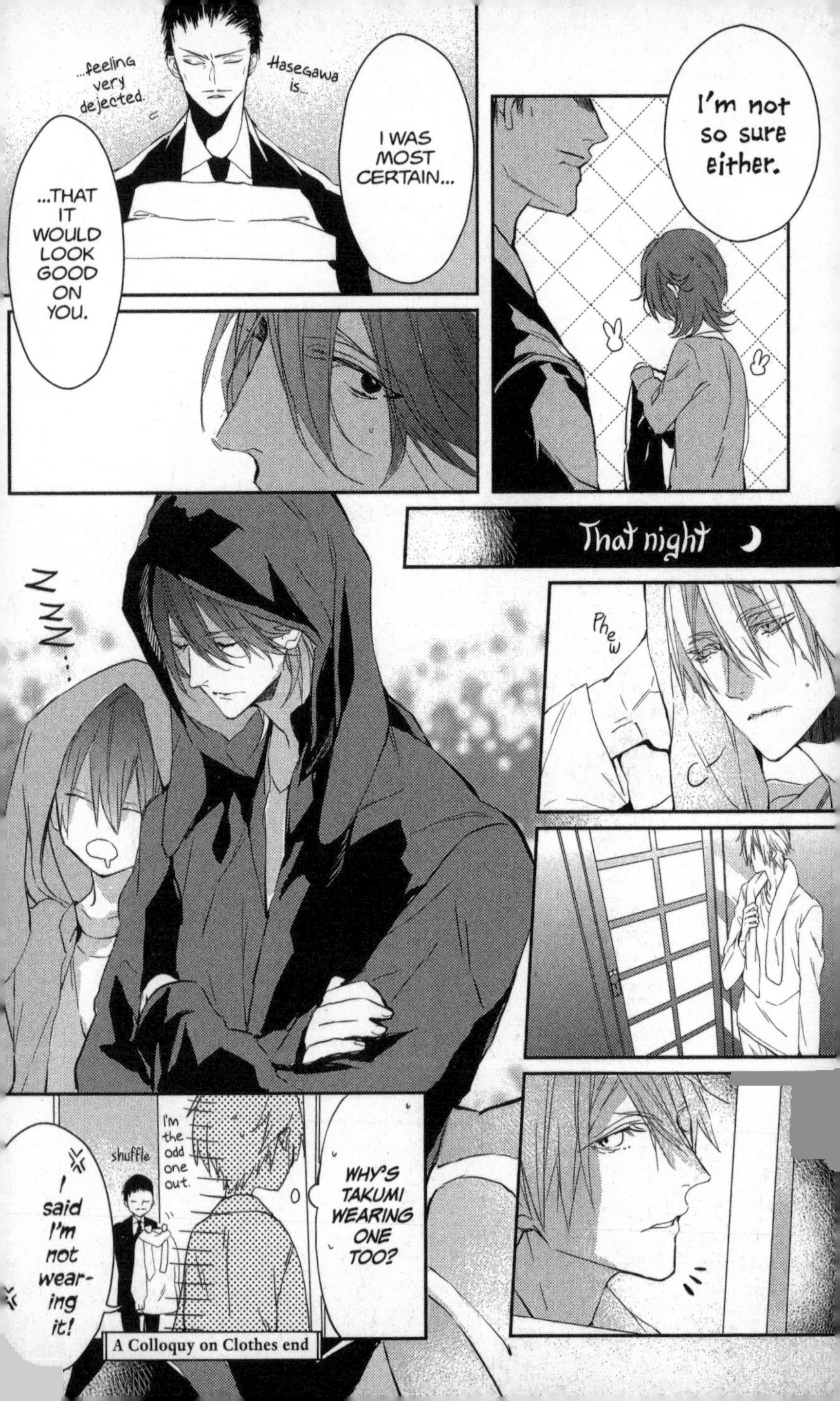
I'm not so sure either.
I WAS MOST CERTAIN...
Hasegawa is...
...feeling very dejected.
...THAT IT WOULD LOOK GOOD ON YOU.
That night
Phew
ZZZ...
WHY'S TAKUMI WEARING ONE TOO?
I'm the odd one out.
shuffle
I said I'm not wearing it!
A Colloquy on Clothes end

Postscript

★ Hello! This is Akaza Samamiya! I always feel down about how difficult it is to draw manga, but thanks to all your support, we've reached volume 4! Thank you so much for picking it up!

RANDOM INFO

★ When it comes to the characters' names, it can get pretty hard to keep them all straight. My editor is always asking me, "Wait. ***Which*** Mary is it?" So we've started calling our regular Mary "the M one" for "masochist."

★ I bought a kettle recently. I'm making progress!

★ Summer or winter, I cook almost every meal in a pot.

We're going to learn more about the mysterious "Mary" in the next volume. I hope you stick around to find out what happens!

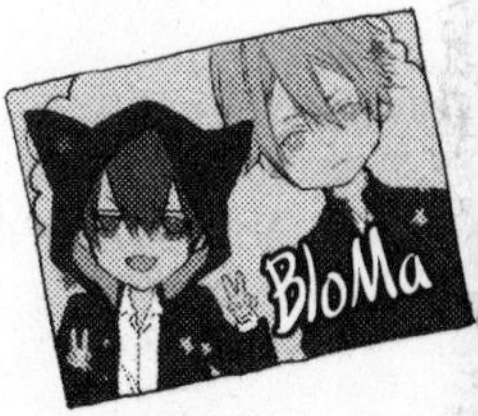
BloMa
The photo booth pictures we gave away at my last autograph session (school-uniform version).

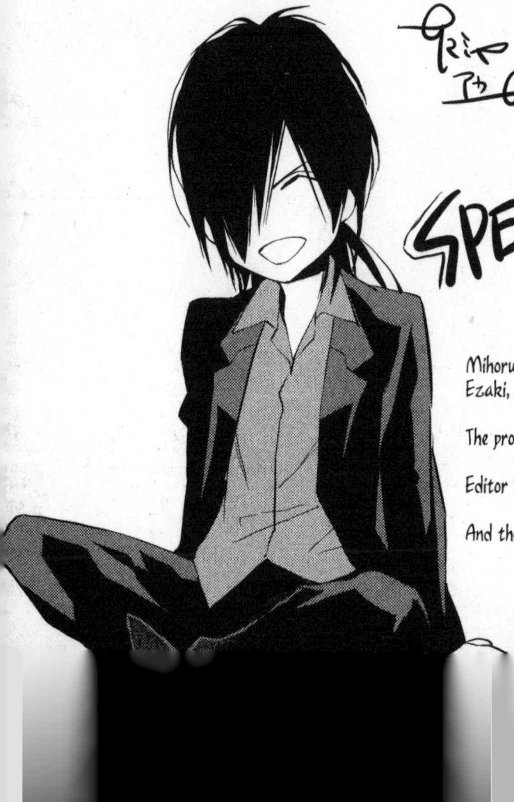

SPECIAL THANKS

Mihoru, H-saka, M-fuchi, H-gawa, T-mizu, Ezaki, Madam, T-ko, Y-tani.

The production team, Haruo, Sumida, M-ika.

Editor S, the designers, everyone who supported me.

And the readers!

twitterID samamiya
http://sama.ciao.jp

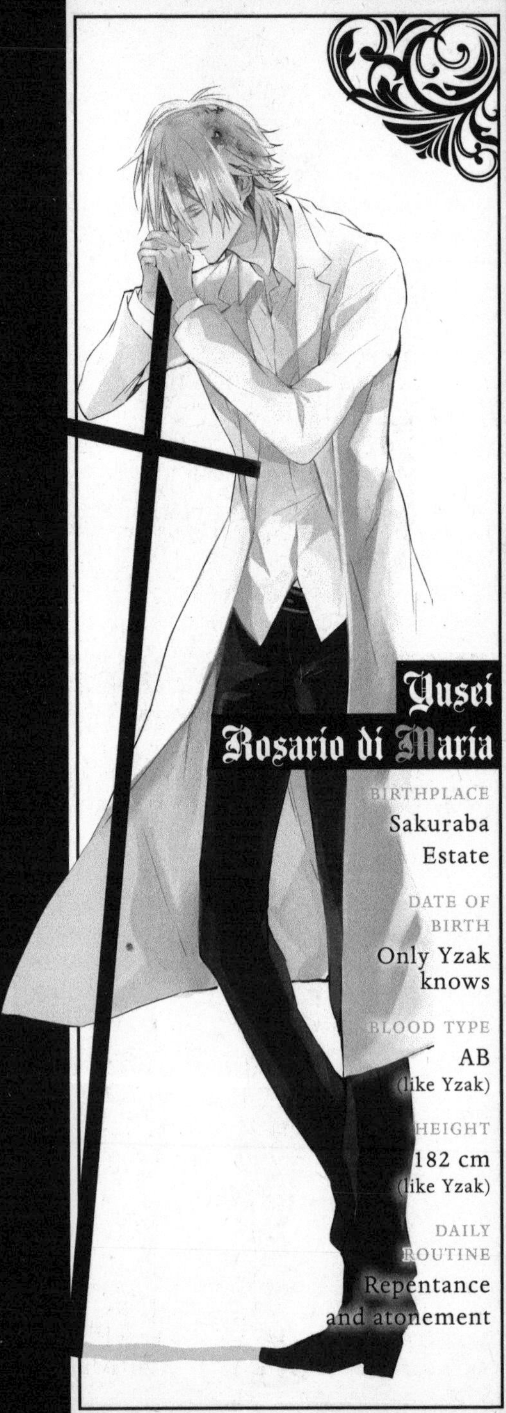

Yusei Rosario di Maria

BIRTHPLACE
Sakuraba Estate

DATE OF BIRTH
Only Yzak knows

BLOOD TYPE
AB
(like Yzak)

HEIGHT
182 cm
(like Yzak)

DAILY ROUTINE
Repentance and atonement

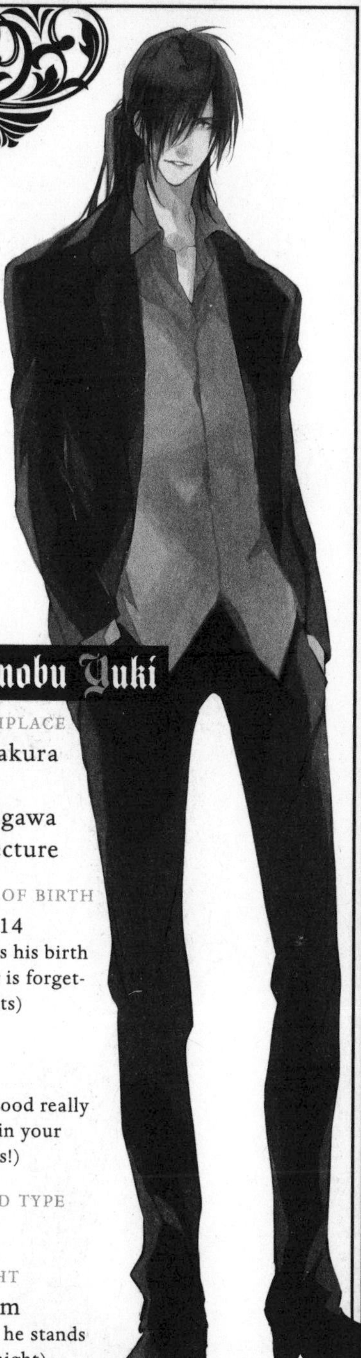

Shinobu Yuki

BIRTHPLACE

Kamakura City, Kanagawa Prefecture

DATE OF BIRTH

May 14
(knows his birth flower is forget-me-nots)

AGE

34
(manhood really starts in your thirties!)

BLOOD TYPE

O

HEIGHT

198 cm
(when he stands up straight)

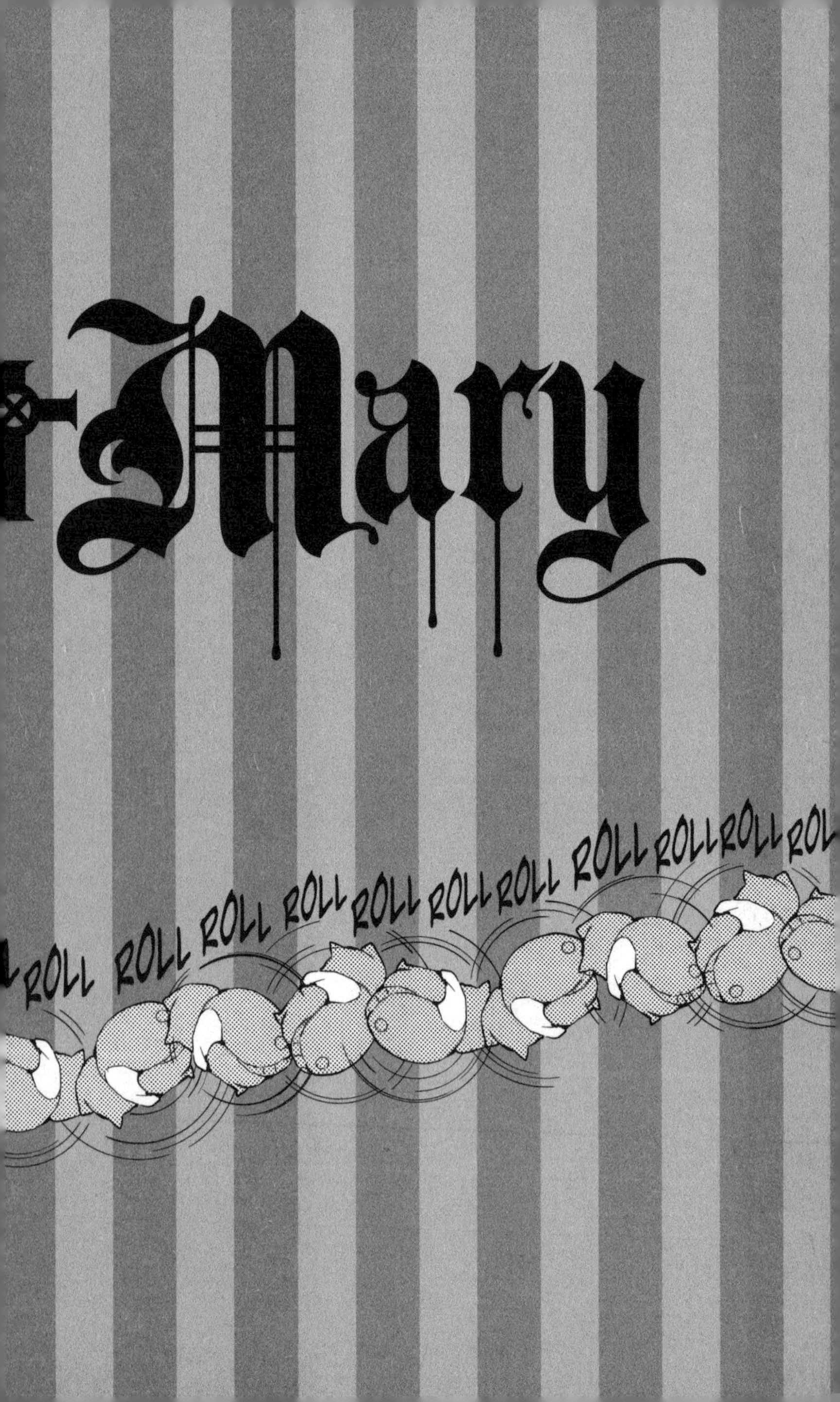
Mary
ROLL
ROLL
ROLL
ROLL
ROLL
ROLL
ROLL
ROLL
ROLL
ROLL

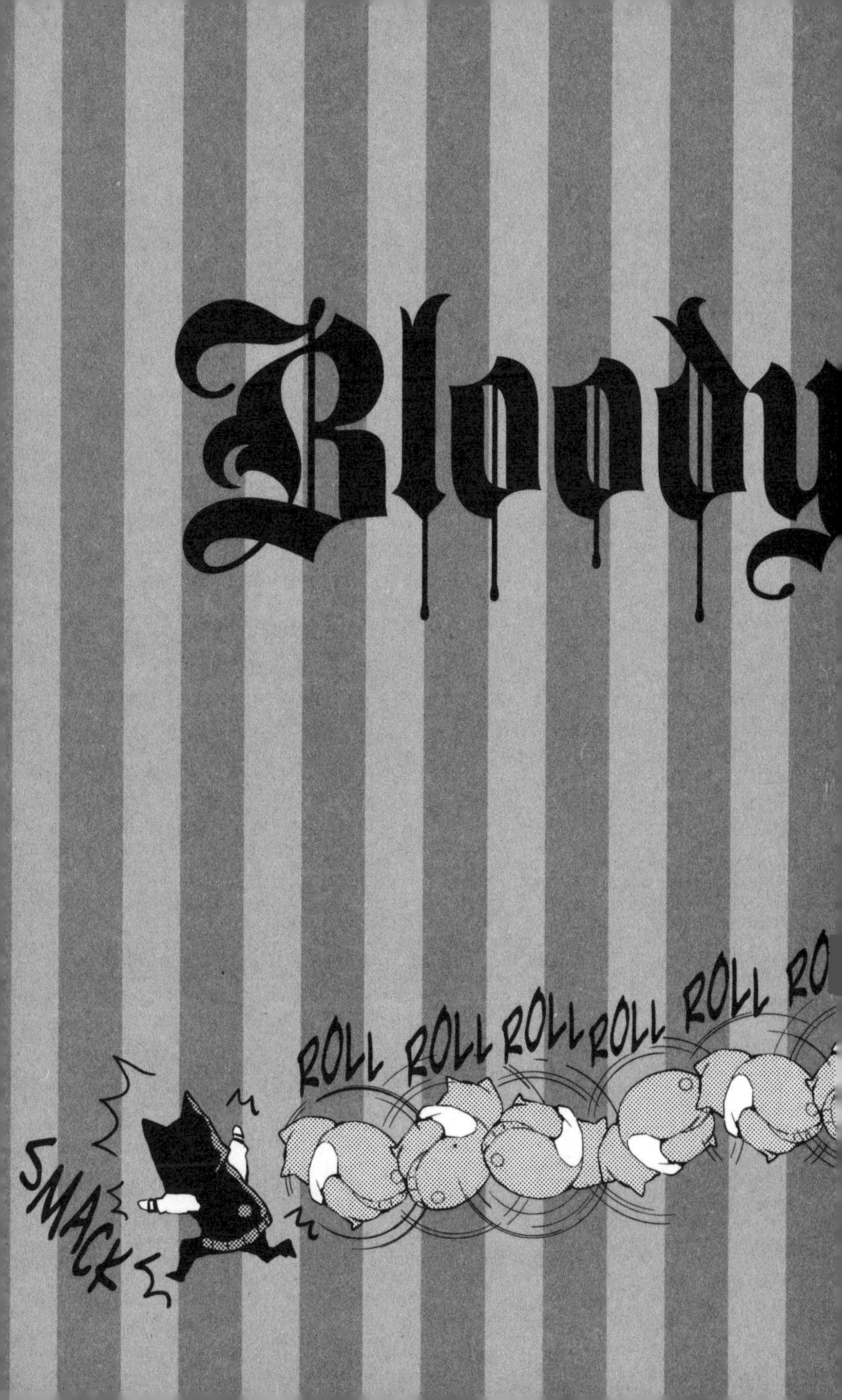
Bloody
ROLL ROLL ROLL ROLL ROLL RO
SMACK

akaza samamiya

Born November 7, Cancer, blood type B.
Vampires are always wearing business
suits, and I think that's because they
all originally came from England.
But they're certainly not gentlemen.

Bloody Mary

Volume 4
Shojo Beat Edition

story and art by Akaza Samamiya

translation Katherine Schilling
touch-up art & lettering Sabrina Heep
design Fawn Lau
editor Erica Yee

BLOODY MARY Volume 4
© Akaza SAMAMIYA 2015
First published in Japan in 2015 by KADOKAWA
CORPORATION, Tokyo.
English translation rights arranged with KADOKAWA
CORPORATION, Tokyo.

The stories, characters and incidents mentioned
in this publication are entirely fictional.

Printed in the U.S.A.

Published by VIZ Media, LLC
P.O. Box 77010
San Francisco, CA 94107

10 9 8 7 6 5 4 3 2 1
First printing, September 2016

www.viz.com   www.shojobeat.com

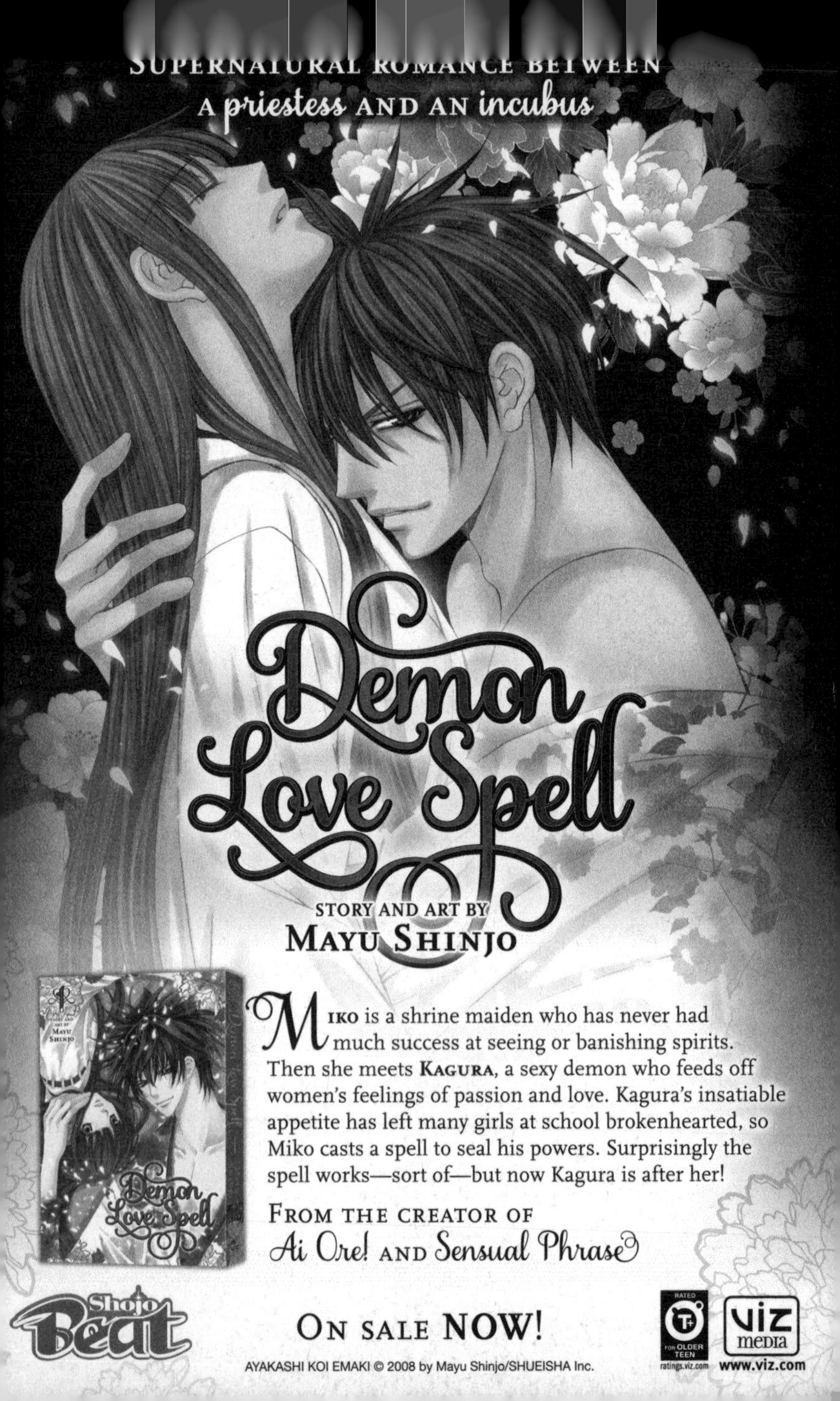
SUPERNATURAL ROMANCE BETWEEN
A priestess AND AN incubus
Demon Love Spell
STORY AND ART BY
MAYU SHINJO
MIKO is a shrine maiden who has never had much success at seeing or banishing spirits. Then she meets KAGURA, a sexy demon who feeds off women's feelings of passion and love. Kagura's insatiable appetite has left many girls at school brokenhearted, so Miko casts a spell to seal his powers. Surprisingly the spell works—sort of—but now Kagura is after her!
FROM THE CREATOR OF
Ai Ore! AND Sensual Phrase
Shojo Beat
ON SALE NOW!
RATED T+ FOR OLDER TEEN
ratings.viz.com
VIZ media
www.viz.com
AYAKASHI KOI EMAKI © 2008 by Mayu Shinjo/SHUEISHA Inc.

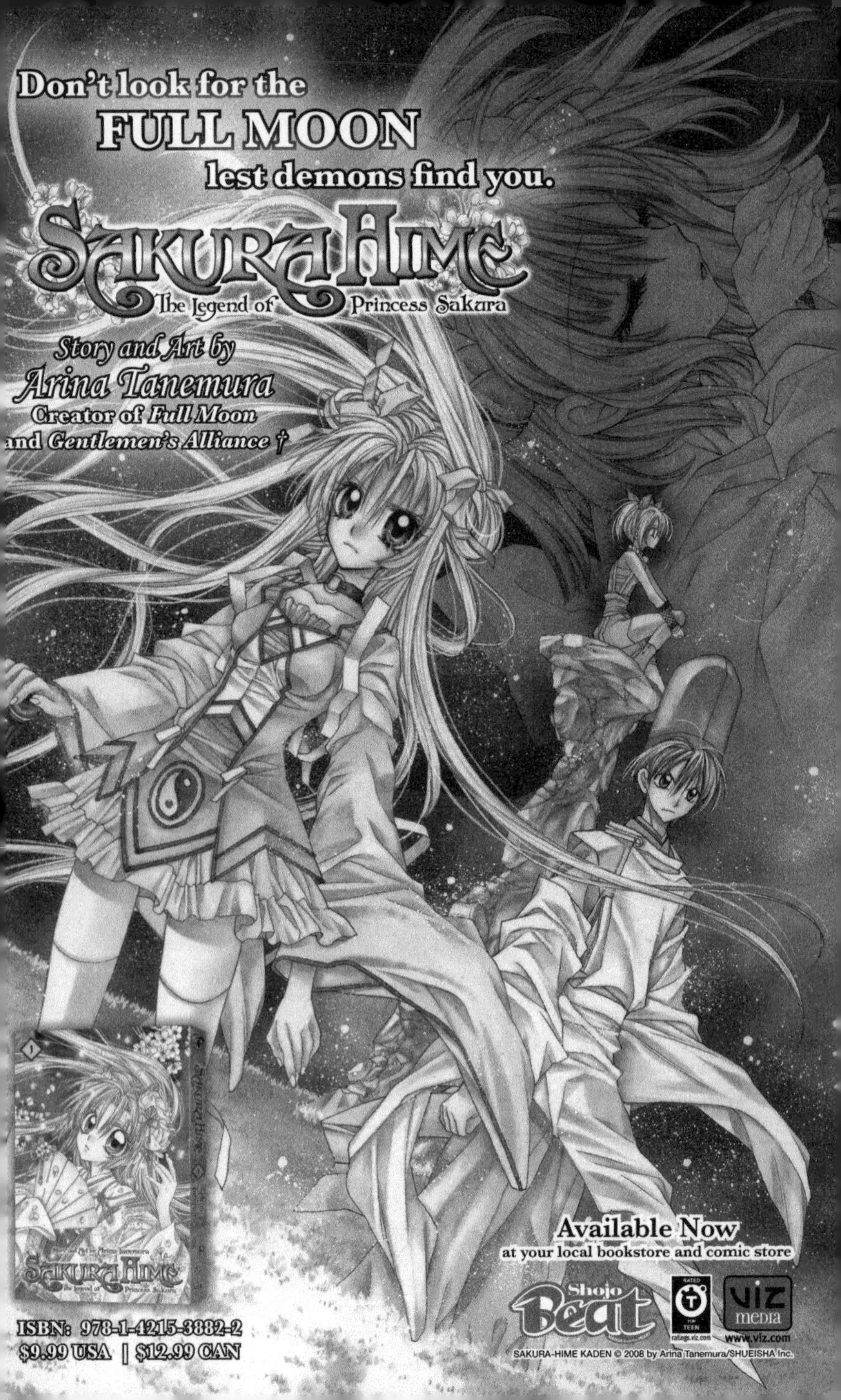
Don't look for the
FULL MOON
lest demons find you.
SAKURA HIME
The Legend of Princess Sakura
Story and Art by
Arina Tanemura
Creator of Full Moon
and Gentlemen's Alliance †
ISBN: 978-1-4215-3882-2
$9.99 USA | $12.99 CAN
Available Now
at your local bookstore and comic store
Shojo Beat
RATED T FOR TEEN
ratings.viz.com
VIZ media
www.viz.com
SAKURA-HIME KADEN © 2008 by Arina Tanemura/SHUEISHA Inc.

stop

YOU MAY BE READING THE

wrong way

IT'S TRUE: In keeping with the original Japanese comic format, this book reads from right to left—so action, sound effects and word balloons are completely reversed. This preserves the orientation of the original artwork—plus, it's fun! Check out the diagram shown here to get the hang of things, and then turn to the other side of the book to get started!

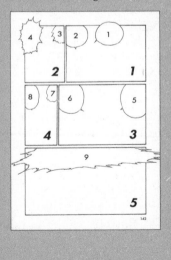